Machine Learning, Animated

The release of ChatGPT has kicked off an arms race in Machine Learning (ML), however, ML has also been described as a black box and very hard to understand. *Machine Learning, Animated* eases you into basic ML concepts and summarizes the learning process in three words: *initialize, adjust* and *repeat.* This is illustrated step by step with animation to show how machines learn: from initial parameter values to adjusting each step, to the final converged parameters and predictions.

This book teaches readers to create their own neural networks with dense and convolutional layers, and use them to make binary and multi-category classifications. Readers will learn how to build deep learning game strategies and combine this with reinforcement learning, witnessing AI achieve super-human performance in Atari games such as Breakout, Space Invaders, Seaquest and Beam Rider.

Written in a clear and concise style, illustrated with animations and images, this book is particularly appealing to readers with no background in computer science, mathematics or statistics.

Dr. Mark Liu is a tenured finance professor and founding director of the Master of Science in Finance program at the University of Kentucky, where he teaches Python Predictive Analytics to graduate students. He has more than 20 years of coding experience and is the author of *Make Python Talk* (No Starch Press, 2021).

Chapman & Hall/CRC Machine Learning & Pattern Recognition

A First Course in Machine Learning
Simon Rogers, Mark Girolami

Statistical Reinforcement Learning: Modern Machine Learning Approaches
Masashi Sugiyama

Sparse Modeling: Theory, Algorithms, and Applications
Irina Rish, Genady Grabarnik

Computational Trust Models and Machine Learning
Xin Liu, Anwitaman Datta, Ee-Peng Lim

Regularization, Optimization, Kernels, and Support Vector Machines
Johan A.K. Suykens, Marco Signoretto, Andreas Argyriou

Machine Learning: An Algorithmic Perspective, Second Edition
Stephen Marsland

Bayesian Programming
Pierre Bessiere, Emmanuel Mazer, Juan Manuel Ahuactzin, Kamel Mekhnacha

Multilinear Subspace Learning: Dimensionality Reduction of Multidimensional Data
Haiping Lu, Konstantinos N. Plataniotis, Anastasios Venetsanopoulos

Data Science and Machine Learning: Mathematical and Statistical Methods
Dirk P. Kroese, Zdravko Botev, Thomas Taimre, Radislav Vaisman

Deep Learning and Linguistic Representation
Shalom Lappin

Artificial Intelligence and Causal Inference
Momiao Xiong

Introduction to Machine Learning with Applications in Information Security, Second Edition
Mark Stamp

Entropy Randomization in Machine Learning
Yuri S. Popkov, Alexey Yu. Popkov, Yuri A. Dubno

Transformers for Machine Learning
Uday Kamath, Kenneth Graham, Wael Emara

The Pragmatic Programmer for Machine Learning
Marco Scutari, Mauro Malvestio

Machine Learning, Animated
Mark Liu

For more information on this series please visit: https://www.routledge.com/Chapman--HallCRC-Machine-Learning--Pattern-Recognition/book-series/CRCMACLEAPAT

Machine Learning, Animated

Mark Liu

CRC Press
Taylor & Francis Group
Boca Raton London New York

CRC Press is an imprint of the
Taylor & Francis Group, an **Informa** business

A CHAPMAN & HALL BOOK

First edition published 2024
by CRC Press
6000 Broken Sound Parkway NW, Suite 300, Boca Raton, FL 33487-2742

and by CRC Press
4 Park Square, Milton Park, Abingdon, Oxon, OX14 4RN

CRC Press is an imprint of Taylor & Francis Group, LLC

Library of Congress Cataloging-in-Publication Data

Names: Liu, Mark (Mark H.), author.
Title: Machine learning, animated / Mark Liu.
Description: First edition. | Boca Raton, FL : CRC Press, 2024. | Includes
   bibliographical references and index.
Identifiers: LCCN 2023016272 (print) | LCCN 2023016273 (ebook) | ISBN
   9781032462141 (hbk) | ISBN 9781032462134 (pbk) | ISBN 9781003441281
   (ebk) | ISBN 9781003380580 (eBook+)
Subjects: LCSH: Neural networks (Computer science)--Problems, exercises,
   etc. | Computer animation--Problems, exercises, etc. | Machine
   learning--Problems, exercises, etc. | Video
   games--Programming--Problems, exercises, etc.
Classification: LCC QA76.87 .L576 2024 (print) | LCC QA76.87 (ebook) |
   DDC 006.3/107--dc23/eng/20230905
LC record available at https://lccn.loc.gov/2023016272
LC ebook record available at https://lccn.loc.gov/2023016273

ISBN: 978-1-032-46214-1 (hbk)
ISBN: 978-1-032-46213-4 (pbk)
ISBN: 978-1-003-44128-1 (ebk)
ISBN: 978-1-003-38058-0 (eBook+)

DOI: 10.1201/b23383

Typeset in Latin Modern font
by KnowledgeWorks Global Ltd.

Publisher's note: This book has been prepared from camera-ready copy provided by the authors.

Access the Support Material: https://www.routledge.com/Machine-Learning-Animated/Liu/p/book/9781032462141
and https://github.com/markhliu/MLA

To Ivey and Andrew.

Contents

Preface

Artificial Intelligence, deep learning, machine learning — whatever you're doing if you don't understand it — learn it. Because otherwise you're going to be a dinosaur within 3 years.

–Mark Cuban, 2021

Machine learning (ML) is redefining the way we live nowadays: it's integrated into an increasing number of products and services in the economy, from recommender systems to language translations, from voice assistants, medical imaging, to self-driving cars... ML, especially deep learning, has made great strides in the last couple of decades, largely due to the advancements in computing power (such as graphics processing unit (GPU) training and distributed computing) and the exploding amount of data available to train deep neural networks.

The recent release of ChatGPT by OpenAI has upped the ante in the game, forcing Google and other competitors to release large language models of their own [5]. Different organizations and institutions have realized that an arms race in the field of ML and artificial intelligence (AI) is on. Everyone in every profession must adapt or face the risk of becoming a dinosaur and getting left behind. A case in point is a recent announcement by the Chartered Financial Analyst (CFA) Institute on March 17, 2023, to add ML and AI in CFA exams to prepare candidates in these fields [26]. The change comes after the CFA Institute "speaking with employers who were bemoaning that while what's in the program was very practical, when they hire new charterholders, they're not quite job ready." [11]

The need to incorporate ML into the college curriculum was clear long before the release of ChatGPT. In the Master of Science in Finance (MSF) program at the University of Kentucky, we have kept a close eye on the market demand for skill sets in these fields so as to keep our graduates competitive on the job market. I created and taught a Python Predictive Analytics course for our finance master students, involving state-of-the-art ML models such as deep neural networks, random forests, gradient boosting machines, and so on. While students are generally amazed by what ML can accomplish, they complain that the learning process in ML is like a black box and hard to understand. To help explain the inner workings of ML algorithms, I have simplified the learning process into three words: initialize, adjust, and repeat.

- Step 1: A machine learning model assigns values to the model parameters (initialize).
- Step 2: It makes predictions based on the current parameters and compares predictions with the actual values; it changes the parameters so that the predictions in the next iteration will move closer to the actual values (adjust).
- Step 3: It repeats step 2 until the parameters converge (repeat).

The teaching experience has sowed the seed for this book. In the early part of the book, I'll discuss the building blocks of ML such as loss functions, activation functions, the gradient descent optimization algorithm, the learning rate... Better yet, the book will use animations to show step by step how machines learn: the initial parameter values, the adjustment in each step, and the final converged parameters and predictions. I attempt to fill the void in the market for an ML book for college students and young professionals with no background in computer science, mathematics, or statistics. As such, the book takes a practical rather than technical approach to ML. The book provides an intuitive explanation of concepts such as deep learning, Q-learning, or the policy-gradient algorithm. You'll learn how to implement these algorithms by following the examples and how to apply them to your own field, be that business, biology, medicine, or something else entirely. While most models are built by using the TensorFlow Keras API, you also learn to create ML models from scratch on your own, without resorting to any API. Along the way, you'll know how ML models are constructed, how the parameter values are initialized and then gradually adjusted during the training process, how parameters converge, and how the trained models make accurate predictions.

This book is divided into six parts. Part I discusses how to install Python and how to create animations with Python libraries. Part II introduces you to ML basics such as the gradient descent optimization algorithm, the learning rate, loss functions, and activation functions. Part III covers binary and multi-category classifications and introduces you to neural networks. In Part IV, we build deep learning game strategies in OpenAI Gym games as well as in multi-player games such as Tic Tac Toe and Connect Four. Part V introduces you to the basics of reinforcement learning. In Part VI, we combine deep learning with reinforcement learning to create deep reinforcement learning game strategies, so you can create a double deep Q-network to train all Atari games (Breakout, Space Invaders, Seaquest, and so on).

Here's an overview of the book:

Part I: Installing Python and Learning Animations

Chapter 1: Installing Anaconda and Jupyter Notebook

This chapter guides you through installing the Python software based on your operating system, whether that's Windows, Mac, or Linux. You'll create a virtual environment just for projects in this book and install Jupyter Notebook as the integrated development environment (IDE). You'll set up a directory to manage files in this book.

Chapter 2: Creating Animations

You learn to create graphics and animations in Python. This prepares you to create graphic representations and animations of the intermediate stages of the ML process later in this book.

Part II: Machine Learning Basics

Chapter 3: Machine Learning: An Overview

You'll learn what ML is and how it's different from the traditional algorithms in artificial intelligence (AI). We'll discuss three types of ML: supervised learning, unsupervised learning, and reinforcement learning. The three types also differ in terms of data, methodologies, and applications.

Chapter 4: Gradient Descent – Where Magic Happens

You'll use animations to show step by step how the parameter values in ML models change based on the gradient descent algorithm so that the ML models make predictions with the lowest forecasting error possible. The forecasting errors are measured by a loss function. Training an ML model is finding parameter values that minimize the loss function. The optimization process is achieved through gradient descent or some variant of it. You'll also know what the learning rate is and how it affects the training process.

Chapter 5: Introduction to Neural Networks

This chapter discusses how neural networks learn from the data and make predictions. You learn to construct a simple neural network from scratch to learn the relation between ten pairs of input and output variables. You use the three steps that we have outlined in ML: initialize, adjust, and repeat. You'll animate the learning process by extracting the parameter values and predictions in each step of the training process in this simple neural network.

Chapter 6: Activation Functions

You'll use the rectified linear unit (ReLU) activation function in a neural network to approximate a nonlinear relationship. The Sigmoid activation function squashes a number to the range between 0 and 1 so that it can be interpreted as the probability of an outcome. The Softmax activation function squeezes a group of numbers into the range [0, 1] so they can be interpreted as the probability distribution of multiple outcomes.

Part III: Binary and Multi-Category Classifications

Chapter 7: Binary Classifications

Binary classification is an ML algorithm to classify samples into one of two categories. In this chapter, you learn binary classifications by classifying images into horses and deer using a neural network. You create an animation to demonstrate how the model weights and the predicted probabilities change in different stages of training.

Chapter 8: Convolutional Neural Networks

A convolutional layer treats an image as a two-dimensional object and finds patterns on the image. It then associates these patterns with the image labels. This significantly improves the predictive power of the model. In this chapter, you learn the basic concepts related to a convolutional layer such as the number of filters, kernel size, zero-padding, strides... Better yet, you learn to create animations to show step by step how to apply a filter on an image and how the convolution operations are conducted.

Chapter 9: Multi-Category Image Classifications

When the target label is a multi-category variable with more than two possible values, we call the machine learning algorithm a multi-category classification problem. In this chapter, you learn to classify images in CIFAR-10 into one of the ten labels using a deep neural network with augmentations and convolutional layers.

Part IV: Developing Deep Learning Game Strategies

Chapter 10: Deep Learning Game Strategies

You learn to use deep learning to train intelligent game strategies in the Frozen Lake game in OpenAI Gym. You first generate game data for training purposes. You then create a deep neural network to train game strategies. The agent picks the action with the highest probability of winning based on the trained model.

Chapter 11: Apply Deep Learning to the Cart Pole Game

You learn to train deep learning game strategies to play the Cart Pole game in OpenAI Gym. You learn to creatively redefine what's considered "winning" in a game so that there are roughly evenly distributed numbers of winning and losing games in the simulated data. You feed the re-labelled data into a deep neural network to train the model. The trained model wins the Cart Pole game 100% of the time.

Chapter 12: Deep Learning in Multi-Player Games

You learn to create a game environment for Tic Tac Toe. You then apply deep learning to Tic Tac Toe with the aim of developing intelligent game strategies. We'll also animate the decision-making process of the agent so we can look under the hood at how deep learning game strategies work.

Chapter 13: Deep Learning in Connect Four

You create a game environment for Connect Four and use simulated games to train a deep neural network. At each step of the game, the deep learning agent iterates through all possible next moves and selects the move with the highest probability of winning. You animate the decision-making process by showing all possible next moves and the associated probabilities of winning in each step of the game.

Part V: Reinforcement Learning

Chapter 14: Introduction to Reinforcement Learning

In reinforcement learning, an agent interacts with an environment through trial and error. The agent learns to achieve the optimal outcome by receiving feedback from the environment in the form of rewards and punishments. In this chapter, you'll train the Q-table in the Frozen Lake game. You create an animation to demonstrate how tabular Q-learning works. In each state, you put the game board on the left and the Q-table on the right. You highlight the row corresponding to the state and compare the Q-values under the four actions. The best action is highlighted in red. The animation repeats this process until the game ends.

Chapter 15: Q-Learning with Continuous States

Tabular Q-learning can solve problems in which both the number of actions and the number of states are finite. In the Mountain Car game, the state variable is continuous so the number of states is infinite. You use a finite number of discrete values to represent the state space and train the Q-table for the game effectively.

Chapter 16: Solving Real-World Problems with Machine Learning

You learn to solve an Amazon Delivery Route problem by using tabular Q-learning. You first find the shortest route between any two households in town by training a Q-table. You need to deliver eight packages a day. You consider all permutations and calculate the total distance traveled with each permutation. You select the one with the shortest total distance.

Part VI: Deep Reinforcement Learning

Chapter 17: Deep Q-Learning

You learn to use a neural network to approximate a Q-table. A deep Q-learning agent chooses an action in a given state by feeding the current game state into a deep Q-network. The network returns Q-values associated with different actions. The agent selects the action with the highest Q-value. You learn to successfully apply deep Q-learning to the Cart Pole game.

Chapter 18: Policy-Based Deep Reinforcement Learning

You learn policy-based reinforcement learning in this chapter: instead of estimating the value functions associated with different actions, you directly train a policy that tells the agent which action to take in a given state. You use the policy gradient method to play the Atari Pong game, earning a perfect score of 21 to 0.

Chapter 19: The Policy Gradient Method in Breakout

You generalize the policy gradient method you learned in Chapter 18 to another Atari game: Breakout. You animate how the agent learns to dig a tunnel on the side of the wall to send the ball to the back of the wall to score more efficiently.

Chapter 20: Double Deep Q-Learning

Q-learning has a well-known problem of overestimating Q-values. To overcome this problem, you learn to use the double Q-learning method in which one deep Q-network is used for training (the training network) and another for prediction (the target network). You animate how the trained agent in Breakout sends the ball to the back of the wall multiple times.

Chapter 21: Space Invaders with Double Deep Q-Learning

You tweak the Q-network you used in Chapter 20 and apply it to another Atari game, Space Invaders. Even though the agent does not know the rules of the Space Invaders game, it can eliminate all invaders on the screen, just by learning from the rewards via repeated interactions with the game environment.

Chapter 22: Scaling Up Double Deep Q-Learning

You scale up the double deep Q-network to play any Atari game. A model with the same network architecture, same hyperparameters, and same training procedure is created that can be applied to any Atari game. You apply the model on two new Atari games: Seaquest and Beam Rider. With these skills, you are ready to train and test any Atari game by using the same model.

All Python programs, along with answers to some end-of-the-chapter questions, are provided in the GitHub repository https://github.com/markhliu/MLA.

Acknowledgments

I have many people to thank for along the journey of making this book a reality. A portion of this book was developed while I was teaching Python Predictive Analytics to Master of Science in Finance students at the University of Kentucky in the past few years. I'd like to thank all MS Finance students for keeping me motivated to find novel ways to explain how Machine Learning works. I'd also like to thank Randi Slack and Solomon Pace-McCarrick at CRC Press for guiding me through the editorial process. Thanks to the production team of Michele Dimont and Riya Bhattacharya for helping me cross the finish line. Finally, I'd like to thank my wife Ivey Zhang and my son Andrew Liu for being so supportive in this journey.

I

Installing Python and Learning Animations

## CHAPTER 1

Installing Anaconda and Jupyter Notebook

> The mechanic, who wishes to do his work well, must first sharpen his tools.
>
> *–Ancient Chinese Proverb*

IN THIS CHAPTER, you'll first learn why Python is a great tool for machine learning (ML). After that, I'll guide you through installing the Python software you need to start running Python programs for this book. There are different ways of installing Python and managing packages on your computer. We'll be using Anaconda as our Python distribution and development environment for this book. I'll guide you through the installation process based on your operating system, whether that's Windows, Mac, or Linux. I'll also discuss the advantages of choosing Anaconda over other ways of installing Python.

You'll learn to create a virtual environment just for projects in this book. After that, you'll install Jupyter Notebook as your integrated development environment (IDE) and start coding in it. At the end of the chapter, you'll set up a directory to manage files in this book.

New Skills in This Chapter

- Setting up Python on your computer by installing Anaconda
- Creating a virtual environment for projects in this book
- Starting coding in Python by using Jupyter Notebook
- Setting up a file system for this book

DOI: 10.1201/b23383-1

1.1   WHY PYTHON FOR MACHINE LEARNING?

In this section, I'll briefly discuss why Python is popular as a programming language in general and why it's the preferred language for ML nowadays in particular.

1.1.1   The Rise of Python

Python has been the world's most popular programming language since late 2018, according to The Economist [25]. Once you start to code in Python, it's easy to see why. Python is a user-friendly, open-source, and cross-platform programming language. Python code is relatively close to plain English, so with only a little experience, you can often guess what a block of code is trying to accomplish.

Python is open source, meaning not only that the software is free to use for everyone but also that other users can create and alter libraries. In fact, Python has a vast ecosystem from which you can get resources and help from members in the community. Python programmers can share their code with one another, so instead of building everything from scratch, you can import modules designed by others, as well as share your modules with others in the Python community.

Python is a cross-platform programming language, meaning you can code in Python whether you use Windows, Mac, or Linux. However, the installation of software and libraries can be slightly different depending on your operating system. I'll show you how to install various libraries in your operating system. Once these are properly installed, Python code works the same in different operating systems.

Python is a high-level interpreted language. It allows users to abstract away from details of the computer such as data type, memory management, and pointers. As a result, the execution of Python code is slower than lower-level compiled languages such as C, C++, or Java. However, nowadays, with the advancements in computer hardware, you'll hardly notice the difference.

Ways to Learn Python Basics

This book assumes you have some basic understanding of the Python programming language. If not, a great place to start is the free online Python tutorial provided by W3Schools. Go to https://www.w3schools.com/python/ and follow the examples and exercises in the tutorial. They also provide a "Try it Yourself" editor and online compiler for you to run the Python code without installing Python on your computer. Alternatively, you can pick up a Python basics book and go over it. The Michigan State University's Professor Charles Severance has a book called Python for Everyone [22], and there is a printed version as well as a free online version https://www.py4e.com/.

1.1.2 Python for Machine Learning

All the ML algorithms in this book are in Python. We choose Python for several reasons.

First, as we mentioned above, Python is an expressive high-level language for general application development. Python's syntax structure is easy to follow. It is easy for ML enthusiasts to understand and process what the code is trying to accomplish. As a result, Python users can focus on solving ML problems without spending too much time and effort on the coding part. The simplicity of Python also allows programmers to collaborate with each other easily because understanding each other's code is not as difficult.

Second, you can easily get support from the Python ML community. There is a large online community with various groups and forums where programmers post their errors or other types of problems and help each other out. You can get resources and help from members in the Python ML community. If you encounter issues for the ML libraries in this book, you can search the forums for the Python packages you are using, or go to sites such as Stack Overflow to look for answers. In the rare case that you couldn't find an answer, feel free to reach out to me for help.

Third, Python is one of the most popular languages for ML. This is mainly because the Python ML ecosystem provides a wide collection of libraries that enable users to create ML models easily. In particular, you'll use extensively the following three libraries in this book: NumPy, TensorFlow, and Keras. Below, I'll briefly discuss what these libraries can accomplish. In a later chapter, we'll go into more details when we use these libraries to create various ML models.

NumPy stands for numerical Python. The NumPy library provides efficient data structures to represent numerical vectors and matrices, which allows Python to handle high-dimensional array objects and perform efficient mathematical operations. It is the bedrock of many of Python's numerical computing libraries such as pandas, matplotlib, and TensorFlow. For example, as you'll see later in this book, pictures are represented as three-dimensional NumPy arrays in Python: the first dimension is the width of the picture, the second the height, and the third the color channels. Even though NumPy is a Python library, most of the code in it is written in C or C++, and this allows for faster execution of the code.

Keras is a deep learning application programming interface (API) developed by Google. It makes the implementations of deep neural networks easy. Specifically, it provides the building blocks for developing state-of-the-art deep neural networks. It provides a convenient way for you to specify neural networks. You can easily add or remove a layer of neurons from the network as you tune your model. When you add a new layer of neurons, you can specify how many neurons to include in the layer, what activation function to use, and so on. You can also choose different types of layers of neurons such as dense layers or convolutional layers. Later chapters cover more details.

TensorFlow is an ML library developed by Google. It uses data flow and differentiable programming to perform different tasks. It allows users to pre-process data. The library takes input data as high-dimensional arrays known as tensors. The TensorFlow library allows you to perform mathematical operations such as matrix multiplications, convolutional operations, and so on. For example, we'll use TensorFlow to calculate the gradients of a function at the current parameter values so that we know how much to adjust the parameters based on the rule of gradient descent. We'll discuss how to implement all these (along with the terminologies I mentioned here) in later chapters.

1.2 INSTALLING ANACONDA

There are different ways of running Python programs and managing packages on your computer. This book uses Anaconda. Anaconda is an open-source Python distribution, package, and environment manager. It is user-friendly and provides for the easy installation of many useful Python libraries and packages that otherwise can be quite a pain (or downright impossible) to compile and install yourself. Specifically, Anaconda allows users to conda install packages in addition to pip installing packages (if you don't know the difference between the two, don't panic; I'll explain later in this chapter). As a matter of fact, many packages and libraries used in this book will be conda installed. Some of them cannot be pip installed. Therefore, if you don't install Anaconda on your computer, many projects in this book won't work. I urge you to follow the instructions in this chapter and install Anaconda so that you can enjoy all projects in this book.

Below, I'll guide you through the process of installing Anaconda on your computer based on your operating system.

1.2.1 Installing Anaconda in Windows

To install Anaconda in Windows, go to https://www.anaconda.com/products/individual/. Scroll down to the section Anaconda Installers. Download the latest version of Python 3 graphical installer for Windows. Make sure you download the appropriate 32- or 64-bit package for your machine. Run the installer and follow the instructions all the way through.

To check if Anaconda is properly installed on your computer, search for the Anaconda Navigator app on your computer. If you can open the app, Anaconda is successfully installed on your computer. The Anaconda Navigator app looks like what you see in Figure 1.1.

1.2.2 Installing Anaconda in macOS

To install Anaconda in macOS, go to https://www.anaconda.com/products/individual/. Scroll down to the section Anaconda Installers. Download the latest

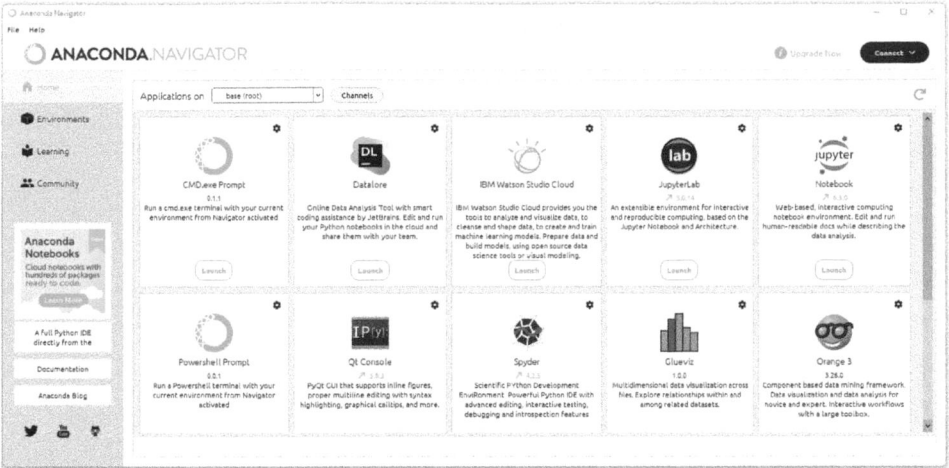

Figure 1.1   The Anaconda Navigator app

version of Python 3 graphical installer for Mac. There is a command line installer option as well. I recommend using the graphical installer instead of the command line installer, especially for beginners, to avoid mistakes. Run the installer and follow the instructions all the way through.

To check if Anaconda is properly installed on your computer, search for the Anaconda Navigator app on your computer. If you can open the app, Anaconda is successfully installed on your computer. The Anaconda Navigator app looks like what you see in Figure 1.1.

1.2.3   Installing Anaconda in Linux

The installation of Anaconda in Linux involves more steps than for other operating systems: there is no graphical installer for Linux. First, go to https://www.anaconda.com/products/individual/, scroll down, and find the latest Linux version. Choose the appropriate x86 or Power8 and Power9 package. Click and download the latest installer bash script. For example, the installer bash script during my installation was https://repo.anaconda.com/archive/Anaconda3-2022.05-Linux-x86_64.sh. This link will change over time, but we'll use this version as our example.

Open a terminal on your computer. By default, the installer bash script is downloaded and saved to the Downloads folder on your computer. You should then install Anaconda by issuing the following command in the terminal (use the path for your bash script if it is different):

```
bash ~/Downloads/Anaconda3-2022.05-Linux-x86_64.sh
```

After pressing the ENTER key on your keyboard, you'll be prompted to review and approve the license agreement. The last question in the installation process is this:

```
installation finished. Do you wish the installer to prepend the
Anaconda3 install location to PATH in your /home/mark/.bashrc ?
[yes|no] [no] >>>
```

You should type yes and press ENTER in order to use the conda command to open Anaconda in a terminal.

Now you need to activate the installation by executing this command:

```
source ~/.bashrc
```

To open Anaconda navigator, enter the following command in the terminal:

```
anaconda-navigator
```

You should see the Anaconda navigator on your machine, similar to Figure 1.1.

1.2.4   Difference between Conda-install and Pip-install

Many people think pip install and conda install are the same, but they're not. Pip is the Python packaging authority's recommended tool for installing packages from the Python packaging index. Pip can be used to install only Python software. In contrast, Conda is a cross-platform package and environment manager that installs not only Python software but also packages in C or C++ libraries, R packages, or other software. One case in point is that the portaudio package is a C package, which cannot be installed using Pip, but can be installed using Conda. In order to make Python connect to your computer microphone, you need the portaudio package. Installing Anaconda is the only way to make speech recognition work in Python. See my book Make Python Talk for details if you are interested [14].

1.3   VIRTUAL ENVIRONMENT FOR THIS BOOK

As you build more and more projects in Python, you'll install many libraries. Some libraries may interfere with other libraries, and different projects may use different versions of the same library. To avoid problems of clashing libraries, I recommend you build a virtual environment for each project. A virtual environment is a way to isolate projects from each other.

1.3.1   Create the Virtual Environment MLA

We'll create a virtual environment to contain all projects in this book. Let's name the virtual environment MLA, as in Machine Learning, Animated.

How to Open the Anaconda Prompt in Windows

Don't confuse the Anaconda prompt in the Windows operating system with the command prompt. To open Anaconda prompt in Windows, search for the Anaconda prompt app and click on the app to open it.

To create a virtual environment, open the Anaconda prompt (in Windows) or a terminal (in Mac or Linux). Enter the following command:

```
conda create -n MLA python==3.9.12
```

After pressing ENTER, follow the instructions onscreen and press y when the prompt asks you y/n. Once you have created the virtual environment on your machine, you need to activate it.

1.3.2 Activate the Virtual Environment

To activate the virtual environment MLA, open the Anaconda prompt (in Windows) or a terminal (in Mac or Linux). Execute the following command:

```
conda activate MLA
```

In Windows, you'll see the following on your Anaconda prompt:

```
(MLA) C:\>
```

You can see the (MLA) prompt, which indicates that the command line is now in the virtual environment MLA that you've just created.

On a Mac, you should see something similar to the following in the terminal (the username will be different):

```
(MLA) Macs-MacBook-Pro:~ macuser$
```

In Linux, you should see something similar to this on your terminal (the username will be different):

```
(MLA) mark@mark-OptiPlex-9020:~$
```

1.3.3 De-activate the Virtual Environment

When the command line is in the virtual environment MLA, there are two ways you can deactivate it.

The first way is to issue the following command:

```
conda deactivate
```

Note that you don't need to put the environment name MLA in the command. Conda automatically goes to the base environment after deactivation. In Windows, you'll see the following on your Anaconda prompt:

```
(base) C:\>
```

You can see the (base) prompt, which indicates that the command line is in the default Python environment.

On a Mac, you should see something similar to the following in the terminal:

```
(base) Macs-MacBook-Pro:~ macuser$
```

In Linux, you should see something similar to this in your terminal:

```
(base) mark@mark-OptiPlex-9020:~$
```

The second way is to issue the following command:

```
conda activate base
```

The above command activates the base environment, which is the default Python environment. This effectively deactivates the virtual environment MLA the command line was in before.

1.4 SET UP JUPYTER NOTEBOOK IN THE VIRTUAL ENVIRONMENT

Now we need to set up Jupyter Notebook in the newly created virtual environment on your computer. First, activate the virtual environment MLA by running the following line of code in the Anaconda prompt (in Windows) or a terminal (in Mac or Linux):

```
conda activate MLA
```

To install Jupyter Notebook in the virtual environment, run the command:

```
conda install notebook==6.4.8
```

To launch Jupyter Notebook, execute the following command in the same terminal with the virtual environment activated:

```
jupyter notebook
```

Jupyter Notebook should open in your default browser. If not, open a browser and put http://localhost:8888 in the address bar, and you should open the Jupyter Notebook.

The Jupyter Notebook app is shown in Figure 1.2.

1.4.1 Write Python in Jupyter Notebook

To get you up and running, I'll show you how to run Python programs in Jupyter Notebook.

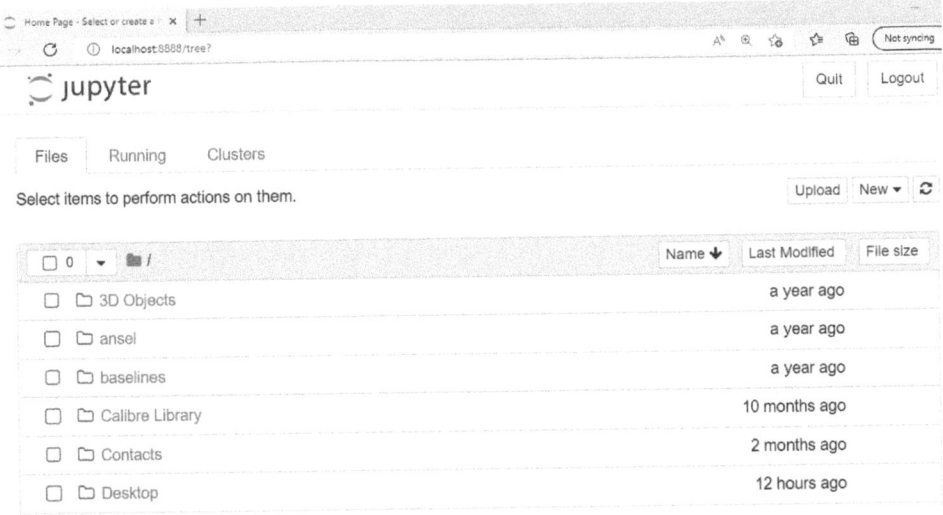

Figure 1.2 The Jupyter Notebook app

How to Download an .ipynb or .py file from GitHub

To download an individual file from GitHub with .ipynb or .py extension, first go to the file's url using your browser. Click on the Raw button and you'll be redirected to a new url that shows the raw code of file. Press CTRL and S simultaneously on your keyboard and a dialog box pops up. Select All Files (*.*) from the Save as type drop-down menu and save the file on your computer.

Download the template file *tmp.ipynb* from the book's GitHub repository https://github.com/markhliu/MLA/blob/main/files/tmp.ipynb. Save it in the folder /mla in your computer's /Desktop folder. Go back to the Jupyter Notebook in your browser, click on Desktop, then the mla folder, then the file *tmp.ipynb*. You should see a cell with the following lines of code in it:

```
[2]: print("I love Python!")
```

```
I love Python!
```

Put your mouse cursor inside the cell and click on the Run button at the top menu (the icon with a black triangle and the word Run in it). You should see a message below the cell as the output. The message says, "I love Python!"

Two Ways to Run the Code in a Cell in Jupyter Notebook

There are two ways you can run the code in a cell in Jupyter Notebook: press the Run button, or press the ENTER and SHIFT keys simultaneously.

1.4.2 Issue Commands in Jupyter Notebook

You can issue certain commands in Jupyter Notebook without going to the Anaconda prompt (in Windows) or a terminal (in Mac or Linux).

For example, if you want to pip install the **matplotlib** library in the virtual environment MLA, you can do it in two different ways. The first way is to open the Anaconda prompt (in Windows) or a terminal (in Mac or Linux) and issuing the following two lines of commands:

```
conda activate MLA
```

```
pip install matplotlib==3.5.2
```

The second way, a shortcut, is to enter the following line of code in a cell:

```
[3]: !pip install matplotlib==3.5.2
```

Run the above cell will install the *matplotlib* library on your computer. Note that since you have opened the Jupyter Notebook in the MLA virtual environment, you have installed the *matplotlib* library in the MLA virtual environment, not in the base Python environment.

Make sure you put an exclamation mark (!) in front of the code in the cell. This tells Python to use the cell as a shortcut to the command line.

Not All Commands Can Be Executed in a Jupyter Notebook Cell

Not all commands can be executed in a Jupyter Notebook cell. For example, you cannot conda install a package by issuing commands in a Jupyter Notebook cell. As a matter of fact, you cannot execute any Conda command in a Jupyter Notebook cell.

1.5 FILE SYSTEM FOR THE BOOK

First, make sure that you have a subfolder /mla in your computer's /Desktop folder. We'll use the folder /mla to contain all files for this book. We'll use a subfolder /utils within the /mla folder for all local packages that we use for this book. We'll use another subfolder /files to contain other files such as graphs and videos. Within the /files directory, we create a sub-directory for each chapter such as /ch01, /ch02, and so on.

> **Python Modules, Packages, and Libraries**
>
> Python modules, packages, and libraries differ slightly. A Python module is a single file with the .py extension. In contrast, a Python package is a collection of Python modules contained in a single directory. The directory must have a file named ___init___.py to distinguish it from a directory that happens to have .py extension files in it. A Python library is a collection of Python packages. We'll use the terms modules, packages, and libraries loosely and sometimes interchangeably.

Next, open a Jupyter notebook in the MLA virtual environment by following instructions earlier in this chapter. Save it as *ch01.ipynb* in the folder /Desktop/mla/. Enter the following lines of code in it and run the cell:

```
[4]: import os

os.makedirs("utils", exist_ok=True)
os.makedirs("files/ch01", exist_ok=True)
```

The *makedirs()* method in the *os* library creates a directory on your computer. The exist_ok=True option tells Python not to return an error message if such a directory already exists. Download the file ___init___.py from the book's GitHub repository https://github.com/markhliu/MLA and save it in the folder /Desktop/mla/utils/ on your computer.

With that, you are all set up. You'll learn how to create pictures and animations in Python in the next chapter.

1.6 GLOSSARY

- **Activate A Virtual Environment:** Go into the subdirectory for a virtual environment so that you can write programs using packages within the virtual environment.
- **Anaconda:** An open-source software distribution, package, and environment manager.
- **Anaconda Navigator:** An app in Windows, Mac, or Linux that you can install on your computer to manage virtual environments, packages, and programs using a user interface.
- **Anaconda Prompt:** An app for the Windows operating system that you can install on your computer to manage virtual environments, packages, and programs via command lines.
- **Conda Install:** Installing packages for Python on your computer. The packages are provided by Anaconda and can be written in either Python, C, C++, or R.

- **IDE:** An integrated development environment. A comprehensive application for computer programming software development. It usually provides a source code editor, a complier, and a debugger.
- **Pip Install:** Installing packages on your computer from the Python Package Index. Only packages written in Python can be installed.

- **Virtual Environment:** An isolated environment on your computer to contain all needed files for a project.

1.7 EXERCISES

1.1 Install Anaconda on your computer. Open the Anaconda Navigator app on your computer.

1.2 Create a new virtual environment and name it MLA.

1.3 Activate the virtual environment MLA you just created in Exercise 2. Then deactivate the virtual environment and go to the base environment using the two methods discussed in this chapter.

1.4 Install Jupyter Notebook in the virtual environment MLA.

1.5 Download the file *tmp.ipynb* from the book's GitHub repository https://github.com/markhliu/MLA/blob/main/files/tmp.ipynb. Open the Jupyter Notebook app on your computer, and open the file *tmp.ipynb* in the Jupyter Notebook app.

1.6 Continue the previous exercise, in a new cell in Jupyter Notebook, write a line of Python code so that the output is a message "Machine Learning is fun!"

1.7 Continue the previous exercise, put the command !pip install matplotlib==3.5.2 in a new cell in Jupyter Notebook, run the code in the cell and see what happens.

1.8 Continue the previous exercise, put the command !conda install yt in a new cell in Jupyter Notebook, run the code in the cell and see what happens. Hint: you should get an error message because you cannot run any Conda command in a Jupyter Notebook cell.

1.9 Use the *makedirs()* method from the *os* library to create a folder named mla on your computer's desktop. Then create two subfolders utils and files inside the mla folder. Make sure you put the exist_ok=True option in the *makedirs()* method so that Python won't return an error message if such a directory already exists.

## CHAPTER 2

Creating Animations

If a picture is worth a thousand words, what is a video worth?

The Huffington Post

–Scott MacFarland

MACHINE LEARNING (ML) is redefining the way we live by integrating into an increasing number of products and services in the economy: from recommendation algorithms to language translation, from voice assistants, medical imaging, to self-driving cars... ML has made great strides in the last couple of decades, largely due to the invention of convolutional neural networks and the advancements in computing power (such as GPU training and distributed computing). However, ML algorithms are like black boxes and hard to understand. Explaining how ML works can be a challenge. As the old saying goes: a picture is worth a thousand words. Using graphics to explain ML is appealing because pictures provide a visual representation of the complex inner workings of the learning process. With just a glance, readers grasp the essence of what's going on at the heart of the matter.

Better still, in the spirit of the opening quote of this chapter from The Huffington Post by Scott MacFarland [15], this book takes the idea one step further. You'll see a graphic representation in multiple stages of the ML process, which forms an animation as the training algorithm progresses. Therefore, you'll not only get to the bottom of what's happening at each stage of the constructed ML model, but you'll also visualize how the model parameters and predictions change over the course of training.

To that end, in this chapter, you'll learn how to create graphics and animations with Python. We'll use the gross domestic product (GDP) data over time for five countries (US, China, Japan, Germany, and UK) as our example. The graphics and animations are generated with the powerful Python *matplotlib* library. After this chapter, you'll know how to create different types of graphs such as line plots, bar charts, and pie charts. You'll also know how to combine multiple graphs into one file and use the Python *imageio* library to convert them into an animation. Further, you'll learn to

DOI: 10.1201/b23383-2

put multiple figures side by side in each frame of an animation to achieve more informative visual representations.

New Skills in This Chapter

- Creating line plots, bar charts, and pie charts in Python
- Putting multiple graphs in a figure as subplots
- Creating animations by combining multiple graphs into gif files
- Combining two animations into one so frames are shown side by side

---

2.1 CREATE PLOTS WITH MATPLOTLIB

An animation is the displaying of a sequence of still images. Therefore, to create animations, you'll first learn how to create still graphics. We'll use the *matplotlib* Python library to generate images. You'll then use the *imageio* library to combine still images into animations in the format of *gif* files. Let's first install these libraries.

Here I assume you have followed the instructions in Section 1.3 and created the virtual environment MLA. If not, refer back to Section 1.3 for details on how to do so. Activate the virtual environment MLA by running the following line of code in the Anaconda prompt (in Windows) or a terminal (in Mac or Linux):

```
conda activate MLA
```

Install the three libraries by running the following lines of commands in the same Anaconda prompt or terminal with the virtual environment activated:

```
pip install matplotlib==3.5.2
```

```
pip install pandas==1.4.2
```

```
pip install imageio==2.16.2
```

To launch Jupyter Notebook you installed in the virtual environment MLA in Section 1.4, execute the following command in the same Anaconda prompt or terminal with the virtual environment activated:

```
jupyter notebook
```

Before you start, open a blank Jupyter notebook and save it as *ch02.ipynb* in the directory /Desktop/mla/ on your computer. Next, we'll create a subdirectory /files/ch02/ to store files for this chapter.

Start a new cell in *ch02.ipynb* and enter the following lines of code in it and run the cell:

```
[1]: import os

os.makedirs("files/ch02", exist_ok=True)
```

2.1.1   A Single Line Plot

We'll use the annual gross domestic product (GDP) data from the World Bank (the Appendix of this chapter provides details on how to download and clean up the data). Download the file GDPs.csv from the book's GitHub repository and place it in the folder /Desktop/mla/files/ch02/ on your computer.

To create a line plot, you can use the *plot()* method and put the x-axis and y-axis values as the first two arguments. Use the *title()* method to put a figure title on top of the line plot so that people know what the figure is about. Similarly, you can label the x- and y-axis using the methods *xlabel()* and *ylabel()* so that people know what variables you use as the x- and y-values.

```
[2]: import pandas as pd
     import matplotlib.pyplot as plt

     df=pd.read_csv("files/ch02/GDPs.csv")
     fig=plt.figure(dpi=100, figsize=(5,4))
     plt.plot(df["year"], df["USA"])
     plt.xlabel('Year')
     plt.ylabel('GDP (in $ Trillion)')
     plt.title('U.S. GDP Over Time')
     plt.show()
```

In the cell above, we first load the file GDPs.csv using the *read_csv()* method from the pandas library. We then create a figure using the *figure()* method in *matplotlib.pyplot*. The dpi=100 argument makes the output 100 pixels per inch. The figsize=(5,4) argument sets the plot five inches wide and four inches tall. As a result, this creates a picture with a resolution of 500 by 400 pixels.

If you run the cell above, you'll see a line plot of the U.S. GDP values over time. The x-axis is the year, from 1970 to 2020. The y-axis is the GDP value in trillion dollars. The title says, "U.S. GDP Over Time." You can also see the line plot under /files/ch02/plot.png in the book's GitHub repository https://github.com/markhliu/MLA.

Use Nicknames When Importing Modules

In Python, it's common to create a short nickname for a module/package/library with a long name. In the cell above, we import the *pandas* library and give it a nickname *pd*. That way, every time we use the library in the program, we only have to write *pd* instead of the longer full name *pandas*. Similarly, we import the *pyplot* package from the *matplotlib* library and give it a nickname *plt*. This way, we can use the short alias *plt* instead of the longer full name *matplotlib.pyplot*.

2.1.2   Multiple Lines in the Same Plot

You can also plot multiple lines in the same figure. We'll add the GDP of China to the previous plot. The *plot()* method has several optional arguments: the color argument specifies the color of the line, which can take values such as blue, red, or green. The linestyle argument can be solid, dashed, dotted, and so on. The linewidth argument determines how thick the line is.

Make sure you use the *show()* method only after you plot all the lines you intend to include in the figure. If you use the *show()* method after each *plot()* method, you'll get multiple one-line plots instead of one plot with multiple lines in it.

The *legend()* method adds a legend to the figure, and the labels for the two lines are U.S.A. and China, respectively. The *grid()* method makes the grid lines visible on the figure, which makes it easier for us to estimate the GDP values each year based on the height of the line plots.

```
[3]:  fig=plt.figure(dpi=100, figsize=(5,4))
      plt.plot(df["year"],df["USA"],color='blue',
              linestyle='solid',linewidth=2)
      plt.plot(df["year"],df["China"],color='red',
              linestyle='dashed',linewidth=1)
      plt.xlabel('Year')
      plt.ylabel('GDP (in $ Trillion)')
      plt.title('U.S. and Chinese GDP Over Time')
      plt.legend(labels=["USA","China"])
      plt.grid()
      plt.show()
```

We first plot U.S. GDP values over time. We use arguments color='blue', linestyle='solid', and linewidth=2 in the *plot()* method. As a result, the line plot for U.S. GDP values is a solid blue line with a thickness of 2. We then plot Chinese GDP values over time, using arguments color='red', linestyle='dashed', and linewidth=1 in the *plot()* method. This leads to a dashed red line with a thickness of 1.

If you run the cell above, you'll see a plot with two lines in it. There is a legend box at the top left corner indicating that the thick blue solid line is for U.S.A. while the thin red dashed line is for China. The plot is also available under /files/ch02/lines.png in the book's GitHub repository.

2.2   CREATE SUBPLOTS

While it's easy to show animations on electronic devices, it's hard to show them in a book. We'll refer you to the book's GitHub repository for animations in the format of *gif* files.

In this book, you'll learn to create the next best thing to an animation: a sequence of graphs. Specifically, you'll learn to create a sequence of graphs of the intermediate steps of the ML process. After that, you'll place them in a single picture on a grid to illustrate how ML works.

In this section, you'll learn how to create a single image using a group of subplots. Specifically, you'll generate nine individual plots by using years 1972, 1978, . . ., 2020, as the ending years. You then place them on a three by three grid in a single picture.

2.2.1 Create Individual Plots

We'll first generate nine individual plots. In each plot, we'll use year 1970 as the starting year. The ending years are 1972, 1978, . . ., and 2020, respectively.

In the cell below, we'll iterate through the nine ending years. In each iteration, we'll plot the GDPs of the five countries (U.S., China, Japan, Germany, and U.K.) over time. The starting year is always 1970. You'll also save the figure on your computer in each iteration.

```
fig=plt.figure(dpi=100, figsize=(5,4))
plt.grid()
# fix the range of the x value and y values
plt.xlim(1968,2022)
plt.ylim(-1,25)
# iterate through the nine ending years
for i in range(1972,2021,6):
    # use years from 1970 to year i
    dfi=df[df["year"]<=i]
    plt.plot(dfi["year"],dfi["USA"],color='b',
            linestyle='-')
    plt.plot(dfi["year"],dfi["China"],color='r',
            linestyle='--')
    plt.plot(dfi["year"],dfi["Japan"],color='m',
            linestyle='-.')
    plt.plot(dfi["year"],dfi["Germany"],color='k',
            linestyle=':')
    plt.plot(dfi["year"],dfi["UK"],color='g',
            linestyle=None)
    plt.legend(
        labels=["USA","China","Japan","Germany","UK"],
            loc="upper left")
    # save individual pictures on your computer
    plt.savefig(f"files/ch02/p{i}.png")
```

Note that we use plt.xlim(1968,2022) and plt.ylim(−1,25) to fix the range of the x-axis to years 1968–2022 and the values of the y-axis to −1 to 25. Without these two lines of commands, the ranges of x and y will change in each picture. We omitted the x-label, y-label, and the picture title so that it's easy to organize individual plots on a grid. Otherwise, we need to leave extra space between plots to accommodate labels and titles. Finally, you use the *savefig()* method to save plots as pictures on your computer.

Run the above cell. After that, if you go to the folder /Desktop/mla/files/ch02/ on your computer, you'll see nine pictures named p1972.png, p1978.png,..., and p2020.png, respectively. Examine them and make sure they look correct.

Next, we'll organize the nine plots in a single picture so that you can visualize the change in GDPs of the five countries over time.

2.2.2 Create Subplots

We'll use the *PIL* library to convert the pictures we just generated into NumPy arrays. Note that the *PIL* library is one of the dependencies for the *imageio* library. When you install the latter, the former is automatically installed. Therefore, you don't need to install the *PIL* library separately. We'll then use the *subplot()* method in *matplotlib.pyplot* to organize the nine plots we just generated.

```
[5]: import imageio, PIL

     plt.figure(dpi=200,figsize=(9,9))
     for i in range(3):
         for j in range(3):
             plt.subplot(3, 3, 3*i+j+1)
             img=f"files/ch02/p{1972+6*(3*i+j)}.png"
             nparray=PIL.Image.open(img)
             plt.imshow(nparray)
             plt.axis("off")
     plt.subplots_adjust(hspace=-0.36,wspace=-0.2)
     plt.show()
```

We first create a figure using the *figure()* method in *matplotlib.pyplot*. We use the dpi=200 argument to make the output 200 pixels per inch. The figure size is 9 inches wide and 9 inches tall, and this creates a picture with a resolution of 1800 by 1800 pixels. The higher resolution is necessary because we'll place nine plots in one picture. If the resolution is too low, individual plots look grainy.

We iterate through three rows and three columns. The command plt.subplot(3,3,1) creates a subplot at the top left corner of the three by three grid, which forms the whole picture. The command plt.subplot(3,3,2) creates a subplot at the top middle, and so on. By the same token, the command plt.subplot(3,3,9) creates a subplot at the bottom right corner of the figure.

We use the *open()* method in *PIL.Image* to open the png files we saved on our computer. The files are opened as NumPy arrays. We then use the *imshow()* method

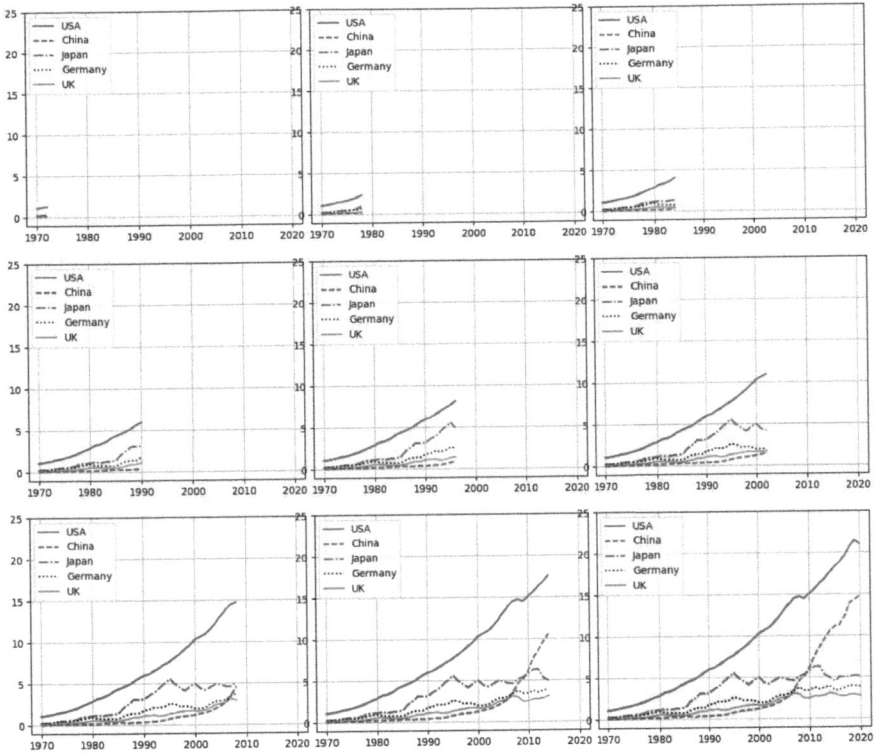

Figure 2.1 A figure with nine subplots

in *matplotlib.pyplot* to convert the NumPy arrays into pictures and place them in the appropriate places on the three by three grid.

Run the above cell, and you'll see an output as in Figure 2.1. The figure is also available under /files/ch02/fig2.1.png in the book's GitHub repository.

Adjusting Space between Subplots

The *subplots_adjust()* method in *matplotlib.pyplot* can be used to adjust the horizontal and vertical space between subplots. Specifically, the argument hspace adjusts the height space (i.e., the vertical space) between subplots while the wspace argument adjusts the width space (i.e., the horizontal space).

2.3 CREATE ANIMATED PLOTS

Next, we'll create an animation of the GDP values of the five countries over time. We'll first generate 50 graphs. In each graph, the starting year is always 1970, while the ending year ranges from 1971 to 2020. We'll then combine the graphs in a single *gif* file so that the graphs will appear sequentially. As a result, you'll see the animation effect.

2.3.1 Generate Annual Line Plots

We'll iterate through the ending years from 1971 to 2020. In each iteration, we'll plot the GDPs of the five countries (U.S., China, Japan, Germany, and U.K.) over time. You'll also save the figure on your computer in each iteration. This creates a total of 50 figures.

```
[6]: fig=plt.figure(dpi=200,figsize=(5,4))
     plt.grid()
     plt.xlabel('Year')
     plt.ylabel('GDP (in $ Trillion)')
     plt.xlim(1968,2022)
     plt.ylim(-1,25)

     for i in range(1971,2021,1):
         dfi=df[df["year"]<=i]
         plt.plot(dfi["year"],dfi["USA"],color='b',linestyle='-')
         plt.plot(dfi["year"],dfi["China"],color='r',linestyle='--')
         plt.plot(dfi["year"],dfi["Japan"],color='m',linestyle='-.')
         plt.plot(dfi["year"],dfi["Germany"],color='k',linestyle=':')
         plt.plot(dfi["year"],dfi["UK"],color='g',linestyle=None)
         plt.legend(labels=["USA","China","Japan","Germany","UK"],
                    loc="upper left")
         plt.title(f'GDPs till Year {i}')
         plt.savefig(f"files/ch02/year{i}.png")
```

We set the range of the x-axis from 1968 to 2022 by using the *xlim()* method. Similarly, we set the range of the y-axis from −1 to 25 trillion dollars by using the *ylim()* method. We iterate the value *i* through years 1971–2020. In each iteration, we extract the GDP values from 1970 to year *i*. Each country is plotted with a different color and line style. The values b, r, m, k, and g are aliases for the colors blue, red, magenta, black, and green, respectively. We do not include the line width option in the *plot()* method so the line width has a default value of 1.

For each iteration, we dynamically set the figure title to reflect the end year. Finally, the plot in each iteration is saved as a picture in the *jpg* format in the subfolder /Desktop/mla/files/ch02/. If you open the subfolder, you'll see the 50 pictures.

2.3.2 Animate the Plots

We'll use the *PIL* library to convert the pictures we just generated into NumPy arrays. We'll then use the *imageio* library to combine the sequence of arrays into an animation in the *gif* format.

```
[7]: import numpy as np

     frames=[]
     for i in range(1971,2021,1):
         frame=PIL.Image.open(f"files/ch02/year{i}.png")
         frame=np.asarray(frame)
         frames.append(frame)
     imageio.mimsave('files/ch02/GDPs.gif', frames, fps=5)
```

We create an empty list *frames* to store all pictures. We iterate through all 50 photos we generated in the last subsection and open each using the *PIL* library. We convert the pictures to NumPy arrays and add them to the list *frames*. Once done, we use the *mimsave()* method to convert the images to the *gif* format. The fps=5 argument generates animation with five frames per second. You can set the value higher or lower based on how fast you want the animation to be: a higher value of fps results in a faster animation.

After you run the above cell, the file *GDPs.gif* is generated and saved in your local folder. To view the animation, you have two options. You can click on the file on your computer to view it. Alternatively, you can view it at the book's GitHub repository in the folder /files/ch02/.

Frames per Second in Animations

The fps argument in the *mimsave()* method controls how fast the animation is. A higher value of fps leads to faster movements in the animation. Most motion pictures we watch have 24 frames per second.

2.4 CREATE ANIMATED BAR CHARTS

Besides line plots, the *matplotlib* library can generated other graphs such as scatter plots, bar charts, pie charts, histograms, and so on. Our purpose here is not to introduce you to all types of figures in the *matplotlib* library. Instead, you are here to learn how to create animations so that you can use the skills to animate the intermediate steps of machine learning algorithms. You can use the same logic to create animations of other graph types.

Nonetheless, in this chapter we'll discuss two more graph types: bar charts and pie charts. In this section, you'll learn how to create animated bar charts. Further, you'll

learn how to put different types of charts side by side and create one single animation
with multiple types of graphs in each frame of the animation.

2.4.1 Create a Horizontal Bar Chart

We'll look at the GDPs of the five countries in year 2009, sort the values, and then
create a horizontal bar chart.

```
[8]: df = df.set_index("year")
     yr2009 = df.loc[2009].sort_values()
     fig = plt.figure(dpi=200, figsize=(6,4))
     colors = plt.cm.Dark2(range(5))
     y = yr2009.index
     width = yr2009.values
     plt.xlim(0,23)
     plt.title("GDP Ranking in Year 2009")
     plt.xlabel("GDP in Year 2009")
     plt.barh(y=y, width=width, color=colors)
```

```
[8]: <BarContainer object of 5 artists>
```

The *set_index()* method in the *pandas* library changes the index value of a DataFrame
from numerical values 0, 1, 2, ... to the values in a column (in this case, the "year"
column). We then retrieve the GDP values of the five countries in 2009 and save it
as a series *yr2009*. The values are sorted based on the GDP values of that year. We
select five different colors for the five countries.

The *barh()* method creates a horizontal bar chart. The y-axis are the names of the
five countries, and the width of the horizontal bar is the GDP value of the country.

2.4.2 Generate Annual Bar Charts

You'll iterate through years 1970–2020. In each iteration, you'll generate a horizontal
bar chart of the GDPs of the five countries, with the highest GDP value on top.
You'll also save the chart on your computer in each iteration. This creates a total of
51 charts.

To get a sense of the data, you can use the *head()* method in pandas to see the first
five observations of the DataFrame *df*. Run the following cell:

```
[9]: df.head()
```

```
[9]:         China    Germany       UK      Japan       USA
     year
     1970  0.092603  0.215838  0.130672  0.212609  1.07330
     1971  0.099801  0.249985  0.148114  0.240152  1.16485
```

1972	0.113688	0.299802	0.169965	0.318031	1.27911
1973	0.138544	0.398374	0.192538	0.432083	1.42538
1974	0.144182	0.445303	0.206131	0.479626	1.54524

The dataset contains five columns, representing five countries. The rows are indexed by years: 1970, 1971, and so on.

```
[10]: # by year, sorted.
for i in range(1970,2021,1):
    yri = df.loc[i].sort_values()
    fig = plt.figure(dpi=200, figsize=(6,4))
    colors = plt.cm.Dark2(range(5))
    y = yri.index
    width = yri.values
    plt.xlim(0,23)
    plt.title(f"GDP Ranking in Year {i}")
    plt.xlabel(f"GDP in Year {i}")
    plt.barh(y=y, width=width, color=colors)
    fig.savefig(f"files/ch02/bar{i}.png")
    # Close figure to save computer memory space
    plt.close(fig)
```

We use the *loc[i]* method to extract year i's values from the dataset *df*, and save it as a data series *yri*. We define *y* as the index values, which are the names of the five countries. The *width* variable is defined as the values in the series, which are the five GDP values. The *plt.barh()* method creates a horizontal bar chart for the year. The charts are saved on your computer. Finally, we use *plt.close(fig)* to close each figure after the chart is saved. Doing so saves the memory space on your computer.

After running the cell, if you go to the folder /files/ch02, you'll see all 51 charts, saved as bar1970.png, bar1971.png, and so on.

```
[11]: yri
```

```
[11]: UK          2.75980
      Germany     3.84641
      Japan       5.05776
      China      14.72270
      USA        20.95300
      Name: 2020, dtype: float64
```

The above cell prints out the *pandas* series *yri*. As you can see, it has five values, with country names as its indexes.

2.4.3   Animate the Bar Charts

The process of converting bar charts into animation is similar to what we have done before for the line plots. We'll use the *PIL* library to convert the charts into NumPy arrays. We'll then use the *imageio* library to combine the sequence of arrays into an animation in the *gif* format.

[12]:
```
frames=[]
for i in range(1970,2021,1):
    frame=PIL.Image.open(f"files/ch02/bar{i}.png")
    frames.append(frame)
imageio.mimsave('files/ch02/bar.gif', frames, fps=5)
```

After you run the above cell, the file *bar.gif* is generated and saved in your local folder. To view the animation, you can click on the file on your computer. Alternatively, you can view it under /files/ch02/ in the book's GitHub repository.

2.5   PUT BAR CHARTS AND PLOTS SIDE BY SIDE

In this section, you'll learn how to put a bar chart and a line plot side by side and create a single picture. After that, you'll create a combined picture each year and then an animation over time.

2.5.1   Combine a Bar Chart and a Plot

First, you'll learn how to put a bar chart and a line plot side by side and combine them into a single picture. We'll use year 2009 as an example. The bar chart for 2009 is saved as *bar2009.png* while the line plot for year 2009 is saved as *year2009.png*. In the cell below, we'll combine them into a picture called combine.png.

[13]:
```
fig = plt.figure(figsize=(11,6),dpi=200)
ax0 = fig.add_subplot(121)
ax1 = fig.add_subplot(122)

# Customize subplots:
frame1=PIL.Image.open("files/ch02/bar2009.png")
frame1=np.asarray(frame1)

frame2=PIL.Image.open("files/ch02/year2009.png")
frame2=np.asarray(frame2)

ax0.imshow(frame1)
ax0.axis('off')
```

```
ax1.imshow(frame2)
ax1.axis('off')
plt.subplots_adjust(wspace=-0.12)
plt.savefig("files/ch02/combine.png")
```

We first use the *plt.figure()* method to create a figure, which is 11 by 4 inches in size. We set the dpi to 200. We then use the *add_subplot()* method to add two subplots to the original figure. The line ax0=plt.add_subplot(121) tells Python to divide the original figure into one row and two columns and put the first picture in position 1 (i.e., on the left). Similarly, the line ax1=plt.add_subplot(122) divides the original figure into one row and two columns and puts the second picture in position 2 (i.e., on the right).

How plt.add_subplot() Works

There are three numbers inside the *plt.add_subplot()* method. The first one is the number of rows, the second the number of columns, and the last number the position of the current subplot. For example, *plt.add_subplot(234)* means you divide the original figure into two rows and three columns and put the subplot in position 4 (i.e., middle row right column). The subplot positions on the grid are numbered from top to bottom and from left to right.

If you run the above cell, the file *combine.png* is generated and saved in your local folder. You can click on the file on your computer to view it. Alternatively, you can view it under /files/ch02/ in the book's GitHub repository.

2.5.2 Create an Animation of the Combined Pictures

Next, we'll combine the bar chart and the line plot for every year from 1971 to 2020. We then form an animation based on the combined pictures.

```
[14]:  frames=[]
       for i in range(1971,2021,1):
           frame1=PIL.Image.open(f"files/ch02/bar{i}.png")
           frame1=np.asarray(frame1)
           frame2=PIL.Image.open(f"files/ch02/year{i}.png")
           frame2=np.asarray(frame2)
           frame=np.concatenate([frame1,frame2],axis=1)
           frames.append(np.array(frame))
       imageio.mimsave('files/ch02/barsplots.gif', frames, fps=5)
```

We first create an empty list *frames* to store all combined pictures. We then iterate through years 1971–2020. Each year, we open the bar chart and the line plot and name them *frame1* and *frame2*, respectively. We use the *concatenate()* method to combine the two pictures. We then append the combined picture in the list *frames*. After that, we create an animation of the pictures over time using the *imageio.mimsave()* method and name it *barsplots.gif*.

If you run the above cell, the file *barsplots.gif* is generated and saved in your local folder. To view the animation, you can click on the file on your computer. Alternatively, you can view it under /files/ch02/ in the book's GitHub repository.

Concatenate NumPy Arrays

The axis=1 argument in the *concatenate()* method in NumPy tells Python to combine the two arrays side by side instead of on top of each other. If you change the argument to axis=0, you'll create an animation with the bar chart on top and the line plot at the bottom.

2.6 ANIMATED PIE CHARTS

In this section, you'll first learn how to create a pie chart. You'll then create a pie chart each year from 1970 to 2000. After that, you'll create an animation of pie charts over time. Finally, you'll create an animation with pie charts and line plots side by side.

2.6.1 Create a Pie Chart

We'll look at the GDPs of the five countries in year 2009, sort the values, and then create a pie chart.

```
[15]: fig = plt.figure(figsize=(12,8),dpi=100)
      colors = plt.cm.Dark2(range(5))
      labels = yr2009.index
      GDPs = yr2009.values
      plt.ylabel("GDP Pie Chart in Year 2009",fontsize=20)
      explode = [0.01, 0.02, 0.03, 0.04, 0.05]
      plt.pie(GDPs,
              labels=labels,
              autopct='%1.1f%%',
              startangle = -45,
              textprops={'fontsize': 15},
              explode=explode)
      plt.savefig(f"files/ch02/pie.png")
```

The *pie()* method in the *matplotlib* library creates a pie chart based on a collection of values. It calculates the percentage of each country's GDP in the combined sum automatically. The labels are the names of the five countries, while the *explode* argument dictates how much each wedge will be plotted away from the center. Finally, the *startangle* argument dictates how many degrees to rotate the pie chart.

2.6.2 Generate Annual Pie Charts

You'll iterate through years 1970–2020. In each iteration, you'll generate a pie chart of the GDPs of the five countries. You'll also save the chart on your computer in each iteration. This creates a total of 51 pie charts.

```
[16]: for i in range(1970,2021,1):
          yri = df.loc[i].sort_values()
          fig = plt.figure(figsize=(12, 8),dpi=100)
          colors = plt.cm.Dark2(range(5))
          labels = yri.index
          GDPs = yri.values
          plt.ylabel(f"GDP Pie Chart in Year {i}", fontsize=20)
          explode = [ 0.01, 0.02, 0.03, 0.04,0.05]
          plt.pie(GDPs,
                  labels=labels,
                  autopct='%1.1f%%',
                  startangle = -45,
                  textprops={'fontsize': 15},
                  explode=explode)
          fig.savefig(f"files/ch02/pie{i}.png")
          plt.close(fig)
```

Note, we have set the dpi to 100 and the size to 12 by 8. This way, later when we put the pie chart and the line plot side by side, their heights are the same (both are 800 pixels). So we can use the *concatenate()* method to combine the two pictures. If the heights of the two pictures are not the same, we cannot directly concatenate them together.

If you run the above cell, 51 pie charts will be generated and saved in your local folder. You can click on the files on your computer to view them.

2.6.3 Animate the Combined Pie Charts and Plots

The process for converting bar charts into animation is similar to what we have done before for the line plots. We'll use the *PIL* library to convert the charts into NumPy arrays. We'll then use the *imageio* library to combine the sequence of arrays into an animation in the *gif* format.

```
[17]: frames=[]
      for i in range(1971,2021,1):
```

```
       frame1=PIL.Image.open(f"files/ch02/pie{i}.png")
       frame1=np.asarray(frame1)
       frame2=PIL.Image.open(f"files/ch02/year{i}.png")
       frame2=np.asarray(frame2)
       frame=np.concatenate([frame1,frame2],axis=1)
       frames.append(np.array(frame))
   imageio.mimsave('files/ch02/pieplot.gif', frames, fps=5)
```

After you run the above cell, the file *pieplot.gif* is generated and saved in your local folder. To view the animation, you can click on the file on your computer. Alternatively, you can view it in the book's GitHub repository.

2.7 APPENDIX: DOWNLOAD AND CLEAN UP THE GDP DATA

Below, you'll learn how to download and clean up the GDP values of the five countries and save it in a CSV file. The raw dataset is downloaded from the World Bank website https://data.worldbank.org/indicator/NY.GDP.MKTP.CD. The dataset is then cleaned up and I only kept data for the five countries (U.S.A., China, Japan, Germany, and UK) from 1970 to 2020. The cleaned-up data is placed under /files/ch02/ in the book's GitHub repository https://github.com/markhliu/MLA. Below is the Python code used to extract the data.

[1]:
```
'''
First, go to this site
https://data.worldbank.org/indicator/NY.GDP.MKTP.CD
Under Download in the middle right, click on the CSV
option to download the CSV files
put the three CSV files in your local folder
'''

import pandas as pd

df=pd.read_csv("API_NY.GDP.MKTP.CD_DS2_en_csv_v2_4019306.csv",
    skiprows=4)
df=df[(df["Country Name"]=="China") |
      (df["Country Name"]=="United States") |
      (df["Country Name"]=="Japan") |
      (df["Country Name"]=="Germany") |
      (df["Country Name"]=="United Kingdom")]
df.loc[df['Country Name']=="United States",\
       'Country Name'] = "USA"
df.loc[df['Country Name']=="United Kingdom",\
       'Country Name'] = "UK"
df=df.drop(['Country Code','Indicator Name','Indicator Code',
```

```
        '1960','1961','1962','1963','1964','1965','1966',
        '1967','1968','1969'], axis=1)
df=df.set_index('Country Name')
df=df.transpose()
df=df/1000000000000
df["year"]=df.index
df.to_csv("GDPs.csv")
```

This creates the file GDPs.csv that we have used earlier in this chapter.

2.8 GLOSSARY

- **Bar Chart:** Also called a bar graph. It is a type of chart representing categorical data in the form of rectangular bars. In a horizontal (vertical) bar chart, the lengths (heights) of the bars are proportional to the values they represent.
- **GDP:** Gross domestic product. The total amount of final goods and services that are produced and sold by a country in a specific period of time (usually in a year).
- **Line Plot:** Also called a line graph. It is a type of chart displaying the relation between variables in the form of straight line segments.
- **Pie Chart:** Also called a circle chart. A circle is divided into slices to represent the numerical proportion.

2.9 EXERCISES

2.1 Install the *matplotlib*, *pandas*, and *imagio* libraries in the MLA virtual environment on your computer.

2.2 Create a subfolder /Desktop/mla/file/ch02/ on your computer to store files for this chapter.

2.3 Add grid lines and a legend box to the single line plot in Section 2.1.1. Also change the dpi to 128 and the figure size to eight by six inches.

2.4 Add a *show()* method after the first *plot()* method in Section 2.1.2. See what output you get.

2.5 Add a third line to the plot in Section 2.1.2 using the GDP data for Germany. Make the new line dotted black with a line width of 2.

2.6 Change the range of x-axis to years 1969–2021 and the range of y-axis to −0.5 to 24.5 in the individual plots in Section 2.2.1.

2.7 Change the height space to −0.3 and width space to −0.22 between subplots in Section 2.2. Re-run the program and see how the new figure looks compared to Figure 2.1.

2.8 Change the frame per second to 8 in the animation in Section 2.3.2. Name the new animation *GPDs_fast.gif*. Compare the new animation to the original animation *GDPs.gif*. Is the new animation faster or slower?

2.9 How to move the bar chart to the right and the line chart to the left in the combined graph in Section 2.5.1?

2.10 How to make the pie chart display two digits after decimal in the percentage numbers in Section 2.6.1?

II

Machine Learning Basics

## CHAPTER 3

Machine Learning: An Overview

[Machine Learning is]... a field of study that gives computers the ability to learn
without being explicitly programmed.
–Arthur Samuel, in 1959

ON MAY 11, 1997, the IBM supercomputer Chess engine, Deep Blue, beat
the world Chess champion, Gary Kasparov [7]. It was the first time a
machine has triumphed over humans in a Chess tournament. The news garnered
much media attention. However, the artificial intelligence (AI) algorithm behind Deep
Blue, though impressive and powerful, was the traditional rule-based techniques, not
machine learning (ML) models.

Fast forward 19 years to May 9, 2016, Google DeepMind's AlphaGo beat the world
Go champion Lee Sedol [4]. AI has again stolen the spotlight and generated a media
frenzy. This time, a new type of AI algorithm, namely machine learning (more specifically, deep reinforcement learning) was the driving force behind the game strategies.
You may wonder: What exactly is ML? How is it related to AI? Why is it so popular
these days?

In this chapter, you'll learn what ML is and how it's different from the traditional
algorithms in AI. We'll discuss three different types of ML, namely supervised learning, unsupervised learning, and reinforcement learning. The three types of ML use
different types of data, different methodologies, and have applications on different
types of problems.

You'll also have an overview of what will be covered in later chapters and how they
fit into the three different types of ML. Finally, we'll lay out a real world example
as a motivation on what ML can achieve and how you can apply ML to real-world
problem solving.

New Skills in This Chapter

- Learning the difference between rule-based AI and machine learning
- Understanding three different types of machine learning
- Getting to know the learning process, common algorithms, and main applications of supervised learning, unsupervised learning, and reinforcement learning
- Understanding deep learning and deep reinforcement learning

---

Before you start, open the Jupyter Notebook app in the virtual environment MLA on your computer. After that, open a blank Jupyter notebook and save it as *ch03.ipynb* in the directory /Desktop/mla/ on your computer. Next, we'll create a subdirectory /files/ch03/ to store files in this chapter.

Start a new cell in *ch03.ipynb* and execute the following lines of code in it:

[1]:
```
import os

os.makedirs("files/ch03", exist_ok=True)
```

You should see the new folder /Desktop/mla/files/ch03/ on your computer.

3.1 ML: A NEW PARADIGM FOR AI

The advancements of AI are quicker than most scientists have imagined. AI has generated much media fanfare and it's redefining the way we live. But exactly what is AI?

In the section, you'll learn what AI is and how ML has emerged as a new paradigm in AI.

3.1.1 What is AI?

It's widely believed that the term AI is coined by John McCarthy in 1955. The word artificial in AI means that it's man-made, instead of naturally occurring in the world. AI is intelligence generated by human-engineered machines. It's different from natural intelligence demonstrated by humans and other animals.

When people hear about AI, the first thing comes to their mind is usually a robot. In reality, AI is much more than that. Nowadays, AI is integrated into every aspect of our lives: examples include recommendations systems, voice assistants, foreign language translators... AI is based on the idea that human intelligence can be replicated by machines. Shortly after the computer was invented, scientists have been working on simulating human intelligence in machines to solve complicated problems.

> ### What is AI?
>
> According to Merriam Webster, AI is "a branch of computer science dealing with the simulation of intelligent behavior in computers."

3.1.2 Rule-Based AI

Broadly speaking, there are two ways to make a machine mimic human intelligence: to program it or to teach it to learn. To program a computer to mimic human intelligence is to lay out the rules and tell the computer what to do in each situation. This is rule-based AI.

Rule-based AI is a traditional AI technique. It is the AI algorithm behind Deep Blue, for example. To achieve rule-based AI, humans code all the rules into a machine and tell the machine what to do in each situation based on the rules. In the case of Deep Blue, the machine calculates hundreds of billions of Chess board positions in the three minutes allotted for a player to make a move, and makes a decision based on which next move has the best chance of winning the game. In other words, in rule-based AI models, we feed the algorithms the rules and the input variables and the machine tells us what the output should be.

Rule-based AI achieved great feats in the late 20th century by automating mundane jobs and increasing productivity. According to Forbes, by 1985, corporations spent $1 billion a year on AI systems [16]. Deep Blue brought AI to headline news when it beat then world Chess champion Gary Gasparov in 1997.

However, rule-based AI has its limitations. In many situations, rules are not known to humans. In other situations, rules are known to humans, but they are hard or even impossible to be programmed onto a computer. For example, humans can tell a dog from a cat at a quick glance. However, if you ask humans to describe all the features that distinguish a dog from a cat, most people will fail. Even if they can articulate a list of features to tell the two apart, it's hard to write a computer program to classify dog and cat images.

This brings us to the new approach in AI, which we'll discuss below.

3.1.3 What is ML? Why ML Matters?

Machine learning (ML) is a new paradigm in AI. The method is very different from the traditional rule-based AI. Instead of programming all the rules onto a computer and telling the computer what to do in each situation, we feed the computer many different examples and let the computer learn what the rules are.

Arthur Samuel, a pioneer in AI, first coined the term ML in 1959. ML takes a diametrically different approach to AI. Instead of coding in a set of rules and telling the machine what to do, humans give the machine a large number of examples and ask the machine what the rules are. It's a process for machines to infer rules from example data.

This new approach to AI is appealing in situations where coding in rules is either too difficult or downright impossible. In some situations, the rules are clear and relatively easy to code in a computer program, such as in a Tic Tac Toe game. Humans can use a MiniMax algorithm (which is rule-based AI) to find a perfect solution to the game. However, in many other situations, the rules are too complicated or even impossible to code in a computer program. For example, in the game of Go, players usually make a move without explicitly knowing why it's a good move. They only know intuitively it makes sense. This makes it difficult to use rule-based AI to program a Go-player.

Rule-Based AI versus ML

In rule-based AI, we hard code the rules into the algorithm and ask the algorithm to tell us what the decision should be. In contrast, in ML, we feed the model with example data and ask the model to learn from the data and tell us what the rules are.

3.1.4 Why is ML so Popular?

If scientists started research in ML since 1950s, why is it becoming so popular only in the last couple of decades? Several factors contributed to the recent rise of ML: advancements in computing power, availability of big data, and breakthroughs in ML research. I'll elaborate below.

Advancements in computing power: As you'll see later in this book, ML algorithms are computationally costly and time-consuming. For example, OpenAI's GPT-3 model has 175 billion parameters. A model with so many parameters was impossible to train a couple of decades ago. The recent advancements in computing power make the training of many complicated ML systems possible. In particular, nowadays deep learning models can be trained using graphics processing units (GPUs) instead of central processing units (CPUs). Since GPUs devote more transistors to arithmetic units than CPUs, they have greatly reduced the training time. Further, distributed deep learning combines the computing power of multiple machines, which has greatly accelerated the ML research and development.

Availability of data: An article in The Economist in 2017 says that "the worlds' most valuable resource is no longer oil, but data" [13]. ML models require a large amount of quality data to train the parameters. In the last couple of decades, the rise of big data has generated a need for ML models to analyze them. At the same time, the availability of big data makes the training of ever more advanced ML models possible.

Breakthroughs in ML research: ML research has seen many breakthroughs in the last few decades. In particular, the invention of Convolutional Neural Networks (CNNs) has greatly improved the power of deep neural networks (DNNs). CNNs have put deep learning at the cutting edge of artificial intelligence. Because of CNNs, deep learning is now the most promising field in machine learning. CNNs use a different type of layers than the regular fully-connected layers of neurons. A convolutional layer treats an image as a two-dimensional object and finds patterns on the image. It then associates these patterns with the image labels. This greatly improves the predictive power of the model. Deep learning is also applied to other types of ML models such as reinforcement learning, which further accelerated the power of ML. Deep reinforcement learning (which is a combination of deep neural networks and reinforcement learning) was the brain behind DeepMind's algorithm that beat the world Go champion Lee Sedol in 2016.

3.2 DIFFERENT TYPES OF ML

There are different types of algorithms used in the field of ML to solve complicated problems. Broadly speaking, ML can be classified into three different types: supervised learning, unsupervised learning, and reinforcement learning. Below, we'll discuss their main characteristics, how the learning process works, different algorithms in each type, and their main applications.

3.2.1 Supervised Learning

Supervised learning uses labeled data to train ML models. Labeled data mean that the output is already known to you. For example, we may have thousands of pictures of dogs and cats. Labeled data tell us whether each picture is a dog or a cat. A supervised learning model learns from labeled data and extracts patterns in the input data. Based on these patterns, the trained model then maps inputs (dog or cat images) to outputs (i.e., labels: whether the picture is a dog or a cat). After learning from thousands of picture-label pairs, the trained model then takes an input, and makes a prediction on what the output should be.

In this book, you'll use supervised learning to classify images into a horse or a deer in a binary classification problem. You'll then extend the technique to a multiple classification problem in which you classify images into one of the ten groups (planes, trucks, frogs, and so on).

The name supervised training reflects the fact that the training process needs human supervision: human curated data (input-output pairs) need to be prepared before the training process.

Classification and Regression Problems in Supervised Learning

Depending on whether the label is a continuous variable or a categorical variable, supervised learning can be grouped into regression problems or classification problems. When the label is a continuous variable, such as the housing price or the temperature, it's a regression problem. On the other hand, when the label is a categorical value such as Yes or No in loan application approval decisions, it is a classification problem.

Below, we summarize the learning process, the common algorithms used, and the applications of supervised learning.

Learning Process: The learning process for supervised learning is as follows. The starting point is the human-curated data. The data contain many pairs of input variables and output variables. We then choose a supervised ML model to learn from the input-output pairs. After the training, we feed the model with inputs and the model tells us what the output should be.

Common Algorithms: There are different algorithms people can use in supervised learning. Some examples include:

- Linear regressions
- Logistic regressions
- Random forests
- Gradient boosting machines
- Neural networks

In this book, we'll focus mainly on neural networks as our supervised learning model. But you'll also see some examples of linear regressions and logistic regressions.

Applications: Supervised learning is used when the human-curated data is relatively easy to obtain. It's widely used in computer vision, image classifications, natural language processing, and genomics.

3.2.2 Unsupervised Learning

Unsupervised learning doesn't use labeled data. Instead, it uses unlabeled data that have no output variable for each observation. An unsupervised learning model uses the input data to identify patterns and features for the purpose of generating the output variable.

The unsupervised learning doesn't need external supervision in the sense that the model doesn't need human curated and labeled data to train the model. While in supervised learning, the data we use to train the model are input-output pairs, in reality, we don't know the labels of the data in many situations. For example, you may have thousands of news articles and you want to sort them into different categories such as sports news, weather news, entertainment news, and so on. Further, we can use unsupervised learning to generate labels for the input data so that the new dataset can be used in supervised learning.

Because there are no pre-assigned target variables for the input data, unsupervised learning models must find naturally-occurring similarities, differences, and other patterns from the input data. Examples of unsupervised learning methods include clustering, principal component analysis, and data visualization (plotting, graphing, and so on). The unsupervised learning has attracted far less attention than the other two types of ML. In this book, we don't cover unsupervised learning in detail.

Below, I summarize the learning process, the common algorithms used, and the applications of unsupervised learning.

Learning Process: The learning process for unsupervised learning is as follows. The starting point is the unstructured, unlabeled data. The data contain many observations of input variables, but each observation has no target variable. We then choose an unsupervised model to learn from the naturally occurring patterns in the input data and generate a label for each observation.

Common Algorithms: Some common algorithms used in unsupervised learning include:

- K-means clustering
- Hierarchical clustering
- Principal component analysis

In this book, we'll not cover any specific unsupervised learning algorithm.

Applications: Unsupervised learning is used when the input variables are easy to obtain but it's hard to generate labels for each observation. It's commonly used in data visualization, dimension reduction, and recommendation systems.

3.2.3 Reinforcement Learning

Reinforcement learning (RL) deals with how intelligent agents should take optimal actions in an environment to maximize cumulative rewards. RL differs from supervised learning in the sense that no labeled input/output pairs are needed for the purpose of training. The training approach is by using trial and error. The agent explores different actions and gets either rewards or penalties for the action taken.

In both supervised and unsupervised learning, we need plenty of data to feed into the model. However, in many situations, the data is hard to come by. All we can observe is the outcome of the actions. In such cases, we need to rely on reinforcement leaning.

In reinforcement learning, an agent operates in an environment through trial and error. The agent learns to achieve the optimal outcome by receiving feedback from the environment in the form of rewards. In Parts V and VI of the book, we'll discuss various types of reinforcement learning methods.

Below, I summarize the learning process, the common algorithms used, and the applications of reinforcement learning.

Learning Process: In RL, we need an environment to train the agent. The agent can choose different actions in each step. The outcome can be observed in the form of a reward or a penalty, and the agent learns from the outcome to maximize the expected cumulative payoff from a sequence of actions.

Common Algorithms: Some common algorithms used in RL include

- Q-learning
- Policy gradients
- Deep Q-learning

In this book, we'll cover all the above three algorithms.

Applications: RL is widely used in the gaming industry to train intelligent game strategies. It's also used to train robots and to develop self driving cars.

3.3 DEEP REINFORCEMENT LEARNING

Deep Learning and Deep Reinforcement Learning are the coolest buzz words these days in the AI world. Exactly what are deep learning and deep reinforcement learning?

In this section, I'll briefly discuss what they are and where you'll learn them in this book.

3.3.1 Deep Learning

Deep learning is a special case of the neural networks algorithm we just mentioned above when we discuss supervised learning. As you'll see later in this book, a neural network has an input layer, an output layer, and any number of hidden layers. When the number of hidden layers in the neural network is small, say, with just 1 or 2 hidden layers, it's called a shallow neural network. On the other hand, if the number of hidden layers is large, say, 5 or 10, we call it a deep neural network. Deep learning is ML with deep neural networks.

3.3.2 Combine Deep Learning and Reinforcement Learning

We discussed that there are different algorithms in RL, such as Q-learning and policy gradients. When we combine deep neural networks with reinforcement learning, we have deep reinforcement learning.

In particular, one type of deep reinforcement learning is deep Q-learning. In many machine learning problems, the number of states is discrete and finite, but huge. Examples include the Chess or Go game, in which the number of possible scenarios is astronomical. It's impractical to create a Q-table for these types of games for two reasons: First, the computer will not have enough memory to save and update a Q-table with so many different states; Second, it will be too computationally costly to explore all possible states to calculate and update the correct Q values. Instead, we'll combine Q-learning and deep learning and use a deep neural network to approximate the Q values. That's the idea behind deep Q-learning.

3.4 APPLY ML IN THE REAL WORLD

In recent years, many companies have greatly improved their products and services using machine learning. These companies become market winners. We'll show in this book that you can apply ML in real-world problem-solving as well. Further, it's actually easy and fun to apply ML in the real world.

3.4.1 The Delivery Route Problem

You can apply machine learning to your daily life.

Here we use a real-world example to illustrate the point. Imagine you live in a small town and deliver packages for Amazon for a living. Residents in your town live on a 10 by 10 grid as shown in Figure 3.1. Each residence is marked by coordinates (x, y). The Amazon Hub is located in H=(x=6, y=6). The green area in the town is a park so there are no households inside. The town has a total of 90 households: There are a total of 10×10=100 coordinates, but nine coordinates fall inside the park ((x=3, y=3), (x=3, y=4), (x=3, y=5), (x=4, y=3), (x=4, y=4), (x=4, y=5), (x=5, y=3), (x=5, y=4), (x=5, y=5)), and the Amazon Hub occupies one. Therefore, we have a total of 100-9-1=90 households. Each day, you'll deliver 8 packages to 8 different households. The 8 households are different each day. You want to use machine learning to find out the shortest route for you each day, no matter what the 8 households are. At the end of the book, you'll be able to use machine learning to solve the problem. Along the way, you'll learn how MLs work.

3.4.2 Try the Problem before You Know the Answer

Later in Chapter 16, we'll provide an answer to the problem using RL. The solution will give you the shortest route no matter what the eight households are. You'll get the answer in one minute or so from an ML model on your computer.

To appreciate the power of ML, I'll let you try it before you know the answer. Suppose the 8 households you have to deliver to are: (x=1, y=2), (x=5, y=0), (x=3, y=2), (x=9, y=9), (x=7, y=2), (x=0, y=7), (x=1, y=5), (x=1, y=3). Remember, you'll start at the Amazon Hub (x=6, y=6) and finish at the Amazon hub as well.

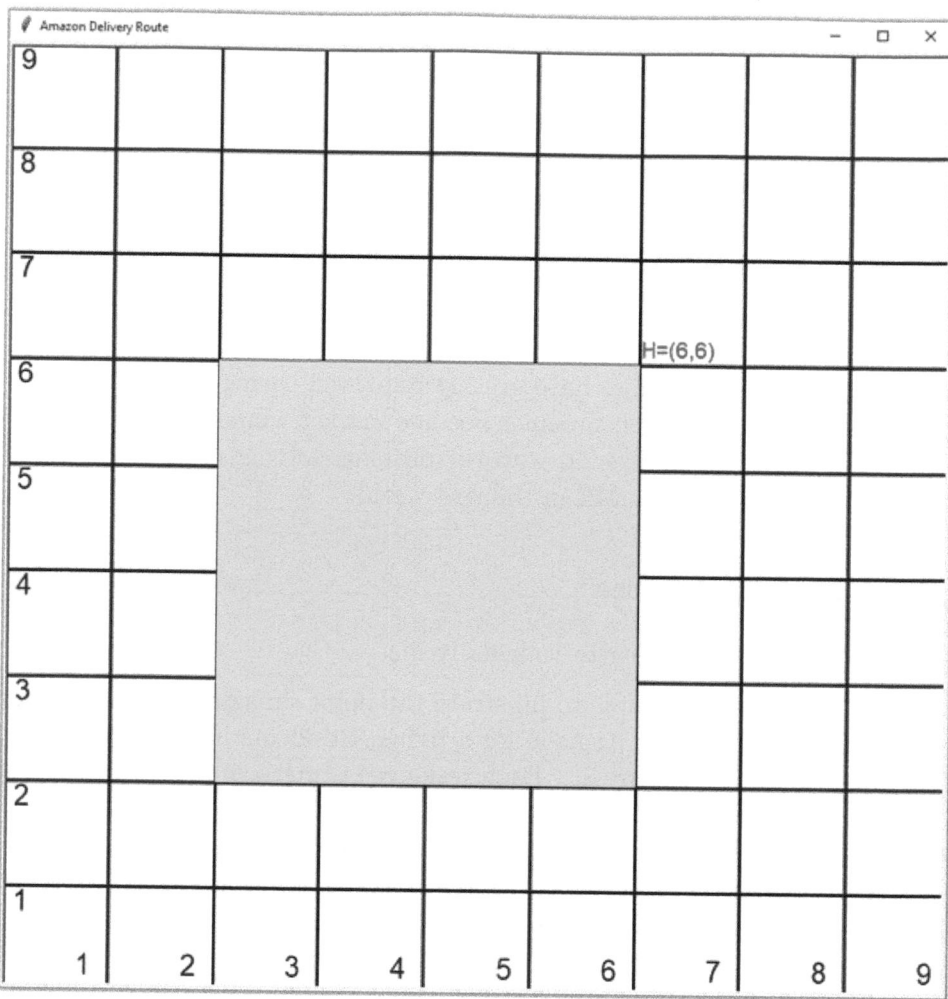

Figure 3.1 The map for the delivery route problem

Spend a few minutes and map out the shortest route. Also calculate how many blocks you have to travel in total. Write your answer in a file called *MyAnswer.txt* and save it in the folder /Desktop/mla/files/ch03/ for comparison with the answer in Chapter 16.

3.5 GLOSSARY

- **Artificial Intelligence (AI):** A branch of computer science dealing with the simulation of intelligent behavior in computers. It is different from natural intelligence from humans and other animals.
- **Machine Learning (ML):** A branch of artificial intelligence (AI) in which humans give computers the ability to learn without being explicitly programmed.
- **Reinforcement Learning (RL):** A type of ML in which agents interact with

an environment to explore different actions. Agents learn to choose actions to maximize the cumulative rewards through trial and error.

- **Rule-Based AI:** A branch of artificial intelligence (AI) in which humans give computers the rules and ask the computers what to do in certain situations.
- **Supervised Learning:** A type of ML in which the model uses labeled data to learn the relation between the input variables and the output variables.
- **Unsupervised Learning:** A type of ML in which the model uses unlabeled data to learn the similarities, differences, and other patterns among the input variables to generate the output variables.

3.6 EXERCISES

3.1 What is artificial intelligence (AI)?

3.2 What is rule-based AI?

3.3 What is machine learning (ML)? How is it different from rule-based AI?

3.4 What are the three types of ML?

3.5 What is supervised learning? What are the learning process, common algorithms, and applications of supervised learning?

3.6 What is the difference between classification problems and regression problems? Find an example for each type of problems.

3.7 What is unsupervised learning? What are the learning process, common algorithms, and applications of unsupervised learning?

3.8 What is reinforcement learning? What are the learning process, common algorithms, and applications of reinforcement learning?

3.9 What are deep learning and deep reinforcement learning?

3.10 Create an answer for the delivery route problem in this chapter. Save your answers (the shortest route and the number of blocks to be traveled) in a file *MyAnswer.txt* in /Desktop/mla/files/ch03/.

## CHAPTER 4

Gradient Descent – Where Magic Happens

In view of all that we have said in the foregoing sections, the many obstacles we appear to have surmounted, what casts the pall over our victory celebration? It is the curse of dimensionality, a malediction that has plagued the scientist from the earliest days.

Adaptive Control Processes: A Guided Tour
–Richard Bellman, 1961

THIS BOOK SUMMARIZES supervised learning in three words: initialize, adjust, and repeat.

The idea behind supervised learning is surprisingly simple. In essence, supervised learning consists of three steps:

- Step 1 (Initialize): Random values are assigned to the model parameters;
- Step 2 (Adjust): The model makes predictions based on the current parameters; the model then compares the predictions with the actual values (i.e., labels); the model adjusts parameters accordingly: if the prediction is too large (small), the model adjusts the parameters so that the prediction will be smaller (larger) in the next iteration;
- Step 3 (Repeat): The model repeats Step 2 thousands or millions of times until the parameters converge.

Such a simple idea leads to amazing results, including beating the world Champion in the Go game, recognizing images, voice assistants, self-driving cars...

Step 2 or the word "adjust" is where the magic of ML happens. It's achieved through gradient descent or some variant of it. This chapter uses animations to show step by step how the parameter values change based on gradient descent so that a certain goal is achieved. Specifically, ML is the process of finding a way to make predictions

DOI: 10.1201/b23383-4

with the lowest forecasting error. In mathematical terms, machine learning is trying to find parameter values that minimize the loss function.

This chapter will show you how gradient descent helps us find the right parameter values quickly and efficiently. You'll learn exactly how ML algorithms make gradual changes to the parameter values: the change is proportional to the negative value of the first derivative of the loss function with respect to the parameters. You'll also know what the learning rate is and how it affects the training process.

New Skills in This Chapter

- Optimization through grid search
- Finding the optimal value through the gradient descent algorithm
- Choosing the right learning rate in gradient descent
- Using the GradientTape API in TensorFlow to calculate gradients

---

Before you start, open the Jupyter Notebook app in the virtual environment MLA on your computer. After that, open a blank Jupyter notebook and save it as *ch04.ipynb* in the directory /Desktop/mla/ on your computer. Next, we'll create a subdirectory /files/ch04/ to store files in this chapter.

Start a new cell in *ch04.ipynb* and execute the following lines of code in it:

[1]:
```
import os

os.makedirs("files/ch04", exist_ok=True)
```

4.1 OPTIMIZATION THROUGH GRID SEARCH

This section discusses how to find the best parameter values though grid search, a brute force method.

4.1.1 How Grid Search Achieves Optimization

Suppose you want to find the value of x to minimize the value of $y = (x - 10)^2$. A brute force approach is to look at many different values of x and see which one leads to the lowest value of y. The method is called grid search. The idea is to look at different values in each parameter, and see which combination of parameters leads to the best result.

The Loss Function in ML

The loss function in ML is the objective function in the mathematical optimization process. Intuitively, the loss function measures the forecasting error of the ML model. By minimizing the loss function, the ML model finds parameter values that lead to the best predictions. In the example above, we can think of $y = (x - 10)^2$ as the loss function, and the objective is to find a value of x that leads to the best prediction for the true value 10.

In our example, we have only one parameter, x. So we look at 2000 different values of x between 0 and 20 and see which value leads to the lowest value of $y = (x - 10)^2$.

This can be easily done in Python as follows:

```
[2]: import numpy as np

# Create 2000 different values of x and y
x=np.linspace(0,20,2000)
y=(x-10)**2
# Find out the lowest value of y
min_y = np.min(y)
print(f"the minimum y is {min_y}")
# Find out the optimal value x
argmin_y = np.argmin(y)
print(f"the minimum y is indexed at {argmin_y}")
best_x = x[argmin_y]
print(f"the optimal x is {best_x}")
```

```
the minimum y is 2.5025018762497603e-05
the minimum y is indexed at 1000
the optimal x is 10.005002501250624
```

We use the *linspace()* method in NumPy to create 2000 different values of x between 0 and 20. For each value of x, we calculate the value of $y = (x - 10)^2$. The *min()* method returns the lowest value of y and we call the value *min_y*. The *argmin()* method returns the index value of the lowest y. The output from the above cell tells us that the 1000th y has the lowest value. We can also find out the optimal x by using the index. The results show that when $x = 10.005$, the minimum value of y is achieved, at $y = 0.000025$, which is very close to the true minimum value of $y = 0$.

Next, you'll create a graph showing the relation between the value of x and the function $y = (x - 10)^2$. The graph will also show the lowest value of y and the optimal value of x found through the grid search algorithm above.

[3]:
```python
from matplotlib import pyplot as plt

fig=plt.figure(dpi=100,figsize=(8,6))
plt.grid()
plt.plot(x,y,color='blue',label="$y=(x-10)^2$")
plt.scatter(best_x, min_y,color='red',s=150)
plt.plot([0,10],[0,0],color='red',linestyle='dashed')
plt.plot([10,10],[-10,0],color='red',linestyle='dashed')
plt.xlim(0,20)
plt.ylim(-10,100)
plt.xlabel("value of x")
plt.ylabel("value of $y=(x-10)^2$")
plt.title("Finding the Minimum $y$ Using Grid Search")
plt.legend(loc="upper right")
# add text to explain
txt=plt.annotate(
    f'Mininum y:    {round(min_y,6)}\nValue of x:\
    {round(best_x,3)}',
    xy=(best_x, min_y),
    xytext=(0.2,0.5),
    textcoords='axes fraction',
    bbox=dict(boxstyle="round", fc="0.9"),
    arrowprops=dict(arrowstyle='->',
        color='g',linewidth = 1),fontsize = 15)
```

We create a figure that is 8 inches wide and 6 inches tall with dpi=100. We use the *grid()* method to include gridlines in the picture. We then plot the values of y against the values of x. To put mathematical equations in the label, you can use the dollar sign ($) around the equation. We use the *scatter()* method to create a large red dot as the solution to the grid search; as a result, a red dot is shown at *(x=10.005, y=0.000025)*. The label for the y-axis is *value of $y = (x - 10)^2$*, with an equation in it. Again, simply put dollar signs around the equation for it to appear in the graph anywhere (title, x-label, y-label, or the legend).

We use the *annotate()* function to create a text box inside the figure. The first argument is the message you want to display in the text box. The xy argument in *annotate()* tells the arrow where to point to. The xytext=() argument in *annotate()* defines the position of the text box in the figure. The textcoords='axes fraction' argument says that the coordinates in the xytext=(0.2, 0.5) argument uses axes fraction system, which means that (0, 0) is lower left of the axes and (1, 1) is upper right of the axes. We also specify that the arrow should be green with a line width of 1, and the font size inside the text box should be 15. You can change the parameters in the *annotate()* function to see how they change the figure.

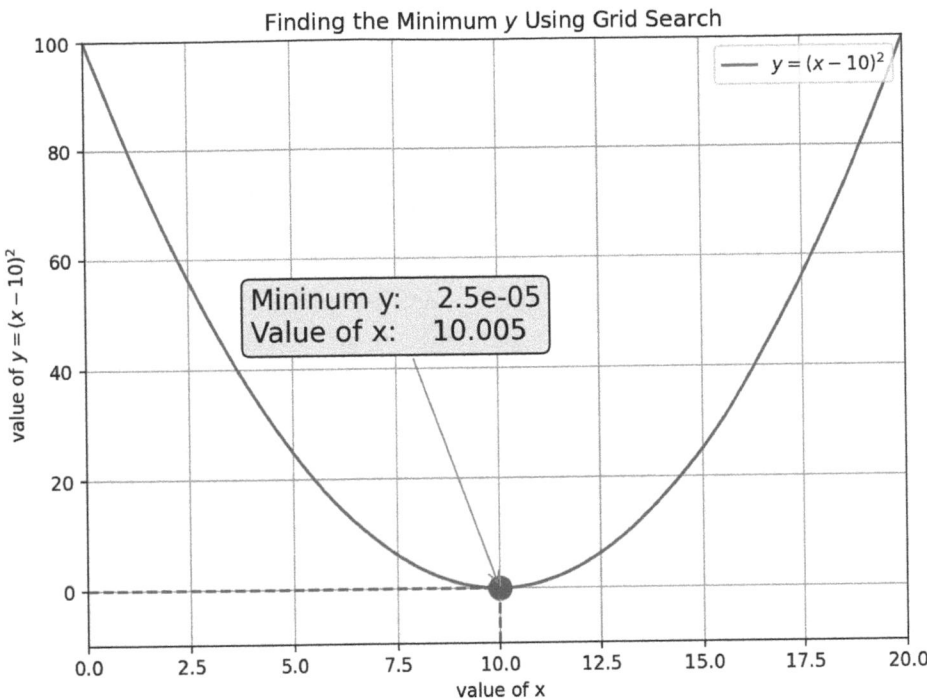

Figure 4.1 Finding minimum $y = (x - 10)^2$ through grid search

---

Two Ways of Importing A Sub-Package

When you import a subpackage from a package, you can use one of the two ways:

- from package import subpackage
- import package.subpackage

For example, when you import the *pyplot* subpackage from *matplotlib* and give it a short name *plt*, you can use one of the two ways:

- from matplotlib import pyplot as plt
- import matplotlib.pyplot as plt

After that, you can call the subpakcage *pyplot* in the program using the short name *plt*.

Run the above cell, and you'll see an output as in Figure 4.1. The figure is also available under /files/ch04/fig4.1.png in the book's GitHub repository.

4.1.2   Curse of Dimensionality and Directional Grid Search

Grid search works only if the number of parameters is small. In the above example, we only need to find out the value of one parameter, x. Many machine learning models, such as neural networks, have thousands or even millions of parameters (OpenAI's third generation generative pre-trained transformer, GPT-3, has about 175 billion parameters). It's infeasible to conduct a grid search with so many parameters.

Curse of Dimensionality

The term curse of dimensionality was coined by mathematician Richard Bellman when considering problems in dynamic programming. See the opening quote of this chapter by Richard Bellman in his 1961 book "Adaptive Control Processes: A Guided Tour" [2]. The curse of dimensionality refers to various problems and complications when dealing with high-dimensional space. In our setting of grid search, it means when the number of parameters increases, the number of searches we have to perform in order to find the optimal parameters grows exponentially.

It is difficult to optimize a function of many variables by searching on a discrete multidimensional grid. The number of possible combinations increases exponentially with dimensionality. To illustrate the point, suppose you want to find the values of 10 parameters, x_1, x_2,...x_{10}, to minimize the value of $y = (x_1 - 1)^2 + (x_2 - 2)^2 + ... + (x_{10} - 10)^2$. If we search 2000 values for each parameter as we did in the above example, the total number of possibilities is 2000^{10}, an astronomical number. This is the so-called curse of dimensionality problem with grid search.

One solution to speed up grid search is to use the gradients to guide us as to which direction to go.

Why Move in the Opposite Direction of the Gradient?

By definition, the first derivative of a function $f(x)$ with respect to x is

$$f'(x) = \lim_{h \to 0} \frac{f(x + h) - f(x)}{(x + h) - x}$$

It tells us when the value of x changes by a small amount, how much will the value of $f(x)$ change. In particular, $f'(x) > 0$ means that when x increases, the value of $f(x)$ increases. In contrast, if $f'(x) < 0$, this means when x increases, the value of $f(x)$ decreases.

Therefore, in order to minimize the value of y, we should move in the opposite direction of the first derivative $\frac{dy}{dx}$. Why? If $\frac{dy}{dx} > 0$, this tells us that when we increase x, the value of y will also increase. But since we want to minimize the value of y, by reducing the value of x (i.e., the opposite direction of $\frac{dy}{dx} > 0$), we'll reduce the value of y to achieve our goal. Similarly, if $\frac{dy}{dx} < 0$, this tells us that when we increase x, the value of y will decrease. Hence we should move in the opposite direction of $\frac{dy}{dx} < 0$, that is, by increasing the value of x to minimize y.

Next, we'll implement the idea of directional grid search. Suppose when the incremental change of y is less than 0.0001, we consider the value to be converged and the minimum is found. If the value of y doesn't converge after 2000 iterations, we consider the directional grid search a failure.

A critical hyper-parameter to choose is how much to change the value of x in each iteration. If we make too small a change to x, it takes too long to converge and it's computationally costly. On the other hand, if we make too large a change to x in each iteration, the value of y will oscillate back and forth around the value of the true minimum. As a result, it may take too long for the values of x and y to converge or they never converge.

We need to consider a moderate value of incremental change. Specifically, we increase the value of x by 0.01 in each iteration.

```
[4]:   # randomly selects an initial value of x
       x0=1.2345
       y0=(x0-10)**2
       # how much to adjust the value of x in each iteration
       step=0.01
       # keep track of the values of x and y
       ys=[]
       xs=[]
       xs.append(x0)
       ys.append(y0)
       # find the derivative; i.e., gradient
       def dydx(x):
           dydx=2*(x-10)
           return dydx
       # starts the directional grid search
       x=x0
       for i in range(1,2001,1):
           # directional grid search
           if dydx(x)>0:
               x=x-step
           else:
               x=x+step
           # calculate the current value of y
           y=(x-10)**2
           # record values of x and y
           xs.append(x)
           ys.append(y)
           # stop if the change is smaller than 0.0001
           if abs(ys[-1]-ys[-2])<=0.0001:
               print(f"find minimum after {i} steps")
               print(f"the minimum y is {ys[-1]}")
```

```
        print(f"the optimal x is {xs[-1]}")
        break
    # quit if not converge after 2000 iterations
    else:
        if i==2000:
            print("fail to find the minimum")
# keep track of values
min_y = y
argmin_y = i
best_x = x
```

```
find minimum after 877 steps
the minimum y is 2.0249999998482748e-05
the optimal x is 10.004499999999831
```

The results show that after 877 steps, the value of y converges. The minimum value of y, 2.025e-5, is even smaller than the one we find using grid search, 2.5e-5.

In the cell below, we draw a picture of the searching process. We plot the value of the function $y = (x - 10)^2$ against the value of x. We also show the result of the optimization process. We use the green arrows to show the process of the search (how the values of x and y change in each step).

[5]:
```
fig, ax=plt.subplots(figsize=(8,6), dpi=100)
plt.grid()
x=np.linspace(0,20,2000)
y=(x-10)**2
ax.plot(x,y,color='blue',label="$y=(x-10)^2$")
plt.scatter(best_x, min_y,color='red',s=150)
ax.plot([0,10],[0,0],color='red',linestyle='dashed')
ax.plot([10,10],[-10,0],color='red',linestyle='dashed')
ax.set_xlim(0,20)
ax.set_ylim(-10,100)
ax.set_xlabel("value of x")
ax.set_ylabel("value of $y=(x-10)^2$")
ax.set_title("Directional Grid Search")
plt.legend(loc="upper right")
# add text to explain
txt = ax.annotate(
    f'Step size: {step}\n# of steps: {argmin_y}',
    xy = (best_x, min_y),
    xytext = (0.4,0.5),
    textcoords = 'axes fraction',
    bbox = dict(boxstyle="round", fc="0.9"),
    arrowprops=dict(arrowstyle = '->',
        color = 'g', linewidth = 1),fontsize = 15)
```

```
# Show the path of the directional grid search
for k in range(len(xs)-1):
    ax.annotate("",xy = (xs[k+1], ys[k+1]),
    xytext = (xs[k], ys[k]),
    textcoords = 'data',
    bbox = dict(boxstyle="round", fc="0.9"),
    arrowprops=dict(arrowstyle='->',color='g',linewidth=1))
```

Note here we are using the *subplots()* method to create a figure with a subplot ax. Since there is only one subplot in the figure, this is equivalent to creating a figure without subplots. You can look at Section 4.1.1 and find out how to create the same figure without using the *subplots()* method. I'll leave that as an exercise.

4.2 GRADIENT DESCENT

The directional grid search approach cuts the searching iterations by more than half, from 2000 to 877. However, when the number of parameters is large, even directional grid search is prohibitively costly in computational power. Therefore, we'll use the gradient descent algorithm to further reduce the computational needs. The idea is that in each iteration, we'll adjust the value of x so that:

- We change the value of x in the opposite direction of the gradient; that is, when the gradient is positive, decrease the value of x; when the gradient is negative, increase the value of x;
- We adjust the value of x proportional to the magnitude (i.e., the absolute value) of the gradient.

When the magnitude of the gradient $\frac{dy}{dx}$ is large, the point (x, y) is far away from the minimum point. Making a large adjustment will not overshoot. The large adjustment will speed up the optimization process. When the magnitude of the gradient $\frac{dy}{dx}$ is small, the point (x, y) is close to the minimum point. Making a large change may lead to over-adjustment. The small adjustment will make sure that the value of x doesn't overshoot to the other side of the minimum point.

In the cell below, we find the lowest value of y by using the gradient descent approach.

In particular, we calculate the gradient at each step, and change the value of x based on the gradient descent rule: change in the opposite direction, also make sure that the change is proportional to the magnitude of the first derivative of the loss function with respect to the parameter. In our example here, the gradient is easy to calculate:

$$\frac{dy}{dx} = \frac{d(x-10)^2}{dx} = 2(x-10)$$

Therefore, it's easy for us to determine how much we should adjust x in each step.

```
[6]: learning_rate=0.1
     # keep track of the values of x and y
     ys=[]
     xs=[]
     xs.append(x0)
     ys.append(y0)
     # starts the gradient descent
     x=x0
     for i in range(1,2001,1):
         # gradient descent
         x=x-learning_rate*dydx(x)
         # calculate current value of y
         y=(x-10)**2
         # record values of x and y
         xs.append(x)
         ys.append(y)
         # stop if the change is smaller than 0.0001
         if abs(ys[-1]-ys[-2])<=0.0001:
             print(f"find minimum after {i} steps")
             print(f"the minimum y is {ys[-1]}")
             print(f"the optimal x is {xs[-1]}")
             break
         # if not converge after 2000 iterations, quit
         else:
             if i==2000:
                 print("fail to find the minimum")
     # save values
     min_y = y
     argmin_y = i
     best_x = x
```

```
find minimum after 30 steps
the minimum y is 0.00011774774744450676
the optimal x is 9.989148836585644
```

The results show that in just 30 steps, the value of y converges. The green arrows in the graph below illustrate the path of (x, y) in each iteration throughout the learning process.

```
[7]: fig, ax=plt.subplots(figsize=(8,6), dpi=100)
     plt.grid()
     x=np.linspace(0,20,2000)
     y=(x-10)**2
     ax.plot(x,y,color = 'blue',label="$y=(x-10)^2$")
```

```
plt.scatter(best_x, min_y, color = 'red', s=150)
ax.plot([0,10],[0,0],color='red',linestyle='dashed')
ax.plot([10,10],[-10,0],color='red',linestyle='dashed')
ax.set_xlim(0,20)
ax.set_ylim(-10,100)
ax.set_xlabel("value of x")
ax.set_ylabel("value of $y=(x-10)^2$")
ax.set_title("Gradient Descent Optimization")
plt.legend(loc="upper right")
# add text to explain
txt = ax.annotate(
    f'Learning rate: {learning_rate}\n# of steps: {argmin_y}',
    xy = (best_x, min_y),
    xytext = (0.4,0.5),
    textcoords = 'axes fraction',
    bbox = dict(boxstyle="round", fc="0.9"),
    arrowprops=dict(arrowstyle = '->',
                color = 'g', linewidth = 1),
    fontsize = 15)
# Show the path of gradient descent
for k in range(len(xs)-1):
    ax.annotate("", xy = (xs[k+1], ys[k+1]),
    xytext = (xs[k], ys[k]),
    textcoords = 'data',
    bbox = dict(boxstyle="round", fc="0.9"),
    arrowprops=dict(arrowstyle = '->',
        color = 'g', linewidth = 1))
```

At the end of the above cell, we start a for loop to iterate through every step in the learning process. In each step, we draw a green arrow. The end of the green arrow is (x,y) before adjustment, and the head of arrow points to (x,y) after adjustment. We set the text box to empty at each iteration so only the arrows are shown, without any actual text in the figure.

Run the above cell, and you'll see a figure in the output cell. The figure is also available under /files/ch04/gd.png in the book's GitHub repository.

4.3   USE TENSORFLOW TO CALCULATE GRADIENTS

While it's easy to calculate the gradient in the above example when $y = (x - 10)^2$, it's extremely complicated to calculate gradients in most machine learning models such as deep neural networks. Luckily, you can use the TensorFlow library for that purpose.

In this section, you'll first install the TensorFlow library. You'll then learn how to calculate gradients using the library. Finally, you'll solve the optimization problem of finding the lowest y value when $y = (x - 10)^2$. You'll use this skill quite often later in this book because you are required to calculate gradients in many machine learning models (deep neural networks, deep Q-learning, policy gradients, and so on).

4.3.1   Install TensorFlow

To install the TensorFlow library, run the following line of command in the Anaconda prompt (Windows) or a terminal (Mac or Linux), with your virtual environment MLA activated:

```
pip install --user tensorflow==2.12.0
```

Or as a shortcut, you can pip install Python libraries in a cell in your Jupyter notebook *ch04.ipynb* directly. Remember to put the exclamation mark (!) in front of the command, as follows:

```
!pip install --user tensorflow==2.12.0
```

Make sure you restart the Jupyter Notebook app on your computer after installation for the library to take effect.

4.3.2   Calculate Gradients Using TensorFlow

The *gradient()* method can be used to calculate the gradient of a function at any point. The cell below calculates the gradient of $y = (x - 10)^2$ when $x = 2$.

```
[8]:  import tensorflow as tf
      from IPython.display import Markdown as md

      tfx = tf.Variable(2, dtype='float32')
      with tf.GradientTape() as tape:
          ty=(tfx-10)**2
      dydx = tape.gradient(ty,tfx).numpy()
      md(f"the gradient of the function \
      $y=(x-10)^2$ at $x=2$ is {dydx}")
```

[8]: the gradient of the function $y = (x - 10)^2$ at $x = 2$ is -16.0

As a custom, we usually import the TensorFlow library and give it a short name *tf*. We import the *Markdown()* method from *Ipython.display* in order to display mathematical equations in the output cell of the Jupyter Notebook app. If you run the above cell, the result shows that the gradient of the function $y = (x - 10)^2$ at $x = 2$ is -16, which is the correct answer since

$$\frac{dy}{dx} = 2(x - 10) = 2(2 - 10) = -16.$$

> **TensorFlow Gradient Tapes**
>
> The TensorFlow library provides the GradientTape API for calculating the gradient of a function at any point. Specifically, the GradientTape API keeps a record of relevant operations executed inside the context of the API as a tape. The API then uses the tape to compute the gradients using reverse mode differentiation. See the documentation here https://www.tensorflow.org/guide/autodiff for details.

Next, you can calculate the gradient of the function $y = (x - 10)^2$ at various point $x = 2$, $x = 4$,... $x = 18$.

```
[9]: x=np.linspace(0,20,2001)
     y=(x-10)**2

     for i in range(2001):
         if x[i]%2==0 and 2<=x[i]<=18:
             tfx = tf.Variable(x[i], dtype='float32')
             with tf.GradientTape() as tape:
                 ty=(tfx-10)**2
             dydx = tape.gradient(ty,tfx).numpy()
             print(f"the gradient at x={x[i]} is {dydx}")
```

```
the gradient at x=2.0 is -16.0
the gradient at x=4.0 is -12.0
the gradient at x=6.0 is -8.0
the gradient at x=8.0 is -4.0
the gradient at x=10.0 is 0.0
the gradient at x=12.0 is 4.0
the gradient at x=14.0 is 8.0
the gradient at x=16.0 is 12.0
the gradient at x=18.0 is 16.0
```

4.3.3 Gradient Descent Optimization with TensorFlow

We'll revisit the problem of finding the minimum value for $y = (x - 10)^2$. This time, we'll use the TensorFlow library to calculate gradients.

Since we'll do this several times with different learning rates, creating a function is more efficient and reduces the amount of coding.

```
[10]: def GD(lr):
          x0=1.2345
          y0=(x0-10)**2
          learning_rate = lr
          ys=[]
```

```
xs=[]
xs.append(x0)
ys.append(y0)
x=x0
for i in range(1,2001,1):
    # gradient descent
    tfx = tf.Variable(x, dtype='float32')
    with tf.GradientTape() as tape:
        ty=(tfx-10)**2
    dydx = tape.gradient(ty,tfx).numpy()
    x=x-learning_rate*dydx
    # calculate current value of y
    y=(x-10)**2
    # record values of x and y
    xs.append(x)
    ys.append(y)
    # if the change is smaller than 0.0001, stop
    if abs(ys[-1]-ys[-2])<=0.0001:
        print(f"find minimum after {i} steps")
        print(f"the minimum y is {ys[-1]}")
        print(f"the optimal x is {xs[-1]}")
        break
    # if y not converge after 2000 steps, quit
    else:
        if i==2000:
            print("fail to find the minimum")
return y, i, x, xs, ys
```

Here we have defined a function *GD()* that takes an argument lr, which is the learning rate. The function uses the TensorFlow library to calculate gradients at the current value of x. At each iteration, it adjusts the value of x by $-lr \times gradient$.

To find the lowest value of y using gradient descent with a learning rate of 0.1, we simply call the function *GD()* using a learning rate of 0.1 as its argument, like so.

[11]:
```
min_y, argmin_y, best_x, xs, ys = GD(0.1)
```

```
find minimum after 30 steps
the minimum y is 0.0001177467707075305
the optimal x is 9.989148881591857
```

We find exactly the same results as before. Here the only difference is that we have used a different way of calculating gradients: in Section 4.2, we calculate the gradient using the closed-form solution $\frac{dy}{dx} = 2(x-10)$; here we use the TensorFlow library to calculate the gradient.

4.3.4 Animate the Optimization Process

Next, we'll create an animation of the intermediate steps of the gradient descent optimization algorithm we just used in Section 4.3.3.

First, we define a *draw()* function to create a sequence of pictures. The *draw()* function takes four arguments: prefix is used to put a prefix in each picture; lr is the learning rate; xs and ys are the intermediate x- and y-values in each iteration during the gradient descent optimization process.

```python
def draw(prefix, lr, xs, ys):
    x_points=np.linspace(0,20,2000)
    y_points=(x_points-10)**2
    for i in range(30):
        xsi, ysi = xs[:i+2], ys[:i+2]
        fig, ax=plt.subplots(figsize=(8,6), dpi=100)
        plt.grid()
        ax.plot(x_points,y_points,color='b',label="$y=(x-10)^2$")
        plt.scatter(xsi[-1], ysi[-1],color ='red',s=150)
        ax.plot([0,10],[0,0],color='red',linestyle='dashed')
        ax.plot([10,10],[-10,0],color='red',linestyle='dashed')
        ax.set_xlim(0,20)
        ax.set_ylim(-10,100)
        ax.set_xlabel("value of x", fontsize=12)
        ax.set_ylabel("value of $y=(x-10)^2$",fontsize=12)
        ax.set_title(f"Gradient Descent with lr={lr}",fontsize=16)
        plt.legend(loc="upper right", fontsize=15)
        # add text to explain
        txt = ax.annotate(
            f'''Learning rate: {lr}''',
            xy = (xsi[-1], ysi[-1]),
            xytext = (0.64,0.1), fontsize=12,
            textcoords = 'axes fraction',
            bbox = dict(boxstyle="round", fc="0.9"))
        txt = ax.annotate(
            f'''Step {i+1}\nx = {round(xsi[-1],5)}''',
            xy = (xsi[-1], ysi[-1]),
            xytext = (0.4,0.8),
            textcoords = 'axes fraction',
            bbox = dict(boxstyle="round", fc="0.9"),
            arrowprops=dict(arrowstyle = '->',
                color = 'm', linewidth = 1),
            fontsize = 15)
        # Show the path of gradient descent
        for k in range(len(xsi)-1):
            ax.annotate("",xy = (xs[k+1], ys[k+1]),
```

```
                 xytext = (xs[k], ys[k]),
                 textcoords = 'data',
                 bbox = dict(boxstyle="round", fc="0.9"),
                 arrowprops=dict(arrowstyle = '->',
                     color = 'g', linewidth = 1))
        fig.savefig(f"files/ch04/{prefix}{i}.png")
        plt.close(fig)
```

Note here we use only the first 30 interactions to create 30 pictures. If we create instead all 2000 pictures when there are 2000 iterations, it takes several hours to generate the data. Further, having so many pictures saved on your computer will take up too much space on your hard drive.

We use a text box to show what the learning rate is. Another text box shows which step the learning process is in and the x- and y-values in that step. At the end, we create a green arrow for each step to go from the before-adjustment (x, y) to after-adjustment (x, y).

Run the above cell and nothing will happen because we just define the *draw()* function here. Next, we call the *draw()* function, and put the prefix as "lr_medium". As a result, all the pictures saved will have a prefix of "lr_medium". The learning rate is 0.1, and the x- and y-values are xs and ys.

[13]:
```
draw("lr_medium", 0.1, xs, ys)
```

Run the above cell, and you'll see 30 pictures in the folder /Desktop/mla/ch04/files/: lr_medium0.png, lr_medium1.png, ..., and lr_medium29.png. Next, we'll combine the png files into an animation.

[14]:
```
import PIL, imageio

def gif(prefix):
    frames=[]
    for i in range(30):
        frame=PIL.Image.open(f"files/ch04/{prefix}{i}.png")
        frame=np.asarray(frame)
        frames.append(np.array(frame))
    imageio.mimsave(f'files/ch04/{prefix}.gif', frames, fps=5)
```

Here we define a *gif()* function to combine pictures into an animation. The prefix argument specifies the prefix used in each of the 30 pictures we use to create the animation. We use the *PIL* library to open the 30 pictures and convert them into NumPy arrays. The 30 arrays are put in a list *frames*. Finally, we use the *mimsave()* method in *imageio* to convert the list of NumPy arrays into an animation, with five frames per second.

Run the above cell so the *gif()* function is defined. Next, call the *gif()* function and put lr_medium as the argument, like so:

```
[15]: gif("lr_medium")
```

Run the above cell, and you'll see an output *lr_medium.gif* in the folder /Desktop/mla/ch04/files/. You can click on the file to see the animation. Alternatively, you can see the animation under /files/ch04/ in the book's GitHub repository.

4.4   CHOOSE THE RIGHT LEARNING RATE

In the above example, we choose a learning rate of 0.1. That is, in each step, we reduce the parameter by the product of 0.1 and the first derivative of the function at that point. However, how do we know to choose a learning rate of 0.1? In general, it comes from experience or trial and error.

Below, I'll show you what happens if the learning rate is too large or too small.

4.4.1   When the Learning Rate is Too Large

If the learning rate is too large, we make large changes to the parameter values in each iteration. This leads to wild swings in the parameter values. As a result, the parameter values may not converge. The code in the cell below shows what happens if we choose a learning rate of 0.95.

```
[16]: min_y, argmin_y, best_x, xs, ys = GD(0.95)
```

```
find minimum after 58 steps
the minimum y is 0.0003781270223312588
the optimal x is 9.980554511517289
```

Here we simply call the *GD()* function and put a learning rate of 0.95 as the argument. Results show that it takes 58 steps to find the minimum, about twice as many steps as when you choose a learning rate of 0.1.

Next, we call the *draw()* function to generate pictures based on a learning rate of 0.95.

```
[17]: draw("lr_large", 0.95, xs, ys)
```

If you run the above cell, you'll see 30 pictures in the folder /Desktop/mla/ch04/files/: lr_large0.png, lr_large1.png, ..., and lr_large29.png. Next, we'll combine the png files into an animation by calling the *gif()* function, like so:

```
[18]: gif("lr_large")
```

If you run the above cell, you'll see an animation *lr_large.gif* in the folder /Desktop/mla/ch04/files/. You can click on the file to see the animation. The animation shows that the value of x swings back and forth wildly, especially in the early stages of the learning process.

4.4.2 When the Learning Rate is Too Small

In contrast, if the learning rate is too small, we make very small changes to the parameters in each iteration. As a result, it may take a long time for the parameter values to converge. If we require the training process to stop after a fixed number of iterations, the parameters may not converge at all. The code in the cell below shows what happens if we choose a learning rate of 0.001.

```
[19]: min_y, argmin_y, best_x, xs, ys = GD(0.001)
```

```
fail to find the minimum
```

The above output shows that at a learning rate of 0.001, the algorithm fails to find the minimum within 2000 iterations. This is because the change the algorithm makes at each step is too small and it takes more than 2000 steps to converge.

For comparison purpose, we create 30 pictures of the learning process at the beginning by calling the *draw()* function below:

```
[20]: draw("lr_small", 0.001, xs, ys)
```

If you run the above cell, you'll see 30 pictures in the folder /Desktop/mla/ch04/files/: lr_small0.png, lr_small1.png, ..., and lr_small29.png. Next, we'll combine the png files into an animation by calling the *gif()* function, like so:

```
[21]: gif("lr_small")
```

If you run the above cell, you'll see an animation *lr_small.gif* in the folder /Desktop/mla/ch04/files/. You can click on the file to see the animation. The animation shows that the value of x changes very slowly.

4.5 COMPARE LEARNING RATES

For comparison purpose, you'll combine the three animations into one. In each frame, you put the three scenarios side by side: on the left is when the learning rate is too large; in the middle, the learning rate is optimal; on the right, the learning rate is too small.

Since you cannot see animations in the book, you'll also create a figure with multiple subplots to show various stages of the gradient descent algorithm with different learning rates.

4.5.1 Combine Animations

To combine three animations into one, we use the *concatenate()* method in NumPy. The argument axis=1 in the method places the three frames side by side horizontally.

First, we open the 30 pictures when the learning rate is small. We then store the pictures as NumPy arrays in a list called *smalls*, like so:

```
22]: smalls=[]
     for i in range(30):
         frame=PIL.Image.open(\
         f"files/ch04/lr_small{i}.png")
         frame=np.asarray(frame)
         smalls.append(np.array(frame))
```

Next, we open the 30 pictures when the learning rate is medium. We store the pictures as NumPy arrays in a list called *mediums*. Similarly, the 30 pictures when the learning rate is large are stored in a list called *larges*, like so:

```
23]: mediums=[]
     for i in range(30):
         frame=PIL.Image.open(\
          f"files/ch04/lr_medium{i}.png")
         frame=np.asarray(frame)
         mediums.append(np.array(frame))
     larges=[]
     for i in range(30):
         frame=PIL.Image.open(\
          f"files/ch04/lr_large{i}.png")
         frame=np.asarray(frame)
         larges.append(np.array(frame))
```

In each of the 30 stages of training, we use the *concatenate()* method in NumPy to combine the three frames side by side horizontally. The combined frames are stored in a list *frames*. The following cell accomplishes that:

```
[24]: frames=[]
      for i in range(30):
          frame=np.concatenate([larges[i],mediums[i],smalls[i]],axis=1)
          frames.append(np.array(frame))
```

Finally, we use the *minsave()* method in *imageio* to convert the 30 frames into an animation in *gif* format, like so:

```
[25]: imageio.mimsave('files/ch04/lrs.gif',frames,fps=6)
```

If you run the above cell, you'll see an animation *lrs.gif* in the folder /Desktop/mla/ch04/files/ on your computer. The animation shows the three scenarios side by side: the case with a large learning rate is on the left, and the case with a small learning rate is on the right. In the middle is the case when the learning rate is moderate.

4.5.2 Subplots of Different Stages

Even though we cannot show animations in the book, we can create a figure with multiple subplots to show various stages of the gradient descent algorithm with different learning rates.

For that purpose, we illustrate vertically four stages of the learning process: stages 1, 10, 20, and 30. In each stage, we'll show three different learning rates horizontally. We can use the list *frames* we just created in the last subsection as follows:

[26]:
```
stacked=np.concatenate([frames[0],frames[9],\
            frames[19],frames[29]],axis=0)
```

The list *stacked* now has 12 pictures in it, with three different learning rates and four different stages.

Next, we'll use *matplotlib.pyplot* to create a figure with the 12 pictures as subplots, like so:

[27]:
```
fig=plt.figure(dpi=100,figsize=(24,24))
plt.imshow(stacked)
plt.axis('off')
plt.show()
```

At the end of the above cell, we start a *for* loop to iterate through the first 30 steps in the learning process. In each step, we draw a green arrow. The end of the green arrow is (x, y) before adjustment, and the head of arrow points to (x, y) after adjustment. Note we set the text message to an empty string in the text boxes so only the arrows are shown, without any actual text in the text boxes.

Run the above cell, and you'll see an output as in Figure 4.2. The figure is also available under /files/ch04/fig4.2.png in the book's GitHub repository.

4.6 GLOSSARY

- **Curse of Dimensionality:** The curse of dimensionality refers to various problems and complications when dealing with high-dimensional space. In the setting of grid search, it means when the number of parameters increases, the number of searches we have to perform in order to find the optimal parameters grows exponentially.
- **Directional Grid Search:** A method to find optimal parameter values by adjusting values in the opposite direction of the first derivative of the loss function with respect to the parameters.

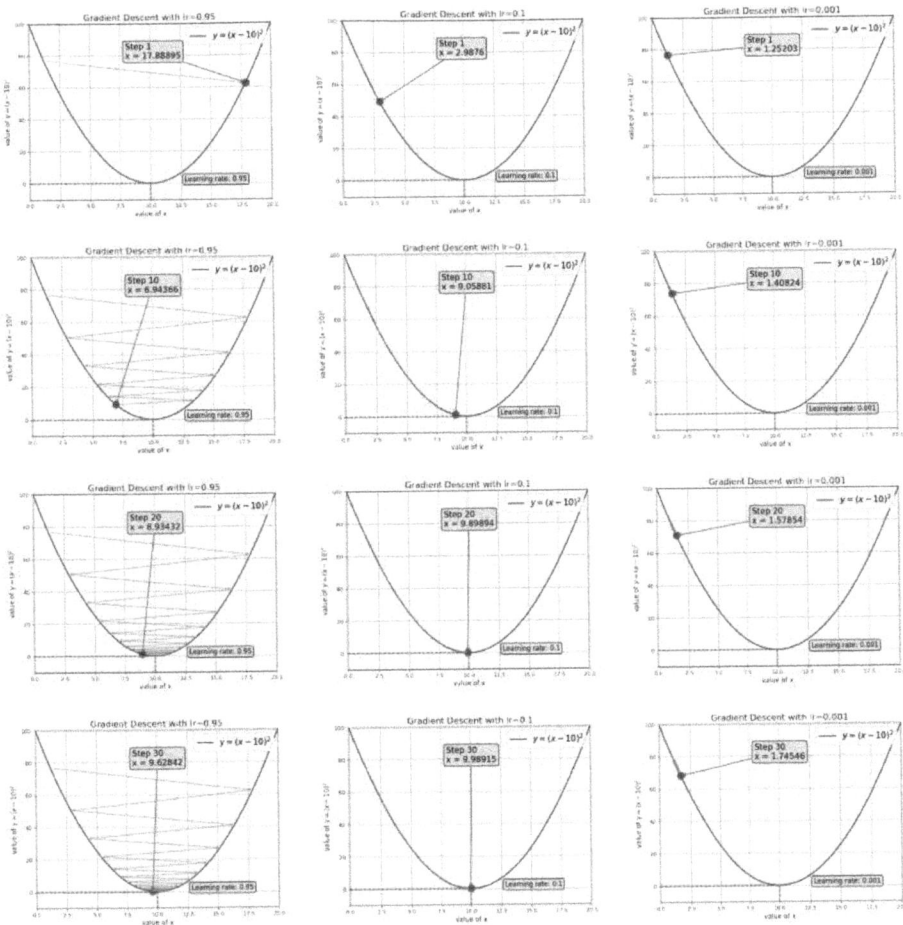

Figure 4.2 How learning rates affect the gradient descent algorithm

- **Gradient Descent:** An optimization algorithm used to minimize the loss function. The method adjusts parameter values proportional to the negative of the first derivative of the loss function with respect to the parameters.
- **Grid Search:** A method to find optimal parameter values by searching over the space of all possible combinations of different parameters.
- **Learning Rate:** A hyperparameter in ML models to control how fast to adjust the parameters in each step. The learning rate is usually a value between 0 and 1.
- **Loss Function:** Also called the cost function. It measures the error between the forecasts from ML models and the actual values. Some commonly used loss functions include mean square error, mean absolute error, and cross entropy.

4.7 EXERCISES

4.1 Explain how grid search works?

4.2 Modify the program in Section 4.1.1 to find the lowest value of $y = cos(x)$ by searching 1000 different values in the range of $0 \leq x \leq 8$.

4.3 What is curse of dimensionality? What is directional grid search?

4.4 What is gradient descent? Why should the parameters move in the opposite direction of the gradient?

4.5 Modify the second program in Section 4.1.2 to plot the directional grid search process by using *figure()* instead of the *subplots()* method. To start, you should change *fig, ax=plt.subplots(figsize=(8,6), dpi=100)* to *fig=plt.figure(figsize=(8,6), dpi=100)*. Modify the rest of the program so that it produces exactly the same graph.

4.6 Use gradient descent to find the lowest value of $y = cos(x)$ in the range of $0 \leq x \leq 8$ without the help of the TensorFlow library. Set the initial value of x to 1 and the learning rate to 0.1. Consider the value of y converged if the incremental change from one iteration to the next is less than 0.001. If the value of y doesn't converge after 2000 iterations, consider the search failed.

4.7 Redo the previous question, but use the TensorFlow library to calculate gradients this time.

## CHAPTER 5

Introduction to Neural Networks

The human brain is estimated to have about a hundred billion nerve cells, two million miles of axons, and a million billion synapses, making it the most complex structure, natural or artificial, on earth.

–T. Green, S.F. Heinemann, and J.F. Gusella (Neuron, 1998)

THE MOST SUCCESSFUL new development in the field of machine learning is neural networks. Since the 1990s, training a deep neural network was considered impossible and most researchers had abandoned the idea. Until in 2006, a paper in the journal *Neural Computation* by Geoffrey Hinton, Simon Osindero, and Yee-Whye Teh demonstrates how to train a deep neural network capable of recognizing handwritten digits with high accuracy [9]. The authors call their technique "deep learning." The 2006 paper opened the floodgate for research in neural networks. Now deep learning is the most powerful tool in the field of Machine Learning.

This chapter discusses how neural networks learn from data and make predictions. You'll learn to construct a simple neural network from scratch to learn the relation between ten pairs of input and output variables. You'll use the three steps that we have outlined in Chapter 4: initialize, adjust, and repeat. You'll see the parameter values and predictions in action in every step of the training process in this simple neural network.

While you can explicitly calculate the gradients in each step and adjust parameters accordingly in this simple example, the calculation of gradients becomes more complex in neural networks with multiple hidden layers. You'll learn how to use TensorFlow and Keras to construct a neural network and calculate the gradients automatically. You'll also learn the skills to manage situations where you have to customize the loss function in the training process to prepare you for deep Q-learning in later chapters.

Specifically, the ten pairs of inputs and outputs that we use to train the model have the following values:

- When $X = -40$, $Y = -40$
- When $X = -30$, $Y = -22$
- When $X = -10$, $Y = 14$
- When $X = 0$, $Y = 32$
- When $X = 5$, $Y = 41$
- When $X = 10$, $Y = 50$
- When $X = 20$, $Y = 68$
- When $X = 40$, $Y = 104$
- When $X = 60$, $Y = 140$
- When $X = 100$, $Y = 212$

You may have noticed a linear relation between Xs and Ys that corresponds to the relation between Celsius and Fahrenheit $Y = 1.8X + 32$. At the end of the chapter, you'll animate exactly how the neural network that you build from scratch "initializes, adjusts, and repeats." The model initializes parameters w and b in a linear model $Y = wX + b$; it makes predictions and adjusts w and b step by step, based on the gradient descent algorithm you learned in Chapter 4. As the training progresses, the model will find the correct relation $Y = 1.8X + 32$. You'll create an animation to show the values of w and b in each step.

New Skills in This Chapter

- Creating a neural network in NumPy to learn the relation between inputs and outputs
- Adjusting parameters in a neural network based on partial derivatives and the gradient descent algorithm
- Creating a neural network using Keras APIs
- Using the Keras API to train a neural network and make predictions
- Customizing training a neural network using the GradientTape API in TensorFlow

---

Before you start, open the Jupyter Notebook app in the virtual environment MLA on your computer. After that, open a blank Jupyter notebook and save it as *ch05.ipynb* in the directory /Desktop/mla/ on your computer. Next, we'll create a subdirectory /files/ch05/ to store files in this chapter.

Start a new cell in *ch05.ipynb* and execute the following lines of code in it:

```
[1]: import os

os.makedirs("files/ch05", exist_ok=True)
```

You should see a new directory /Desktop/mla/files/ch05/ on your computer.

5.1 ANATOMY OF A NEURAL NETWORK

Despite their widespread use, one common criticism for neural networks (or most ML models, for that matter) is that they are like black boxes and hard to understand. Indeed, nowadays, when building a neural network, you can simply use APIs from the Keras library without fully understanding what's going on within the model.

To look under the hood and have a better understanding of the logic behind a neural network without using any APIs, you'll create one from scratch and dissect its components with the NumPy library only.

A neural network is trying to mimic how human brains work. According to a paper in 1998 in the journal *Neuron* by Tim Green, Stephen F. Heinemann, and Jim F. Gusella, the human brain consists of billions of neurons that are connected by synapses [24]. Neural networks try to model this process by creating a machine learning model on a computer. A neural network consists of an input layer, an output layer, and some hidden layers in between. The powerful neural networks usually have many hidden layers, hence the name "deep neural networks." We'll start with a shallow one with no hidden layers, just one input layer and one output layer.

5.1.1 Elements of a Neural Network

The problem we're trying to solve is as follows. Suppose you have ten pairs of Xs and Ys, and their values are as follows: $(X = -40, Y = -40)$, $(X = -30, Y = -22)$, ..., $(X = 100, Y = 212)$. You may have noticed a linear relationship between the values of X and Y that corresponds to the relation between Celsius and Fahrenheit

$$Y = 1.8 * X + 32$$

The question is: can you create a machine learning model to learn the relationship between the two variables? Further, after training the model, what's the model's prediction of Y when the input value is $X = 50$?

In this section, you'll construct a neural network from scratch for that purpose. Along the way, you'll learn all the basics of a neural network.

Specifically, we'll construct a neural network with one input layer, one output layer, and no hidden layers by using the NumPy library only. In general, each layer in a neural network has one or more neurons. We'll include two neurons in the input layer and one neuron in the output layer in our simple model. We'll draw a diagram of the neural network we have constructed. The Python code in the cell below creates the diagram using the *matplotlib* library.

```
[2]: from matplotlib import pyplot as plt

fig=plt.figure(figsize=(12,6),dpi=200)
ax=fig.add_subplot(111)
# Draw the two input neurons
```

```
circle=plt.Circle((-3,2),radius=0.8,color='white',ec="m")
ax.add_artist(circle)
circle=plt.Circle((-3,-2),radius=0.8,color='white',ec="m")
ax.add_artist(circle)
# Draw the output neuron
circle=plt.Circle((1,0),radius=0.8,color='white',ec="m")
ax.add_artist(circle)
# Draw connections between neurons
ax.annotate("",xy=(0.2,0),xytext=(-2.2,2),
    arrowprops=dict(arrowstyle='->',
    color='b',linewidth=2))
ax.annotate("",xy=(0.2,0),xytext=(-2.2,-2),
    arrowprops=dict(arrowstyle='->',
    color='b',linewidth=2))
ax.annotate("",xy=(-3.8,-2),xytext=(-5.5,-2),
    arrowprops=dict(arrowstyle='->',
    color='b',linewidth=2))
ax.annotate("",xy=(-3.8,2),xytext=(-5.5,2),
    arrowprops=dict(arrowstyle='->',
    color='b',linewidth=2))
ax.annotate("",xy=(3.5,0),xytext=(1.8,0),
    arrowprops=dict(arrowstyle='->',
    color='b',linewidth=2))
# Create explanations in the graph
plt.text(-5.25,2.1,"bias",fontsize=20,color="k")
plt.text(-5.25,-1.9,"input",fontsize=20,color="k")
plt.text(2,0.1,"output",fontsize=20,color="k")
plt.text(-1.7,-1.9,f"w",fontsize=20,color="r",rotation=39)
plt.text(-1.7,0.9,f"b",fontsize=20,color="r",rotation=-39)
plt.text(-3.2,1.8,"1",fontsize=30,color="k")
plt.text(-3.2,-2.2,"X",fontsize=30,color="k")
plt.text(0.5,-0.1,"wX+b",fontsize=20,color="k")
plt.text(3.8,-0.1,f"Y",fontsize=20,color="r")
ax.set_xlim(-6,6)
ax.set_ylim(-3,3)
plt.axis("off")
plt.savefig(f"files/ch05/nn.png")
```

We create a figure that is 12 inches wide and 6 inches tall with dpi=200. We use the *add_subplot()* method to add a subplot in the figure. The argument 111 in the *add_subplot()* method means that the original figure is divided into one row and one column, with the subplot in position 1. We use the *add_subplot()* method so that

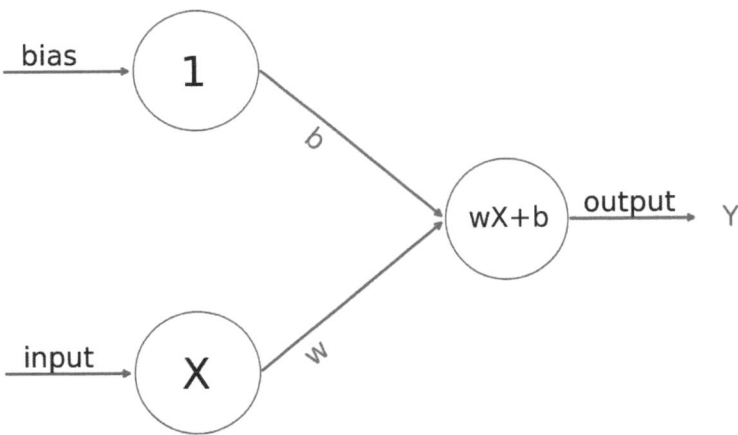

Figure 5.1 The diagram of a simple neural network

we can use the *add_artist()* method later to add circles and other art shapes in the subplot. We use three circles of radius 0.8 to denote the two input neurons and the one output neuron. We draw blue arrows to show that the neurons are connected.

The values for the two input neurons are a constant (i.e., the bias) and the variable X. The two input neurons are connected to the output neuron and this process generates a value $Y = w * X + b$, where b is the bias term and w the weight on the variable X. Here w and b are model parameters. The job of the model is to learn what the correct values of w and b should be based on the input-output pairs.

We use the *annotate()* function to create a text box inside the figure. The first argument of the *annotate()* function is the message you want to display in the text box. The xy argument in *annotate()* tells the arrow where to point to. The xytext=(0.2, 0.5) argument in *annotate()* defines the position of the textbox in the figure. The textcoords='axes fraction' argument says that the coordinates in the xytext=(0.2, 0.5) argument use the axes fraction system. We also specify that the arrow should be green with a line width of 1, and the font size inside the text box should be 15. You can change the parameters in the *annotate()* function to see how they change the figure.

If you run the above cell, you'll see an output as in Figure 5.1. The figure is also available under /files/ch05/ in the book's GitHub repository.

Next, we'll use this simple neural network to solve the problem of figuring out the relation between Xs and Ys in the example above, based on the ten pairs of values.

5.1.2 How Does a Neural Network Learn?

A neural network takes in input-output pairs and finds out the relation between the input and output variables. Since the relation between the input and output variables is governed by parameter values of the model, training a neural network boils down to estimating the model parameter values. In the example above, the model takes in the values of X and Y. It also takes in a bias term (that is, a constant value) through the other neuron in the input layer. Both neurons in the input layer are connected to the output neuron. The model learns the relation between X and Y by finding out the correct values of w and b in the following formula:

$$Y = w * X + b$$

To solve the problem in the above example, the neural network model follows the steps below:

1. Randomly assigns values to the weight w and the bias term b;
2. Takes the input data Xs and generates predictions for Ys based on the formula $\hat{Y} = w * X + b$;
3. Compares the predictions $\hat{Y}$ with the actual values of Y and calculates the forecasting error based on the loss function (more on this later);
4. Calculates the gradients of the loss function with respect to w and b at the current values;
5. Adjusts the parameters w and b based on the gradient descent algorithm (or a variant of it) that we learned in Chapter 4;
6. Repeats Steps 2 to 5 above for many iterations till the value of w and b converge.

After the above steps, the model is considered trained. To make a prediction using the trained model for any value of X, simply use the values of w and b in the trained model, and the prediction is $\hat{Y} = w * X + b$.

The Mean Squared Error Loss Function

The loss function is a measure of how good the prediction is. The mean squared error (MSE) is one of the most widely used loss functions in ML. MSE is defined as

$$MSE = \frac{1}{N} \sum_{i=1}^{N} (Y_n - \hat{Y}_n)^2$$

where Y_n is the actual value of the target variable (i.e., the label) and $\hat{Y}_n$ is the predicted value of the target variable. To calculate MSE, we look at the forecasting error: the difference between the model's predictions and the actual values. We then square the forecasting error for each observation, and average it across all observations. In short, it is the average squared forecasting error in each observation.

We'll modify the code we used in Chapter 4 and apply a similar algorithm of gradient descent to find out the values of w and b that minimize the loss function. We'll then use the trained model to make predictions.

First, run the Python code in the cell below to train the model:

```
[3]: import numpy as np

# the values of X and Y
X=np.array([-40, -30, -10, 0, 5, 10, 20, 40, 60, 100]\
            ).reshape(-1,1)
Y=np.array([-40.0, -22.0, 14.0, 32.0, 41.0, 50.0, 68.0,\
            104.0, 140.0, 212.0]).reshape(-1,1)
# create a vector of ones as the bias term
const=np.tile(1,[len(X),1])
# randomly assign values to w and b
w=1
b=1
# reshape w and b to matrix form
w=np.array([w]).reshape(1,1)
b=np.array([b]).reshape(1,1)
print(f"the initial weights are w={w[0,0]} and b={b[0,0]}")
# set the learning rate
lr=0.0005
# record results
ws, bs, yhats, losses = [], [], [], []
# train the model
for i in range(10000):
    # make predictions; forward propagation
    pred=np.matmul(X, w) + b
    # calculate loss as MSE
    loss=(Y-pred).T@(Y-pred)/len(Y)
    # calculate gradients
    dldw=-2*X.T@(Y-pred)/len(X)
    dldb=-2*const.T@(Y-pred)/len(X)
    # perform gradient descent; backward propagation
    w = w - lr*dldw
    b = b - lr*dldb
    if (i+1)%1000==0:
        print(f"iteration: {i+1}, loss: {loss[0,0]:.2f},",end="")
        print(f" weights: w={w[0,0]:.4f}, b={b[0,0]:.4f}")
    ws.append(w[0,0])
    bs.append(b[0,0])
    yhats.append(pred)
    losses.append(loss[0,0])
```

```
the initial weights are w=1 and b=1
iteration: 1000, loss: 146.96, weights: w=1.9100, b=19.0060
iteration: 2000, loss: 25.84, weights: w=1.8461, b=26.5518
iteration: 3000, loss: 4.54, weights: w=1.8193, b=29.7157
iteration: 4000, loss: 0.80, weights: w=1.8081, b=31.0422
iteration: 5000, loss: 0.14, weights: w=1.8034, b=31.5984
iteration: 6000, loss: 0.02, weights: w=1.8014, b=31.8316
iteration: 7000, loss: 0.00, weights: w=1.8006, b=31.9294
iteration: 8000, loss: 0.00, weights: w=1.8003, b=31.9704
iteration: 9000, loss: 0.00, weights: w=1.8001, b=31.9876
iteration: 10000, loss: 0.00, weights: w=1.8000, b=31.9948
```

Note that everything is done with the NumPy library. We didn't use the TensorFlow or the Keras library. This way, you can create a neural network from scratch and have a better understanding of how it works.

We define the values of Xs and Ys. We also create a vector of ones with the *tile()* method in NumPy. To train the model, we follow the three steps outlined at the beginning of Chapter 4: initialize, adjust, and repeat. Specifically, we first initialize the parameters w and b with some random values: we set $w=1$ and $b=1$. Setting them to other values leads to almost identical results. As an exercise, you can change the initial values to $w=0$ and $b=0$ and see what the outcome is.

We then adjust the values of w and b each iteration based on the rule of gradient descent. We set the learning rate to $lr=0.0005$. We calculate the gradients explicitly in each iteration, and change w and b based on the following formula:

$$\Delta w = -lr \times \frac{\partial \mathbf{L}(w, b)}{\partial w}$$

and

$$\Delta b = -lr \times \frac{\partial \mathbf{L}(w, b)}{\partial b}$$

Note here we explicitly calculate the first derivatives of the loss function with respect to the parameters w and b. To simplify notation, we use the matrix operations when adjusting the parameter values. Note here that when you multiple two matrices, you can use either *np.matmul()* or @: they produce identical results.

After 10000 epochs of training, the values of w and b converge to around 1.8 and 32, their true values.

Calculate Gradients in the Example

Training the neural network in this case boils down to finding the values of w and b that minimize the loss function $MSE = \frac{1}{N}\sum_{i=1}^{N}(Y_n - \hat{Y}_n)^2$. Based on what we learned in Chapter 4, we can adjust the parameter values explicitly by using the gradient descent algorithm. In particular, we can calculate the gradients of the loss function at any given point. Since the loss function is:

$$\mathbf{L}(w,b) = MSE = \frac{1}{N}\sum_{i=1}^{N}(Y_n - \hat{Y}_n)^2 = \frac{1}{N}\sum_{i=1}^{N}(Y_n - b - w*X_n)^2$$

The gradients are:

$$\frac{\partial \mathbf{L}(w,b)}{\partial w} = \frac{1}{N}\sum_{i=1}^{N} -2X_n(Y_n - b - w*X_n)$$

and

$$\frac{\partial \mathbf{L}(w,b)}{\partial b} = \frac{1}{N}\sum_{i=1}^{N} -2(Y_n - b - w*X_n)$$

In the Python code above, the gradients are represented in matrix form.

5.1.3 Make Predictions

Now that the model is trained, we can print out the final, converged, values of the parameters w and b. As a result, we also know the exact relation between X and Y, as follows:

```
[4]: # Obtain the converged values of w and b
w=ws[-1]
b=bs[-1]
print(f"the values of w and b are w={w:.2f} and b={b:.2f}")
```

the values of w and b are w=1.80 and b=31.99

Results show that the neural network learns from the data that the parameters should be $w=1.80$ and $b=31.99$.

Round Floating Numbers

In the cell above, we use *:.2f* after the variables w and b to round the float numbers to two digits after the decimal point. If you want to round them to, say, 3 digits after decimal, use *:.3f*. Alternatively, you can use the Python built-in function *round()* for that purpose. For example, replacing *w:.2f* with *round(w,2)* leads to the same result.

To make a prediction on what's the value of Y when $X=50$, we can plug in the values of w and b into the linear model $Y = wX + b$ and use the formula to make predictions, like so:

```
[5]: print(f"the relation between X and Y is Y={w:.2f}X+{b:.2f}.")
     pred_Y=w*50+b
     print(f"when X=50, the prediction is Y={pred_Y:.2f}")
```

```
the relation between X and Y is Y=1.80X+31.99.
when X=50, the prediction is Y=122.00
```

The result above shows that the prediction is 122.00, a perfect prediction for the true value of 122 degrees Fahrenheit.

5.2 ANIMATE THE LEARNING PROCESS

Next, we'll create an animation of the intermediate steps of the ML process we just implemented in the last section. First, we create a sequence of pictures. In each picture, we'll show the values of w and b, as well as the predicted values of Y and the squared forecasting error. We then combine the sequence of pictures into an animation.

5.2.1 Generate Graphs

The following cell creates a graph every 200 epochs, and this creates a total of 51 pictures since we include the first epoch as well. Specifically, we show the values of the parameters w and b in each epoch, as well as the predicted Y value.

```
[6]: from matplotlib import pyplot as plt
     from matplotlib.patches import Rectangle

     # select the steps to create graphs
     steps=[x for x in range(len(ws)) if x==0 or (x+1)%200==0]
     for k in steps:
         w=round(ws[k],3)
         b=round(bs[k],1)
         loss=round(losses[k],3)
         yhat=yhats[k]
         fig = plt.figure(figsize=(12,6), dpi=200)
         ax = fig.add_subplot(111)
         # add rectangle to plot
         ax.add_patch(Rectangle((2.2,-2.5), 1.5, 5,
                     edgecolor = 'k',alpha=0.1))
         ax.add_patch(Rectangle((4,-2.5), 1.7, 5,
                     edgecolor = 'k',alpha=0.1))
```

```
# Draw the two input neurons
c=plt.Circle((-3,2),radius=0.8,color='white',ec="m")
ax.add_artist(c)
c=plt.Circle((-3,-2),radius=0.8,color='white',ec="m")
ax.add_artist(c)
# Draw the output neuron
c=plt.Circle((1,0),radius=0.8,color='white',ec="m")
ax.add_artist(c)
# Draw connections between neurons
ax.annotate("",xy = (0.2,0),xytext = (-2.2,2),
                    arrowprops=dict(arrowstyle = '->',
                    color = 'b', linewidth = 2))
ax.annotate("",xy = (0.2,0),xytext = (-2.2,-2),
                    arrowprops=dict(arrowstyle = '->',
                    color = 'b', linewidth = 2))
ax.annotate("",xy = (-3.8,-2),xytext = (-5.5,-2),
                    arrowprops=dict(arrowstyle = '->',
                    color = 'b', linewidth = 2))
ax.annotate("",xy = (-3.8,2),xytext = (-5.5,2),
                    arrowprops=dict(arrowstyle = '->',
                    color = 'b', linewidth = 2))
ax.annotate("",xy = (2.2,0),xytext = (1.8,0),
                    arrowprops=dict(arrowstyle = '->',
                    color = 'b', linewidth = 2))
# put epoch number and losses up
plt.text(-0.7, 2.2, f"epoch={k+1}\nloss={loss}",
        fontsize=20, color="g")
# Put explanation texts on the graph
plt.text(-5.25, 2.1, "bias", fontsize=20, color="k")
plt.text(-5.25, -1.9, "input", fontsize=20, color="k")
plt.text(2.3, 2.6, "output", fontsize=20, color="k")
plt.text(4.3, 2.6, "loss", fontsize=20, color="k")
plt.text(-1.7, -1.9, f"w={w}", fontsize=20,
        color="r",rotation=39)
plt.text(-1.7, 0.9, f"b={b}", fontsize=20,
        color="r",rotation=-39)
plt.text(-3.2, 1.8, "1", fontsize=30, color="k")
plt.text(-3.2, -2.2, "X", fontsize=30, color="k")
plt.text(0.5, -0.1, "wX+b", fontsize=20, color="k")
plt.text(2.3, -2.92, "$\hat{Y}$", fontsize=15, color="r")
plt.text(4, -2.92, "$(\hat{Y}-Y)^2$",
        fontsize=15, color="r")
for i in range(10):
    plt.text(4, 2.2-i*0.5,
```

```
        f"$({round(Y[i,0],1)}-({round(yhat[i,0],1)})"+")^2$",
        fontsize=10, color="k")
    plt.text(2.3, 2.2-i*0.5, f"{i+1}: "+
    "$\hat{Y}$"+f"={round(yhat[i,0],3)}",
            fontsize=10, color="k")
ax.set_xlim(-6, 6)
ax.set_ylim(-3, 3)
plt.axis("off")
plt.savefig(f"files/ch05/nn{k}.png")
plt.close(fig)
```

First, we create a list of indexes to represent the epochs in which we want to create the pictures. The 51 indexes are stored in a list called *steps*. We then use a *for* loop to iterate through the 51 steps. In each step, we extract the values of the parameter values w and b, the predicted value of Y, as well as the value of the loss function. We draw a diagram of the simple neural network we created. The values of w and b are placed close to the connections between the neurons so that you understand the concept of forward propagation.

Forward Propagation and Backward Propagation

In neural networks, forward propagation is when input data are fed in the forward direction through the network, starting from the input layer, then hidden layers, and finally the output layer. Backward propagation is when the weights in each layer are adjusted based on gradient descent (or a variant of it).

We also create a shaded box to show the values of the ten predicted Y values, as well as the squared forecasting error. The value of the MSE loss function is shown at the top center of the picture, along with the epoch number.

If you run the above code cell, you'll see 51 pictures on your computer in the folder /Desktop/mla/files/ch05/: they are named as *nn0.png, nn199.png...*, and *nn9999.png*.

5.2.2 Create Animation Based on Graphs

Next, we'll create an animation of the training process using the 51 pictures we just generated.

```
[7]: import imageio, PIL

frames=[]
for k in steps:
    frame=PIL.Image.open(f"files/ch05/nn{k}.png")
    frame=np.asarray(frame)
```

```
        frames.append(np.array(frame))
imageio.mimsave('files/ch05/nn.gif', frames, fps=6)
```

We create an empty list *frames* to store all pictures. We iterate through the 51 pictures we generated in the last subsection and open each one using the *PIL* library. We convert the pictures to NumPy arrays and add them to the list *frames*. Once done, we use the *mimsave()* method in the *imageio* library to convert the images to the *gif* format. The fps=6 argument generates animation with six frames per second.

After you run the above cell, the file *nn.gif* is generated and saved in your local folder. To view the animation, you can click on the file on your computer. Alternatively, you can view it at the book's GitHub repository under the folder /files/ch05/.

5.2.3 Subplots of Different Stages

Even though we cannot show animations in the hard copy of the book, we can create a figure with multiple subplots to show various stages of the training process. For that purpose, we showcase four pictures in four stages: 1, 4000, 7000, and 10000. The Python code in the cell below creates the subplots.

```
[8]:  frames=[]
      frame1=PIL.Image.open(f"files/ch05/nn0.png")
      frame2=PIL.Image.open(f"files/ch05/nn3999.png")
      frame3=PIL.Image.open(f"files/ch05/nn6999.png")
      frame4=PIL.Image.open(f"files/ch05/nn9999.png")
      frames.append(frame1)
      frames.append(frame2)
      frames.append(frame3)
      frames.append(frame4)

      plt.figure(dpi=200,figsize=(12,24))
      for i in range(4):
              plt.subplot(4,1,i+1)
              plt.imshow(frames[i])
              plt.axis("off")
      plt.subplots_adjust(hspace=-0.25)
      plt.show()
```

We first create an empty list *frames* to store the four pictures we want to show. We use the *PIL* library to open the four pictures and add them to the list *frames*. We use the *plt.figure()* method to create a figure, which is 12 by 24 inches in size. We set the dpi to 200. We then use the *subplot()* method to add four subplots to the original

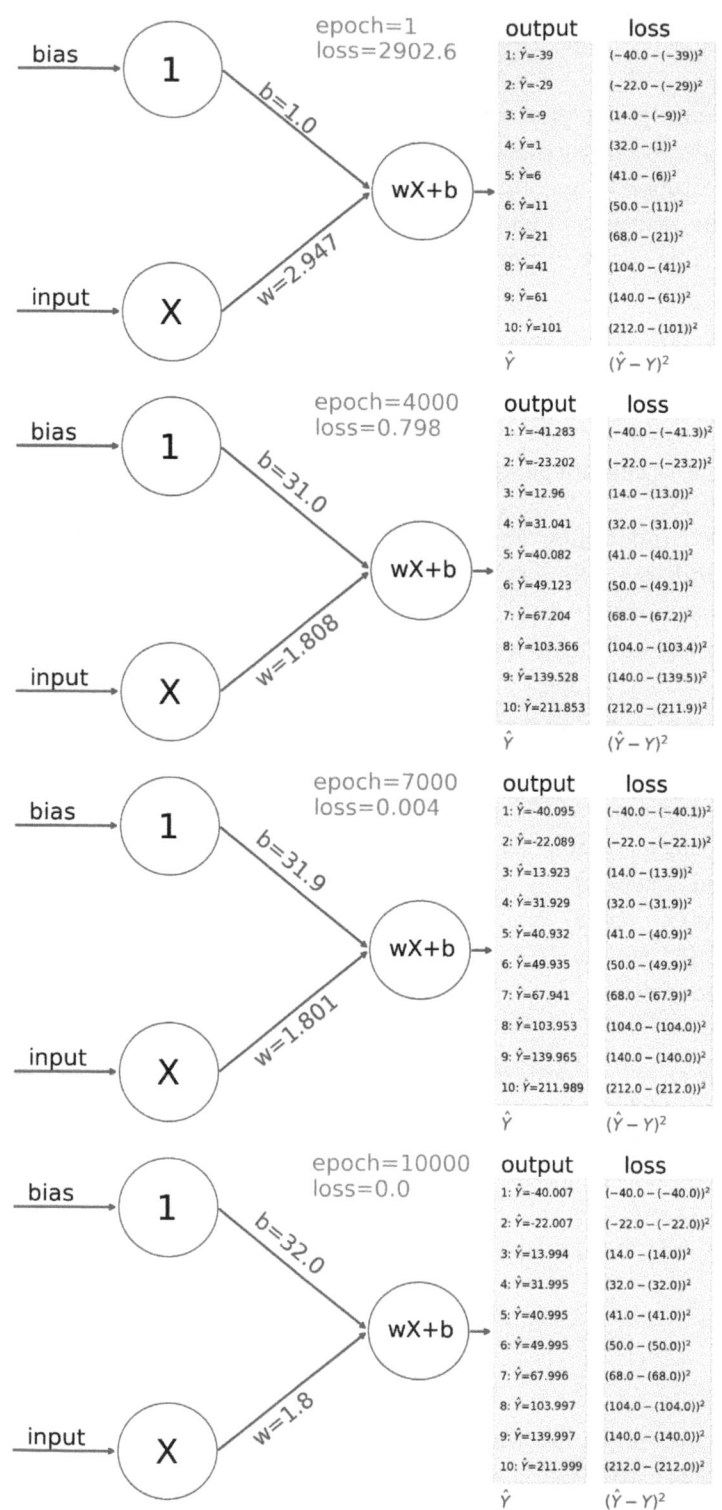

Figure 5.2 How parameters change during the training process

figure, organized vertically to form a four by one grid. We adjust the vertical space between the four pictures so they line up with proper amount of spaces in between.

Run the above cell, and you'll see an output as in Figure 5.2. The figure is also available under /files/ch05/ in the book's GitHub repository.

5.3 CREATE A NEURAL NETWORK WITH KERAS

The example we have shown above is relatively simple. In particular, there is a closed-form solution to the gradients so we can implement the gradient descent algorithm by calculating the gradients ourselves in the Python code.

However, to solve more complicated problems, we need to construct neural networks with more layers. Calculating the gradients is too complicated and time-consuming. Therefore, for the rest of the book, we'll rely on the Keras library to implement all optimizations.

In this section, you'll learn how to use Keras to solve the same problem we just solved in the last section. As we discussed in Chapter 1, Keras is a Python library for developing and evaluating neural networks. The newest version of the TensorFlow library has already integrated Keras in it. Therefore, no separate installation of Keras is needed.

In particular, Keras provides built-in APIs for training, evaluating, and utilizing neural network models. You can use the *fit()* method to pass data to the built-in training loops of a model. Once the training is finished, you can use the *predict()* method to make predictions. The *evaluate()* method allows you to evaluate the performance of the model, either on the training data or the testing data.

5.3.1 Construct the Model

The easiest way to construct a neural network in Keras is to use the Sequential model. The Sequential model constructs a linear stack of layers of neurons.

We first import the Sequential model and the Dense class from Keras, like so:

```
[9]: from tensorflow.keras.models import Sequential
     from tensorflow.keras.layers import Dense
```

As you'll see later in this book, there are different types of layers in neural networks such as convolutional layers, dropout layers, fully-connected layers, recurrent layers, and so on. Fully connected layers are also called dense layers, and we'll use it below to construct our neural network.

Run the above cell to import the Sequential model and the Dense class. Next, we construct the model using Keras as follows:

```
[10]: first_nn=Sequential()
      first_nn.add(Dense(1,input_shape=[1]))
```

We first create a sequential model and call it *first_nn*. We then add a fully-connected dense layer to the model. The first argument, 1, in *Dense()* says that there is only one neuron in the output layer, because the prediction Y is a scalar. The second argument, input_shape=[1], specifies the shape of the input layer. Note that there is a default bias term in the input layer, so we use input_shape=[1] instead of input_shape=[2]. It says that there is only one input variable besides the bias term in the input layer.

5.3.2 Compile and Train the Model

Next, we'll compile the model. We need to specify what loss function to use, and which optimizer to pick to adjust the parameters (it's usually a variant of the gradient descent algorithm).

```
[11]: import tensorflow as tf

      # Fix the random state so results are reproducible
      tf.random.set_seed(0)
      first_nn.compile(loss='mean_squared_error',
        optimizer=tf.keras.optimizers.Adam(learning_rate=0.1),
                       metrics=['mse'])
```

We use the *compile()* method to compile the model. We use MSE as our loss function. We also choose the Adam optimizer. The Adam optimizer is a variant of the gradient descent algorithm based on adaptive estimation of first-order and second-order moments. See the documentation here https://keras.io/api/optimizers/adam/ for details about the Adam optimizer. Finally, we use MSE as our metrics of the performance of the model (that is, how good the predictions are).

To train the model, we'll specify the values of X and Y. We'll also tell the model how many iterations to run, and the batch size in the training process. The batch size determines how many observations of data to consider before the model weights are adjusted. The default batch size is 32. Since we only have 10 observations, we set the batch size to 10.

```
[12]: X=np.array([-40, -30, -10, 0, 5, 10, 20,\
                    40, 60, 100],dtype=float).reshape(-1,1)
      Y=np.array([-40, -22, 14, 32, 41, 50,\
          68, 104, 140, 212],dtype=float).reshape(-1,1)
      history=first_nn.fit(X, Y, verbose=0, \
                       epochs=10000, batch_size=10)
```

Run the above cell to train the model. You'll not see any output from the above cell because we set *verbose* to 0 in the *fit()* method. You can change *verbose* to 1 and the output will show the training time length and the value of the loss function in each epoch.

5.3.3 Make Predictions

Now that the model is trained, you can use the *predict()* method from Keras to directly make predictions based on the value of X. In the cell below, we predict the value of Y when $X = 50$. Make sure you put the value of X in matrix form because the input data to the neural network must be two-dimensional with a shape of $(-1,1)$: the first value -1 in the shape means the data can have any number of rows and the second value means the data must have exactly one column. Here for simplicity, I use row and column to denote the two dimensions of the input data, which is a NumPy array.

```
13]: w, bias = first_nn.layers[-1].get_weights()
     print(f"weights are {w[0,0], bias[0]}")

     pred = first_nn.predict([[50]])
     print(f"when X=50, the prediction is Y={round(pred[0,0],2)}")
```

```
weights are (1.8, 32.0)
when X=50, the prediction is Y=122.0
```

The output shows that the values of w and b are 1.8 and 32, respectively. When the value of X is 50, the model's prediction of Y is 122, a perfect prediction. Note here that the prediction is a two-dimensional NumPy array, so we use [0,0] to extract the numerical value from the element in the first row and first column.

Further, we can use the *evaluate()* method from Keras to measure the performance of the trained model, like so:

```
14]: MSE = first_nn.evaluate(X, Y)
```

```
1/1 [==============================] - 0s 76ms/step
- loss: 0.0000e+00 - mse: 0.0000e+00
```

The output shows that the model does an almost perfect job in making predictions: the value of the loss function is zero.

Since we have saved the training history, we can plot the value of MSE over the course of the training process, like so:

```
15]: import matplotlib.pyplot as plt

     plt.plot(history.history["mse"],label='MSE',color="r")
     plt.legend()
     plt.show()
```

If you run the above cell, you'll see a plot of the value of the loss function MSE during the training process. The value of MSE goes to zero after about 50 epochs of training. The figure is also available under /files/ch05/MSE_plot.png in the book's GitHub repository.

5.4 CUSTOMIZE TRAINING WITH GRADIENTTAPE

While Keras built-in APIs make the training, evaluation, and utilization of neural network models easy, there are limitations to these APIs. One limitation of the Keras high-level APIs is the fact that it's very challenging for us to write custom training loops in various situations.

For example, the loss functions provided by Keras APIs can only be used to calculate the difference between the predicted target values and the actual target values. In some situations, we need to construct our own custom loss functions. A case in point is later in this book when we train deep Q-learning models, the loss function is the difference between the current Q value and the updated Q value. Therefore, we cannot use Keras APIs to train deep Q-learning models. Instead, we need to use the GradientTape function to write custom training loops.

In this section, you'll learn how to use the GradientTape function in TensorFlow to calculate the gradients in each step of the training loop and then use the optimizer to adjust parameters step by step. This way, you'll be familiar with how to use the GradientTape function for training purposes instead of relying on Keras built-in APIs. You'll use these skills later in the book when you train deep Q-learning models.

5.4.1 Construct the Model

The model construction part is the same as in the last section. We create a Sequential model with one input layer and one output layer, as follows:

```
[16]: g_tape_nn=Sequential()
      g_tape_nn.add(Dense(1,input_shape=[1]))
```

Next, we specify the loss function and the optimizer. We still use the mean squared error loss function, and the Adam optimizer with a learning rate of 0.1.

```
[17]: mse = tf.keras.losses.MeanSquaredError()
      optimizer=tf.keras.optimizers.Adam(learning_rate=0.1)
```

5.4.2 Train the Model

To train the model, we'll write a loop with 10000 iterations. In each iteration, we calculate the prediction of the model based on the current parameters. We then calculate the value of the loss function explicitly. Specifically, we'll use the GradientTape function to record operations and auto differentiate so that we can calculate the partial derivatives of the loss function with respect to the parameters. We then use the Adam optimizer (a variant of the gradient decent algorithm) to adjust the parameters, like so:

```
18]: for i in range(10000):
         with tf.GradientTape() as t:
             pred = g_tape_nn(X)
             loss=mse(Y, pred)
         # Update using backpropagation
         gs = t.gradient(loss,g_tape_nn.trainable_variables)
         optimizer.apply_gradients(zip(gs,\
                 g_tape_nn.trainable_variables))
```

In the above cell, *g_tape_nn.trainable_variables* is a vector of parameters that we need to train in the neural network. In our case, they are w and b in the linear relation $y = w * X + b$.

We calculate the partial derivatives of the loss function with respect to the two parameters, and record them as *gs*. The adjustment of the parameter values is done through the last line of code in the above cell

```
optimizer.apply_gradients(zip(gs,g_tape_nn.trainable_variables)).
```

Specifically, the *apply_gradients()* method ajusts the values of the parameters based on the learning rate and the gradients.

5.4.3 Make Predictions

You can make predictions using the trained model as before by replying on the predict() function:

```
19]: pred = g_tape_nn.predict([[50]])
     print(f"when X=50, the prediction is Y={round(pred[0,0],2)}")
```

```
when X=50, the prediction is Y=122.0
```

As you can see, the prediction of the model is $Y = 122.0$ when the input is $X = 50$. However, you cannot use the *evaluate()* method from Keras in this case since the model is not compiled. Further, you may see a warning message saying that the model is not compiled when you write custom training loops.

5.5 GLOSSARY

- **Backward Propagation:** Backward propagation is when the weights in each layer of a neural network are updated based on the gradients and the optimizer.
- **Deep Learning:** A machine learning method based on deep neural networks that are characterized by many hidden layers of neurons, in addition to an input layer and an output layer.
- **Deep Neural Networks:** Neural networks consist of many hidden layers of connected neurons, besides an input layer and an output layer.
- **Forward Propagation:** Forward propagation is when input data are fed in the forward direction through the neural network, from the input layer, to the hidden layers, and finally the output layer.
- **Hidden Layer:** The hidden layer is located between the input layer and the output layer in a neural network. It receives processed data from the input layer, further processes it, and passes them on to the output layer.
- **Input Layer:** The input layer is the first layer of neurons in a neural network. It brings the input data into the system for further processing by hidden layers and the output layer.
- **Mean Squared Error (MSE) Loss Function:** A commonly used loss function in machine learning. It is the average squared value of the difference between the actual value and the predicted value from the model.
- **Neural Networks:** A type of machine learning models inspired by the biological neural networks of human brains. They are also called artificial neural networks or simply neural nets. Neural networks consist of multiple layers of connected neurons: an input layer, an output layer, and in most cases a number of hidden layers.
- **Output Layer:** The output layer is the last layer of neurons in a neural network. It produces the predictions from the model.

5.6 EXERCISES

5.1 What is an input layer? An output layer? A hidden layer?

5.2 What is the mean squared error (MSE) loss function?

5.3 Modify the program in Section 5.1.2 so that the initial parameter values are $w = 0, b = 0$. Also make changes so that the values of the loss function, w, and b are all three digits after the decimal point.

5.4 Modify the last code cell in Section 5.4.3 to predict the Y value when $X = -40$.

## CHAPTER 6

Activation Functions

The number of possible "on-off" patterns of neuronal firing is immense, estimated as a staggering ten times ten one million times (ten to the millionth power). The brain is obviously capable of an imponderably huge variety of activity; the fact that it is often organized and functional is quite an accomplishment!
The Developing Mind: Toward a Neurobiology of Interpersonal Experience
–Daniel J. Siegel, 1999

THE ARTIFICIAL NEURAL network in ML is modeled after human brains. A human brain consists of about 100 billion neurons, which are connected by synapses. Biological neurons receive stimuli (called action potentials) from the outside world or other neurons. When a neuron receives a sufficiently large amount of stimuli in a short amount of time, it turns on and fires its own chemical signals. The on-off patterns of neurons in human brains are as important as the shear number of neurons in them, as the opening quote of this chapter states [23].

In artificial neural networks, activation functions transform inputs into outputs. As the name suggests, the activation functions activate the neuron when the input reaches a certain threshold. Simply put, activation functions are on-off switches in artificial neural networks. These on-off switches play an important role in making artificial neural networks powerful. The activation functions allow a network to learn more complex patterns in the data. Without activation functions, neural networks can only learn linear relationships in the data.

In Chapter 5, you have seen how a neural network makes accurate predictions on a linear relation between the input and the output variables. However, we could have done it with a linear regression and achieved similar results. You may wonder, what's the advantage of neural networks? Neural networks are function approximation algorithms. Feed a neural network with enough data, it can figure out the relation between any input-output pairs even if the relation is nonlinear and very complicated. Or even if we human beings don't know the exact functional form between the inputs and outputs.

DOI: 10.1201/b23383-6

You'll learn why we need activation functions to model a nonlinear relationship in this chapter. You'll first try to create a neural network to predict the relation between X and $y = sin(X)$ without an activation function. The neural network does a poor job because it can only predict a linear relation between inputs and outputs without activation functions. You'll then add the rectified linear unit (ReLU) activation function to the neural network and show that the model can now approximate the nonlinear relation between X and $y = sin(X)$.

You'll also learn the sigmoid activation function and how it squashes a number to the range between 0 and 1 so that it can be interpreted as the probability of an outcome. Similarly, the softmax activation function squeezes a group of numbers into the range $[0, 1]$ with the property that the numbers in the group add up to 100%. Therefore, the output from a softmax function can be interpreted as the probability distribution of multiple outcomes. Because of these properties, we use sigmoid and softmax activation functions in binary and multi-category classifications, respectively.

You'll create an animation to show how the ReLU activation function creates a nonlinear relationship between the inputs and outputs. You'll also create an animation to show how the sigmoid activation function takes a number between $-\infty$ and ∞ and squashes it so the output is between 0 and 1, which can in turn be interpreted as the probability of an outcome. You'll then combine these two animations into one so that the two activation functions are displayed side by side. Finally, you'll also learn what is a softmax activation function and why the output from the softmax function can be interpreted as the probability distribution of multiple outcomes.

New Skills in This Chapter

- Understanding what is the ReLU activation function
- Adding the ReLU activation function to a neural network to create a nonlinear relation
- Getting to know the sigmoid activation function and why it's used in binary classifications
- Getting to know the softmax activation function and why it's used in multi-category classifications

---

Before you start, open the Jupyter Notebook app in the virtual environment MLA on your computer. After that, open a blank Jupyter notebook and save it as *ch06.ipynb* in the directory /Desktop/mla/ on your computer. Next, we'll create a subdirectory /files/ch06/ to store files in this chapter. Start a new cell in *ch06.ipynb* and execute the following lines of code in it:

```
[1]: import os

os.makedirs("files/ch06", exist_ok=True)
```

You should see a new directory /Desktop/mla/files/ch06/ on your computer.

6.1 WHY DO WE NEED ACTIVATION FUNCTIONS?

Activation functions help us create a nonlinear relationship between the inputs and outputs. Without them, we can only approximate linear relations. No matter how many hidden layers we add to the neural network, we cannot achieve a nonlinear relationship.

To illustrate the point, let's try to train a deep neural network to learn the relationship between X and $y = sin(X)$. The structure of the neural network we use has two hidden layers, with 7 and 5 neurons, respectively. We'll soon generate a diagram of the structure of this specific neural network. You'll see that without activation functions, the neural network cannot learn a nonlinear relationship: the linear transformation of a linear relationship is still linear.

We then add in the ReLU activation function in the two hidden layers in the neural network. The model successfully generates a nonlinear relationship between the inputs and outputs that resembles a sine function.

6.1.1 Construct a Neural Network

To predict the relation between X and $y = sin(X)$, we'll create a neural network with four layers: an input layer with two neurons, two hidden dense layers with seven and five neurons in them, respectively, and an output layer with just one neuron.

First, we draw a diagram to visualize the structure of the above neural network. Since this neural network has a total of 15 neurons, and neurons in adjacent layers are fully connected, drawing all the neurons and connections can be tedious and time-consuming work. Luckily, you can borrow from online sources in the Python community. For example, Professor Colin Raffel's post below discusses how to draw a neural network with different numbers of layers with any number of neurons in each layer:

https://gist.github.com/craffel/2d727968c3aaebd10359

The Python code below is inspired by Professor Colin Raffel's post. It draws the neural network that we'll use to predict the relation between X and $y = sin(X)$ (with four layers of neurons):

```
[2]: import matplotlib.pyplot as plt

     fig=plt.figure(figsize=(10,7.6),dpi=300)
     ax=fig.add_subplot(111)
     v=(0.9-0.1)/7
     h=(0.9-0.1)/(4-1)
     # iterate through layers
     for n, s in enumerate([2,7,5,1]):
         t=v*(s-1)/2+0.5
```

```python
    # Draw neurons
    for m in range(s):
        c=plt.Circle((0.1+n*h,t-m*v),v/4,
                       color='g',ec='r',zorder=4)
        ax.add_artist(c)
    # add input lines
    if n==0:
        for m in range(2):
            ax.annotate("",xy=(0.074,t-m*v),xytext=(0,t-m*v),
            arrowprops=dict(arrowstyle='->',color='r'))
            plt.text(x=0.02,y=t+0.01,fontsize=20,color="k",s="1")
            plt.text(x=0.02,y=t-v+0.01,fontsize=20,color="k",s="X")
    # add output lines
    if n==3:
        plt.text(x=3*h+0.15,y=t-m*v+0.01,
                 fontsize=20,color="k",s="y")
        ax.annotate("",xy=(3*h+0.2,t),xytext=(3*h+0.1,t),
        arrowprops=dict(arrowstyle='->',color='r'))
# draw connections
for n, (a,b) in enumerate(zip([2,7,5],[7,5,1])):
    ta=v*(a-1)/2+0.5
    tb=v*(b-1)/2+0.5
    for m in range(a):
        for o in range(b):
            line=plt.Line2D([n*h+0.1,(n+1)*h+0.1],
                             [ta-m*v,tb-o*v],c='b')
            ax.add_artist(line)
ax.axis('off')
ax.set_ylim(0.12,0.88)
ax.set_xlim(0,1)
fig.savefig('files/ch06/dnn-sin.png')
```

We first calculate the horizontal and vertical spaces between neurons, h and v, respectively, based on the maximum number of neurons in a layer (in our case, seven), and the number of layers (in our case, four). We then iterate through the four layers. The *enumerate()* method in Python produces all elements in a list with their corresponding indexes. Therefore, *enumerate*($[2, 7, 5, 1]$) gives us the indexes of the layers, (0, 1, 2, and 3), as well as the number of neurons in each layer (2, 7, 5, and 1).

We then draw the neurons in each layer as circles. The two input lines and the output line are drawn as arrows, using the *annotate()* method in the *matplotlib* library. Finally, the connections between neurons are straight lines, drawn using the *Line2D()* method.

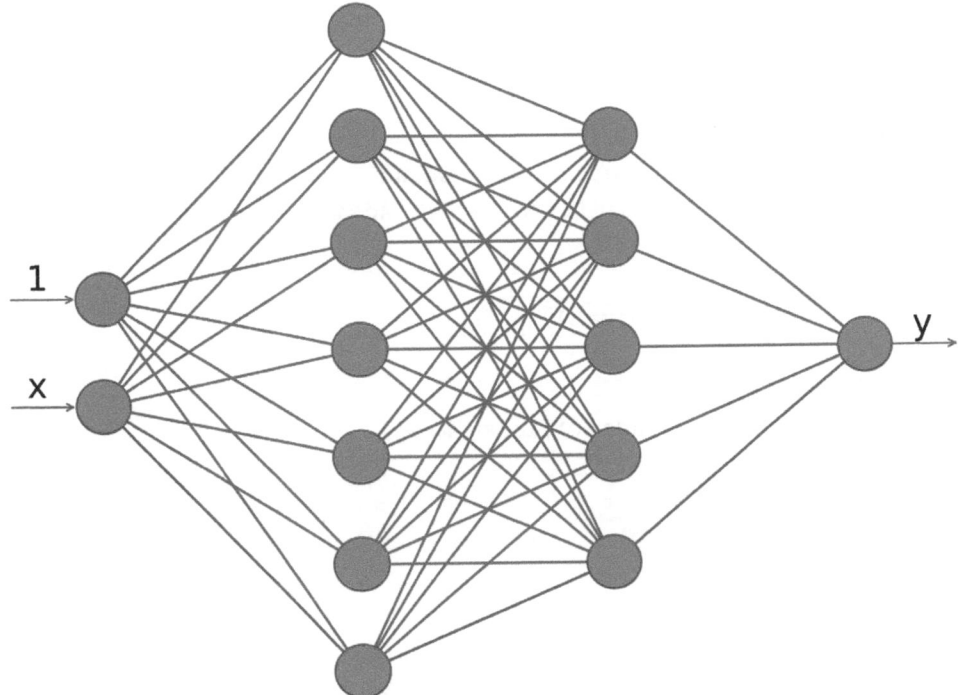

Figure 6.1 A diagram of a neural network with two hidden layers

---

The zip() Function in Python

The *zip()* function in Python combines items from multiple collections and returns a series of tuples with items from each collection. In the code cell above, we use *zip*([2, 7, 5], [7, 5, 1]) to produce three tuples (2, 7), (7, 5), and (5, 1). The multiple collections in the *zip()* function must have the same length.

If you run the Python code in the above cell, you'll see an output as in Figure 6.1. The figure is also available under /files/ch06/ in the book's GitHub repository.

As an exercise, modify the above cell and change the number of neurons in the two hidden layers to 8 and 4, respectively. Rerun the cell and see if the diagram reflects the change.

Next, we'll use this neural network to approximate the relation between X and $y = sin(X)$.

6.1.2 Learn a Nonlinear Relation without Activation

First, we create a neural network using *keras* based on what we learned in Chapter 5. We then create 1000 pairs of inputs and outputs that have a nonlinear relationship of

$y = sin(X)$. We don't use any activation functions in any of the layers in the neural network.

[3]:
```python
import numpy as np
from tensorflow.keras.models import Sequential
from tensorflow.keras.layers import Dense
from tensorflow.keras.optimizers import Adam

model=Sequential()
model.add(Dense(7,input_dim=1))
model.add(Dense(5))
model.add(Dense(1))
model.compile(optimizer=Adam(),loss='mse')

# Generate 1000 numbers in [-5,5]
X = np.linspace(-5,5,1000)
# Gnerate y as sine X
y = np.sin(X)
# Train the model using the X, y as inputs
hist = model.fit(X, y, epochs= 150, verbose=1)
```

In the cell above, we first import the NumPy library. We then import the Sequential model, the Dense layer, and the Adam optimizer from Keras that's embedded in the TensorFlow library. We then create the neural network using the Keras API as we did in Chapter 5. We use the mean squared error as the loss function in the neural network when compiling the model.

Upper Case and Lower Case (X, y) in ML

In machine learning models, it's customary to use a lower case y to denote the output variable (i.e., the target) since the output is usually a one-dimensional vector. In contrast, it's customary to use an upper case X to denote the input variable since there are usually more than one feature. Therefore, the input is a two-dimensional matrix. We'll follow this custom for the rest of this book.

We create 1000 X values between -5 and 5 using the *linspace()* method in NumPy. The 1000 corresponding y values are generated as $y = sin(X)$. To train the model, we use the *fit()* method and put the 1000 pairs of inputs and outputs (X, y) we generated as the arguments. We train the model for 150 epochs. We save the training history in a Python callbacks history object called *hist*.

Below, you can view the value of the loss function in the training process by retrieving the information from the object *hist* we just created.

```
[4]:   # View the loss through the training process
       fig=plt.figure(dpi=100)
       plt.plot(hist.history["loss"],label='Loss',color="r")
       plt.legend()
       plt.show()
```

In the above cell, we use the *matplotlib* library to plot the values of the loss function during the process of training. If you run the cell, you'll see a plot as the output. Alternatively, you can view the loss during the training process at the book's GitHub repository by looking for the picture /files/ch06/loss1.png. The plot shows that the loss, as measured by mean squared error, ranges from 0.5005 and 0.5035. The value of the loss didn't come down significantly after 150 epochs of training. This indicates that the model is not doing a good job of approximating the relationship between X and y.

Next, we'll create an out of sample dataset to test the performance of the trained model.

```
[5]:   # Create the testing dataset
       X_test=np.linspace(-np.pi,np.pi,200)
       y_test=np.sin(X_test)
```

We use the *linspace()* method in NumPy to create 200 points between $-\pi$ and π. We use them as the values of X_test in the testing dataset. The true value of y in the testing sample is $y\_test = sin(X\_test)$. Next, we'll predict the value of y based on the trained model, like so:

```
[6]:   # Make predictions on the test dataset
       y_pred=model.predict(X_test)
```

```
7/7 [==============================] - 0s 1ms/step
```

We use the *predict()* method to make predictions. The predicted values of y are saved as y_pred.

The Python code in the cell below plots both the actual values of y and the predicted values of y to show how good the predictions are.

```
[7]:   # Compare the actual y value and the prediction
       fig = plt.figure(figsize=(12,6), dpi=200)
       plt.scatter(X_test,y_test,label='Actual')
       plt.plot(X_test,y_pred,label='Prediction',marker="D",color="r")
       plt.legend()
       plt.show()
```

We first create a figure that is 12 by 24 inches in size, with a dpi of 200. We then create a scatter plot of y_test against X_test and label it *Actual*. In the same figure, we plot the values of y_pred against X_test and label it *Prediction*. We set the marker argument to D and the color argument to r. As a result, the prediction plot appears as a string of red diamonds.

If you run the above cell, you'll see a figure comparing the predictions with the actual values of $y = sin(X)$. You can also view the figure at the book's GitHub repository by looking for the picture /files/ch06/compare1.png. The figure shows that the predictions (the red diamonds) form a straight line, while the relation between y_test against X_test form a sine curve.

The above results show that the neural network is doing a poor job of predicting the relation between X and $y = sin(X)$.

Why the Predicted Relation Is Still Linear with Multiple Layers?

Without an activation function, the values in each layer of the neural network are simply a linear transformation of the inputs from the previous layer. We cannot generate a nonlinear relation even if we use multiple layers. Why? Because the linear transformation of a linear relation is still linear.

Here is an intuitive illustration of why a linear transformation of a linear relation is still linear. Suppose y is a function of x, and z is a function of y, like so

$$y = f(x)$$

$$z = g(y)$$

If both $f(.)$ and $g(.)$ are linear, we have

$$y = w_f * x + b_f$$

$$z = w_g * y + b_g$$

where w_f, b_f, w_g, and b_g are all constants. Then we have

$$z = w_g * (w_f * x + b_f) + b_g = w_g w_f * x + w_g b_f + b_g$$

which shows that z is still a linear function of x.

Without an activation function, a neural network can only predict a linear relationship between inputs and outputs. No matter how many hidden layers we include in the neural network, we cannot generate a nonlinear relationship between X and y. As an exercise, modify the Python code cells in this subsection so that the neural network has three hidden layers with 8, 6, and 5 neurons, respectively. Rerun the cells and see if the neural network can generate a nonlinear relationship.

Next, we'll talk about the ReLU activation function and how it can help neural networks achieve nonlinear approximations.

6.2 THE RELU ACTIVATION FUNCTION

In this section, we'll first discuss what the ReLU activation function is. We then show that with the ReLU activation function, we can successfully approximate a nonlinear relation with a neural network.

6.2.1 What is ReLU?

ReLU is short for rectified linear unit activation function. It returns the original value if it's positive, and 0 otherwise. That is, the ReLU function is defined as follows mathematically:

$$ReLU(x) = \begin{cases} x & \text{for } x > 0 \\ 0 & \text{for } x \leq 0 \end{cases}$$

It's widely used in many neural networks, and you'll see it in this book more often than any other type of activation function.

In essence, the ReLU activation function activates the neuron when the value of x reaches the threshold value of zero. When the value of x is below zero, the neuron is switched off. This simple on-off switch is able to create a nonlinear relation between inputs and outputs.

The following program plots the ReLU activation function in the range of -6 to 6.

```
[8]: # Generate x values
xs = np.linspace(-6,6,31)
# Define the ReLU function
def relu(x):
    y=np.zeros(len(x))
    for i in range(len(x)):
        if x[i]>0:
            y[i]=x[i]
    return y
ys=relu(xs)
# Plot the ReLU function
fig, ax = plt.subplots(figsize=(12,8),dpi=200)
plt.xlim(-6,6)
plt.ylim(-1,6.5)
plt.grid()
plt.plot(xs, ys, color = 'blue')
legend='$ReLU(x)\
=\{\genfrac{}{}{0}{}{x\ if \ x>0}{0\ if \ x\leq 0}$'
plt.legend([legend],fontsize=15)
plt.xlabel("value of x")
```

```
plt.ylabel("value of $y=ReLU(x)$")
plt.title("The ReLU Activation Function")
plt.savefig("files/ch06/relu.png")
```

We create 31 values of x between -6 and 6. We then create the corresponding 31 values of $y = ReLU(x)$. The values of x and y are plotted in blue in a figure created with the *matplotlib* library. The functional form of the ReLU activation function appears in the legend box in the graph. To use LaTex code to create mathematical equations, simply put dollar signs ($) around the LaTex code.

If you run the above cell, the plot will be saved on your computer as *relu.png* in the folder /Desktop/mla/files/ch06/. The figure is also available under /files/ch06/ in the book's GitHub repository. The plot is piece-wise linear: it's linear for values below zero; it's also linear for values greater than zero. Since the two linear lines don't have the same slope, the overall pattern is nonlinear.

6.2.2 Animate the ReLU Function

Better yet, you can create an animation of the ReLU activation function, showing how the value of $y = ReLU(x)$ changes as the value of x changes from -6 to 6.

The Python code in the cell below creates a series of pictures of the ReLU function when the value of x changes from left to the right on the horizontal axis.

```
[9]:  # Generate the ReLU function at different (x, y)
      for i in range(31):
          # add the current position of (x,y)
          x = xs[i]
          y = ys[i]
          # Plot a pic of the relu function as background
          fig, ax = plt.subplots(figsize=(12, 8), dpi=200)
          plt.xlim(-6,6)
          plt.ylim(-1,6.5)
          plt.grid()
          plt.plot(xs, ys, color = 'blue')
          plt.legend([legend],fontsize=20)
          plt.xlabel("value of x", fontsize=20)
          plt.ylabel("value of $y=ReLU(x)$", fontsize=20)
          plt.title("The ReLU Activation Function",fontsize=30)
          plt.scatter(x,y,color='red',s=150)
          # add text to explain
          txt=ax.annotate(
          f'value of x: {round(x,2)}\nvalue of y: {round(y,2)}',
              xy=(x,y),xytext=(0.2,0.6),textcoords='axes fraction',
              bbox=dict(boxstyle="round",fc="0.9"),
              arrowprops=dict(arrowstyle='->',color='g'),
```

```
                fontsize=20)
        plt.savefig(f"files/ch06/relu{i}.png")
        plt.close(fig)
```

We iterate through the 31 points of (x, y) from the left to right of the horizontal axis. In each iteration, we first plot the ReLU function as the background. We plot the point (x, y) as a red dot in the graph. We create a text box to show the values of X and y. The text box points to the red dot so you know which point the graph is focusing on.

If you run the above code cell, you'll see 31 pictures on your computer in the folder /Desktop/mla/files/ch06/: they are named as *relu0.png, relu1.png...*, and *relu30.png*.

Next, we combine the 31 graphs we just created into an animation.

```
10]: import imageio, PIL


     frames=[]
     for i in range(31):
         frame=PIL.Image.open(f"files/ch06/relu{i}.png")
         frame=np.asarray(frame)
         frames.append(np.array(frame))
     imageio.mimsave('files/ch06/relu.gif',frames,fps=6)
```

We create an empty list *frames* to store all pictures. We then iterate through the 31 pictures we generated in the last code cell and open each one using the *PIL* library. We convert the pictures to NumPy arrays and add them to the list *frames*. Once done, we use the *mimsave()* method in the *imageio* library to convert the images to the *gif* format.

After you run the above cell, the file *relu.gif* will be generated and saved in your local folder. To view the animation, you can click on the file on your computer. Alternatively, you can view it at the book's GitHub repository under the folder /files/ch06/.

6.2.3   Use ReLU to Model Nonlinearity

Now that you understand what the ReLU function is, you'll put it to good use by generating a nonlinear relation between the input and output variables. Specifically, you'll use the same neural network you built in Section 6.1.2 and add the ReLU activation function in the two hidden layers, and retrain the model.

```
11]: model = Sequential()
     model.add(Dense(7, activation="relu", input_dim=1))
     model.add(Dense(5, activation="relu"))
     model.add(Dense(1))
     model.compile(optimizer=Adam(),loss='mse')
```

```
# Generate 1000 numbers in [-5,5]
X = np.linspace(-5,5,1000)
# Gnerate y as sine X
y = np.sin(X)
# Train the model using the X, y as inputs
hist = model.fit(X,y,epochs=150,verbose=0)
# View the loss through the training process
plt.plot(hist.history["loss"],label='Loss',color="r")
plt.legend()
plt.show()
```

In particular, we add the argument activation="relu" in the two hidden dense layers. We then retrain the model and save the training history.

We can now make predictions using the newly trained model, like so.

[12]:
```
# Make predictions on the test set
X_test = np.linspace(-np.pi,np.pi,200)
y_test = np.sin(X_test)
pred = model.predict(X_test)
# Compare the actual y value and the prediction
fig = plt.figure(figsize=(12,6), dpi=100)
plt.scatter(X_test,y_test,label='Actual')
plt.plot(X_test,pred,label='Prediction',marker="D",color="r")
plt.legend()
plt.show()
```

```
7/7 [==============================] - 0s 665us/step
```

We generate 200 points between $-\pi$ and π as the values of X_test in the testing sample. The true value of y in the testing sample is $y\_test = sin(X\_test)$. We predict the value of y based on the re-trained model.

If you run the above cell, you'll see a figure showing that the predictions (the red diamonds) form a curve resembling a sine curve. You can also view the figure at the book's GitHub repository by looking for the picture /files/ch06/compare2.png. The predictions now match the true y values pretty well. Most importantly, the shape of the prediction is now nonlinear. The above results show that the neural network is doing a good job of predicting the relation between X and $y = sin(X)$, with the help of the ReLU activation function.

Here you do have a lot of flexibility in how many hidden layers you want to include in the neural network and how many neurons each hidden layer should have. As an exercise, remove the second hidden layer from the neural network. Make sure you keep the first hidden layer intact with the ReLU activation function. Rerun the cells and see if the predictions match the actual sine shape.

6.3 THE SIGMOID ACTIVATION FUNCTION

The second most-used activation function in this book is the sigmoid function. It's widely used in many machine learning models. In particular, it's a must-have in any binary classification problem.

The sigmoid function has the form

$$y = \frac{1}{1 + e^{-x}}$$

The sigmoid function has an S-shaped curve. It has this nice property: for any value of input x between $-\infty$ and ∞, the output value y is always between 0 and 1. Because of this property, we use the sigmoid activation function to model the probability of an outcome, which also falls between 0 and 1 (0 means there is no chance of the outcome occurring, while 1 the outcome occurring with 100% certainty).

6.3.1 Plot the Sigmoid Function

We plot the sigmoid function when the value of x ranges from -6 to 6.

```
13]:  xs=np.linspace(-6,6,31)
      def sigmoid(x):
          p=1/(1+np.exp(-x))
          return p
      ys=sigmoid(xs)
      fig,ax=plt.subplots(figsize=(12,8),dpi=200)
      plt.grid()
      plt.plot(xs, ys, color='blue',
      label='The Sigmoid Function $y= \dfrac{1}{1 + e^{-x}}$')
      plt.legend(loc="upper left",fontsize=20)
      plt.title("The Sigmoid Activation Function",fontsize=30)
      plt.savefig("files/ch06/sigmoid.png")
```

We create 31 different values of x between -6 and 6 using the *linspace()* method in NumPy. We then define the sigmoid function and create 31 values of $y = sigmoid(x)$. The values of x and y are plotted in blue in a figure created with the *matplotlib* library. The mathematical formula of the sigmoid activation function appears in the legend box in the graph by using the LaTex code.

If you run the above cell, the plot will be saved on your computer as *sigmoid.png* in the folder /Desktop/mla/files/ch06/. The figure is also available under /files/ch06/ in the book's GitHub repository. As you can see, the value of the sigmoid function is between 0 and 1, which can be interpreted as the probability of an outcome.

6.3.2 Animate the Sigmoid Function

Next, we'll animation the sigmoid activation function, showing how the value of $y = sigmoid(x)$ changes as the value of x changes from -6 to 6. We'll first generate a series of pictures and then combine them into an animation.

The Python code in the following cell generates 31 pictures.

```python
[14]: xs = np.linspace(-6,6,31)
      for i in range(31):
          # add the current position of (x,y)
          x=xs[i]
          y=sigmoid(x)
          # Plot a pic of the sigmoid function as background
          fig,ax=plt.subplots(figsize=(12,8),dpi=200)
          plt.grid()
          plt.plot(xs,sigmoid(xs),color='blue',
          label='The Sigmoid Function $y= \dfrac{1}{1 + e^{-x}}$')
          plt.legend(loc="upper left",fontsize=20)
          plt.xlabel("value of x",fontsize=20)
          plt.ylabel("value of $y= \dfrac{1}{1 + e^{-x}}$",
                  fontsize=20)
          plt.title("The Sigmoid Activation Function",fontsize=30)
          plt.scatter(x,y,color='red',s=150)
          # add text to explain
          txt=ax.annotate(
          f'value of x: {round(x,5)}\nvalue of y: {round(y,5)}',
              xy=(x,y),xytext=(0.65,0.1),textcoords='axes fraction',
              bbox=dict(boxstyle="round",fc="0.9"),
              arrowprops=dict(arrowstyle='->',color='g'),
              fontsize=20)
          plt.savefig(f"files/ch06/sigmoid{i}.png")
          plt.close(fig)
```

We iterate through the 31 points of (x, y) from the left to the right of the horizontal axis. In each iteration, we first plot the sigmoid function as the background. We then plot the point (x, y) as a red dot in the graph. We create a text box to show the values of x and y. The text box points to the red dot so you know which point the graph is focusing on.

If you run the above code cell, you'll see 31 pictures on your computer in the folder /Desktop/mla/files/ch06/: they are named as *sigmoid0.png, sigmoid1.png...*, and *sigmoid30.png*.

Next, we combine the 31 graphs we just created into an animation.

```
[5]: frames=[]
     for i in range(31):
         frame=PIL.Image.open(f"files/ch06/sigmoid{i}.png")
         frame=np.asarray(frame)
         frames.append(np.array(frame))
     imageio.mimsave('files/ch06/sigmoid.gif',frames,fps=6)
```

We iterate through the 31 pictures we just generated and open them using the *PIL* library. We convert the pictures to NumPy arrays and use the *mimsave()* method in the *imageio* library to convert the images to an animation in the *gif* format.

After you run the above cell, the file *sigmoid.gif* will be generated and saved in your local folder. To view the animation, you can click on the file on your computer. Alternatively, you can view it at the book's GitHub repository under the folder /files/ch06/.

6.3.3 Combine Animations

Next, let's combine the two animations in one so that you can see the ReLU function and the sigmoid function side by side in the animation.

To combine two animations into one, we use the *concatenate()* method in NumPy. The argument axis=1 in the method places the two frames side by side horizontally, like so:

```
[16]: frames=[]
      for i in range(31):
          frame1=PIL.Image.open(f"files/ch06/relu{i}.png")
          frame1=np.asarray(frame1)
          frame2=PIL.Image.open(f"files/ch06/sigmoid{i}.png")
          frame2=np.asarray(frame2)
          frame=np.concatenate([frame1,frame2],axis=1)
          frames.append(np.array(frame))
      imageio.mimsave('files/ch06/relusig.gif',frames,fps=5)
```

We start a *for* loop to iterate through different phases of the animation. In each of the 31 iterations, we first open a picture of the ReLU function and convert it into NumPy arrays. We then open a picture of the sigmoid function and use the *concatenate()* method in NumPy to combine it with the RuLU function picture horizontally. The combined frames are stored in a list *frames*. We then use the *imageio* library to convert the combined frames into an animation.

If you run the above cell, you'll see an animation *relusig.gif* in the folder /Desktop/mla/ch06/files/ on your computer. The animation shows the two activation functions side by side, when the value of x moves from the left to the right of the horizontal axis.

6.3.4 A Picture with Subplots of Different Stages

Even though we cannot show animations in the book, we can create a figure with multiple subplots to compare the two functions at different x values.

For that purpose, we showcase eight pictures to form a four by two grid. The four pictures in the left column illustrates the ReLU function, while the four in the right column the sigmoid function, like so:

```
[17]: stacked=np.concatenate([frames[0],frames[10],\
              frames[20],frames[30]],axis=0)
```

The NumPy array *stacked* now has 8 pictures in it, with 2 different functions and four different stages. Note that in the above cell, we use the argument axis=0 in the *concatenate()* method in NumPy so that the four frames are organized vertically.

Next, we'll use *matplotlib.pyplot* to create a figure with eight pictures in it, like so:

```
[18]: fig=plt.figure(dpi=300,figsize=(24,32))
plt.imshow(stacked)
plt.axis('off')
plt.show()
```

Here we create a figure that is 24 inches wide and 32 inches tall. We set the dpi as high as 300 so that the picture is clear with high resolutions. Since the NumPy array *stacked* is a combination of eight pictures, all we need is to use the *imshow()* method in *mapplotlib* to generate the graph.

Run the above cell, and you'll see an output as in Figure 6.2. The figure is also available under /files/ch06/ in the book's GitHub repository.

6.4 THE SOFTMAX ACTIVATION FUNCTION

The third most-used activation function in this book is the softmax function. It's a must-have in any multi-category classification problem.

6.4.1 What is the Softmax Function?

The softmax function has the form

$$y(x) = \frac{e^x}{\sum_{k=1}^{K} e^{x_k}}$$

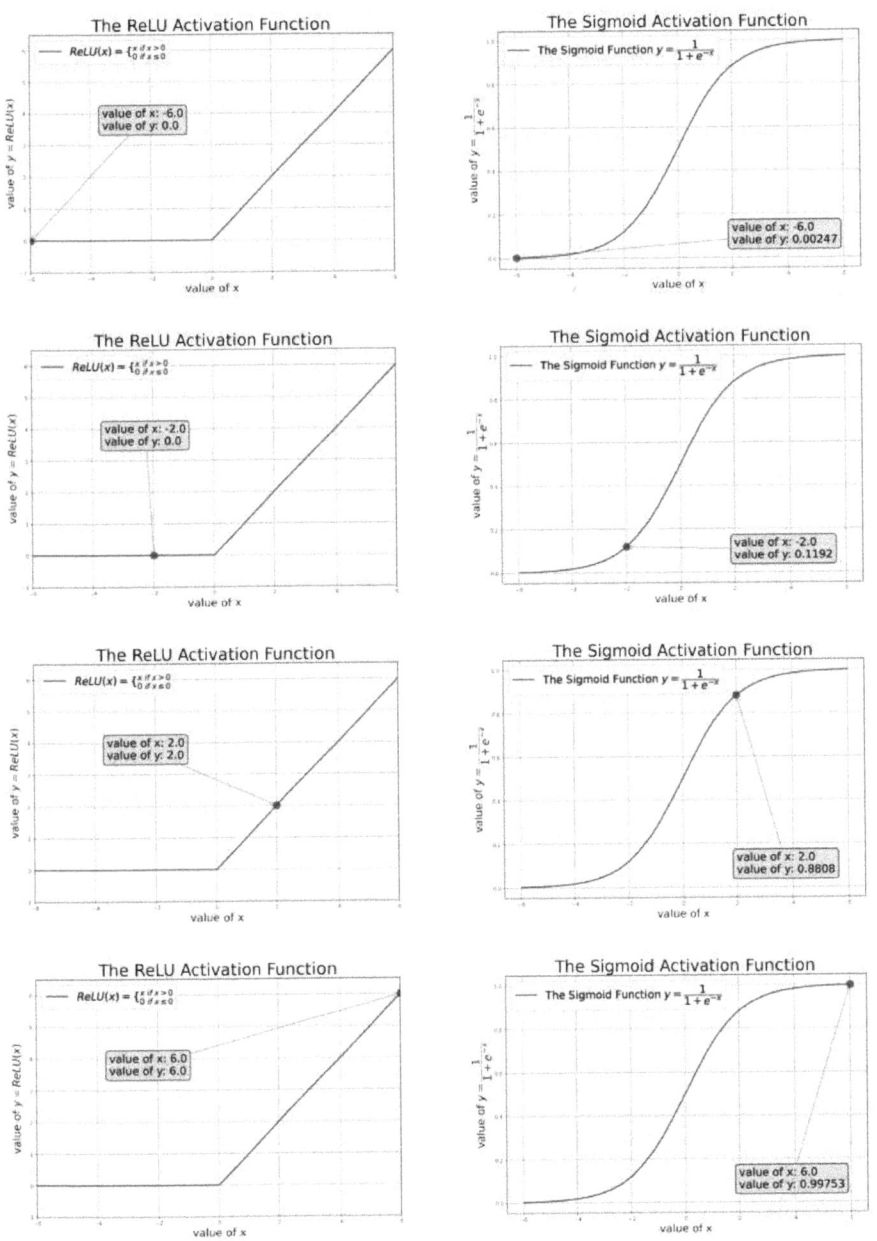

Figure 6.2 Compare the ReLU and sigmoid functions

where $x = [x_1, x_2, ..., x_K]$ and $y = [y_1, y_2, ..., y_K]$ are K-element lists. The i-th element of y is

$$y_i(x) = \frac{e^{x_i}}{\sum_{k=1}^{K} e^{x_k}}$$

The softmax function has the following properties:

- The softmax function can take a K-element vector x as the input; each element in the vector x can be any value between $-\infty$ and ∞.
- The softmax function generates a K-element vector y as the output; each element in the vector y has a value between 0 and 1.
- The elements in the output vector y add up to 1 (i.e., 100%).

Because of these properties, we use the softmax activation function to model the probability distribution of a multiple-category outcome. You'll notice later in this book that the activation function in the output layer is always the softmax function when we model multi-category classification problems.

To illustrate the above three properties of the softmax function, we next show how the softmax function converts $x = [-1.3, 7.9, -0.8, 5.1]$ into the probability distribution of four possible outcomes.

```
[19]:  xs = [-1.3, 7.9, -0.8, 5.1]
       # Define the softmax() function
       def softmax(x):
           xi=np.exp(x)
           return xi/xi.sum()
       # Converts them into four values
       ys = softmax(xs)
       for y in ys:
           print(0<=y<=1)
```

```
True
True
True
True
```

In the above cell, we first define the vector x with the four input values. We then define the softmax function and use it to generate a vector y with four output values. Finally, we check each of the four elements in y to see if they are between 0 and 1. The above results show *True* four times, indicating that all four values in y are indeed between 0 and 1.

Next, we check if the values of the elements in y add up to 1, i.e., 100%.

```
[20]:  # The sum of the four values
       print("the sum of the four values in ys is", ys.sum())
```

```
the sum of the four values in ys is 1.0
```

In the above cell, we use $ys.sum()$ to calculate the sum of the four values in the NumPy array ys. The output shows that the sum of the four values is 1.0. That is, the four values in the output vector of the softmax activation function add up to 100%.

6.4.2 A Diagram of the Softmax Function

Next, we'll draw a diagram of the softmax activation function. In particular, we'll draw the four values in the input vector x on the left of the diagram. The mathematical formula of the softmax activation function will be placed in the middle of the diagram. Finally, we'll put the four values in the output vector y on the right of the diagram, like so:

```python
from matplotlib.patches import Rectangle

# Create a figure
fig = plt.figure(figsize=(12,4), dpi=200)
ax = fig.add_subplot(111)
# Add rectangles to the figure
ax.add_patch(Rectangle((-6,-2), 3, 4,
            edgecolor = 'r',alpha=0.2))
ax.add_patch(Rectangle((3,-2), 2.8, 4,
            edgecolor = 'r',alpha=0.2))
ax.add_patch(Rectangle((-2,-1), 4, 2,
            edgecolor = 'k',
            facecolor = 'g',
            alpha=0.2))
# Add text boxes
plt.text(-1.9, -0.1,
        r"$\frac {e^{x_i}} {e^{x_1}+e^{x_2}+e^{x_3}+e^{x_4}} $",
        fontsize=32, color="k")
plt.text(-1.8, 1.1, r"Softmax Activation",
        fontsize=21.5, color="r")
plt.text(-1.85, -1.5, r"$y_1+y_2+y_3+y_4=100\%$",
        fontsize=17.5, color="r")
# Add x and y values
for i in range(4):
    plt.text(-5.8, 1.35-i, f"$x_{i}={xs[i]}$",
        fontsize=22, color="k")
    plt.text(3.1, 1.35-i, f"$y_{i}={ys[i]:.5f}$",
        fontsize=22, color="k")
ax.annotate("", xy=(-2,0), xytext = (-3,0),
                arrowprops=dict(arrowstyle = '->',
                color = 'b', linewidth = 2))
```

```
ax.annotate("", xy = (3,0), xytext = (2,0),
                 arrowprops=dict(arrowstyle = '->',
                 color = 'b', linewidth = 2))
ax.set_xlim(-6, 6)
ax.set_ylim(-2, 2)
plt.axis("off")
```

[21]: (-6.0, 6.0, -2.0, 2.0)

We first create a figure that is 12 inches wide and 4 inches tall with dpi=200. The *Rectangle* class in *matplotlib* creates a shaded rectangle in the figure. The first argument in the *Rectangle* class is the lower left corner co-ordinates, the second and third arguments are the width and height of the rectangle, respectively. For example, $Rectangle((-6, -2), 3, 4, edgecolor =' r', apha = 0.2)$ creates a rectangle that is 3 inches wide and 4 inches tall, with the point $(-6, -2)$ as left lower corner. The $edgecolor =' r'$ argument means the edge color is red, and $alpha = 0.2$ dictates the transparency of the face color.

We put two blue arrows in the graph. The first arrow points from the input values x to the softmax activation function. The second arrow points from the softmax function to the output values y. We also show on the diagram that the values in the output vector y add up to 100%.

Run the above cell, you'll see a diagram with three rectangle boxes. The first contains the four values in the input vector x, the second the mathematical formula of the softmax function, and the third the four values in the output vector y. Alternatively, you can see it under /files/ch06/softmax.png in the book's GitHub repository.

6.5 GLOSSARY

- **Activation Functions:** Functions in neural networks that are used to determine the output of neurons in the network. Commonly used activation functions include ReLU, sigmoid, and softmax.
- **ReLU Activation Function:** ReLU is short for rectified linear unit activation function. It returns the original value if the input is positive, and 0 otherwise.
- **Sigmoid Activation Function:** The sigmoid function has the form

$$y = \frac{1}{1 + e^{-x}}$$

  It has this nice property: for any value of input x between $-\infty$ and ∞, the output value y is always between 0 and 1. Because of this property, it is used to model the probability of an outcome.
- **Softmax Activation Function:** The softmax function has the form

$$y(x) = \frac{e^x}{\sum_{k=1}^{K} e^{x_k}}$$

where $x = [x_1, x_2, ..., x_K]$ and $y = [y_1, y_2, ..., y_K]$ are K-element lists. Each element in the output vector has a value between 0 and 1. The elements in the output vector add up to 1. Because of these properties, we use the softmax activation function to model the probability distribution of a multiple-category outcome.

6.6 EXERCISES

6.1 Explain what an activation function is. Give three examples of commonly used activation functions.

6.2 Modify the program in Section 6.1.1 so that the numbers of neurons in the neural network are [2, 8, 4, 1] instead of [2, 7, 5, 1].

6.3 Modify the cells in Section 6.1.2 so that the neural network contains three hidden layers with 8, 6, and 5 neurons, respectively. Don't add an activation function in any layer. See if the predictions form a nonlinear relationship and explain why the predicted relationship is still linear even with more hidden layers.

6.4 What is the ReLU activation function?

6.5 Modify the programs in Section 6.2.3 to remove the second hidden layer in the neural network. Make sure you keep the ReLU activation function in the first hidden layer. Rerun the Python code in the cells and see if the predicted relationship is nonlinear.

6.6 What is the sigmoid activation function? Why do we use it as the activation function when we model binary classification problems?

6.7 What is the softmax activation function? Why do we use it as the activation function when we model multi-category classification problems?

III

Binary and Multi-Category Classifications

## CHAPTER 7

Binary Classifications

To be, or not to be: that is the question.

Hamlet

−William Shakespeare

BINARY CLASSIFICATION IS one of most important and most common types of supervised learning problems. Examples of binary classifications include whether an email is a spam, whether a credit card transaction is fraudulent, whether a customer will buy a certain product, or whether a loan application will be approved. . .

In this chapter, you'll learn binary classification by classifying images into two categories: a horse or a deer. You'll build a simple neural network from scratch for the task. In Chapter 4, we summarized ML in three words: initialize, adjust, and repeat. You'll follow the three steps to train the neural network for your binary classification task in this chapter. Specifically, you'll build a neural network and retrieve the initialized weights in the model. As you start to train the model using images and their corresponding labels, the model weights are adjusted to fit the data. You'll see how the weights and the predictions change as the training progresses.

In the early stages of training, if you feed a picture of a horse into the model, the predicted probability is about 35%. As the training progresses, the probability increases steadily since the model gradually learns from the data. After training, the predicted probability is more than 88%. Similarly, in the early stages of training, if you feed a picture of a deer into the model, the predicted probability of it being a deer is around 60%. This probability increases over the course of training. After training, the predicted probability is 94%. You'll create an animation to demonstrate how the model weights and the predicted probabilities change in different stages of training.

DOI: 10.1201/b23383-7

New Skills in This Chapter
- Downloading and processing the CIFAR-10 image data
- Using a logistic regression for binary classification
- Creating and training a neural network for binary classification
- Retrieving model weights and predictions from different stages of training
- Creating graphs and animations to show model weights and predictions
- Evaluating binary classification models using accuracy and confusion matrix

---

Before you start, open the Jupyter Notebook app in the virtual environment MLA on your computer. After that, open a blank Jupyter notebook and save it as *ch07.ipynb* in the directory /Desktop/mla/ on your computer. Next, we'll create a subdirectory /files/ch07/ to store files in this chapter. Start a new cell in *ch07.ipynb* and execute the following lines of code in it:

[1]:
```
import os

os.makedirs("files/ch07", exist_ok=True)
```

You should see a new directory /Desktop/mla/files/ch07/ on your computer.

In addition, you'll need to install the *scikit-learn* library on your computer to run logistic regressions and to split data into train and test subsets. First activate the virtual environment MLA. Run the following command in the Anaconda prompt (Windows) or a terminal (Mac or Linux):

```
pip install scikit-learn==1.2.2
```

or simply run the following line of code in a new cell in *ch07.ipynb*:

```
!pip install scikit-learn==1.2.2
```

You need to restart the Jupyter Notebook app on your computer for the installation to take effect.

7.1   WHAT IS A BINARY CLASSIFICATION PROBLEM

When the target label is a binary variable with two possible values (such as 0 or 1, yes or no), we call the ML algorithm a binary classification problem. This is very common in the real-world, ranging from credit card fraud prediction, two-class image classification, to disease detection. The ML algorithm first learns the relationship between the input features and the output label. The algorithm then makes predictions based on input features and classifies each observation into one of the two categories.

7.1.1 Sigmoid Activation in Binary Classifications

In binary classifications, since the target label is 0 or 1, we predict the probability that the target variable is of class 1. With complementary probability, the target is of class 0. In this chapter, you'll use a neural network to classify an image into either a horse (value 1) or a deer (value 0).

You'll use the sigmoid activation function to squash the output from the last layer in the neural network (which can take values from $-\infty$ to ∞) to the range $[0, 1]$. This way, the final output from the neural network can be interpreted as the probability of the target being class 1 (in our example, the probability that the image is a horse).

The idea can be illustrated in the graph below. Here we assume a linear relationship between the input and the output before activation. The inputs are the raw pixels of an image plus a bias term. The output is the probability that the image is a horse. We use a neural network with no hidden layer as our prediction model. We put the sigmoid activation function in the output layer as explained above.

The Python code in the cell below creates a diagram for the neural network that we'll use for the binary classification problem in this chapter.

```
[2]: from matplotlib import pyplot as plt
     from matplotlib.patches import Rectangle

     fig=plt.figure(figsize=(12,6),dpi=200)
     ax=fig.add_subplot(111)
     # Draw the two input neurons
     circle=plt.Circle((-3,2),radius=0.8,color='white',ec="m")
     ax.add_artist(circle)
     circle=plt.Circle((-3,-2),radius=0.8,color='white',ec="m")
     ax.add_artist(circle)
     # Draw the output neuron
     circle=plt.Circle((1,0),radius=0.8,color='white',ec="m")
     ax.add_artist(circle)
     # Draw connections between neurons
     ax.annotate("",xy=(0.2,0),xytext=(-2.2,2),
         arrowprops=dict(arrowstyle='->',color='b',linewidth=2))
     ax.annotate("",xy=(0.2,0),xytext=(-2.2,-2),
         arrowprops=dict(arrowstyle='->',color='b',linewidth=2))
     ax.annotate("",xy=(-3.8,-2),xytext=(-5.5,-2),
         arrowprops=dict(arrowstyle='->',color='b',linewidth=2))
     ax.annotate("",xy=(-3.8,2),xytext=(-5.5,2),
         arrowprops=dict(arrowstyle='->',color='b',linewidth=2))
     ax.annotate("",xy=(4.5,0),xytext=(4,0),
         arrowprops=dict(arrowstyle='->',color='b',linewidth=2))
     # Put explanation texts on the graph
     plt.text(-5.25,2.1,"bias",fontsize=20,color="k")
```

```
plt.text(-5.25,-1.9,"input",fontsize=20,color="k")
plt.text(-1.7,-1.9,f"w",fontsize=20,color="r",rotation=39)
plt.text(-1.7,0.9,f"b",fontsize=20,color="r",rotation=-39)
plt.text(-3.2,1.8,"1",fontsize=30,color="k")
plt.text(-3.2,-2.2,"X",fontsize=30,color="k")
plt.text(0.5,-0.1,"wX+b",fontsize=20,color="k")
plt.text(4.6,-0.1,f"Y",fontsize=20,color="r")
plt.text(2.05,-0.1,r"$\frac{1}{1+e^{-(wX+b)}}$",
    fontsize=25,color="k")
# add text to explain
txt=ax.annotate('Sigmoid\nActivation',xy=(3,-1),
    xytext=(0.65,0.1),textcoords='axes fraction',
    bbox=dict(boxstyle="round",fc="0.9"),
    arrowprops=dict(arrowstyle='->',color='g',linewidth=1),
    fontsize=20)
# add rectangle to plot
ax.add_patch(Rectangle((2,-1),2,2,edgecolor='k',alpha=0.1))
ax.set_xlim(-6,6)
ax.set_ylim(-3,3)
plt.axis("off")
plt.savefig("files/ch07/binary.png")
```

The graph is generated using the *matplotlib* library. We draw two circles on the left to represent the input neurons. The first is the bias term and the second the vector of raw pixels of an image. The input data is then propagated forward to the output layer based on the weights w and b: the value in the output layer before activation is $wX + b$. Since we use sigmoid activation, the output after activation is

$$Y = \frac{1}{1 + e^{-(wX+b)}},$$

which is a value between 0 and 1, the probability that the image is a horse.

If you run the above cell, you'll see an image *binary.png* in the folder /Desktop/mla/ch07/files/ on your computer. The image shows the structure of the neural network we'll use for binary classification in this chapter.

7.1.2 The Binary Cross-Entropy Loss Function

In binary classification problems, the preferred loss function is the binary cross-entropy function, which measures the average difference between the predicted probabilities and the actual labels (1 or 0). If a model makes a perfect prediction and assigns a 100% probability to all observations labeled 1 and a 0% probability to all observations labeled 0, the binary cross-entropy loss function will have a value of 0.

Mathematically, the binary cross-entropy loss function is defined as

$$Binary\ Cross\ Entropy = \sum_{n=1}^{N} -[y_n \times log(\hat{y}_n) + (1 - y_n) \times log(1 - \hat{y}_n)]$$

where $\hat{y}_n$ is the estimated probability of observation n being class 1, and y_n is the actual label of observation n (which is either 0 or 1).

7.2 PROCESS IMAGE DATA

You'll use CIFAR-10, a popular dataset to train ML and computer vision algorithms, to learn how to make binary and multiple classification predictions in this book. Note that TensorFlow now has included CIFAR-10 in its standard dataset so you can load it directly from TensorFlow. In the Appendix at the end of this chapter, you'll learn how to do that.

However, it's a good idea to learn how to download data in a zip format from the origin, process it, and visualize it. Along the way, you'll pick up valuable skills in data science libraries such as NumPy, *matplotlib*, and others.

Let's go to Alex Krizhevsky's home page at University of Toronto https://www.cs.toronto.edu/~kriz/cifar.html to have a look at the dataset. CIFAR-10 provides 60,000 images in ten different classes: planes, cars, birds, cats, deer, dogs, frogs, horses, ship, and trucks.

You can manually download the data from the website and unzip it. But we'll use Python to do all those steps so you can learn how to handle similar problems in the future.

7.2.1 Download Data

The Python code in the cell below downloads the data and saves the data on your computer.

```
[3]: import requests
# Use the requests library to fetch the file from the URL
url='https://www.cs.toronto.edu/~kriz/cifar-10-python.tar.gz'
file=requests.get(url)
# Download the file content
with open('files/ch07/cifar-10-python.tar.gz','wb') as f:
    f.write(file.content)
```

We first import the *requests* library and use the *get()* method to retrieve the content of the zip file from the website based on the url provided. We then use the built-in Python function *write()* to save the data content to a file on your computer.

Run the above cell and then go to /Desktop/mla/files/ch07/ and you should see the zip file *cifar-10-python.tar.gz* in the folder.

Next, we'll unzip the file and place the content in a local folder, like so:

```
[4]:  import tarfile
      # Unzip it and save it in the subfolder /cifar10
      cifar=tarfile.open('files/ch07/cifar-10-python.tar.gz')
      cifar.extractall('files/ch07/cifar10')
      cifar.close()
```

We use the *tarfile* library to unzip the file and save the content in the subfolder /cifar10. The library *tarfile* is in the Python Standard Library, so no installation is needed.

If you go to the subfolder /file/ch07/cifar10/cifar-10-batches-py/, you'll see 8 files there. We'll discuss how to use these files below.

7.2.2 Convert NumPy Arrays to Pictures and Back

Next, you'll learn to convert a group of integers such as 0, 2, 144, or 255 into pictures that you can see on your computer. In the process, you'll understand how the RGB color model works to create images. You'll also learn to convert a picture back into a group of numbers in the format of NumPy arrays.

The Python code in the cell below loads up one batch of data and prints out the number of pictures under each label.

```
[5]:  import pickle
      import numpy as np

      # The unpickle function from Krizhevsky's page
      def unpickle(file):
          with open(file, 'rb') as fo:
              dict = pickle.load(fo, encoding='bytes')
          return dict
      # Use only one batch to speed up training
      path="files/ch07/cifar10/cifar-10-batches-py/"
      batch1=unpickle(path+"data_batch_1")
      # Put b before column since they are bits literal
      data=batch1[b"data"]
      labels=batch1[b'labels']
      # Look at ten pictures
      for i in range(10):
          num = labels.count(i)
          print(f"there are {num} pictures of label {i}")
```

```
there are 1005 pictures of label 0
there are 974 pictures of label 1
there are 1032 pictures of label 2
```

```
there are 1016 pictures of label 3
there are 999 pictures of label 4
there are 937 pictures of label 5
there are 1030 pictures of label 6
there are 1001 pictures of label 7
there are 1025 pictures of label 8
there are 981 pictures of label 9
```

The CIFAR-10 data we just downloaded are organized in five batches of training data and one batch of test data, plus a file of meta data, and a ReadMe file. We open only the first batch for the moment to save time. However, we'll use all five batches in later chapters. Note that since the data are bit literals, we need to put letter b in front of the column names when we load them up. Each batch contains both the data (X) and labels (y), with 10000 pictures. There are ten different labels: 0, 1, ..., 9. We count how many pictures under each label. The results above show that about 1000 pictures are under each label.

Next, we reshape the NumPy arrays that represent these pictures and visualize one of them.

```
[6]: X=data.reshape(10000,3,32,32)
     X=X.transpose(0,2,3,1).astype("uint8")
     y=np.array(labels)
     # Visualize the first picture
     X0=X[0]
     print(X0)
     plt.imshow(X0)
     plt.show()
```

```
[[[ 59  62  63]
  [ 43  46  45]
  [ 50  48  43]
  ...
  ...
  [216 184 140]
  [151 118  84]
  [123  92  72]]]
```

The picture data, i.e., the Xs, are NumPy arrays in the shape of 3 by 32 by 32. There are three color channels (red, green, and blue), and each picture has a resolution of 32 by 32 pixels. The data is in a channel-first format, so we have switched the positions of the 2nd and the fourth axis in the original data by using the *transpose()* method in NumPy.

We then use the *imshow()* method in *matplotlib* to convert NumPy arrays into a picture. Run the above cell and you'll see the numbers that represent the first picture, and they are numbers ranging from 0 to 255. We use the *imshow()* method in the *matplotlib* library to show the first picture in the dataset. The output shows a picture of a frog.

The RGB Color Model

The RGB color model has three color channels: red, green, and blue. Hence the name RGB. The value in each color channel ranges from 0 to 255. For example, [0, 0, 0] results in the color black since it lacks any color; [0, 0, 255] is blue; [255, 255, 0] is a mixture of red and green, which results in yellow. For more details, see, e.g., https://en.wikipedia.org/wiki/RGB_color_model.

7.2.3   Match Pictures with Labels

The labels you just saw are ten numbers from 0 to 9. Next, you'll convert these numbers into meaningful object names and match them with the pictures.

```
[7]:  # Names of the ten types of objects
      names = ['plane', 'car', 'bird', 'cat', 'deer',
              'dog', 'frog', 'horse', 'ship', 'truck']
      # Create a 5 by 5 grid of pictures
      plt.figure(figsize=(10,10),dpi=300)
      for i in range(5):
          for j in range(5):
              plt.subplot(5,5, 5*i+j+1)
              plt.imshow(X[5*i+j])
              plt.axis('off')
              plt.title(names[y[5*i+j]], fontsize=12)
      plt.subplots_adjust(hspace=0.20)
      plt.show()
      plt.savefig("files/ch07/25pics.png")
```

Here we use the $axis('off')$ option to turn off the axis so you only see the pictures. The *subplot()* method puts the 25 pictures in a 5 by 5 matrix. We extract the name of each picture, and put it as the title of the picture, so you can see it on top of each picture here.

If you run the above cell, you'll see a figure as in Figure 7.1. The figure contains 25 pictures of trucks, frogs, horses, and so on. The figure is saved on your computer as *25pics.png* in the folder /Desktop/mla/files/ch07/.

Figure 7.1 Sample pictures from the CIFAR-10 dataset

7.3 BINARY CLASSIFICATION WITH A LOGIT REGRESSION

In this section, we'll use a traditional logistic regression to classify images into horses and deer.

7.3.1 Prepare the Data

A color picture uses three channels: red, green, and blue. Below, you'll separate the three channels and see what the picture looks like if we use just one channel instead of three.

```
[8]: # Keep deer and horses only
     # Change y to a dummy of 1 (horse) or 0 (deer)
     X=[]
     y=[]
     for i in range(1000):
         if labels[i]==4:
             X.append(data[i])
             y.append(0)
         if labels[i]==7:
             X.append(data[i])
             y.append(1)
     # Reshape X
     X=np.array(X,dtype=float)
     # change channel first to channel last
     X=X.reshape(-1,3,32,32).transpose(0,2,3,1)
     # Change X to a float between 0 and 1
     X=X/255
     # Reshpae y
     y=np.array(y,dtype=float).reshape(-1,)
```

The Python code in the above cell goes through the 1000 pictures in the first batch and selects the ones that are labeled as 4 (deer) or 7 (horse). We then change the label to 0 (deer) or 1 (horse) so that the target variable is binary. We do this in order to create a data set to train a binary classification model.

Next, we select a picture of a horse and a picture of a deer as our examples to create subplots, like so:

```
[9]: # Select one example of horse and one example of deer
     horse=X[1]
     deer=X[7]
     # Look at three channels separately
     horse_channel1=horse[:,:,0]
     horse_channel2=horse[:,:,1]
     horse_channel3=horse[:,:,2]
     deer_channel1=deer[:,:,0]
     deer_channel2=deer[:,:,1]
     deer_channel3=deer[:,:,2]
     # Plot them channel by channel
     horses=[horse,horse_channel1,horse_channel2,horse_channel3]
     deers=[deer,deer_channel1,deer_channel2,deer_channel3]
     horse_labels = ["horse in color", "first channel only",
                     "second channel only", "third channel only"]
     deer_labels = ["deer in color", "first channel only",
                    "second channel only", "third channel only"]
```

```
plt.figure(figsize=(12,6),dpi=300)
for i in range(4):
    plt.subplot(2,4,i+1)
    plt.imshow(horses[i])
    plt.title(horse_labels[i], fontsize=12)
    plt.axis('off')
    plt.subplot(2,4,i+5)
    plt.imshow(deers[i])
    plt.title(deer_labels[i-4], fontsize=12)
    plt.axis('off')
plt.subplots_adjust(hspace=0.20)
plt.show()
plt.savefig("files/ch07/channels.png")
```

The subplots have two rows and four columns of pictures. The first row are four pictures of a horse. The first one has all three color channels so it looks colorful. The last three are the same picture but with only one color channel. The second row are four pictures of a deer. The first one has all three color channels while the other three have one color channel each. As you can see, not much information is lost with just one channel and you can easily identify them as a horse and a deer. Therefore, we'll use only the first channel to reduce the data size and training time. However, in later chapters of this book, you'll use all three channels to train the model so as to have a more accurate prediction.

Run the above cell and the image *channels.png* will be saved in the folder /Desktop/mla/ch07/files/ on your computer.

7.3.2   Train the Logit Model

Next, we use the logistic regression in *scikit-learn* to train the model. To avoid overfitting, it's customary to split the data into train and test subsets. We then train the model using the train set and make the out-of-sample predictions on the test set.

The Python code below splits the data (X, y) we generated in the last section into the train set (x_train, y_train) and testing samples (x_test, y_test). We then use the first color channel of the images in x_train and x_test and reshape them to a size of $(-1, 1024)$, meaning the NumPy arrays can have any number of rows and 1024 columns. The processed images are then saved as X_train and X_test and they are ready to be fed into our neural network.

```
[10]:  from sklearn.model_selection import train_test_split

       # Split data into train and test
       x_train,x_test,y_train,y_test=train_test_split(X,y,
           test_size=0.2,random_state=0)
       # Use only the first channel to reduce data size
```

```
X_train=x_train[:,:,:,0].reshape(-1,32*32)
X_test=x_test[:,:,:,0].reshape(-1,32*32)
print("X_train shape is", X_train.shape)
print("X_test shape is", X_test.shape)
print("y_train shape is", y_train.shape)
print("y_test shape is", y_test.shape)
# Save the data for later use
pickle.dump((X_train,X_test,y_train,y_test),
            open('files/ch07/train_test.p','wb'))
```

```
X_train shape is (160, 1024)
X_test shape is (41, 1024)
y_train shape is (160,)
y_test shape is (41,)
```

We use the *train_test_split()* method in *scikit-learn* to split the original sample into train and test subsets. The argument *test_size=0.2* means 80% of the original sample goes to the train set and the remaining 20% to the test set. We use the *random_state=0* argument to fix the random generator seed at 0 to make the results reproducible. Without the argument, the sample will be split differently each time you run the program. We save the data as *train_test.p* in the folder /files/ch07/ so that we can use the same data for training and testing in later chapters.

The output above shows that there are 160 images in the train set and 41 in the test set. Since we use only one color channel, each image has 32*32=1024 features and we use them to predict whether the image is a horse or a deer.

Next, we train the logistic regression model by using the train subset we just created, like so:

[11]:
```
# Logit regression;
# Set max_iter to 5000 so that the model converges
from sklearn.linear_model import LogisticRegression
logit=LogisticRegression(max_iter=5000)
logit.fit(X_train,y_train)
```

Make sure that you put the *max_iter=5000* argument when you call the *Logistic-Regression()* class. This ensures that the model parameters converge.

The Logit model is now trained. Next, we make predictions in the out-of-sample test dataset.

7.3.3   Predict Using the Logit Model

Next, we use the trained logistic regression model to make out-of-sample predictions. We also evaluate the performance of the model.

```
[12]: from sklearn.metrics import confusion_matrix
      from sklearn.metrics import accuracy_score

      # Make predictions
      pred_test = logit.predict(X_test)
      # Print out the confusion matrix
      ma5=confusion_matrix(y_test,pred_test)
      print("the confusion matrix is\n", ma5)
      # Print out the accuracy score
      accuracy=accuracy_score(y_test,pred_test)
      print(f"the accuracy of the prediction is {accuracy}")
```

```
the confusion matrix is
 [[13 11]
 [ 7 10]]
the accuracy of the prediction is 0.5609756097560976
```

The *predict()* method generates a label of either 1 or 0 based on the predicted probability, using 0.5 as the cutoff. The labels are 1 for horses and 0 for deer.

We use the accuracy score and the confusion matrix to evaluate the performance of the predictions. The output above shows the confusion matrix by comparing the predictions with the actual labels. The four values in the confusion matrix indicate that there are 13 cases of true negatives (TNs, the image is a deer and the prediction is a deer), 10 cases of true positives (TPs, the image is a horse and the prediction is a horse), 11 cases of false positives (FPs, the image is a deer and the prediction is a horse), and 7 cases of false negatives (FNs, the image is a horse and the prediction is a deer).

The accuracy is the total number of correct predictions (TPs + TNs) divided by the total number of images (TPs + TNs + FPs + FNs). The trained Logit model has an accuracy of around 56.10%.

Confusion Matrix and the Accuracy Score

Both the confusion matrix and the accuracy score are measures of the performance of a classification model.

The confusion matrix in a binary classification is defined as

$$Confusion\ Matrix = \begin{bmatrix} TNs & FPs \\ FNs & TPs \end{bmatrix},$$

where True negatives (TNs) are cases when the label is 0 and the prediction is also 0; True positives (TPs) are cases when the label is 1 and the prediction is also 1; False negatives (FNs) are cases when the label is 1 and the prediction is 0; False positives (FPs) are cases when the label is 0 and the prediction is 1.

The accuracy score is defined as

$$Accuracy = \frac{TPs + TNs}{TPs + TNs + FPs + FNs}$$

The numbers in the numerator are correct predictions (TPs+TNs), while the denominator is the total number of cases.

An accuracy score of 56% is not very high. Since there are only two classes, if one were to randomly predict, the accuracy score should be around 50%.

There are at least three reasons for the low accuracy here:

- The sample size is small: we use only 160 pictures to train the model. Therefore, the amount of information for the model to learn from is limited.
- The model is not sophisticated enough. We assume a simple linear relation between the image pixels and the output (before squashing the output into the range of 0 and 1).
- We use only one channel of the image, and some information is lost in the process.

We'll address all three weaknesses in later chapters. The purpose of this chapter is to introduce you to the basics of binary classifications.

7.4 BINARY CLASSIFICATION WITH A SIMPLE NEURAL NETWORK

Next, we'll use a neural network with no hidden layers to make predictions on the same dataset. Theoretically, it works the same as a Logit regression.

After that, we'll create a diagram of the neural network, with weights and biases, as well as the predicted probabilities on a picture of a horse, and on a picture of a deer, separately.

Finally, we'll record the model weights during the training process, and demonstrate how the predictions change as the training progresses.

7.4.1 Train and Test Using a Neural Network

The script below builds a simple neural network using the TensorFlow library and trains the model using the train subset we just generated.

```
13]: import tensorflow as tf

tf.random.set_seed(0)
model = tf.keras.Sequential()
model.add(tf.keras.layers.Dense(1,
    activation='sigmoid',input_shape=(32*32,)))
model.compile(optimizer="adam",loss="binary_crossentropy")
model.fit(X_train,y_train,verbose=0,epochs=125)
```

Here we fix the random seed generator in TensorFlow to state 0 so that the results are reproducible. We use the sequential model in Keras to create the simple neural network. We use the Aadm optimizer and train the model for 125 epochs using the train set (X_train, y_train).

Run the above cell and wait till the training is finished. Next, we make predictions based on the trained neural network.

```
14]: pred_model=model.predict(X_test)
    # Convert values between 0 and 1 to Y or N
    pred_yn=np.where(pred_model>0.5,1,0)
    ma5=confusion_matrix(y_test,pred_yn)
    print("the confusion matrix is\n", ma5)
    # Print out the accuracy score
    accuracy=accuracy_score(y_test,pred_yn)
    print(f"the accuracy of the prediction is {accuracy}")
```

```
the confusion matrix is
 [[11 13]
 [ 4 13]]
the accuracy of the prediction is 0.5853658536585366
```

We use the *predict()* method to make predictions on the test set (X_test). Note that the prediction from the model is a continuous number between 0 and 1. We need to convert the prediction to a 1 or 0 based on a cutoff value of 0.5 since there are roughly the same number of horses and deer in our sample. The output above shows the confusion matrix and the accuracy score from the predictions of the trained neural network.

The accuracy score is now 58.54%, better than that from the Logit regression. The confusion matrix looks different. The neural network makes 13 TP predictions and 11

TN predictions. You may wonder, why the differences in predictions between the Logit regression and the neural network? There are at least two main reasons. The first is that each model initializes parameters differently so the models may converge to different values. Second, and more importantly, different variants of gradient descent algorithms are used as optimizers in the Logit regression and in the neural network above. The Logit regression in scikit-learn uses the L-BFGS optimizer, while the neural network above uses the Adam optimizer.

7.4.2   Focus on Two Examples

Next, we'll focus on a horse and a deer in the test set and see how the predicted probabilities on them change over the course of training.

```
[15]:   # A picture of a horse
        plt.imshow(x_test[9])
        plt.show()
        # A picture of a deer
        plt.imshow(x_test[2])
        plt.show()
        # Save the two examples for later use
        pickle.dump((x_test[9], x_test[2]),
                    open('files/ch07/horsedeer.p','wb'))
```

The 10th picture in the test set is a horse, and the 3rd one is a deer. If you run the above cell, you should see two pictures, one with a horse in it and the other a deer.

7.4.3   Diagrams of the Network and Predictions

We now look under the hood and dive into the neural network and see how the prediction model works. Specifically, we'll keep all the data in the intermediate steps of the training process. We obtain the weights of the model and the predicted probabilities on the above two pictures before training. We then again obtain the information after 5 epochs, 10 epochs, ... and 125 epochs.

```
[16]:   # create lists for weights and epochs
        ws=[]
        bs=[]
        epochs=[]
        p_horse=[]
        p_deer=[]
        # record weights before training
        tf.random.set_seed(0)
        model = tf.keras.Sequential()
        model.add(tf.keras.layers.Dense(1,
            activation='sigmoid',input_shape=(32*32,)))
```

```
model.compile(optimizer="adam",loss="binary_crossentropy")
w0, bias0 = model.layers[-1].get_weights()
bs.append(bias0[0])
ws.append(w0.reshape(1024,))
epochs.append(0)
# record predictions before training
pred_horse=model.predict(X_test[9].reshape(-1,1024))
pred_deer=model.predict(X_test[2].reshape(-1,1024))
p_horse.append(pred_horse[0,0])
p_deer.append(pred_deer[0,0])
```

The Python code in the above cell first generates two lists *ws* and *bs* to store the weights and bias terms during the training process. Similarly, the list *epochs* is used to store the epoch number. The lists *p_horse* and *p_deer* will store the predicted probabilities on the example horse and deer images.

We then re-create the neural network and retrieve the weights and probabilities before training begins. We use *model.layers[-1].get_weights()* to retrieve the weights in the last layer of the neural network.

Next, we train the model for five epochs at a time, and record information at each stage.

```
[17]:   # Train 5 epochs at a time
        for i in range(1,26,1):
            model.fit(X_train,y_train,verbose=0,epochs=5)
            # record weights after training
            w,bias=model.layers[-1].get_weights()
            bs.append(bias[0])
            ws.append(w.reshape(1024,))
            epochs.append(i*5)
            # record predictions after training
            pred_horse=model.predict(X_test[9].reshape(-1,1024))
            pred_deer=model.predict(X_test[2].reshape(-1,1024))
            p_horse.append(pred_horse[0,0])
            p_deer.append(pred_deer[0,0])
```

After every five epochs of training, we retrieve five pieces of information: the weights, the bias term, the epoch number, and the predicted probabilities on the example horse and deer images. We store these five pieces of information in the following five lists: *ws, bs, epochs, p_horse,* and *p_deer.*

Next, we'll generate 26 pictures of the intermediate stages of training. In each picture, we'll draw the neural network, the weights and the bias term at that stage, the epoch number, and the predictions.

The code to generate the 26 pictures is too long. To save space, we define a function in the local *utils* package and call the function below to generate the pictures.

Specifically, we define a *horse_pic()* function in the file *ch07util.py* inside the *utils* local package. Go to the book's GitHub repository, download the file *ch07util.py* under /utils/ and save it in the folder /Desktop/mla/utils/ on your computer. As we discussed in Chapter 1, you should save an empty file ___*ini*___.*py* inside the folder /utils/ so that Python knows that *utils* is a local Python package.

If you open the file *ch07util.py*, you'll see how the function *horse_pic()* is defined in the file. The function draws 26 pictures at different stages of training and saves a picture on your computer at each stage.

Run the following lines of code in the cell below:

[18]:
```
from utils.ch07util import horse_pic

# Call the horse_pic() function
horse_pic(p_horse,ws,bs,epochs,x_test[9])
```

We first import the *horse_pic()* function from the local *ch07util* module inside the local *utils* package that we defined earlier. We then call the *horse_pic()* function to generate the 26 pictures. The *horse_pic()* function takes five arguments: the first four are from the five lists we generated above, and the last argument is the example horse image *x_test[9]*.

After running the above cell, if you go to the folder /files/ch07/ on your computer, you'll see the 26 pictures generated by the program above. For example, if you open the picture *p_horse0.png*, you'll see the weights of the model, plus the model's prediction on the horse picture, before training starts. The picture shows that before training, the model assigns a 34.74% chance that it's a horse. In contrast, if you look at the *p_horse25.png*, you'll see the weights of the model, plus the model's prediction on the horse picture after 25 rounds (i.e., 125 epochs) of training. The probability has increased to 88%, a fairly accurate prediction.

7.4.4   Animate the Training Process

Better yet, you can create an animation of the training process and see how the weights and predicted probabilities change over the course of training.

The Python code below combines the 26 png files into a gif file using the *imageio* library.

[19]:
```
import imageio, PIL

frames=[]
for i in range(26):
    frame=PIL.Image.open(f"files/ch07/p_horse{i}.png")
    frame=np.asarray(frame)
    frames.append(np.array(frame))
imageio.mimsave('files/ch07/p_horse.gif', frames, fps=3)
```

Run the above cell, and you'll see an animation *p_horse.gif* saved in the folder /Desktop/mla/files/ch07/ on your computer. The animation is also available under /files/ch07/ in the book's GitHub repository.

7.4.5 Animate the Predictions for the Deer

We can also animate how the predicted probability for the deer image changes over the course of training.

First, we define a function *deer_pic()* and call it to generate 26 pictures. If you open the file *ch07util.py* inside the *utils* local package, you'll see the definition of the function. The function draws 26 pictures at different stages of training and saves a picture on your computer at each stage. The pictures focus on the predicted probabilities for the deer image instead of the horse image.

Run the following lines of code in the cell below:

```
[20]: from utils.ch07util import deer_pic

deer_pic(p_deer,ws,bs,epochs,x_test[2])
```

We first import the *deer_pic()* function from the local *ch07util* module inside the local *utils* package that we defined earlier. We then call the *deer_pic()* function to generate the 26 pictures. The last argument in the *deer_pic()* function is the example deer image we have selected, *x_test[2]*.

After running the above cell, if you go to the folder /files/ch07/ on your computer, you'll see the 26 pictures generated by the cell above. For example, if you open the picture *p_deer0.png*, you'll see that before training, the model assigns a 39.76% chance that the picture is a horse. This is equivalent to predicting that the picture is a deer with a 60.24% probability. In contrast, if you look at the picture *p_deer25.png*, you'll see that the model now places a 94.08% probability that the picture is a deer, a very accurate prediction!

Next, we can create an animation to show the whole process

```
[21]: frames=[]
for i in range(26):
    frame=PIL.Image.open(f"files/ch07/p_deer{i}.png")
    frame=np.asarray(frame)
    frames.append(np.array(frame))
imageio.mimsave('files/ch07/p_deer.gif',frames,fps=3)
```

The cell above combines the 26 png files into a gif file using the *imageio* library. Run the above cell, and you'll see an animation *p_deer.gif* in the folder /Desktop/mla/files/ch07/ on your computer. The animation is also available under /files/ch07/ in the book's GitHub repository.

7.5   COMBINE THE ANIMATIONS

Now we can combine the animations for the horse and for the deer, and put them side by side for comparison. We'll also use subplots to compare the two predictions.

7.5.1   Animate the Two Predictions

To combine two animations into one, we use the *concatenate()* method in NumPy. The argument *axis=1* in the method places the two frames side by side horizontally at each stage of training, like so:

```
[22]:   frames=[]
        for i in range(26):
            frame1=PIL.Image.open(f"files/ch07/p_horse{i}.png")
            frame1=np.asarray(frame1)
            frame2=PIL.Image.open(f"files/ch07/p_deer{i}.png")
            frame2=np.asarray(frame2)
            frame=np.concatenate([frame1, frame2], axis=1)
            frames.append(np.array(frame))
        imageio.mimsave('files/ch07/p_horse_deer.gif',frames,fps=3)
```

We start a *for* loop to iterate through different stages of training. In each of the 26 iterations, we first open a picture of the prediction for the horse image that we generated earlier and convert it into NumPy arrays. We then open a picture of the prediction for the deer image and use the *concatenate()* method in NumPy to combine the two pictures horizontally. The combined frames are stored in a list *frames*. We then use the *imageio* library to convert the combined frames into an animation.

If you run the above cell, you'll see an animation *p_horse_deer.gif* in the folder /Desktop/mla/files/ch07/ on your computer. The animation is also available in the book's GitHub repository under /files/ch07/.

7.5.2   Subplots

While it's easy to view animations on electronic devices, it's difficult to view them in a hard copy of a book. Instead, we'll create a graph with multiple subplots to illustrate different stages of training. Specifically, you'll create a figure with eight subplots that form a four by two grid. The two columns are for horse and deer image predictions, respectively. The four rows represent four different stages of training.

```
23]: rows=[0,8,16,25]
     cols=["horse","deer"]
     plt.figure(dpi=300,figsize=(28,40))
     for i in range(4):
         for j in range(2):
             plt.subplot(4,2,2*i+j+1)
             img=f"files/ch07/p_{cols[j]}{rows[i]}.png"
             nparray=PIL.Image.open(img)
             plt.imshow(nparray)
             plt.axis("off")
     plt.subplots_adjust(hspace=-0.06,wspace=-0.2)
     plt.savefig('files/ch07/horsedeer.png')
     plt.show()
```

The Python code in the above cell first creates a list *rows* to store the four stages of training that we want to highlight. The list *cols* contains the two prefixes that we'll use to retrieve the saved images: *horse* and *deer*. We then iterate through the four rows and two columns to draw the eight subplots one by one. We use the method *subplots_adjust()* to adjust the horizontal and vertical spaces between subplots.

Run the above cell and go to the folder /Desktop/mla/files/ch07/ on your computer, you'll see the subplots *horsedeer.png*, as shown in Figure 7.2.

7.6   BINARY CLASSIFICATION WITH A DEEP NEURAL NETWORK

Next, we'll add two hidden layers to the neural network with ReLU activations. We'll use the same train set to train the new network.

The Python code in the cell below creates the new neural network, trains the model, and prints out the model summary.

```
[24]: tf.random.set_seed(0)
      model=tf.keras.Sequential()
      model.add(tf.keras.layers.Dense(1024,activation='relu',
                               input_shape=(32*32,)))
      model.add(tf.keras.layers.Dense(32,activation='relu'))
      model.add(tf.keras.layers.Dense(1,activation='sigmoid'))
      model.compile(optimizer="adam",loss="binary_crossentropy")
      model.fit(X_train,y_train,verbose=0,epochs=125)
      print(model.summary())
```

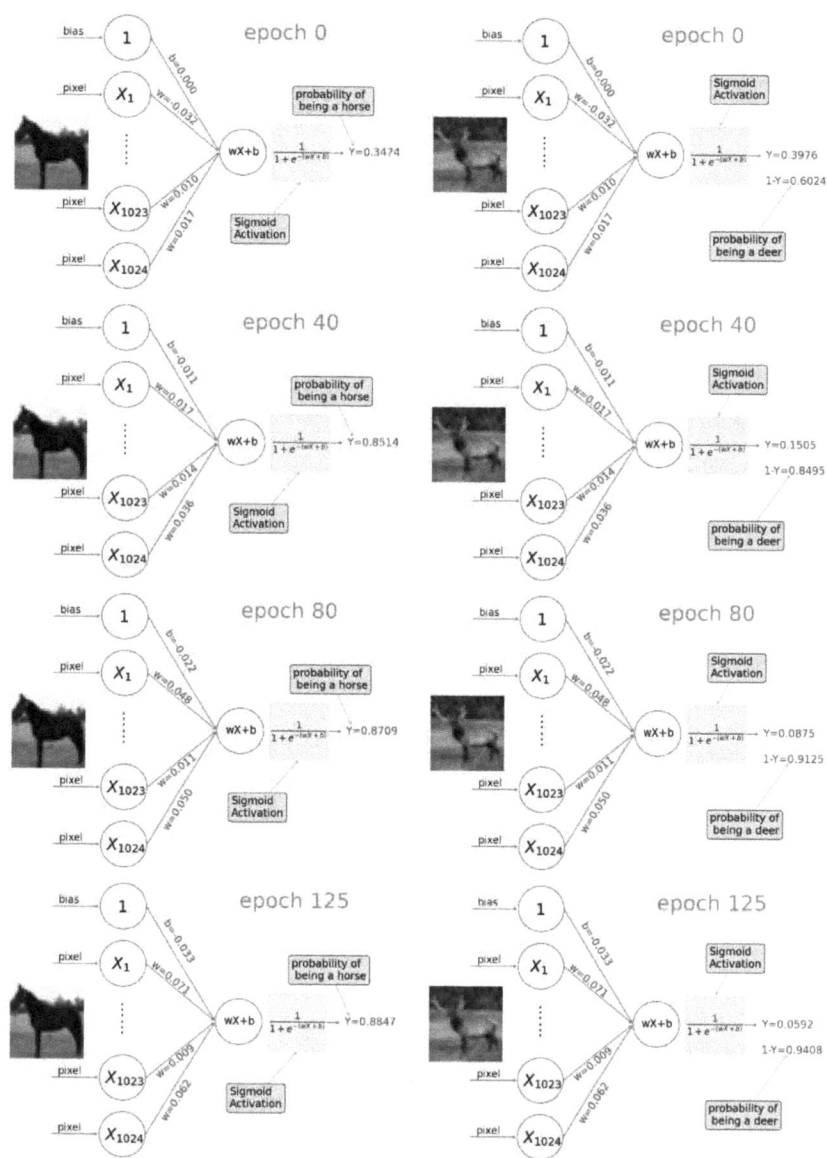

Figure 7.2 How the predictions change during training process

```
Model: "sequential_3"
```

Layer (type)	Output Shape	Param #
dense_3 (Dense)	(None, 1024)	1049600
dense_4 (Dense)	(None, 32)	32800
dense_5 (Dense)	(None, 1)	33

```
Total params: 1,082,433
Trainable params: 1,082,433
Non-trainable params: 0
```

None

The output above shows that the new neural network has three dense layers in it, with 1024, 42, and 1 neurons in them, respectively. Since the input shape is 32*32=1024 and the first layer has 1024 neurons in it, there are a total of 1024*(1024+1)=1049600 parameters in the first layer (the +1 part represents the bias term in the first layer). The second layer has (1024+1)*32=32800 parameters. The third layer has 32+1=33 parameters. The model has a total of 1082433 trainable parameters.

We'll make predictions using the new model on the test set X_test, like so:

```
25]: pred_model=model.predict(X_test)
     # Convert values between 0 and 1 to Y or N
     pred_yn=np.where(pred_model>0.5,1,0)
     ma5=confusion_matrix(y_test,pred_yn)
     print("the confusion matrix is\n", ma5)
     accuracy=accuracy_score(y_test,pred_yn)
     print(f"the accuracy of the prediction is {accuracy}")
```

```
the confusion matrix is
 [[15  9]
 [ 7 10]]
the accuracy of the prediction is 0.6097560975609756
```

The above results show that the new model has an accuracy of 60.98%, a small increase from the 58.54% accuracy we had earlier when we don't use hidden layers. The results show that using more hidden layers to generate non-linear relations between inputs and outputs helps the prediction in this case.

7.7 APPENDIX: LOAD CIFAR10 FROM TENSORFLOW DIRECTLY

You can also choose to load up the CIFAR10 dataset directly from TensorFlow. Here is how.

```
[26]: (x_train, y_train), (x_test, y_test) = \
            tf.keras.datasets.cifar10.load_data()
assert x_train.shape == (50000, 32, 32, 3)
assert x_test.shape == (10000, 32, 32, 3)
assert y_train.shape == (50000, 1)
assert y_test.shape == (10000, 1)
```

The dataset has four parts. We use the *assert* command above to make sure that the train subset has 60000 images in it and the test subset has 10000 images in it.

Next, we look at the first two images, like so:

```
[27]: # Look at the first two pictures
pic1=x_train[0]
pic2=x_train[1]
plt.imshow(pic1)
plt.show()
plt.imshow(pic2)
plt.show()
```

The output shows that the first picture is a frog and the second a truck.

7.8 GLOSSARY

- **Accuracy Score:** In binary classification, the accuracy score is the percentage of correct predictions among all cases.
- **Binary Classification:** Binary classification is the machine learning algorithm with the task of classifying samples into one of the two categories.
- **Binary Cross Entropy:** A loss function used to measure average difference between the predicted probabilities of an outcome and the actual labels (1 or 0). It's the preferred loss function in binary classifications.
- **Binary Variable:** A variable with two possible values, such as 1 or 0, or Yes or No.
- **Confusion Matrix:** In binary classification, the confusion matrix is a two by two matrix with the numbers of true negatives, true positives, false positives, and false negatives in the four positions, respectively.
- **False Negatives:** False negatives (FNs) are cases when the label is 1 and the prediction is 0.
- **False Positives:** False positives (FPs) are cases when the label is 0 and the prediction is 1.

- **Logistic Regression:** A binary classification method that uses regression analysis. It assumes a linear relation between features X and the label y before activation. It then uses the logistic function to transform the value to a probability, as follows:
$$y = \frac{1}{1 + e^{-(wX+b)}}.$$
- **The RGB Color Model:** The color model with three color channels: red, green, and blue. The value in each channel ranges from 0 to 255.
- **True Negatives:** True negatives (TNs) are cases when the label is 0 and the prediction is also 0.
- **True Positives:** True positives (TPs) are cases when the label is 1 and the prediction is also 1.

7.9 EXERCISES

7.1 What is binary classification? Give two examples.

7.2 What is the binary cross entropy loss function? What's the formula to calculate it?

7.3 Modify the code in the second cell in Section 7.2.2 to print out the NumPy array that represents the tenth picture in the dataset X. Also use *matplotlib* to show the picture in a graph.

7.4 Modify the code cell in Section 7.2.3 to show the 26th to the 50th picture in the dataset X.

7.5 Explain what the confusion matrix is in binary classification.

7.6 What are true negatives, true positives, false negatives, and false positives?

7.7 Explain what the accuracy score is in binary classification.

7.8 Add a third hidden layer with 16 neurons to the deep neural network just before the output layer in Section 7.6. Rerun the code cells in the section and see if there is any improvement in predictions.

## CHAPTER 8

Convolutional Neural Networks

> The pooling operation used in convolutional neural networks is a big mistake, and the fact that it works so well is a disaster.
>
> *–Geoffrey Hinton*

THE USE OF Convolutional Neural Networks (CNNs) has greatly improved the power of deep neural networks (DNNs). CNNs have put deep learning at the cutting edge of artificial intelligence. Because of CNNs, deep learning is now the most promising field in machine learning.

CNNs use a different type of layers than dense layers. A convolutional layer treats an image as a two-dimensional object and finds patterns on the image. It then associates these patterns with the image labels. This significantly improves the predictive power of the model. Even though CNNs are mainly used for image classification and computer vision, they are also widely used in other tasks such as speech recognition, video classification, and other data analysis problems.

In this chapter, you'll learn the basic concepts related to a convolutional layer such as the number of filters, kernel size, zero-padding, strides. . . Better yet, you'll learn to create animations to show step by step how to apply a three by three filter on a three by three image with zero-padding and a stride of one. Similarly, you'll also apply a two by two filter on a six by six image without zero-padding and with a stride of two. Along the way, you'll have a deep understanding of how CNNs work and learn to use them for pattern recognition and feature extraction. Later in this book, you'll use these skills to design intelligent game strategies by treating game boards as a two-dimensional image and extra spatial features from them.

DOI: 10.1201/b23383-8

New Skills in This Chapter

- Applying filters on images and performing convolution operations
- Understanding kernel size, zero-padding, and strides
- Creating and training neural networks with convoluational layers
- Getting to know the max pooling layer
- Applying convolutional and max pooling layers in image classifications

---

Before you start, open the Jupyter Notebook app in the virtual environment MLA on your computer. After that, open a blank Jupyter notebook and save it as *ch08.ipynb* in the directory /Desktop/mla/ on your computer. Next, we'll create a subdirectory /files/ch08/ to store files in this chapter. Start a new cell in *ch08.ipynb* and execute the following lines of code in it:

[1]:
```
import os

os.makedirs("files/ch08", exist_ok=True)
```

8.1 WHAT ARE CONVOLUTIONAL NEURAL NETWORKS (CNNS)?

Convolutional layers use filters (also called kernels) to find patterns on the input data. A convolutional layer can automatically detect a large number of patterns and associate certain patterns with the target label. This is useful in both image classifications and game strategy developments in this book.

For simplicity, we'll use game boards as examples to explain how convolutional layers work. Game boards have relatively fewer pixels compared to images. Therefore, it's easier for us to apply filters on them and perform convoluation operations. In particular, we'll use the Tic Tac Toe game board, something everyone knows, as our example in this chapter. We can focus on certain patterns on a game board that we know are associated with game outcomes (vertical, horizontal, or diagonal lines in Tic Tac Toe and Connect Four games, for example). Later in this book, we'll design intelligent game strategies for Tic Tac Toe and Connect Four by using CNNs to extract spatial features on game boards. You'll also use CNNs to detect patterns on the screenshots of Atari games such as Breakout and Space Invaders and design deep Q-learning game strategies.

8.1.1 Our Running Example

Let's say that the input data is a Tic Tac Toe game board. For simplicity, let's assume the board has three Xs in the top row while the other six squares are all empty. Of course, in a real Tic Tac Toe game, Player O takes turns too so you won't see such a board in a real game. But let's simplify things to make the calculations simple.

We need to encode the game board into numbers so that the Python program can process it. We use 1 to denote a square on the board with an X in it, −1 a square with an O in it, and 0 an empty square.

Run the code in the cell below.

```
[2]: import numpy as np

     inputs = np.array([[1,1,1],
                        [0,0,0],
                        [0,0,0]]).reshape(-1,3,3,1)
```

We represent the board with a three by three matrix: the first row has three ones in it since they are occupied by Xs. The remaining positions are all zeros since they are all empty.

We use *reshape(-1,3,3,1)* to reshape the matrix to a four dimensional array: the first dimension represents how many images we have; the second and third dimensions are the width and height of the image. The last dimension is the color channel. For a color picture, there are three channels (RGB, i.e., red, green, and blue), but here we put the number of channels as one for simplicity.

8.1.2 A Horizontal Filter

Below, we'll create a horizontal filter with a size of three by three. The middle row has values one, while the other two rows have zeros in them. Run the Python code in the cell below to create a horizontal filter:

```
[3]: # Create a horizontal filter
     h_filter = np.array([[0,0,0],
                          [1,1,1],
                          [0,0,0]]).reshape(3,3,1,1)
```

A horizontal filter highlights the horizontal features in the image and blurs the rest. We'll apply the three by three horizontal filter on the Tic Tac Toe game board as follows by using the *conv2d()* function from TensorFlow:

```
[4]: import tensorflow as tf

     # Apply the filter on the game board
     outputs=tf.nn.conv2d(inputs,h_filter,strides=1,padding="SAME")
     # Convert output to numpy array and print it output
     print(outputs.numpy().reshape(3,3))
```

```
[[2 3 2]
 [0 0 0]
 [0 0 0]]
```

In the output, the values are large in the first row. The values are all 0 in the other two rows. So the horizontal filter has correctly detected the horizontal pattern in the first row of the game board.

But how exactly does the conv2d layer generate the output through the filter? We'll explain in detail below.

The game board is a three by three matrix. The padding="SAME" argument in the *conv2d()* function adds 0s around the input image so the padded image now is a five by five matrix. To draw the padded image in *matplotlib*, we'll first define a few helper functions.

The first helper function, *sqr()*, draws squares at a given location in a figure that's generated by *matplotlib*. The definition is as follows:

```
[5]:   # Define sqr() function to draw a square
       def sqr(ax,x,y,size=1,linestyle="-",color="gray",linewidth=1):
           ax.plot([x,x+size],[y,y],linestyle=linestyle,
               color=color,linewidth=linewidth)
           ax.plot([x,x],[y+size,y],linestyle=linestyle,
               color=color,linewidth=linewidth)
           ax.plot([x+size,x+size],[y,y+size],linestyle=linestyle,
               color=color,linewidth=linewidth)
           ax.plot([x,x+size],[y+size,y+size],linestyle=linestyle,
               color=color,linewidth=linewidth)
```

The *sqr()* function takes seven arguments. The first argument, ax, is the subplot in which to place the square. The second and third arguments are the x- and y-coordinates of the bottom left corner of the square. The size argument is the side length of the square, with a default value of 1. The last three arguments are line style, color, and line width of the square, with default values of a dash, gray, and one, respectively.

The next helper function, *padded_board()*, draws the five by five padded board. The definition of the function is as follows:

```
[6]:   # A function to draw the padded board
       def padded_board(ax):
           # Draw solid squares
           for i in range(3):
               for j in range(3):
                   sqr(ax,-5+i,j,color="k",linewidth=2)
           # Draw dotted gray squares
           for i in range(5):
               for j in range(5):
                   sqr(ax,-6+i,-1+j,linestyle="dotted")
           # Put values inside squares
           for x in range(5):
```

```
        for y in range(5):
            if 1<=x<=3 and y==3:
                ax.text(x-5.6,y-0.6,r"1",size=16,color="gray")
            else:
                ax.text(x-5.6,y-0.6,r"0",size=16,color="gray")
```

The *padded_board()* function uses the *sqr()* function we just defined. It first draws a three by three grid with solid black lines. It then draws a five by five dotted gray grid on top of the original board. Finally, it places numbers 1 or 0 inside each of the 25 squares.

With the two helper functions defined, we can now draw the padded board as follows:

[7]:
```
import matplotlib.pyplot as plt

fig = plt.figure(figsize=(7,5),dpi=200)
ax = fig.add_subplot(111)
# Draw the padded board
padded_board(ax)
ax.set_xlim(-6, -1)
ax.set_ylim(-1, 4)
# Keep the scale of x and y axis the same
plt.axis('equal')
plt.axis('off')
```

If you run the above cell, you'll see a five by five table, with the edge squares all in gray. The inside three by three squares have solid lines. The outside squares of the padded image all have zeros in them, hence the name zero-padding.

Terminology in Convolutional Layers

Filters are also called kernels, and they come in different sizes. We'll use filters of sizes 3 by 3 and 2 by 2 in this chapter. Zero-padding means we put 0s around the edges of the image. Stride in CNN indicates how many pixels we move the filter in each step when we scan the filter over an image. A stride of 1 means the filter shifts one pixel to the right or down at a time on the image. You'll see examples of stride=1 and stride=2 in this chapter.

With zero-padding, the 3 by 3 image now becomes a 5 by 5 image. We then apply the 3 by 3 filter on the image. With a stride of 1, the filter will scan cover the image 9 times. We can create an animation to show how it works.

The Python code in the cell below first defines a *scan()* function to generate an image in once location. We then call the function nine times to cover nine different areas on the padded image, like so:

```
[8]: from matplotlib.patches import Rectangle

     def scan(h,v):
         fig=plt.figure(figsize=(7,5),dpi=200)
         ax=fig.add_subplot(111)
         ax.set_xlim(-6,-1)
         ax.set_ylim(-1,4)
         plt.axis('equal')
         plt.axis('off')
         padded_board(ax)
         # Draw the red scanner
         for i in range(3):
             for j in range(3):
                 sqr(ax,-6+i+h,1+j-v,color="r",linewidth=3)
         # Save the picture
         plt.savefig(f"files/ch08/scan{h}{v}.png")
         plt.close(fig)
     # Scan different areas
     for v in range(3):
         for h in range(3):
             scan(h,v)
```

The *scan()* function first draws the padded board. It then focuses on one particular area, (h,v), on the padded board, where h is the number of times the filter moved to the right and v the number of times the filter moved down. For example, (h=0,v=0) is the top left corner, while (h=2,v=2) the bottom right corner. The function then applies the filter on the area by drawing a red 3 by 3 table over the area.

Once the function *scan()* is defined, we iterate different values of h and v and call the function nine times to cover all nine areas on the padded board. If you run the code in the above cell, nine pictures *scan00.png, scan01.png, ..., scan22.png* will be saved in the folder /Desktop/mla/files/ch08/ on your computer.

Next, we'll combine the nine pictures into an animation as follows:

```
[9]: import PIL
     import imageio

     frames=[]
     for v in range(3):
         for h in range(3):
             frame=PIL.Image.open(f"files/ch08/scan{h}{v}.png")
             frame=np.asarray(frame)
             frames.append(frame)
     imageio.mimsave('files/ch08/filter.gif', frames, fps=1)
```

If you open the file *filter.gif* in your local folder, you'll see an animation of the red 3 by 3 filter scanning on different areas of the padded board.

8.2 CONVOLUTION OPERATIONS

Exactly what is a convolutional operation? What is the output when we apply a filter on an image? We'll answer these questions in this section.

8.2.1 Calculations in a Convolution Operation

In the running example above, we use a 3 by 3 horizontal filter, which has values

$$\begin{bmatrix} 0 & 0 & 0 \\ 1 & 1 & 1 \\ 0 & 0 & 0 \end{bmatrix}$$

We apply the filter on the game board, which has values

$$\begin{bmatrix} 1 & 1 & 1 \\ 0 & 0 & 0 \\ 0 & 0 & 0 \end{bmatrix}$$

Since we use zero-padding, the padded board is a five by five matrix with the following values:

$$\begin{bmatrix} 0 & 0 & 0 & 0 & 0 \\ 0 & 1 & 1 & 1 & 0 \\ 0 & 0 & 0 & 0 & 0 \\ 0 & 0 & 0 & 0 & 0 \\ 0 & 0 & 0 & 0 & 0 \end{bmatrix}$$

We end up with an output of

$$\begin{bmatrix} 2 & 3 & 2 \\ 0 & 0 & 0 \\ 0 & 0 & 0 \end{bmatrix}$$

When the filter scans the top left corner of the padded board, the covered area represents a 3 by 3 matrix with values

$$\begin{bmatrix} 0 & 0 & 0 \\ 0 & 1 & 1 \\ 0 & 0 & 0 \end{bmatrix}$$

The convolution operation finds the tensor dot of the two tensors (in this case, one tensor is the filter, and the other is the covered area). Specifically, the convolution operation performs element-wise multiplication in each of the nine cells, then adds up the values in the nine cells, like so:

$$tensor\_dot\left(\begin{bmatrix} 0 & 0 & 0 \\ 1 & 1 & 1 \\ 0 & 0 & 0 \end{bmatrix}, \begin{bmatrix} 0 & 0 & 0 \\ 0 & 1 & 1 \\ 0 & 0 & 0 \end{bmatrix}\right) = \begin{bmatrix} 0 \times 0+ & 0 \times 0+ & 0 \times 0+ \\ 0 \times 1+ & 1 \times 1+ & 1 \times 1+ \\ 0 \times 0+ & 0 \times 0+ & 0 \times 0 \end{bmatrix} = 2$$

To verify the above result, we can use the *tensordot()* function in *numpy* to calculate the output, like so:

[10]:
```python
# Create a horizontal filter
filter_array = np.array([[0,0,0],
                         [1,1,1],
                         [0,0,0]])
# Covered area
covered_area = np.array([[0,0,0],
                         [0,1,1],
                         [0,0,0]])
# Calculate the tensor dot
tensordot = np.tensordot(filter_array, covered_area)

print(f"the output at the top left corner is {tensordot}")
```

```
the output at the top left corner is 2
```

The result is also 2; this is why the value at the top left corner of the output matrix is 2.

Next, we use the same method to calculate the value in all nine cells of the output matrix. First, we generate a padded board

[11]:
```python
# Create a 5 by 5 matrix of zeros
padded_image=np.zeros((5,5))
# The board
image=np.array([[1,1,1],
                [0,0,0],
                [0,0,0]])
# Insert the board to the center of the padded board
padded_image[1:4,1:4]=image
print(f"the padded board has values \n{padded_image}")
```

```
the padded board has values
[[0. 0. 0. 0. 0.]
 [0. 1. 1. 1. 0.]
 [0. 0. 0. 0. 0.]
 [0. 0. 0. 0. 0.]
 [0. 0. 0. 0. 0.]]
```

We then move the filter over the padded board from left to right and from top to bottom to cover the nine areas. In each area, we conduct the convolution operation by calculating the tensordot value, like so:

```
12]: output=np.zeros((3,3))
     for row in range(3):
         for col in range(3):
             area=padded_image[row:row+3,col:col+3]
             output[row,col]=np.tensordot(filter_array,area)
     print(f"the output is\n {output}")
```

```
the output is
 [[2. 3. 2.]
 [0. 0. 0.]
 [0. 0. 0.]]
```

As you can see, the output matrix generated using NumPy is the same as the output matrix generated from the *conv2d()* function in TenforFlow.

Next, we'll create an animation on how the output matrix is generated step by step.

8.2.2 Animate the Convolution Operations

We'll create an animation of the convolution operations when the 3 by 3 horizontal filter is applied on the padded board.

First, we'll create several functions to draw different features on a figure to illustrate how the convolution operations work.

The first function *draw_text()*, draws text in the figure to state that we are applying a 3 by 3 filter on a 3 by 3 image with zero padding and a stride of 1. Run the Python code in the cell below so that the function can be called later when we create figures.

```
13]: # add text to explain
     txt='Apply a 3 by 3 filter on a 3 by 3 image\
     \nwith zero-padding\nstride=1'
     def draw_text(ax,txt):
         ax.annotate(txt,xy=(0,0),xytext=(0.02,0.1),
             textcoords='axes fraction',
             bbox=dict(boxstyle="round",fc="0.9"),
             fontsize=20)
```

The second function, *draw_output_matrix()*, creates a three by three table at the lower right corner of the figure. The values in the table are from the output matrix we generated above in the last subsection.

```
[14]: def draw_output_matrix(ax):
          # Draw the output matrix
          for i in range(3):
              for j in range(3):
                  sqr(ax,2+i,j-3,linewidth=2,color="k")
                  ax.text(2.4+i,-0.6-j,f"{output[j,i]}",\
                          size=16,color="gray")
```

The third function, *draw_filter()*, creates a three by three table at the top right corner of the figure. The values in the table are from the horizontal filter we used above.

```
[15]: def draw_filter(ax):
          # Draw filter on the side
          for i in range(3):
              for j in range(3):
                  sqr(ax,3+i,j+1,color="r",linewidth=3)
          ax.text(2,2.5,"filter=",size=16,color="r")
          # Put numbers in the filter
          for x in range(3):
              for y in range(3):
                  if y==1:
                      ax.text(x+3.4,y+1.3,"1",size=16,color="gray")
                  else:
                      ax.text(x+3.4, y+1.3,"0",size=16,color="gray")
```

The fourth function, *apply_filter(ax, h, v)*, applies the horizontal filter to an area on the padded board. It draws a 3 by 3 red table to represent the filter in a certain area on the board. The function *apply_filter(ax, h, v)* takes three arguments. The first argument, ax, is which axis of the figure to apply the filter. The second and third arguments, h and v, determine where on the padded board to apply the filter. For example, when h=0 and v=0, we apply the filter to the top left corner; when h=1 and v=1, we apply the filter to the middle center area.

```
[16]: def apply_filter(ax,h,v):
          # Apply filter
          for i in range(3):
              for j in range(3):
                  sqr(ax,-6+i+h,1+j-v,color="r",linewidth=3)
```

Next, we define the main function, *slide(h,v)*. The function slides over the padded board from left to right and from top to bottom to scan nine areas. In each area, it creates three pictures. In the first picture, with the suffix *step1*, it draws how the filter is applied to an area on the padded board. In the second picture, with the suffix *step2*, it draws two arrows pointing to the corresponding cell in the output matrix. In the third picture, with the suffix *step3*, it highlights the corresponding value in the output matrix.

The function *slide(h,v)* is defined as follows:

```
17]: def slide(h,v):
         fig = plt.figure(figsize=(12,8), dpi=200)
         ax = fig.add_subplot(111)
         ax.set_xlim(-6, 6)
         ax.set_ylim(-4, 4)
         plt.axis("off")
         # Draw the padded board
         padded_board(ax)
         # Put text in the figure
         draw_text(ax,txt)
         # Draw the output matrx table
         draw_output_matrix(ax)
         # Draw the filter on the top right
         draw_filter(ax)
         # Applies the filter on the board
         apply_filter(ax,h,v)
         # Save the first step in the position h,v
         plt.savefig(f"files/ch08/slide{h}{v}step1.png")
         # Draw two arrows
         ax.annotate('',xy=(2.3+h,-0.3-v),xytext=(-3+h,4-v),
             arrowprops=dict(arrowstyle ='->',color='g',linewidth=1))
         ax.annotate('',xy=(2.3+h,-0.3-v),xytext=(-6+h,1-v),
             arrowprops=dict(arrowstyle='->',color='g',linewidth=1))
         # Save the second step in the position h,v
         plt.savefig(f"files/ch08/slide{h}{v}step2.png")
         # Highlight the value in the output table
         ax.text(2.4+h,-0.6-v,f"{output[v,h]}",size=16,color="r")
         # Save the third step in the position h,v
         plt.savefig(f"files/ch08/slide{h}{v}step3.png")
         plt.close(fig)
```

Make sure you have run all the preceding Python cells so that the functions *sqr()*, *draw_text()*, *draw_output_matrix()*, *draw_filter()*, *apply_filter()*, and *slide()* are all defined.

Next, we'll call the *slide(h,v)* function with different values of h, v to cover nine areas on the padded board to generated 27 pictures, like so:

```
[18]: for v in range(3):
          for h in range(3):
              slide(h,v)
```

Run the above cell, and you'll see 27 pictures, *slide00step1.png, slide00step2.png,...,* *slide22step3.png*, saved in the folder /Desktop/mla/files/ch08/ on your computer.

Next, we'll combine the 27 pictures into a gif file so that we can create an animation.

```
[19]: import PIL
      import imageio

      frames=[]
      for v in range(3):
          for h in range(3):
              for step in range(1,4,1):
                  file=f"files/ch08/slide{h}{v}step{step}.png"
                  frame=PIL.Image.open(file)
                  frame=np.asarray(frame)
                  frames.append(frame)
      imageio.mimsave('files/ch08/slidefilter.gif',frames,fps=2)
```

Run the above cell and you'll see the animation *slidefilter.gif* in the folder /Desktop/mla/files/ch08/ on your computer. It has 27 frames and illustrates how the filter slides over the padded board to cover 9 different areas and generates the nine values in the output matrix.

8.2.3 Subplots

We also create a figure with eight subplots to include in the hard copy of the book. Specifically, we focus on step 3 of the above 27 pictures. We omit the central area so that we have eight pictures to form a four by two grid in the figure.

```
[20]: pics=["00","10","20","01","21","02","12","22"]
      plt.figure(figsize=(24,32),dpi=300)
      for i in range(8):
          plt.subplot(4,2,i+1)
          file=f"files/ch08/slide{pics[i]}step3.png"
          frame=PIL.Image.open(file)
          plt.imshow(frame)
          plt.axis('off')
      plt.subplots_adjust(bottom=0.001,right=0.999,top=0.999,
              left=0.001, hspace=-0.16,wspace=-0.02)
      plt.savefig("files/ch08/slidestep3.png")
```

Figure 8.1 has eight subplots in it. The first one illustrates the value in the top left corner of the output matrix. The rest seven subplots illustrate how the values in the other seven cells in the output matrix are generated. Again, we omit the middle center value in order to form a four by two grid in the figure.

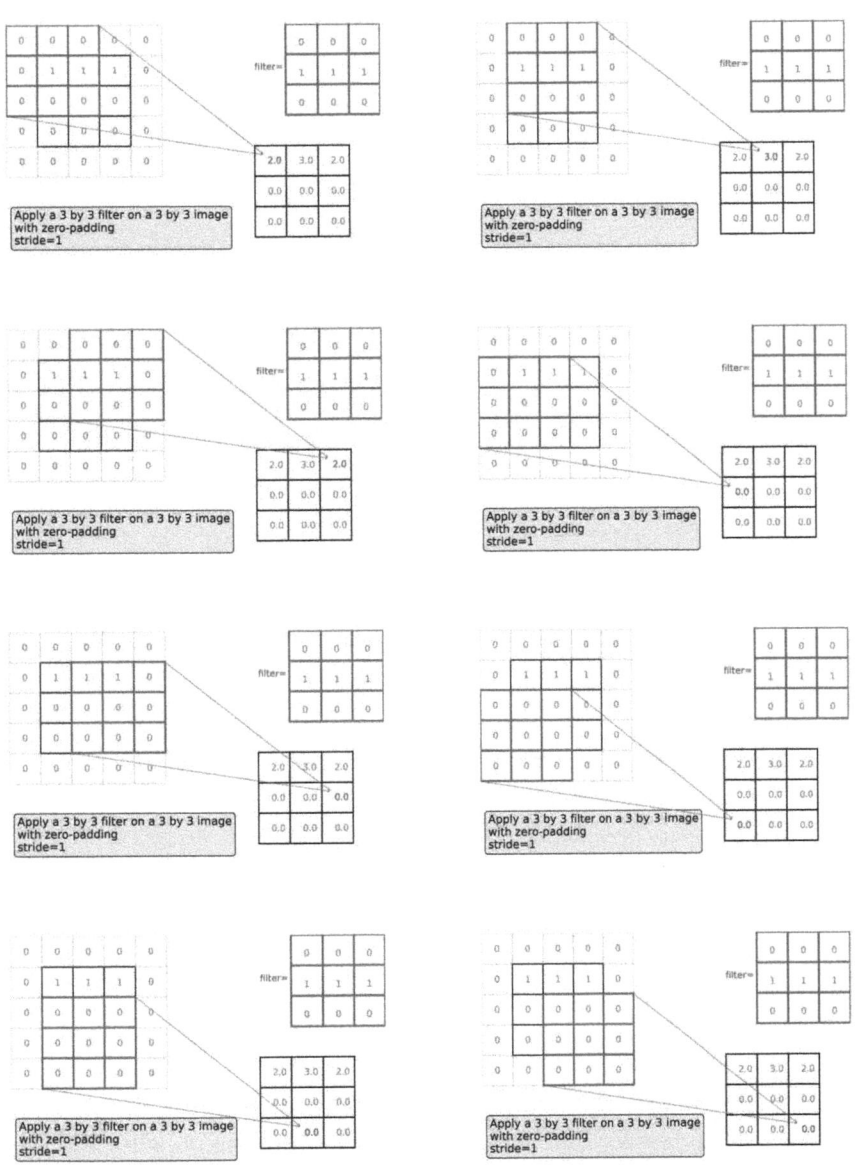

Figure 8.1 A horizontal filter applies on a padded image of three by three

8.3 STRIDE AND PADDING

In the example we just saw, we use zero-padding and a stride of one. Next, we'll discuss what happens if we don't use zero-padding and change the stride size to a value greater than one.

8.3.1 A Filter without Padding and a Stride of 2

We'll apply a two by two diagonal filter on a six by six image without zero-padding. We'll set the stride size to 2.

[21]:
```
# Create a 2 by 2 diagonal filter and a 6 by 6 image
d_filter = np.array([[1,0],
                     [0,1]]).reshape(2,2,1,1)
image = np.array([[1,0,0,1,1,0],
                  [1,0,1,0,0,1],
                  [0,0,0,1,1,0],
                  [0,1,1,0,1,0],
                  [1,0,1,1,0,0],
                  [0,1,0,0,1,0]]).reshape(-1,6,6,1)
```

The code cell above defines the diagonal filter and the six by six image. A diagonal filter finds out and highlights the diagonal features in the image. We'll apply it on the 6 by 6 image as follows:

[22]:
```
# Apply the filter on the image
outputs=tf.nn.conv2d(image,d_filter,strides=2,
                     padding="VALID")
# Convert output to a numpy array and print the output
outputs=outputs.numpy().reshape(3,3).astype(float)
print(outputs)
```

```
[[1. 0. 2.]
 [1. 0. 1.]
 [2. 1. 0.]]
```

The argument stride=2 in the *conv2d()* function means the filter moves two pixels each step. The padding="VALID" argument means there is no zero-padding around the image. Therefore, there will be nine covered areas when the two by two diagonal filter is applied on the image. We can create an animation to show how it works.

8.3.2 Animate the Diagonal Filter

First, we define the function *stride(h,v)* to show how the two by two filter scans over nine different areas (h,v) on the image. The arguments h and v indicate how many steps the filter has moved to the right and to the bottom, respectively, from the top left corner. The function *stride(h,v)* is defined as follows:

```
23]:  image=image.reshape(6,6)
      def stride(h,v):
          fig = plt.figure(figsize=(6,6),dpi=200)
          ax = fig.add_subplot(111)
          # Draw the 6 by 6 image
          for i in range(6):
              for j in range(6):
                  sqr(ax,-6+i,-2+j)
                  ax.text(i-5.6,3.4-j,image[j,i],
                          size=16,color="gray")
          # Draw the filter
          for i in range(2):
              for j in range(2):
                  sqr(ax,-6+i+2*h,2+j-2*v,color="b",linewidth=2)
          ax.set_xlim(-6,0)
          ax.set_ylim(-2,4)
          plt.axis('equal')
          plt.axis('off')
          plt.savefig(f"files/ch08/stride{h}{v}.png")
          plt.close(fig)
```

Next, we'll call the *stride(h,v)* function with different values of h, v to cover nine areas on the six by six image to generated nine pictures, like so:

```
24]:  for v in range(3):
          for h in range(3):
              stride(h,v)
```

Run the above cell, and you'll see nine pictures, *stride00.png*, *stride01.png*,..., *stride22.png*, in the folder /Desktop/mla/files/ch08/ on your computer.

We can combine the pictures into an animation as follows:

```
25]:  frames=[]
      for v in range(3):
          for h in range(3):
              file=f"files/ch08/stride{h}{v}.png"
              frame=PIL.Image.open(file)
              frame=np.asarray(frame)
              frames.append(frame)
      imageio.mimsave('files/ch08/stride.gif',frames,fps=1)
```

If you open the file *stride.gif* in your local folder, you'll see an animation of the two by two diagonal filter moving through nine areas on a six by six image. The filter moves two pixels to the right or to the bottom each time it moves.

8.3.3 Animate the Diagonal Filter Convolution Operation

Next, we'll create an animation on how the output matrix is generated step by step when the two by two diagonal filter is applied on the six by six image.

Specifically, we first define a function *stride_steps()*, which is similar to the *slide()* function we defined previously in this chapter. The function is called to cover nine areas on the six by six image. In each area, the function creates three pictures. In the first picture, with the suffix *step1*, it draws how the filter is applied to an area. In the second picture, with the suffix *step2*, it draws two arrows pointing to the corresponding cell in the output matrix. In the third picture, with the suffix *step3*, it highlights the corresponding value in the output matrix.

To save space, we define the function *stride_steps()* in the local *utils* package. Go to the book's GitHub repository, download the file *ch08util.py* under /utils/ and save it in the folder /Desktop/mla/utils/ on your computer. If you open the file *ch08util.py*, you'll see the exact definition of the function *stride_steps()*.

Next, we call the *stride_steps()* function with different values of h, v to cover nine areas on the six by six image to generate 27 pictures:

```
[26]: from utils.ch08util import stride_steps

for v in range(3):
    for h in range(3):
        stride_steps(h,v,image,outputs)
```

Run the above cell, and you'll see 27 pictures, *stride00step1.png*, *stride00step2.png*,..., *stride22step3.png*, saved in the folder /Desktop/mla/files/ch08/ on your computer.

Next, we'll combine the 27 pictures into a gif file so that we can create an animation.

```
[27]: frames=[]
for v in range(3):
    for h in range(3):
        for step in range(1,4,1):
            file=f"files/ch08/stride{h}{v}step{step}.png"
            frame=PIL.Image.open(file)
            frame=np.asarray(frame)
            frames.append(frame)
imageio.mimsave('files/ch08/stridesteps.gif',frames,fps=2)
```

After running the above cell, you'll see the animation *stridesteps.gif* in the folder /Desktop/mla/files/ch08/ on your computer. It has 27 frames and illustrates how the two by two filter scans over the six by six image to cover 9 different areas and generates the nine values in the output matrix.

8.3.4 Subplots for Strides

We also create a figure with eight subplots to include in the hard copy of the book. Specifically, we focus on step 3 of the above 27 pictures. We omit the central area so that we have eight pictures to form a four by two grid in the figure.

```
28]: pics=["00","10","20","01","21","02","12","22"]
plt.figure(figsize=(24,32),dpi=300)
for i in range(8):
    plt.subplot(4,2,i+1)
    file=f"files/ch08/stride{pics[i]}step3.png"
    frame=PIL.Image.open(file)
    plt.imshow(frame)
    plt.axis('off')
plt.subplots_adjust(bottom=0.001,right=0.999,top=0.999,
        left=0.001, hspace=-0.16,wspace=-0.02)
plt.savefig("files/ch08/stridestep3.png")
```

Figure 8.2 has eight subplots in it. The first one illustrates the value in the top left corner of the output matrix. The rest seven subplots illustrate how the values in the other seven cells in the output matrix are generated.

8.4 COMBINE THE TWO ANIMATIONS

Next, you'll put the two animations, *slidefilter.gif* and *stridesteps.gif*, side by side in one single animation. We'll use the *concatenate()* function from NumPy to combine two frames into one in each of the 27 stages of the two animations.

8.4.1 Combine the Animations

```
29]: frames=[]
for v in range(3):
    for h in range(3):
        for step in range(1,4,1):
            f1=f"files/ch08/slide{h}{v}step{step}.png"
            frame1=PIL.Image.open(f1)
            frame1=np.asarray(frame1)
            f2=f"files/ch08/stride{h}{v}step{step}.png"
```

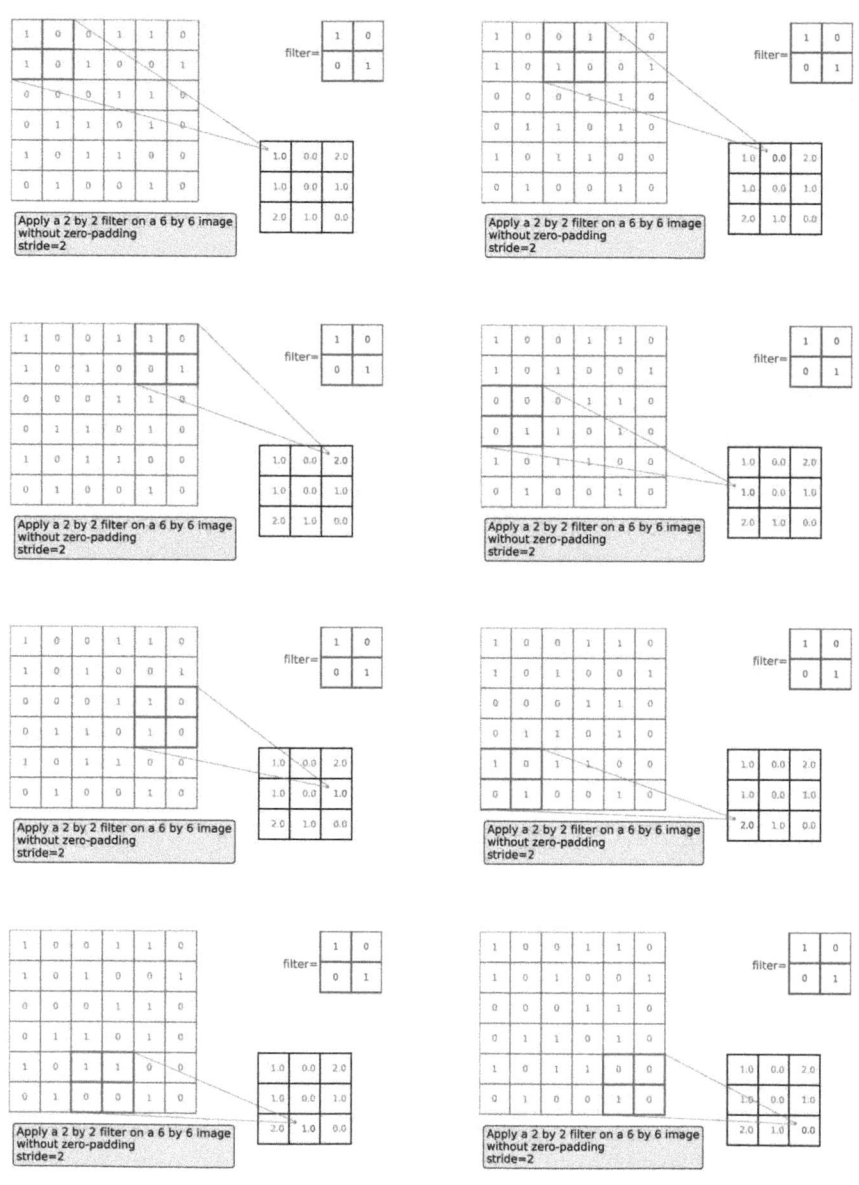

Figure 8.2 How a diagonal filter applies on an image

```
        frame2=PIL.Image.open(f2)
        frame2=np.asarray(frame2)
        frame=np.concatenate([frame1,frame2],axis=1)
        frames.append(frame)
imageio.mimsave('files/ch08/slide_stride.gif',frames,fps=2)
```

If you run the above code cell and open the file *slide_stride.gif* in your local folder, you'll see an animation of the two different filters scanning over two images side by side in each frame.

8.5 MAX POOLING

After we process the images with convolutional layers, we can also use the MaxPooling2D layer to further highlight patterns by taking the maximum value over an input window.

Recall that in the last section, after we apply a 2 by 2 diagonal filter on a 6 by 6 image, the output is a 3 by 3 matrix. We can apply a max_pool2d layer on the output and see what the output looks like:

```
[30]: # Before max pooling
print("the output before max pooling is \n",\
      outputs.numpy().reshape(3,3))
# After max pooling
outputs=outputs.numpy().reshape(-1,3,3,1)
pooled_outputs=tf.nn.max_pool2d(input=outputs,\
            ksize=2,strides=1,padding="VALID")
print("the output after max pooling is \n",\
      pooled_outputs.numpy().reshape(2,2))
```

```
the output before max pooling is
 [[1. 0. 2.]
 [1. 0. 1.]
 [2. 1. 0.]]
the output after max pooling is
 [[1. 2.]
 [2. 1.]]
```

After we apply the two by two max pooling filter on the three by three input matrix, the outcome is a two by two matrix. Here is how it works:

- The two by two max pooling filter first scans the top left corner of the matrix *outputs*, which has four numbers [[1, 0], [1, 0]]. The maximum number among the four cells is 1, hence the value 1 in the top left corner of the *pooled_outputs* matrix.

- The max pooling filter then scans the top right corner of *outputs*, which has four numbers [[0, 2], [0, 1]]. The maximum number among the four cells is 2, hence the value 2 in the top right corner of the *pooled_outputs* matrix.
- The max pooling filter scans the bottom left corner of *outputs*, which has four numbers [[1, 0], [2, 1]]. The maximum number is 2, hence the value 2 in the bottom left corner of the *pooled_outputs* matrix.
- The max pooling filter finally scans the bottom right corner of *outputs*, which has four numbers [[0, 1], [1, 0]]. The maximum number is 1, hence the value 1 in the bottom right corner of the matrix after max pooling.

In the opening quote of this chapter, Professor Geoffrey Hinton thinks that the max pooling is a disaster because valuable information is lost in the process of max pooling. While it is true that only a fraction of the information is used after max pooling, it helps the model to see the big picture and abstract away from unnecessary details. Otherwise, the model gets lost in the jungle of too much information. A good analogy is how a map works. A map intentionally leaves out details in the landscape so users can focus on the larger picture of the landscape and find their way. Similarly, by ignoring small details in the images, the deep learning algorithm can detect big picture patterns and identify the objects in the image.

8.6 BINARY CLASSIFICATIONS WITH CONVOLUTIONAL LAYERS

Now that you know how convolutional layers work, we'll apply them (along with max pooling layers) to the binary classification problem outlined in Chapter 7.

To compare apples with apples, we'll use the same input data to train the model and to make predictions. We'll then compare the confusion matrix as well as the accuracy scores in the out-of-sample testing.

First, we load up the data set we generated in Chapter 7:

```
[31]: import pickle

      # Load the saved data from Chapter 7
      X_train,X_test,y_train,y_test=pickle.load(
          open('files/ch07/train_test.p', 'rb'))
      X_train = X_train.reshape(-1,32,32,1)
      X_test = X_test.reshape(-1,32,32,1)
```

We use the Keras API to create a new deep neural network to train the model. The neural network has two CNN layers and two max pooling layers. After that, we flatten the output from a two-dimensional matrix to a one-dimensional vector and feed the data into a dense layer with 128 neurons.

```
[32]: # Training the model
      import tensorflow as tf
```

```
from tensorflow.keras import layers
tf.random.set_seed(0)
dnn = tf.keras.Sequential()
dnn.add(layers.Conv2D(filters=64, kernel_size=(3,3),\
      activation="relu", input_shape=(32,32,1)))
dnn.add(layers.MaxPooling2D(pool_size=(2,2)))
dnn.add(layers.Conv2D(filters=32, kernel_size=(3,3),
                      activation="relu"))
dnn.add(layers.MaxPooling2D(pool_size=(2,2)))
dnn.add(layers.Flatten())
dnn.add(layers.Dense(units=128, activation="relu"))
dnn.add(layers.Dense(1, activation='sigmoid'))
dnn.compile(optimizer="adam",
            loss="binary_crossentropy",
            metrics=["accuracy"])
hist = dnn.fit(X_train, y_train,
               validation_data=(X_test, y_test),
               verbose=0, epochs=125)
dnn.save('files/ch08/binary_conv.h5')
```

We train the model for 125 epochs and save the model in an h5 file in case you want to make predictions later using the trained model.

Now that the model is trained, we can look at the accuracy of the model during the training process.

```
[33]: # View the training and validation loss
plt.plot(hist.history["accuracy"],
         label='Traning Accuracy',color="r")
plt.plot(hist.history["val_accuracy"],
         label='Validation Accuracy',color="g")
plt.legend()
plt.show()
```

If you run the above code cell, you'll see a graph of the accuracy of the model predictions on the in-sample data (X_train) and the out-of-sample data (X_test). The graph shows that the accuracy in the in-sample predictions reaches 100% after about 50 epochs, possibly due to overfitting. The accuracy in the out-of-sample predictions is close to 70% after about 70 epochs.

Below, we print out the confusion matrix and the accuracy score of the out-of-sample predictions.

```
[34]: from sklearn.metrics import confusion_matrix
from sklearn.metrics import accuracy_score
pred_model=dnn.predict(X_test)
# Convert values between 0 and 1 to Y or N
```

```
pred_yn = np.where(pred_model > 0.5, 1, 0)

ma5=confusion_matrix(y_test,pred_yn)
print("the confusion matrix is\n", ma5)

# Print out the accuracy score
accuracy=accuracy_score(y_test,pred_yn)
print(f"the accuracy of the prediction is {accuracy}")
```

```
2/2 [==============================] - 0s 6ms/step
the confusion matrix is
 [[17  7]
 [ 6 11]]
the accuracy of the prediction is 0.6829268292682927
```

The confusion matrix shows that the new model now predicts 17 true negative, 11 true positives, 7 false positives, and 6 false negatives. The accuracy score is 68.29%.

This is quite an improvement over the predictions in Chapter 7, when we used only dense layers in the neural network. If you recall, the accuracy score with only dense layers is 60.98%. The results show that convolutional layers and max pooling layers help improve the performance of the ML model.

8.7 GLOSSARY

- **Convolutional Neural Network (CNN):** A class of neural networks with at least one convolutional layer. The network is able to detect spatial patterns in the input data.
- **Convolution Operation:** A mathematical operation between two matrices to show how the shape of one matrix is modified by the other.
- **Convolutional Layer:** A layer of neurons that forms the main building block of a convolutional neural network. The convolutional layer uses filters to scan over different parts of the input data to detect patterns.
- **Filter:** Also called a kernel. A matrix with a certain size that moves over the input data to extract features.
- **Max Pooling:** An operation to calculate the maximum value for patches of a feature map.
- **Stride:** Number of pixels to move in each step when the filter moves over the input data.
- **Zero-Padding:** The process of adding zeros around the edges of the input matrix.

8.8 EXERCISES

8.1 Explain what a convolutional neural network is.

8.2 What is a filter? Explain the filter size, zero-padding, and stride.

8.3 Modify the code in Section 8.1.2 so that you apply a three by three vertical filter with values

$$\begin{bmatrix} 0 & 1 & 0 \\ 0 & 1 & 0 \\ 0 & 1 & 0 \end{bmatrix}$$

to the same three by three padded game board. Write down the output matrix before running the code cells. Then check if your answer is the same as the results from running the code cells.

8.4 Continue with the previous question. Modify the code cell in Section 8.2.1 to calculate the output matrix using the *tensordot()* function in NumPy. Verify that the result is the same as that from the previous question when you use the *conv2d()* function from TensorFlow.

8.5 Modify the second code cell in Section 8.3.1 so that you use zero padding and a stride of 1. Write down the output matrix before running the code cell. Then check if your answer is the same as the output from running the code cell.

8.8 EXERCISES

## CHAPTER 9

Multi-Category Image Classifications

> Learning to choose is hard. Learning to choose well is harder. And learning to choose well in a world of unlimited possibilities is harder still, perhaps too hard.
>
> The Paradox of Choice: Why More Is Less
>
> *–Barry Schwartz*

IT IS QUITE often that we need to classify instances into more than two categories in our lives. After you bought something from Amazon, you rate your purchase as one star, two stars,... and all the way to five stars. Financial analysts typically make a recommendation of buy, sell, or hold to investors on a particular stock. A book review can be positive, negative, or neutral... In ML, these are called multi-category classifications.

When the target label is a multi-category variable with more than two possible values (such as 0, 1, or 2, buy, sell, or hold), we call the ML algorithm a multi-category classification problem. In this chapter, you'll learn to classify images in CIFAR-10 into one of the ten labels. To do that, you'll first learn different image augmentation techniques such as rotations, width and height shifts, horizontal flips, and so on. You'll also learn the preferred loss function and activation function to use in multi-category classifications. You'll use a deep neural network with augmentations and convolutional layers to make accurate predictions of the images.

You'll use multi-category classifications often in this book. For example, you'll predict the game outcome (which can be either a win, a loss, or a tie) of Tic Tac Toe or Connect Four based on board positions. You'll also predict the best move in Atari games (moving left, moving right, firing...). Relative to binary classifications, multi-category classifications are more difficult in the sense that the chance of making a correct prediction is smaller. While the unconditional probability of making the right prediction is 50% in binary classifications, that probability decreases to just 10% in a classification with ten different types of target labels. The opening quote of this

DOI: 10.1201/b23383-9

chapter by Barry Schwartz summarizes the difficulty of making the right predictions when the number of choices is large [20].

After you finish this chapter, you'll be able to create an animation to show how the predictions of the model change when the training progresses. On the left of the animation, you'll see that before training, the deep neural network assigns a 12.17% probability to a truck image that it is a truck. After 125 epochs of training, the prediction from the model changes to 98.76%. On the right, you see that the model's predictions on a frog image are 8.78% and 99.86% that it is a frog before and after training, respectively.

New Skills in This Chapter

- Augmenting images through rotations, shifts, and flips
- One-hot encoding labels
- Choosing activation and loss functions in multi-category classifications
- Training, testing, and evaluating a deep neural network for multi-category classifications

---

Before you start, open the Jupyter Notebook app in the virtual environment MLA on your computer. After that, open a blank Jupyter notebook and save it as *ch09.ipynb* in the directory /Desktop/mla/ on your computer. Next, we'll create a subdirectory /files/ch09/ to store files in this chapter. Start a new cell in *ch09.ipynb* and execute the following lines of code in it:

[1]:
```
import os

os.makedirs("files/ch09", exist_ok=True)
```

9.1 IMAGE AUGMENTATIONS

Image augmentations work by modifying the original training data in order to have better predictions. For example, if you perform a horizontal flip on a picture of a horse, it's a mirror image of the original picture but it's still a horse. Similarly, if you tilt a picture of a cat 45 degrees clockwise or counterclockwise, it is still a cat. Image augmentations therefore provide more training data for the model to learn from. This, in turn, improves the performance of the ML model.

The Keras API in TensorFlow has several built-in image augmentation techniques that we can readily use to improve the prediction accuracy. You'll learn a few examples here.

9.1.1 The Keras Image Generator

The Keras API documentation site, https://bit.ly/3OWB6S4, provides details on the *ImageDataGenerator()* method, which generates batches of tensor image data with augmentations. The site provides the following sample code on how to generate augmented image data

```
datagen = ImageDataGenerator(
    featurewise_center=True,
    featurewise_std_normalization=True,
    rotation_range=20,
    width_shift_range=0.2,
    height_shift_range=0.2,
    horizontal_flip=True,
    validation_split=0.2)
```

The above code uses four different augmentation methods: rotation, width shift, height shift, and horizontal flip. If you rotate a picture of a horse 20 or 30 degrees clockwise or counter clockwise, it's still a horse. By doing this, you feed more pictures to the model and this improves the model's ability to identify an object. You can also shift the image vertically up or down, or horizontally to the left or to the right, to augment the image. A horizontal flip means that you flip a picture horizontally to create a mirror image of the original picture.

9.1.2 Visualize Image Augmentations

You can go to the book's GitHub repository to download a sample image of a horse in the folder /files/ch09/. Save the image as *horse.jpg* in the folder /Desktop/mla/files/ch09/ on your computer. We'll use this image as our example in the section. It's a high resolution picture of a horse. The high resolution helps magnify the augmentation effects so that we understand what augmentations do to the original picture.

The following script rotates the original picture up to 20 degrees, conducts horizontal and vertical shifts of the image, and randomly flips the image horizontally. It creates 20 augmented images.

```
[2]:  import numpy as np
      import tensorflow as tf
      import PIL

      # Load the image from the folder
      image=PIL.Image.open('files/ch09/horse.jpg')
      pics=[]
      # Convert the image to a numpy array
      nparray=np.asarray(image)
      nparray=np.expand_dims(nparray,0)
```

```
for i in range(20):
    datagen=tf.keras.preprocessing.image.ImageDataGenerator(
        rescale=1./255,
        featurewise_center=True,
        featurewise_std_normalization=True,
        rotation_range=20,
        width_shift_range=0.1,
        height_shift_range=0.1,
        horizontal_flip=True)
    img_iterator=datagen.flow(nparray,batch_size=1)
    pic=img_iterator.next()
    pics.append(pic)
```

We use the *ImageDataGenerator()* method 20 times on the original horse picture. As a result, we created 20 augmented pictures of the horse. You can use the *matplotlib* library to plot four randomly picked pictures in a two by two grid, as follows:

```
[3]: import matplotlib.pyplot as plt
from random import choice

plt.figure(figsize=(10,10),dpi=100)
for i in range(2):
    for j in range(2):
        plt.subplot(2,2, 2*i+j+1)
        idx=choice(range(20))
        plt.imshow(pics[idx][0])
        plt.axis('off')
plt.subplots_adjust(wspace=0.01,hspace=-0.36)
plt.show()
```

Run the above code cell multiple times. Each time you'll see four augmented horse pictures. Some pictures are rotated clockwise and others counter-clockwise, add - and change sise to wise, due to the argument rotation_range=20 in the *ImageDataGenerator()* method. Similarly, some pictures are shifted left and some shifted right horizontally due to the width_shift_range=0.1 argument. The augmented pictures are also shifted up or down due to the height_shift_range=0.1 argument. Finally, some horses face left and others face right because of the horizontal_flip=True argument. Note that the *ImageDataGenerator()* method above performs the four techniques on the same image simultaneously and randomly. As a result, some images are rotated ten degrees clockwise, shifted slightly to the left and up.

9.2   WHAT IS MULTI-CATEGORY CLASSIFICATION?

When the target label is a multi-category variable with more than two possible values (such as 0, 1, or 2, buy, sell, or hold), we call the ML algorithm a multi-category classification problem.

The CIFAR-10 data set contains ten classes of objects: Planes, cars, birds, cats, deer, dogs, frogs, horses, ship, and trucks. We'll create a neural network to predict which category an image belongs to. Since an image in the data set can belong to any one of the ten categories of objects, we are dealing with a multi-category classification problem.

Compared to binary classifications, we need to change a few things in the neural network when making multi-category classifications. Specifically, we need to change the label, the activation function, and the loss function. We'll discuss them one by one below.

9.2.1   One-Hot Encoder for Labels

In binary classification problems, we use a dummy variable to differentiate the targets: the variable takes value 1 for the positive class and 0 for the negative class. For example, in Chapter 7, we use 1 to denote a horse and 0 a deer.

Once we have more than two classes of objects, one single variable isn't enough: a frog has a value of 6 while a dog has a value of 5 in the labels provided by CIFAR-10. However, the magnitude of the variable may cause confusion: a frog is not greater than a dog in any sense. The label here is an ordinal number instead of a cardinal one. If we feed the variable to the computer, the model will mistakenly think that there is a meaning associated with the magnitude of the target variable and make wrong conclusions.

The solution is to create one variable for each object (one-hot encoders). The script below shows us how to do that.

```
[4]: labels=[0,4,9]
     y=tf.keras.utils.to_categorical(labels,10)
     print(y)
```

```
[[1. 0. 0. 0. 0. 0. 0. 0. 0. 0.]
 [0. 0. 0. 0. 1. 0. 0. 0. 0. 0.]
 [0. 0. 0. 0. 0. 0. 0. 0. 0. 1.]]
```

In the example above, we have three labels: 0, 4, and 9. They represent a plane, a deer, and a truck in the CIFAR-10 data set.

We can use the *to_categorical()* method in TensorFlow to change them into one-hot variables (i.e., categorical variables). The second argument in the *to_categorical()* method, 10, indicates the depth of the categorical variable. This means each categorical variable will be a vector with a length of 10, with value 1 in one position and 0 in all others.

A plane, which has an initial label of 0, now has a one-hot encoder label: a 10-value vector

$$[1, 0, 0, 0, 0, 0, 0, 0, 0, 0]$$

The first value (i.e., index 0) is turned on as 1, and all the rest are turned off as 0. Similarly, a deer, which has a label of 4 originally, now has a one-hot encoder label of

$$[0, 0, 0, 0, 1, 0, 0, 0, 0, 0]$$

The fifth value (i.e., index 4) is turned on as 1, and all the rest are turned off as 0. By the same logic, a truck, with a label of 9, is now represented by

$$[0, 0, 0, 0, 0, 0, 0, 0, 0, 1]$$

9.2.2 The Activation and Loss Functions

In binary classification problems, we use sigmoid as our activation function. For multi-category classification problems, we'll change it to the softmax activation function.

We have discussed the softmax activation function in Chapter 6. If you recall, the softmax function has the form

$$y(x) = \frac{e^x}{\sum_{k=1}^{K} e^{x_k}}$$

where $x = [x_1, x_2, ..., x_K]$ and $y = [y_1, y_2, ..., y_K]$ are K-element vectors. The i-th element of y is

$$y_i(x) = \frac{e^{x_i}}{\sum_{k=1}^{K} e^{x_k}}$$

The softmax function has a nice property: each element in the output vector y is always between 0 and 1. Further, elements in the output vector y sum up to 100%. Because of this property, we can interpret the output vector y as the probability distribution of an outcome with K possible values. Hence, we'll use the softmax activation function to model the probability distribution of a multi-category outcome. As a result, the activation function in the output layer is always the softmax function when we model multi-category classification problems.

The preferred loss function to use in multi-category classifications is the categorical cross-entropy function. It measures the average difference between the predicted distribution and the actual distribution.

Mathematically, the categorical cross-entropy loss function is defined as

$$Categorical\ Cross\ Entropy = \sum_{n=1}^{N} \sum_{k=1}^{K} -y_{n,k} \times log(\hat{y}_{n,k})$$

where $\hat{y}_{n,k}$ is the predicted probability of observation n being class k, and $y_{n,k}$ is the actual label of observation n belonging to category k (which can only take values 0 or 1).

9.3 TRAIN THE MULTI-CATEGORY CLASSIFICATION MODEL

We'll train a DNN model with convolutional layers and image augmentations. We'll use the whole CIFAR-10 train data set. Further, we'll use all three channels of the image, instead of just one, to improve prediction accuracy.

9.3.1 Load the Full Data Set

We'll use all five train batches in CIFAR-10 as our train data set. We'll use the test batch in CIFAR-10 as our test set.

The script in the cell below loads up all the data from CIFAR-10.

```
[5]: import pickle

def unpickle(file):
    with open(file, 'rb') as fo:
        dict=pickle.load(fo, encoding='bytes')
    return dict

X=np.array([]).reshape(-1,32,32,3)
y=np.array([]).reshape(-1,)
path="files/ch07/cifar10/cifar-10-batches-py"

for n in (1,2,3,4,5):
    dn=unpickle(f"{path}/data_batch_{n}")
    Xn=dn[b"data"].reshape(10000,3,32,32)
    Xn=Xn.transpose(0,2,3,1)/255
    yn=np.array(dn[b'labels'])
    # concatenate the batches
    X=np.concatenate((X,Xn),axis=0)
    y=np.concatenate((y,yn),axis=0)
X_train=X.reshape(-1,32,32,3)
y_train=y.reshape(-1,)

# load the test data set
test=unpickle(f"{path}/test_batch")
X_test=test[b"data"].reshape(10000,3,32,32)
X_test=X_test.transpose(0,2,3,1)/255
y_test=np.array(test[b'labels'])

print(X_train.shape)
print(y_train.shape)
print(X_test.shape)
print(y_test.shape)
```

```
(50000, 32, 32, 3)
(50000,)
(10000, 32, 32, 3)
(10000,)
```

The output above shows that there are 5000 training images and 1000 testing images. Let's visualize some images from both the train and the test data set.

```
[6]: plt.imshow(X_train[60])
     plt.show()
     plt.imshow(X_train[88])
     plt.show()
     plt.imshow(X_test[100])
     plt.show()
     plt.imshow(X_test[868])
     plt.show()
```

Run the code in the above cell and you'll see four images. The first two are from the train set: one is a car and the other a truck. The last two are from the test set: one deer and one plane.

9.3.2 Convert Labels to One-Hot Variables

Next, we'll one-hot encode the labels so that the neural network can process them.

```
[7]: y_train=tf.keras.utils.to_categorical(y_train,10)
     y_test=tf.keras.utils.to_categorical(y_test,10)
```

Let's have a look at the shapes of the new *y_train* and *y_test* data sets and print out the first five observations from each set.

```
[8]: print(y_train.shape)
     print(y_train[0:5])
     print(y_test.shape)
     print(y_test[0:5])
```

```
(50000, 10)
[[0. 0. 0. 0. 0. 0. 1. 0. 0. 0.]
 [0. 0. 0. 0. 0. 0. 0. 0. 0. 1.]
 [0. 0. 0. 0. 0. 0. 0. 0. 0. 1.]
 [0. 0. 0. 0. 1. 0. 0. 0. 0. 0.]
 [0. 1. 0. 0. 0. 0. 0. 0. 0. 0.]]
(10000, 10)
[[0. 0. 0. 1. 0. 0. 0. 0. 0. 0.]
 [0. 0. 0. 0. 0. 0. 0. 0. 1. 0.]
 [0. 0. 0. 0. 0. 0. 0. 0. 1. 0.]
```

```
[1. 0. 0. 0. 0. 0. 0. 0. 0. 0.]
[0. 0. 0. 0. 0. 0. 1. 0. 0. 0.]]
```

The shape of the new *y_train* data set is now (50000, 10). The first dimension, 50000, means that there are 50000 image labels in the data set. The second dimension, 10, means that each label is a ten-value array. The first five observations look correct. They are all one-hot variables: a ten value vector with value 1 in one place and 0 in all others. The shape of the new *y_test* dataset is now (10000,10). The first five observations are also all confirmed to be one-hot variables.

Now we are ready to feed the data into the DNN model for training.

9.3.3 Train the Model

First, we create a deep neural network with convolutional layers and max pooling as we did in Chapter 8. We make a few changes to adapt to the new situation.

```
[9]: # Create the model
from tensorflow.keras import layers

tf.random.set_seed(0)
dnn=tf.keras.Sequential()
dnn.add(layers.Conv2D(filters=64,kernel_size=(3,3),\
      activation="relu",input_shape=(32,32,3)))
dnn.add(layers.MaxPooling2D(pool_size=(2,2)))
dnn.add(layers.Conv2D(filters=32,kernel_size=(3,3),
      activation="relu"))
dnn.add(layers.MaxPooling2D(pool_size=(2,2)))
dnn.add(layers.Flatten())
dnn.add(layers.Dense(units=128,activation="relu"))
dnn.add(layers.Dropout(rate=0.2))
dnn.add(layers.Dense(10,activation='softmax'))
dnn.compile(optimizer=\
      tf.keras.optimizers.RMSprop(learning_rate=0.0001),
      loss="categorical_crossentropy",
      metrics=["accuracy"])
```

Four things are worth mentioning here. First, the input shape is now (32, 32, 3) instead of (32, 32, 1) because we use all three color channels of the images. Second, the output layer now has 10 neurons instead of just one because the *y* variable is now one-hot encoded as a ten-value vector. Third, the activation function in the output layer is now softmax instead of sigmoid since the output now is a variable with a depth of ten. Lastly, the loss function now is *categorical_crossentropy* instead of *binary_crossentropy* since we are conducting multi-category classifications instead of binary classifications here.

Next, we add image augmentations before training. We also train five epochs at a time and save the intermediate models so that we can see the predictions as the training progresses. We do this for animation purposes.

[10]:
```
datagen=tf.keras.preprocessing.image.ImageDataGenerator(
    rotation_range=20,
    width_shift_range=0.1,
    height_shift_range=0.1,
    horizontal_flip=True)
datagen.fit(X_train)
training_data=datagen.flow(X_train,y_train)

# Save the model after each five epochs of training
dnn.save('files/ch09/multi_epoch0.h5')
for i in range(1,26,1):
    dnn.fit(training_data,verbose=0,epochs=5)
    dnn.save(f'files/ch09/multi_epoch{i*5}.h5')
```

The above model takes about an hour to train because the Keras API creates augmented images for training just in time. This reduces memory usage but it takes longer to train the model. Once the training is finished, you'll find 26 trained models, *multi_epoch0.h5*, *multi_epoch5.h5*,..., *multi_epoch125.h5*, in the folder /Desktop/mla/file/ch09/ on your computer.

9.3.4 Evaluate the Model

Now that the model is trained, we can evaluate the performance of the model during the training process.

[11]:
```
print(dnn.evaluate(X_train, y_train))
print(dnn.evaluate(X_test, y_test))
```

```
1563/1563 [==============================] - 6s 4ms/step
- loss: 0.5887 - accuracy: 0.7983
[0.5887085199356079, 0.7983199954032898]
313/313 [==============================] - 1s 4ms/step
- loss: 0.7230 - accuracy: 0.7653
[0.7230285406112671, 0.7652999758720398]
```

The above results show that the accuracy scores in the train and test data sets are 79.83% and 76.53%, respectively. Even though we fixed the random state generator in TensorFlow, the Dropout layer in Keras still generates randomness in results. Therefore, you may get a slightly different result from above.

The high accuracy of the model, relative to the model in Chapter 7, comes from several factors. First, we have used the whole data set instead of just 160 observations to train the model. Second, we have used three color channels of the image instead of just one channel to train the model. Third, we have used convolutional layers, max pooling layers, and image augmentations to improve the performance of the model.

We can also calculate the accuracy of the model during the training process as follows.

```
12]:  epochs = []
      train_accuracy =[]
      test_accuracy =[]
      for i in range(26):
          epochs.append(i*5)
          file=f'files/ch09/multi_epoch{i*5}.h5'
          model=tf.keras.models.load_model(file)
          # Accuracy on the training dataset
          train_acc=model.evaluate(X_train,y_train)[1]
          train_accuracy.append(train_acc)
          # Accuracy on the testing dataset
          test_acc=model.evaluate(X_test,y_test)[1]
          test_accuracy.append(test_acc)
      # Plot the accuracies
      plt.plot(epochs,train_accuracy,
              label='Traning Accuracy',color="r")
      plt.plot(epochs,test_accuracy,
              label='Testing Accuracy',color="g")
      plt.legend()
      plt.show()
```

Run the above code cell and you'll see a plot of the prediction accuracy against the epochs. The accuracy score is above 70% for both the training and testing data sets after about 10 epochs of training.

9.4   ANIMATE THE LEARNING PROCESS

We'll create animations to show the learning process of the DNN model we have created above.

Specifically, we find a picture of a truck and a picture of a frog from the test data set. We then look at the predicted probabilities on these two pictures during the training process. We create a graph to show the model's predictions after every five epochs of training. We then combine the graphs to form an animation.

9.4.1   Select Example Pictures

We'll select two example pictures from the test data set.

```
[13]:  # Select a picture of a truck
       truck=X_test[23]
       # Select a picture of a frog
       frog=X_test[29]
       # Visualize them
       plt.imshow(truck)
       plt.show()
       plt.imshow(frog)
       plt.show()
```

We have selected a picture of a truck and a picture of a frog as our examples. If you run the above cell, you'll see an image of a truck and an image of a frog.

Next, we'll save the two pictures on the computer for later use, as follows:

```
[14]:  with open('files/ch09/truck_frog.p', 'wb') as fp:
           pickle.dump((truck, frog), fp)
```

9.4.2 Animate Prediction Changes

Next, we'll create a graph of the model prediction on the truck picture after every five epochs of training.

Specifically, we first define a function *p_truck()*, which generates 26 pictures of the predictions in various stages of training. In each picture, we place the example truck image on the left, the deep neural network in the middle, and the ten output values on the right. The ten output values are the predicted probabilities of the truck image being one of the ten items (a plane, a car, a cat...).

To save space, we place the function *p_truck()* in the local *utils* package. Go to the book's GitHub repository, download the file *ch09util.py* under /utils/ and save it in the folder /Desktop/mla/utils/ on your computer. If you open the file *ch09util.py*, you'll see the exact definition of the function *p_truck()*.

Next, we call the *p_truck()* function to generated 26 pictures:

```
[15]:  from utils.ch09utils import p_truck

       # Call the p_truck function and geneate 26 pictures
       p_truck(truck)
```

If you go to the local folder /Desktop/mla/files/ch09/ and open the file *p_truck0.png*, you'll see a picture showing that before training starts, the model assigns a 12.17% probability that the example image is a truck. In contrast, if you open the file *p_truck25.png*, the picture shows that after 125 epochs of training, the model assigns a 98.76% probability that the example image is a truck.

Next, you'll create an animation of the changing predictions over the course of training.

```
16]: import imageio

frames=[]
for stage in range(26):
    frame=PIL.Image.open(f"files/ch09/p_truck{stage}.png")
    frame=np.asarray(frame)
    frames.append(frame)
imageio.mimsave('files/ch09/p_truck.gif', frames, fps=2)
```

If you go to the local folder /Desktop/mla/files/ch09/ and open *p_truck.gif*, you'll see an animation of the model's prediction on the truck image over the course of training. The predicted probability changes gradually from 12.17% to 98.76%. It's worth noting that after five epochs of training, the model assigns a high probability (at 54.37%) that the image is a car. Given that trucks and cars do look alike, we can understand why the model makes such a prediction. The probability of being a car then gradually decreases after further training: after 35 epochs, the model assigns only a 7.93% probability that the image is a car.

9.4.3 Subplots of the Predictions on the Truck Image

We also create a figure with eight subplots to include in the hard copy of the book. Specifically, we select eight images out of the above 26 pictures we just created and put them in a four by two matrix to form a single picture.

```
17]: pics=["0","3","9","12","15","18","21","25"]
plt.figure(figsize=(24,32),dpi=300)
for i in range(8):
    plt.subplot(4,2,i+1)
    file=f"files/ch09/p_truck{pics[i]}.png"
    frame=PIL.Image.open(file)
    plt.imshow(frame)
    plt.axis('off')
plt.subplots_adjust(bottom=0.001,right=0.999,top=0.999,
        left=0.001, hspace=-0.16,wspace=-0.02)
plt.savefig("files/ch09/p_truck.png")
```

Figure 9.1 has eight subplots in it. The first one, at the top left, illustrates the model prediction on the truck image before training begins. The second one, at top right, shows the model prediction after 15 epochs of training. The last one, at bottom right, shows the model prediction after 125 epochs of training. The figure of subplots, therefore, provides a sense of how the model predictions gradually change as the training progresses.

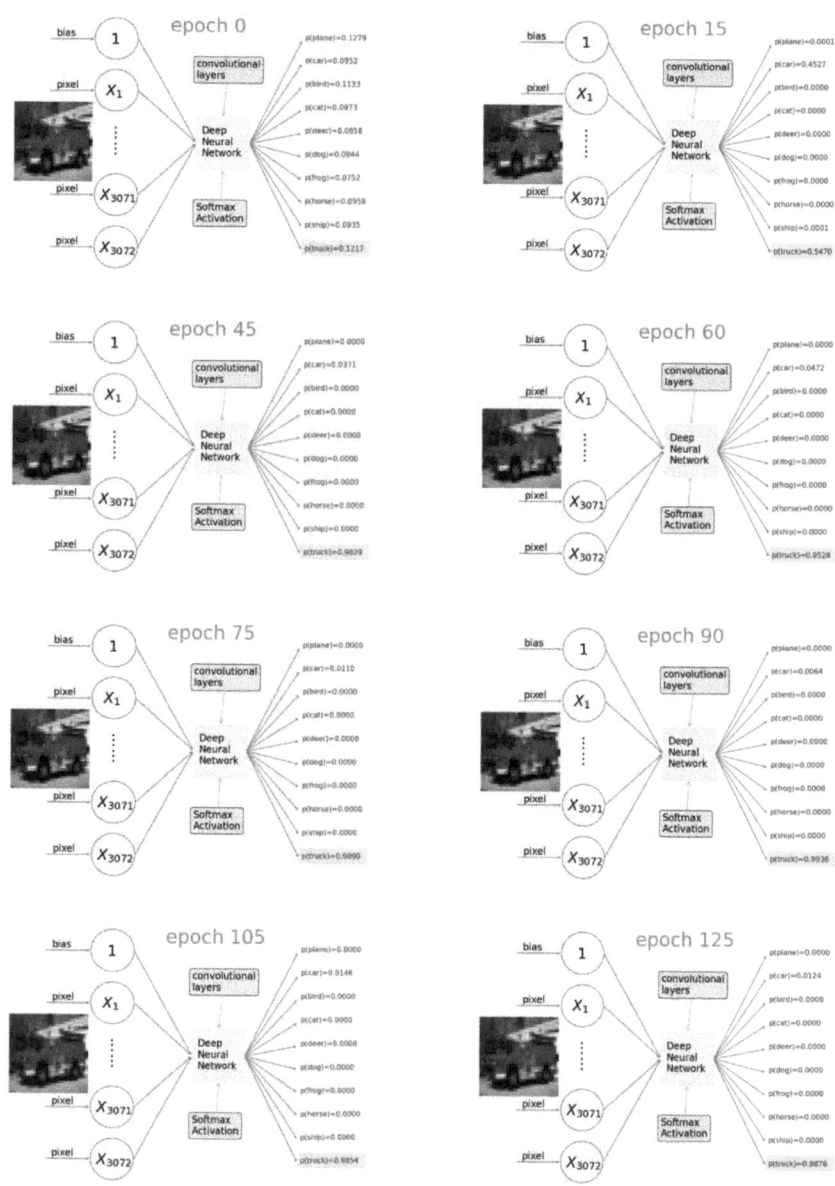

Figure 9.1 Model predictions on a truck image over the course of training

9.4.4 Animate Predictions on the Frog Image

Similarly, you can create an animation of the changing predictions on the frog image during the training process. To do that, we first define a function *p_frog()* to generate 26 pictures of the model predictions on the frog image in different stages of training. We then combine the 26 pictures into an animation in the format of a gif file.

To save space, we place the function *p_frog()* in the local *utils* package. It is in the same file *ch09util.py* you just downloaded from the book's GitHub page. The function *p_frog()* is similar to the function *p_truck()* except that we put the frog image in the picture and highlight the probability that the image is a frog.

To generate the 26 pictures, we call the *p_frog()* function after importing it from the local package, like so:

```
18]: from utils.ch09util import p_frog

     p_frog(frog)
```

Run the above cell to generate the 26 pictures. The file *p_frog0.png* in the folder /Desktop/mla/files/ch09/ on your computer shows that before training starts, the model assigns a 8.78% probability that the image is a frog. After 125 epochs of training, the picture *p_frog25* shows that the model assigns a 99.86% probability that it's a frog.

We can combine the 26 pictures into an animation of the changing predictions over the course of training, as follows:

```
19]: frames=[]
     for stage in range(26):
         frame=PIL.Image.open(f"files/ch09/p_frog{stage}.png")
         frame=np.asarray(frame)
         frames.append(frame)
     imageio.mimsave('files/ch09/p_frog.gif', frames, fps=2)
```

After running the above code cell, if you go to the local folder on your computer and open the file *p_frog.gif*, you'll see an animation of the model's predictions on the frog image over the course of training. The predicted probability changes gradually from 8.78% to 99.86%.

9.4.5 Subplots of the Predictions on the Frog Image

We select eight images out of the 26 pictures we just created and put them in a four by two matrix to form a single picture, like so:

```
20]: plt.figure(figsize=(24,32),dpi=300)
     for i in range(8):
         plt.subplot(4,2,i+1)
```

```
        file=f"files/ch09/p_frog{pics[i]}.png"
        frame=PIL.Image.open(file)
        plt.imshow(frame)
        plt.axis('off')
plt.subplots_adjust(bottom=0.001,right=0.999,top=0.999,
        left=0.001, hspace=-0.16,wspace=-0.02)
plt.savefig("files/ch09/p_frog.png")
```

Figure 9.2 has eight subplots in it. The first one, at the top left, shows the model prediction on the frog image before training. The top right subplot illustrates the model prediction after 15 epochs of training. The bottom right one shows the model prediction after 125 epochs of training. The subplots show that as training progresses, the model assigns a higher and higher probability that the image is a frog.

9.4.6   Combine the Animations

We can now combine the two animations into one so that we can see the changing predictions for the two pictures side by side.

[21]:
```
frames=[]
for stage in range(26):
    frame1=PIL.Image.open(f"files/ch09/p_truck{stage}.png")
    frame1=np.asarray(frame1)
    frame2=PIL.Image.open(f"files/ch09/p_frog{stage}.png")
    frame2=np.asarray(frame2)
    frame=np.concatenate([frame1,frame2],axis=1)
    frames.append(frame)
imageio.mimsave('files/ch09/p_truck_frog.gif',frames,fps=2)
```

In each of the 26 stages of training, we concatenate the graph for the prediction on the truck image and the graph for the prediction on the frog image and combine them into one single frame. We then use the *imageio* library to convert the 26 combined frames into an animation in the gif format.

Run the above code cell and go to the folder /Desktop/mla/files/ch09/ on your computer. You'll see the file *p_truck_frog.gif* in the folder. Open the file to see the animation. It shows the model's prediction on the truck image on the left and prediction on the frog image on the right. As the training progresses, the model makes more and more accurate predictions on the two images.

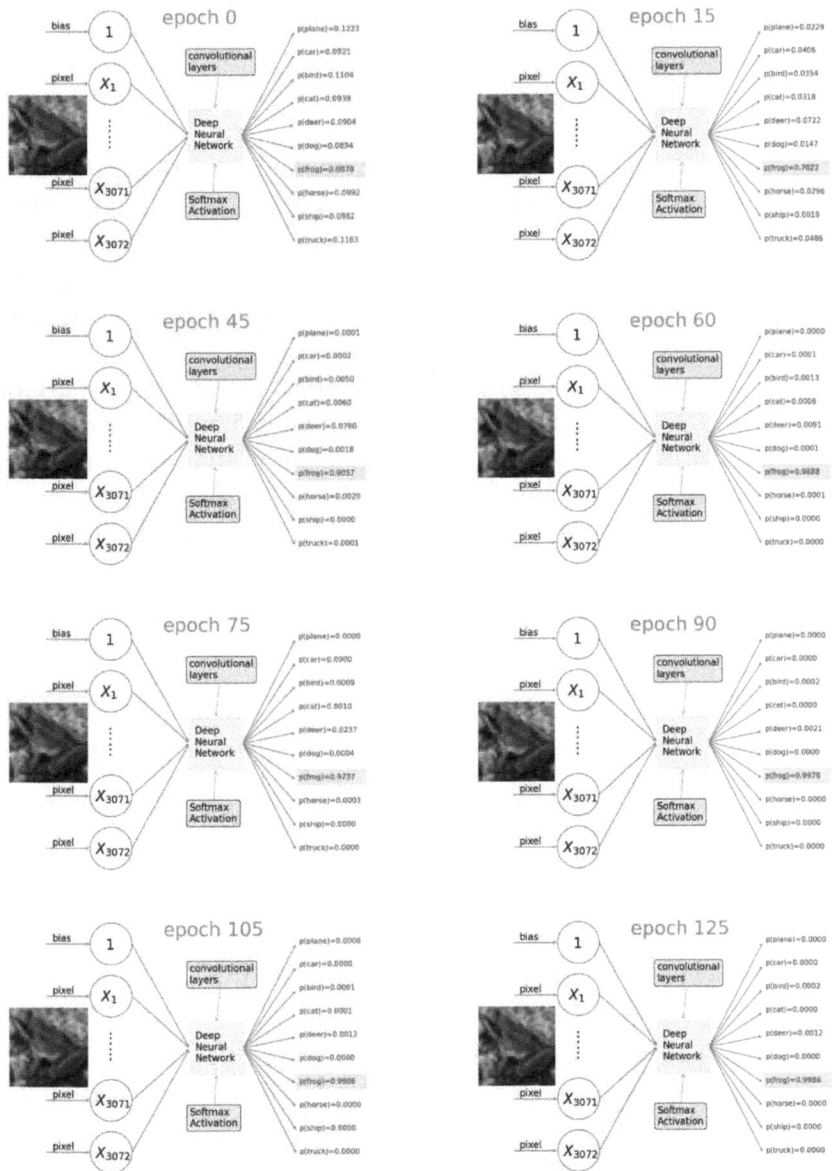

Figure 9.2 Model predictions on a frog image over the course of training

9.5 GLOSSARY

- **Categorical Cross-Entropy:** The loss function used in multi-category classifications. It measures the average difference between the predicted distribution and the actual distribution.
- **Height Shift:** An image augmentation method by moving the image up or down vertically.
- **Horizontal Flip:** A image augmentation method by creating a mirror image of the original picture horizontally.
- **Image Augmentation:** A process of artificially generating training images through methods such as random rotations, width shifts, height shifts, horizontal flips, and so on.
- **Multi-Category Classification:** A machine learning algorithm to classify instances into one of multiple categories. The number of categories is three or more.
- **One-Hot Encoding:** The process of changing a categorical variable into a vector, the values of which are 1 in one place and 0 in all other places.
- **Rotation:** An image augmentation method by randomly rotating the image clockwise or counterclockwise a certain number of degrees.
- **Width Shift:** An image augmentation method by moving the image to the left or to the right horizontally.

9.6 EXERCISES

9.1 Explain what a multi-category classification is. Give two examples.

9.2 What is image augmentation? Explain random rotations, width shifts, height shifts, and horizontal flips.

9.3 Explain what the categorical cross-entropy loss function is.

9.4 Modify the first code box in Section 9.1.2 so that you generate 30 augmented images. Further, change the rotation range to 30 degrees and the width shift range to 0.15.

9.5 Suppose you have three labels in a list *three_labels=[1, 5, 7]*. Change them to one-hot variables using the *to_categorical()* method from TensorFlow.

IV

Developing Deep Learning Game Strategies

## CHAPTER 10

Deep Learning Game Strategies

> Play is the highest form of research.
> *—Albert Einstein*

IN THE NEXT few chapters, you'll learn to creatively apply deep neural networks to various situations. In particular, you'll use deep learning to train intelligent game strategies in different games. You'll learn from A to Z on how to train a game strategy using neural networks. You'll learn to play games in OpenAI Gym. Even though games in the OpenAI Gym environment are designed for reinforcement learning, you'll learn to creatively design deep learning game strategies and win the games. Along the way, you'll have a better understanding of the inner workings of deep learning.

In this chapter, we'll use the Frozen Lake game as an example. You'll learn how to generate game data for training purposes. Once you have a trained model, you'll learn to use the model to design a best-move strategy and play in the OpenAI Gym environment. Finally, you'll test the effectiveness of the strategy. You'll see that the deep learning game strategy works perfectly and wins every game.

At the end of this chapter, you'll create an animation to show how the agent uses the trained model to make decisions on what's the best next move. You'll first draw a game board with the current position of the agent. The agent then hypothetically plays all four next moves, and lets the trained model predict the probability of winning if the agent were to take that action. The agent then picks the action with the highest probability of winning. We'll highlight the best action in the animation in each stage of the game.

> ### New Skills in This Chapter
>
> - Setting up the OpenAI Gym game environment
> - Generating training data by simulating games
> - Designing game strategies using deep neural networks
> - Testing the efficacy of game strategies

Before you start, open the Jupyter Notebook app in the virtual environment MLA on your computer. After that, open a blank Jupyter notebook and save it as *ch10.ipynb* in the directory /Desktop/mla/ on your computer. Next, we'll create a subdirectory /files/ch10/ to store files in this chapter. Start a new cell in *ch10.ipynb* and execute the following lines of code in it:

```
[1]: import os

os.makedirs("files/ch10", exist_ok=True)
```

10.1   GET STARTED WITH THE OPENAI GYM ENVIRONMENT

OpenAI Gym provides the needed working environment for various games. Many machine learning enthusiasts use games in OpenAI Gym to test their algorithms. In this section, you'll learn how to install the libraries needed in order to access games that we'll use in this book. After that, you'll learn how to play a simple game, the Frozen Lake, in this environment.

Before you get started, install the OpenAI Gym library as follows with your virtual environment activated:

```
pip install gym==0.15.7
```

Or you can simply use the shortcut and run the following line of code in a new cell in this notebook:

```
[2]: !pip install gym==0.15.7
```

You need to restart the Jupyter Notebook app for the installation to take effect.

Python Package Version Control

There are newer versions of the OpenAI gym library, but they are not compatible with Baselines, a library that we need to train Breakout and other Atari games (such as Space Invaders, Seaquest, Beam Rider). Therefore, you need to install version 0.15.7 of the OpenAI Gym library. In case you accidentally installed a different version, run the following lines of code to correct it, with your virtual environment activated.

```
pip uninstall gym
pip install gym==0.15.7
```

10.1.1 Basic Elements of a Game Environment

The OpenAI Gym game environments are designed mainly for testing reinforcement learning (RL) algorithms. Later in this book, you'll test various RL algorithms in OpenAI Gym. But for now, we'll use them to test deep learning game strategies.

Let's first discuss a few basic concepts related to a game environment:

- Environment: the world in which agent(s) live and interact with each other or nature. More importantly, an environment is where agent(s) explore and learn the best strategies. Examples of game environments include the Frozen Lake game we'll discuss in this chapter, or the popular Breakout Atari game, or a real-world problem that we need to solve. You'll mostly use game environments from OpenAI Gym, but you'll also learn to create your own game environments later in this book.
- Agent: the player of the game. In most games, there is one player and the opponent is embedded into the environment. But we'll also discuss two-player games such as Tic Tac Toe and Connect Four later in this book.
- State: the current situation of the game. The current game board in the Connect Four game, for example, is the current state of the game. We'll explain more as we go along.
- Action: what the player decides to do given the current game situation. In a Tic Tac Toe game, your action is to choose which cell to place your game piece, for example.
- Reward: the payoff from the game. You can assign a numerical value to each game outcome. For example, in a Tic Tac Toe game, we can assign a reward of 0 to all situations except when the game ends, at which point you can assign a reward of 1 if you win, -1 if you lose the game.

If these concepts sound too abstract at the moment, don't worry. They will become clearer as we move along. Below, you'll see a concrete example of a game environment and the above concepts in this environment.

10.1.2   The Frozen Lake Game

Let's start with the Frozen Lake game environment in OpenAI Gym. In short, an agent moves on the surface of a frozen lake, which is simplified as a four by four grid. The agent starts at the top left corner and tries to get to the lower right corner without falling into one of the four holes on the lake surface. The condition of the lake surface is illustrated in the picture *lake_surface.png* under /files/ch10/ in the book's GitHub repository. If you open the picture, you'll see four gray circles, which are the four holes on the lake surface.

The code in the cell below will get you started:

```
[3]:  import gym

      env=gym.make("FrozenLake-v0",is_slippery=False)
      env.reset()
      env.render()
```

```
SFFF
FHFH
FFFH
HFFG
```

The *make()* method creates the game environment for us. We set the *is_slippery* argument to *False* so that the game is deterministic, meaning the game will always use the action that you choose. The default setting is *is_slippery=True* and this means that you may not go to your intended location since the frozen lake surface is slippery. For example, when you choose to go left on the surface, you may end up going to the right. The *reset()* method starts the game and puts the player at the starting position. The *render()* method shows the current game state.

If you run the above cell, you'll see an output with 16 letters in the form of a four by four grid, which represents the lake surface. The letters have the following meanings:

- S: the starting position.
- H: a hole; the player will fall into the hole and lose the game at this position.
- F: frozen, meaning it's safe to ski on.
- G: goal, the player wins the game if reaching this point.

The current position of the agent is highlighted in red. The above output shows that the player is at the top left corner of the lake, which is the starting position of the agent at the beginning of the game.

We can also print out all possible actions and states of the game as follows:

```
[4]:  # Print out all possible actions in this game
      actions=env.action_space
      print(f"The action space in Frozen Lake is {actions}")
```

```
# Print out all possible states in this game
states=env.observation_space
print(f"The state space in Frozen Lake is {states}")
```

```
The action space in Frozen Lake is Discrete(4)
The state space in Frozen Lake is Discrete(16)
```

The action space in the Frozen Lake game has four values: 0, 1, 2, and 3, where 0 means going left, 1 going down, 2 going right, and 3 going up. The state space has 16 values: 0, 1, 2, ..., 15. The top left square is state 0, the top right is state 3,..., and the bottom right corner is state 15, as shown in the picture *game_states.png* under /files/ch10/ in the book's GitHub repository.

You can play a complete game as follows:

[5]:
```
while True:
    action=actions.sample()
    print(action)
    new_state,reward,done,info=env.step(action)
    env.render()
    print(new_state,reward,done,info)
    if done==True:
        break
```

```
1
    (Down)
SFFF
FHFH
FFFH
HFFG
4 0.0 False {'prob': 1.0}
2
    (Right)
SFFF
FHFH
FFFH
HFFG
5 0.0 True {'prob': 1.0}
```

The code cell above uses several methods in the game environment. The *sample()* method randomly selects an action from the action space. That is, it returns one of the values among {0, 1, 2, 3}. The *step()* method is where the agent interacts with the environment, and it takes the agent's action as input. The output from the *step()* method has four values: the new state, the reward, a variable *done* indicating whether the game has ended, and a variable *info* with some description about the game state. In this case, it provides the probability that the agent reaches the intended state.

Since we are using the nonslippery version of the game, the probability is always 100%. The *render()* method shows a diagram of the resulting state.

The game loop is an infinite *while* loop. If the *done* variable returns a value *True*, the game ends, and we stop the infinite *while* loop.

Note that since the actions are chosen randomly, when you run the above cell, you'll most likely get a different result.

10.1.3 Play the Frozen Lake Game Manually

Next, you'll learn how to manually interact with the Frozen Lake game, so that you have a better understanding of the game environment. This will prepare you to design winning strategies for the Frozen Lake game.

The following lines of code show you how.

```
[6]: print('''
enter 0 for left, 1 for down
2 for right, and 3 for up
''')
env.reset()
env.render()
while True:
    try:
        action=int(input('how do you want to move?\n'))
        new_state,reward,done,_=env.step(action)
        env.render()
        if done==True:
            if new_state==15:
                print("Congrats, you won!")
            else:
                print("Better luck next time!")
            break

    except:
        print('please enter 0, 1, 2, or 3')
```

Use your keyboard to play the game a couple of times. After that, play a game by choosing the following actions: 1, 1, 2, 1, 2, 2 (meaning down, down, right, down, right, right sequentially). As a result, you'll reach the destination without falling into one of the holes and win the game. This is one of the shortest paths that you can take to win the game.

Now, the question is: can you train your computer to win the game by itself?

The answer is yes, and you'll learn how to do that by using the deep learning method via deep neural networks.

10.2 DEEP LEARNING GAME STRATEGIES: GENERATING DATA

In the next few sections, you'll learn to use deep neural networks to train intelligent game strategies.

You'll learn from A to Z on how to train a game strategy using the Frozen Lake game as an example. You'll apply the strategies to other games later in the book.

First, you'll learn to generate simulated game data for training purposes. Once you have a trained model, you'll use the model to design a best-move game strategy and win the game. Finally, you'll test the effectiveness of the strategy.

10.2.1 Summary of the Game Strategy

How to use a neural network to train a game strategy in this case? Here is a summary of what we'll do to train the game strategy:

- We'll let the player randomly choose actions and complete a full game. We'll record the whole game history, which contains all the intermediate states and actions from the beginning to the end of the game.
- We associate each state-action pair with a game outcome (winning or losing). The state-action pair is similar to X (i.e., image pixels) in our image classification problem and the outcome, winning or losing, is similar to y (i.e., image labels such as horse, deer, airplane, and so on) in the image classification problem.
- We'll simulate a large number of games, say, 10000 of them. Use the histories of the games and the corresponding outcomes as (X, y) pairs to feed into a Deep Neural Network. After training is done, we have a trained model.
- At each move of the game, we look at all possible next moves, and feed the hypothetical state-action pair into the pre-trained model. The model will tell you the probability of winning the game if the particular state-action pair were chosen.
- You select the move with the highest chance of winning based on the model's predictions.

Essentially, we convert the problem into a binary classification problem. In each state, we look at each potential action and use the model to classify it into two possible outcomes: winning or losing. We select the action with the highest probability of winning.

10.2.2 Simulate One Game

First, we'll simulate one game and record the whole game history and the game outcome. The script below accomplishes that:

```
[7]:  import numpy as np

      # Define one_game() function
      def one_game():
          # create lists to record game history and outcome
          history=[]
          winlose=[0]
          # start the game
          state=env.reset()
          while True:
              # randomly choose an action
              action=env.action_space.sample()
              # make a move
              new_state,reward,done,_=env.step(action)
              # recording game hisotry
              history.append([state,action,new_state,reward,done])
              # prepare for the next round
              state=new_state
              # stop if the game is over
              if done==True:
                  # if end up in state 15, change outcome to 1
                  if new_state==15:
                      winlose[0]=1
                  break
          return history, winlose
      # Play one game
      history,outcome=one_game()
      print(history)
      print(outcome)
```

```
[[0, 2, 1, 0.0, False], [1, 1, 5, 0.0, True]]
[0]
```

In the cell above, we first define the *one_game()* function, which simulates one full Frozen Lake game. The function returns the game history and the game outcome. For example, the output above shows that the agent made two moves and lost the game. So the game outcome has a value of 0 in it (meaning the agent has lost the game). If the player wins, the value is 1. The game history is a list of lists that records all intermediate steps. In each step, we have values of current state, action taken, next state, reward, and whether the game is over. For example, *[0, 2, 1, 0.0, False]* means that the current state is 0 (i.e., the top left corner), the agent takes an action of 2 (going right), the next state is 1 (the second square in the top row), the reward is 0, and the variable *done* has value *False* (game is not ended).

10.2.3   Simulate Many Games

Next, we'll simulate 10,000 games and record all the intermediate steps and outcomes.

```
[8]: histories=[]
     outcomes=[]
     # Play 10,000 games
     for i in range(10000):
         history,outcome=one_game()
         # record history and outcome
         histories.append(history)
         outcomes.append(outcome)
```

We called the function *one_game()* 10,000 times. The intermediate steps of all games are stored in the list *histories*. The game results (winning or losing) are stored in the list *outcomes*.

Next, we'll save the simulated data on the computer for later use. Specifically, we save the data in the file *frozen_games.pickle* under /Desktop/mla/files/ch10/ on your computer.

```
[9]: import pickle
     # save the simulation data on your computer
     with open('files/ch10/frozen_games.pickle', 'wb') as fp:
         pickle.dump((histories, outcomes), fp)
```

You can load up the saved simulation data from your computer, and print out the first five games.

```
10]: # read the data and print out the first 10 games
     with open('files/ch10/frozen_games.pickle', 'rb') as fp:
         histories, outcomes=pickle.load(fp)

     from pprint import pprint
     pprint(histories[:5])
     pprint(outcomes[:5])
```

```
[[[0, 3, 0, 0.0, False],
  [0, 1, 4, 0.0, False],
  ...
  [6, 0, 5, 0.0, True]]]
[[0], [0], [0], [0], [0]]
```

The output shows all the intermediate steps as well as the outcomes of the first five games. In particular, the five zeros indicate that the agent has failed in the first five games. Note that since the games are generated randomly, your output is likely to be different.

Next we'll train the deep neural network using the simulated data.

10.3 TRAIN THE DEEP NEURAL NETWORK

We'll train the deep neural network so that it can learn from the simulated data. To do that, we'll first prepare the data so that we can feed them into the neural network.

10.3.1 Preprocess the Data

Next, you'll learn how to convert the game history and outcome data into a form that the computer understands before you feed them into the deep neural network.

We'll associate each state-action pair with the final game outcome so that the model can predict the probability of winning for each state-action combination. We'll use the first game above as an example. In the first game, the outcome is 0, meaning the player lost the game. There are 16 steps in game 1 (the number of steps in your data is likely to be different), so we'll create 16 values of X and y, as follows.

```
[11]: game1_history = histories[0]
      game1_outcome = outcomes[0]
      # Print out each state-action pair
      for i in game1_history:
          print(i)
```

```
[0, 3, 0, 0.0, False]
...
[4, 2, 5, 0.0, True]
```

The output above shows that the player started at state 0 (top left corner), and chose action 3 (going up), ended up in the same position (state 0)... In the last round, the player started at state 4, and chose action 2, ended up in state 5, which is a hole, so the game ended as a result. We'll create variables X and y for game 1 as follows:

```
[12]: # Create empty X and y lists
      game1_X, game1_y = [], []
      # Create X and y for each game step
      for i in game1_history:
          game1_X.append([i[0], i[1]])
          game1_y.append(game1_outcome)
      # Print out X, y
      pprint(game1_X)
      pprint(game1_y)
```

```
[[0, 3],
...
 [4, 2]]
[[0], ..., [0]]
```

The above output reflects the 16 steps in game 1. X shows state-action pairs, while y contains the eventual game outcome.

However, if we feed the data into a neural network, the algorithm will mistakenly think that state 14 is greater than 13. Action 3 is greater than action 2. To avoid such confusions, we need to use the one-hot encoder to convert them into a vector of 1s and 0s.

```
13]:  # Define a onehot_encoder() function
      def onehot_encoder(value, length):
          onehot=np.zeros((1,length))
          onehot[0,value]=1
          return onehot
      # Change state and action into onehot_encoders
      game1onehot_X=[]
      for s, a in game1_X:
          print(s,a)
          onehot_s=onehot_encoder(s, 16)
          onehot_a=onehot_encoder(a, 4)
          sa=np.concatenate([onehot_s,onehot_a],axis=1)
          game1onehot_X.append(sa.reshape(-1,))
      # Print out new X
      pprint(game1onehot_X)
```

We convert the state into a 16-value vector and the action a 4-value vector. We then concatenate the two one-hots into a 20-value vector of state-action pair. We'll use this as the input of the deep neural network.

Next, we convert the 10,000 simulated games to the above format, like so:

```
[14]:  # Create empty X and y lists
       X,y=[],[]
       # Create X and y for each game step
       for gamei, yi in zip(histories, outcomes):
           for step in gamei:
               s,a=step[0], step[1]
               onehot_s=onehot_encoder(s, 16)
               onehot_a=onehot_encoder(a, 4)
               sa=np.concatenate([onehot_s,onehot_a],axis=1)
               X.append(sa.reshape(-1,))
               y.append(yi)
```

Now that the dataset is preprocessed, we are ready to train our deep neural network.

10.3.2 Train Deep Learning Game Strategies

Here we are essentially performing a binary classification. We classify each state-action pair into winning or losing. The output layer has one neuron with sigmoid activation. So we can think of the output as the probability of winning the game.

To create a deep neural network, we use four hidden layers, with 128, 64, 32, and 16 neurons in them, respectively. But fewer layers with different numbers of neurons in each layer will generate similar results.

Later, we'll use the trained model to play the Frozen Lake game. When playing, at each state, we'll ask the following question: if I were to choose action 0 (i.e., move left), what's the probability of winning the game? We'll combine the current state and action 0 and feed this state-action pair to the trained deep neural network. The model returns a probability and let's call it $p(win\ s, a0)$. Similarly, if we were to choose actions 1, 2, or 3, the predicted probabilities are $p(win\ s, a1)$, $p(win\ s, a2)$, and $p(win\ s, a3)$, respectively. We then compare the four probabilities and pick the action that leads to the highest probability of winning the game.

Next, we create the neural network using Keras and train the model using the data from the 10,000 simulated games.

```
[15]:  from tensorflow.keras.models import Sequential
       from random import choice
       from tensorflow.keras.layers import Dense

       X = np.array(X).reshape((-1, 20))
       y = np.array(y).reshape((-1, 1))
       # Create a model
       model = Sequential()
       model.add(Dense(128,activation='relu',
                       input_shape=(20,)))
       model.add(Dense(64,activation='relu'))
       model.add(Dense(32,activation='relu'))
       model.add(Dense(16,activation='relu'))
       model.add(Dense(1,activation='sigmoid'))
       model.compile(loss='binary_crossentropy',
                     optimizer='adam',
                     metrics=['accuracy'])
       # Train the model for 50 epochs
       model.fit(X,y,epochs=50,verbose=0)
       model.save('files/ch10/trained_frozen.h5')
```

After 50 epochs of training, we save the model in the local folder on the computer. Next, we'll use the trained model to play the Frozen Lake game.

10.4   PLAY GAMES WITH THE TRAINED MODEL

To play the game with the trained model, we'll look at the current state when deciding each move. We hypothetically take actions 0, 1, 2, and 3, respectively, and use the trained model to predict the probability of winning with each of the four state-action pairs. We'll pick the action that leads to the highest probability of winning. We repeat this process at each step of the game until the game ends.

10.4.1   Test One Game

Below we test one game using the trained model:

```
16]:   action0=onehot_encoder(0, 4)
       action1=onehot_encoder(1, 4)
       action2=onehot_encoder(2, 4)
       action3=onehot_encoder(3, 4)
       # save the predictions in each step
       predictions=[]
       state=env.reset()
       env.render()
       while True:
           # Convert state and action into onehots
           state_arr=onehot_encoder(state, 16)
           # Predict the probability of winning
           sa0=np.concatenate([state_arr,action0],axis=1)
           sa1=np.concatenate([state_arr,action1],axis=1)
           sa2=np.concatenate([state_arr,action2],axis=1)
           sa3=np.concatenate([state_arr,action3],axis=1)
           sa=np.concatenate([sa0,sa1,sa2,sa3],axis=0)
           prediction=model.predict(sa)
           action=np.argmax(prediction)
           predictions.append(prediction)
           print(action)
           new_state,reward,done,info=env.step(action)
           env.render()
           print(new_state,reward,done,info)
           state=new_state
           if done==True:
               break
```

SFFF
FHFH
FFFH
HFFG

```
1
   (Down)
SFFF
FHFH
FFFH
HFFG
4 0.0 False {'prob': 1.0}
1
   (Down)
SFFF
FHFH
FFFH
HFFG
8 0.0 False {'prob': 1.0}
2
   (Right)
SFFF
FHFH
FFFH
HFFG
9 0.0 False {'prob': 1.0}
1
   (Down)
SFFF
FHFH
FFFH
HFFG
13 0.0 False {'prob': 1.0}
2
   (Right)
SFFF
FHFH
FFFH
HFFG
14 0.0 False {'prob': 1.0}
2
   (Right)
SFFF
FHFH
FFFH
HFFG
15 1.0 True {'prob': 1.0}
```

The player wins the game with the shortest possible path: 1, 1, 2, 1, 2, and 2 (meaning down, down, right, down, right, and right sequentially). As a result, the agent reaches the destination without falling into one of the holes. So the deep learning game strategy works!!!

But how, you might ask, was the agent making decisions at each step of the game? We'll look under the hood and see how the model makes predictions for the agent. For that purpose, we save the predictions in each stage of the game for later use. We'll use these probabilities to create an animation in the next section.

```
17]:  with open('files/ch10/frozen_predictions.p','wb') as fp:
          pickle.dump(predictions,fp)
```

The predictions are saved as a pickle file *frozen_predictions.p* on your computer. Note that pickle files can have either .p or .pickle extensions.

10.4.2 Test the Efficacy of the Game Strategy

Winning one game can be a coincidence. We need a scientific way of testing the efficacy of our deep learning game strategy. For that, we'll let the trained model play the game 1000 times, and record how many times the model wins and how many times the model loses.

To save space, we defined a *test_one_game()* function in the local *utils* package. Download the file *ch10util.py* from the book's GitHub repository and save it in the folder /Desktop/mla/utils/ on your computer. The code cell below imports the *test_one_game()* function from the local *utils* package and calls the function 1000 times to test the efficacy of the deep learning game strategy, like so:

```
[18]:  from utils.ch10util import test_one_game

       winloses = []
       for i in range(1000):
           winlose = test_one_game()
           winloses.append(winlose)
       # Print out the number of winning games
       wins = winloses.count(1)
       print("the number of winning games is", wins)
       # Print out the number of losing games
       losses = winloses.count(0)
       print("the number of losing games is", losses)
```

```
the number of winning games is 1000
the number of losing games is 0
```

We record the outcome of each game. If the deep learning game strategy wins, we record an outcome of 1; otherwise, we record an outcome of 0. The output above shows that the deep learning game strategy has won all 1000 games. This shows that our game strategy design works extremely well in this simple game.

10.5   ANIMATE THE DECISION-MAKING PROCESS

We'll create an animation to show how the agent uses the trained model to make decisions on what's the best next move in each stage of the Frozen Lake game.

10.5.1   Generate Figures

We'll first draw a game board with the current position of the agent. We'll then hypothetically play all four next moves, and let the trained DNN model tell us the probability of winning with each hypothetical action. The agent will pick the action with the highest probability of winning. We'll highlight the best action in the animation in each stage of the game.

To save space, we place the function *froze_lake_steps()* in the local *utils* package. It is in the same file *ch10util.py* you just downloaded from the book's GitHub repository.

The following code cell imports the *frozen_lake_steps()* function from the local *utils* package and calls the function to generate 19 pictures.

```
[19]:  from utils.ch10util import frozen_lake_steps

       # Call the function to generate pictures
       frozen_lake_steps()
```

After running the above code cell, if you open the file *frozen_stage0step1.png*, you'll see the starting position of the game. The file *frozen_stage0step2.png* adds the four probabilities to the right of the picture. You can see that the probability of winning for the agent are 0.0145, 0.0214, 0.0139, and 0.0187, respectively if the agent were to go left, down, right, and up. The file *frozen_stage0step3.png* highlights the highest probability of winning for the agent, which is associated with the action of going down. This is why the agent chooses to go down in the first step.

Figure 10.1 is the same as the picture frozen_stage0step3.png we just discussed. It shows why the agent chooses to go down from the starting position: doing so has the highest probability of winning the game.

The file *frozen_stage1step3.png*, *frozen_stage2step3.png*,... highlight the highest probability of winning for the agent in later stages of the game.

We can combine the above pictures into an animation.

10.5.2   Create the Animation

We combine the above 19 pictures into an animation in the form of a gif file by using the *imageio* library, like so:

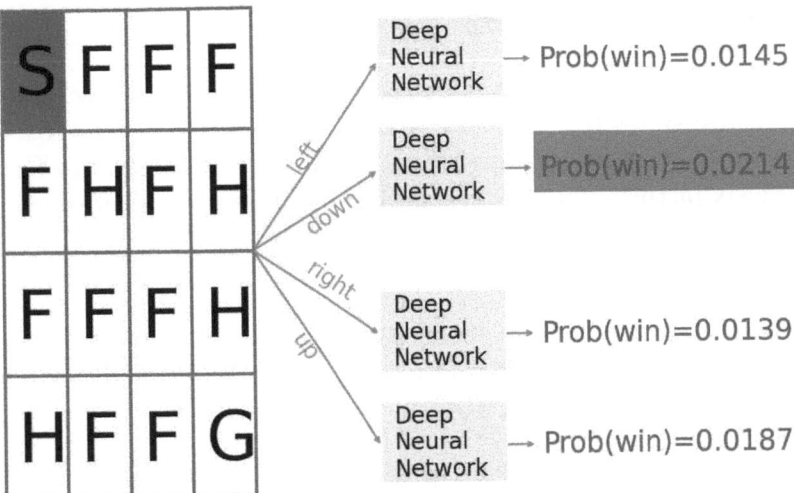

Figure 10.1 Winning probabilities in the first stage of the game

```
20]: import imageio, PIL

     frames=[]
     for stage in range(6):
         for step in range(3):
             file=f"files/ch10/frozen_stage{stage}step{step+1}.png"
             frame=PIL.Image.open(file)
             frame=np.asarray(frame)
             frames.append(np.array(frame))
     frame=PIL.Image.open(f"files/ch10/frozen_stage6step1.png")
     frame=np.asarray(frame)
     # put three frames at the end to highlight the game result
     frames.append(np.array(frame))
     frames.append(np.array(frame))
     frames.append(np.array(frame))
     imageio.mimsave('files/ch10/frozen_stages.gif',frames,fps=2)
```

After running the above code cell, if you go to the local folder on your computer and open the file *frozen_stages.gif*, you'll see an animation of the model's predictions on the winning probabilities of taking different actions. Specifically, in each stage, we first show the current state of the game. We then show the model's predictions of winning if the agent were to take one of the four actions. We then highlight the action with the highest probability of winning.

10.5.3 Create a Figure with Subplots

When playing the game, the agent uses the trained model to make predictions in six different states: states 0, 4, 8, 9, 13, and 14. We'll select six pictures out of the 19 pictures we just created and put them in a three by two matrix to form a single picture. These six pictures illustrate the decision-making process of the whole game.

[21]:
```python
from matplotlib import pyplot as plt

pics=["03","13","23","33","43","53"]
plt.figure(figsize=(28,30),dpi=200)
for i in range(6):
    plt.subplot(3,2,i+1)
    p=f"files/ch10/frozen_stage{pics[i][0]}step{pics[i][1]}.png"
    frame=PIL.Image.open(p)
    plt.imshow(frame)
    plt.axis('off')
plt.subplots_adjust(bottom=0.001,right=0.999,top=0.999,
        left=0.001, hspace=-0.26,wspace=-0.12)
plt.savefig("files/ch10/frozen_stages.png")
```

Figure 10.2 has six subplots in it. The first one, at the top left, shows the model's predictions of winning the game if the agent were to take each of the four actions in the first stage of the game. The top right subplot shows the probabilities in the second stage of the game, and so on. Each subplot highlights the highest probability, hence the optimal action the agent should take. As you can see from the six subplots, the optimal actions are down, down, right, down, right, and right, respectively. Those were the actions taken by the agent to win the game in Section 10.4.1.

10.6 GLOSSARY

- **Action:** What the player decides to do given the current game situation.
- **Agent:** The player of the game. In most games, there is one player and the opponent is embedded into the environment. But there can be more than one agent in a game environment.
- **Environment:** The world in which agent(s) live and interact with each other or nature, and explore and learn the best strategies.
- **Reward:** The payoff to the agent from the game. This is a numerical value based on the game outcome.
- **State:** The current situation of the game.

Figure 10.2 Winning probabilities in the six stages of the game

10.7 EXERCISES

10.1 Install OpenAI Gym in the virtual environment MLA on your computer. Make sure you install version 0.15.7. If you have installed a different version, uninstall it first and then install version 0.15.7.

10.2 What is a game environment? Explain the terms agent, action, state, and reward in a game environment.

10.3 Play a complete Frozen Lake game using your keyboard. What is the minimum number of steps you have to take to win the game?

10.4 Modify the last code box in Section 10.3.2 so that the deep neural network has three hidden layers with 100, 50, and 25 neurons in them, respectively. Retrain the model and save the trained model as *trained_frozen2.h5* on your computer.

10.5 Modify the first code box in Section 10.4.1 to use the newly trained neural network from the previous exercise to play a game.

## CHAPTER 11

Deep Learning in the Cart Pole Game

My powers are ordinary. Only my application brings me success.
—Isaac Newton

DEEP NEURAL NETWORKS (DNNs) are function approximators. If you feed DNNs with enough data, they can figure out the relation between any inputs and outputs no matter how complicated the relation is. Or even if we human beings don't know the exact functional form between the two. Because of this property, DNNs have become ubiquitous in all fields of machine learning: from image classifications, natural language processing, to speech recognition. Later in this book, we'll combine DNNs with reinforcement learning to create deep reinforcement learning models that can solve complicated Atari games.

In Chapter 10, you have applied deep learning to the Frozen Lake game. In essence, you designed a deep learning game strategy based on a binary classification: you associate state-action pairs with the game outcome: a win or a loss. Based on the trained model, you predict the probability of a win with different next moves. You then choose the move with the highest probability of winning. This leads to a perfect game strategy and you win the game 100% of the time.

In the Frozen Lake game, the definition of a win or a loss is clear: if you reach the bottom right corner without falling into one of the holes, it's a win; otherwise, it's a loss. However, in many situations, the definition of a win or a loss is not so black and white. We need to creatively generate the proper labels so that we can convert the problem into binary or multi-category classifications to design game strategies.

The Cart Pole game in OpenAI Gym is such a case. Winning a game is defined as making the Cart Pole stand upright for at least 195 consecutive time steps. However, without random moves, the game will never reach a winning state. Therefore, we cannot use simulated data to train our game strategy. In such cases, we need to creatively redefine what's considered "winning." Specifically, in this chapter, you'll redefine the last ten steps of each game as "losing" and others as "winning" steps. You can think of winning as the ability to keep the cart pole upright for at least another ten steps.

After that, you'll feed the relabeled data into a deep neural network to train the model. Once the model is trained, the agent uses the model to predict the probability of winning with each possible next move. The agent will pick the action with the higher probability of winning. Such a strategy will help the agent win the game 100% of the time. That is, the agent can make the cart pole stay upright for at least 195 steps in every game.

New Skills in This Chapter

- Re-labeling game outcomes as winning and losing
- Simulating games and preprocessing the data for training
- Training game strategies based on simulated games
- Designing best moves based on trained deep neural networks

Before you start, open the Jupyter Notebook app in the virtual environment MLA on your computer. After that, open a blank Jupyter notebook and save it as *ch11.ipynb* in the directory /Desktop/mla/ on your computer. Next, we'll create a subdirectory /files/ch11/ to store files in this chapter. Start a new cell in *ch11.ipynb* and execute the following lines of code in it:

```
[1]:  import os

      os.makedirs("files/ch11", exist_ok=True)
```

11.1   PLAY THE CART POLE GAME IN OPENAI GYM

As we discussed in Chapter 10, you need to install the *gym* library first. Further, we'll use version 0.15.7 of the library because newer versions are not compatible with the *Baselines* package, which we'll use later in this book to play the Atari games. If you haven't already done so, refer back to Chapter 10 on how to install the right version of *gym*.

11.1.1   Features of the Cart Pole Game

We'll first learn the basic features of the Cart Pole game so we know how to design the proper game strategies to win the game.

The code in the cell below creates the Cart Pole game environment:

```
[2]:  import gym

      env = gym.make("CartPole-v0")
      env.reset()
      env.render()
```

[2]: True

The *render()* method generates a graphical rendering of the game window. You should see a separate game window with a cart and a pole in it.

To figure out how many possible actions the agent can take, we print out the *action_space* attribute of the game environment. Similarly, the *observation_space* attribute tells us what variables represent the game state. Run the Python code in the cell below:

```
[3]:  # Print out all possible actions in this game
      actions = env.action_space
      print(f"The action space in the Cart Pole game is {actions}")

      # Print out all possible states in this game
      states = env.observation_space
      print(f"The state space in the Cart Pole game is {states}")
```

```
The action space in the Cart Pole game is Discrete(2)
The state space in the Cart Pole game is Box(4,)
```

The action space in the Cart Pole game is discrete with two values: 0 and 1, with the following meanings:

- 0: moving left
- 1: moving right

The state in the Cart Pole game is a collection of four values, with the following meanings:

- The position of the cart, represented by a value between -4.8 and 4.8;
- The velocity of the cart, represented by a value between -4 and 4;
- The angle of the pole, represented by a value between -0.42 and 0.42;
- The angular velocity of the pole, represented by a value between -4 and 4;

The agent earns a reward of 1 for every time step that the pole stays upright. If the pole is more than 15 degrees away from being vertical or the cart moves more than 2.4 units from the center, the agent loses the game. To win the game, the agent needs to keep the cart pole upright for at least 195 consecutive time steps.

To close the game environment, you can use the *close()* method as follows:

```
[4]:  env.close()
```

If you run the above cell, the graphical rendering of the game window disappears.

11.1.2   Play a Full Game

To familiarize yourself with the game, you can choose random actions and play a complete game as follows:

```
[5]:  env.reset()
      while True:
          action = actions.sample()
          print(action)
          new_state, reward, done, info = env.step(action)
          env.render()
          print(new_state, reward, done, info)
          if done == True:
              break
      env.close()
```

```
0
[ 0.02625933 -0.22749511 -0.01677167  0.30765606] 1.0 False {}
1
[ 0.02170942 -0.03213824 -0.01061855  0.00973133] 1.0 False {}
...
0
[ 0.12443856 0.76014567 -0.20265336 -1.44688204] 1.0 False {}
1
[ 0.13964147  0.95710018 -0.231591    -1.79544121] 1.0 True {}
```

The above code cell uses a couple of methods in the game environment. The *sample()* method randomly selects an action from the action space. That is, it randomly returns one of the values among {0, 1}. The *step()* method is where the agent interacts with the environment, and it takes the agent's action as the input. The output has four values: the new state, the reward, a variable *done* indicating whether the game has ended, and the *info* variable providing some information about the game. Finally, the *render()* method shows an image of the game window.

The game loop is an infinite *while* loop. If the *done* variable returns a value *True*, the game ends and we stop the infinite *while* loop by using the loop command *break*.

Note that since the actions are chosen randomly, when you run the code cell, you'll most likely get different results.

11.2   GENERATE DATA TO TRAIN THE MODEL

In the next few sections, you'll learn how to use deep neural networks to train intelligent strategies for the Cart Pole game.

First, you'll generate simulated game data for training purposes. However, if the agent chooses random moves, the cart pole can never stay upright for anywhere close to

195 consecutive steps. As a result, we'll have all games labeled as losing (i.e., a value of 0). We cannot train game strategies without winning labels. Therefore, we need to creatively redefine what's considered winning. That is, we need to recreate our own labels for the binary classification.

11.2.1   How to Define Winning and Losing?

In the Frozen Lake game in Chapter 10, winning and losing are clearly defined: if the agent reaches the goal without falling into one of the holes, it's a win. On the other hand, if the agent falls into one of the holes before reaching the bottom right corner, it's a loss.

In the Cart Pole game, however, winning is defined as staying upright for at least 195 consecutive steps. If we use random plays to generate training data, the agent will lose all games. None of the games will be classified as winning. Therefore, we need to redefine the label so that some of the observations are defined as winning and others as losing.

Instead of labeling the whole game, we'll label each game state as a win or a loss. We'll define a time step as a win if the cart pole stays upright for at least another ten steps. Otherwise, the time step is defined as losing.

11.2.2   Prepare Data for the Neural Network

How to use a deep neural network to train a game strategy in this case? Here is a summary of what we'll do:

- We'll let the agent randomly choose actions and complete a full game. We'll record the whole game history. The game history will contain all the intermediate states and actions from the very first time step to the very last time step.
- We then associate each state-action pair with a game outcome (a win or a loss). The state-action pairs are similar to image pixels in our image classification problem, and the outcome variables are similar to image labels (such as horses, deer, airplanes and so on).
- We'll simulate a large number of games, say, 10,000 of them. We'll use the histories of the games and the corresponding outcomes as (X, y) pairs to feed into a Deep Neural Network to train the model.
- We then use the trained model to design game strategies. Specifically, at each step in a game, we look at all possible next moves, and feed the hypothetical state-action pairs into the trained model. The model will tell us the probability of winning the game if a certain state-action pair were chosen.
- You select the move with the highest chance of winning based on the model's predictions.

First, we'll simulate one game and record the whole game history plus the game outcome. The Python code in the cell below accomplishes that:

[6]:
```
# Define one_game() function
def one_game():
    # lists to record all game histories and outcomes
    history = []
    winlose = []
    state = env.reset()
    while True:
        # randomly choose an action
        action = env.action_space.sample()
        # make a move
        new_state, reward, done, _ = env.step(action)
        # recording game hisotry
        history.append([state,action,new_state,reward,done])
        # temporarily record the step as winning
        winlose.append(1)
        # prepare for the next round
        state = new_state
        # stop if the game is over
        if done==True:
            break
    return history, winlose
```

Before the game ends, we don't know if a step is a win or a loss. After the game is ended, we'll retroactively label the last ten steps as losing steps (with a label of 0). The remaining steps are classified as winning steps (with a label of 1).

The Python code below reclassifies the last ten steps of the game as losing. As a result, we change the last ten values in the list *winlose* to 0.

[7]:
```
from pprint import pprint

history, winlose = one_game()
# The last ten steps are considered not winning
for i in range(len(history)):
    if len(history)-i<=10:
        winlose[i] = 0

print("the game history is")
pprint(history)
print("the win/loss history is", winlose)
print(f"the game has lasted {len(history)} steps")
env.close()
```

```
the game history is
[[array([-0.01803612,  0.03064895, -0.01890753, -0.03903495]),
  0,
  array([-0.01742315, -0.16419684, -0.01968823,  0.24762301]),
  1.0,
  False],
 ...
 [array([ 0.10135805,  1.20762311, -0.20314459, -1.96610583]),
  1,
  array([ 0.12551051,  1.40423254, -0.24246671, -2.31427023]),
  1.0,
  True]]
the win/loss history is [1, 1, 1, 1, 1, 1, 1, 0, 0, 0, 0,
0, 0, 0, 0, 0, 0]
the game has lasted 17 steps
```

The results above show that the last ten values of the win/loss history of game steps are all 0. The first seven steps are labeled as 1. When you run the above code cell on your computer, the number of time steps in the game is likely to be different since the game is generated randomly.

In a way, the data set tells us what state-action combinations are likely to survive another ten steps and what combinations are likely to fail in the next ten steps. If we feed the data set into a neural network, the model will learn the pattern. We can later use the pattern to choose the best actions based on the state so that the cart pole stays upright as long as possible.

Next, we'll simulate 10,000 games and record all the intermediate steps and outcomes.

[8]:
```python
# create lists to record all game histories and outcomes
histories = []
winloses = []

# Play 10,000 games
for j in range(10000):
    # play a game
    history, winlose = one_game()
    for i in range(len(history)):
        if len(history)-i <= 10:
            winlose[i] = 0
    # record history and outcome
    histories.append(history)
    winloses.append(winlose)
```

We then save the simulated data on the computer for later use.

```
[9]:  import pickle
      # save the simulation data on your computer
      with open('files/ch11/CartPole_games.pickle', 'wb') as fp:
          pickle.dump((histories,winloses), fp)
```

The data set is saved as a pickle file in the folder /Desktop/mla/files/ch11/ on your computer.

You can load up the saved simulation data from your computer, and print out the first game, like so:

```
[10]:  with open('files/ch11/CartPole_games.pickle', 'rb') as fp:
           histories, outcomes=pickle.load(fp)

       pprint(histories[:1])
       pprint(outcomes[:1])
```

Next we'll train the deep neural network using the simulated data.

11.3 TRAIN THE DEEP NEURAL NETWORK

We'll train the deep neural network so that it can learn from the simulated data to predict game outcomes. To do that, we'll first need to preprocess the data so that we can later feed them into the neural network.

11.3.1 Preprocess the Data

We'll create Xs and ys for each game step and put them together for training. Since the outcome variable is either 1 or 0, this is essentially a binary classification problem.

We associate each state and action combination (s, a) with the outcome 1 or 0.

```
[11]:  import numpy as np

       # Create empty X and y lists
       X, y = [], []
       # Create X and y for each game step
       for history, winlose in zip(histories, outcomes):
           for i in range(len(history)):
               state, action, new_state, reward, done = history[i]
               s = np.array(state).reshape((4,1))
               a = np.array(action).reshape((1,1))
               sa = np.concatenate([s, a], axis = 0)
               # Each observation of X is a (state, action) combination
               X.append(sa.reshape(-1,))
```

```
        # Each y is the outcome for the state action combination
        y.append(winlose[i])

# Print the first five observations of X and y
from pprint import pprint
pprint(X[:5])
pprint(y[:5])
# See what's the average value of y
print(np.mean(np.array(y).reshape(-1,)))
```

```
...
[1, 1, 1, 1, 1]
0.5558438552844154
```

The output above shows that the average value of y is about 0.556. This means 55.6% of steps are wins and the rest are losses. Because games are generated randomly, your numbers are likely to be different.

Finally we save the processed data for later use:

[12]:
```
# save the processed data on your computer
with open('files/ch11/CartPoleXy.pickle', 'wb') as fp:
    pickle.dump((X,y),fp)
```

The data set is now ready to be fed into a deep neural network.

11.3.2 Train the Deep Neural Network with Data

Next, we use the preprocessed data set to train our deep neural network.

We classify each state-action pair into a win or a loss. The output layer has one neuron with the sigmoid activation. So we can think of the output as the probability of winning.

There are two hidden layers in the model, with 64 and 16 neurons, respectively. More layers with various numbers of neurons will generate similar results.

Later, we'll use the trained model to play the Cart Pole game. When playing, at each time step, we'll ask the following questions:

- If I were to choose action 0 (i.e., move left), what would be the probability of winning the game? We'll combine the current state and action 0 and feed this state-action pair to the trained deep neural network and get a probability; let's call it $p(win\ s, a0)$.
- If I were to choose action 1 (i.e., move right), what would be the probability of winning the game? We'll use the trained neural network and get $p(win\ s, a1)$.
- Which action leads to a higher probability of winning? We compare $p(win\ s, a0)$ with $p(win\ s, a1)$ and pick the action that leads to the higher $p(win\ s, a)$.

```
[13]:  from tensorflow.keras.models import Sequential
       from tensorflow.keras.layers import Dense

       # load the data
       with open('files/ch11/CartPoleXy.pickle', 'rb') as fp:
           X, y = pickle.load(fp)

       X = np.array(X).reshape((-1, 5))
       y = np.array(y).reshape((-1, 1))

       # Create a model
       model = Sequential()
       model.add(Dense(64,activation='relu',input_shape=(5,)))
       model.add(Dense(16,activation='relu'))
       model.add(Dense(1,activation='sigmoid'))
       model.compile(loss='binary_crossentropy',
                       optimizer='adam',
                       metrics=['accuracy'])

       model.fit(X,y, epochs=50)
       model.save('files/ch11/trained_cartpole.h5')
```

We use Keras to create a sequential model with two hidden layers. Since it's a binary classification problem, we use sigmoid as the activation function in the output layer and binary cross entropy as the loss function. We train the model for 50 epochs and save the trained model in the folder /files/ch11/.

Now that the model is trained, we can use it to play the Cart Pole game.

11.4   PLAY THE GAME WITH THE TRAINED MODEL

To play the game with the trained model, we'll look at the current state and all possible next moves. For each state-action combination, we use the trained model to predict the probability of winning. The action that leads to the highest probability of winning is selected.

Based on this logic, we define a *best_move()* function.

11.4.1   A *best_move*() Function

The following function *best_move()* takes the game environment and the pre-trained model as the two arguments. It then returns the best action in the current game state.

```
[14]:  def best_move(env,model):
           # curret state
           s = np.array(env.state).reshape((4,1))
           # action 0
           a0 = np.array([0]).reshape((1,1))
           sa0 = np.concatenate([s, a0], axis=0).reshape(-1,5)
           # action 1
           a1 = np.array([1]).reshape((1,1))
           sa1 = np.concatenate([s, a1], axis=0).reshape(-1,5)
           # concatenate two state-action combinatoins
           sa = np.concatenate([sa0, sa1], axis=0).reshape(-1,5)
           # make predicitons using the trained model
           predictions = model.predict(sa, verbose=0)
           # pick the action with higher probability of winning
           return np.argmax(predictions)
```

The input to the trained model is a state-action combination. Since the state is a vector with four values and the action is a scalar, the state-action combination is a vector with five values. There are two possible actions at each step: action 0 (moving left) and action 1 (moving right). We hypothetically take one action at a time and use the trained model to predict the hypothetical probability of winning if a certain action were taken. The *best_move*() function returns the best action in this step: the action with higher probability of winning.

11.4.2 Play One Cart Pole Game with the Trained Model

Next, we play a full game using the *best_move*() function to select moves at each step. Further, we record the graphical rendering of the game window at each step, like so:

```
[15]:  from tensorflow.keras.models import load_model

        trained_model = load_model("files/ch11/trained_cartpole.h5")

        state = env.reset()
        frames = []
        for i in range(1,201):
            # Save the screen for later use
            frames.append(env.render(mode='rgb_array'))
            # Use the trained model to select move
            action = best_move(env,trained_model)
            state, reward, done, info = env.step(action)
            if done == True:
                # score is the number of steps staying upright
```

```
        print(f"score is {i}")
        break
env.close()
```

```
score is 200
```

When we put *mode='rgb_array'* in the *render()* method, it returns the game window as a NumPy array. We record the game window in each step and put them in a list *frames*. Later, we'll use these NumPy arrays to create an animation.

The output above shows that the cart pole stays upright for all 200 steps. So the deep learning game strategy works really well!

Next, we'll create an animation to compare two games: one with random moves, and the other with deep learning game strategies.

11.5   COMPARE TWO GAMES

We have already recorded all the frames in a game with deep learning strategies. Next, we'll record all the frames in a game with random moves. We'll then put the frames from the two games side by side so that we can compare the difference in the game outcome.

11.5.1   Record a Game with Random Moves

We'll select random moves and play the Cart Pole game for 200 time steps. We then record all game windows in a list called *random_frames*, like so:

```
[16]: state=env.reset()
      random_frames=[]
      # Record 200 frames
      for i in range(1,201):
          random_frames.append(env.render(mode='rgb_array'))
          # pick a random action
          action=env.action_space.sample()
          # play the game
          state, reward, done, info=env.step(action)
      env.close()
```

If you run the above cell, the list *random_frames* records 200 windows in a random-move game.

11.5.2   Combine Frames

We now have two lists: *frames* and *random_frames*. Each list has 200 game windows/frames. We want to combine the frames from the two lists in each step, with the left frame from the random-move game and the right frame from the game with deep learning strategies.

For that purpose, we defined a *combine_frames()* function in the local *utils* package. You can download the file *ch11util.py* from the book's GitHub repository and save it in the folder /Desktop/mla/utils/ on your computer. Open the file and take a look. In particular, we have used the *frombuffer()* method in NumPy to save data to your computer's memory. If we instead save each combined frame on your computer's hard drive, it's time-consuming. Further, it takes up too much space on your computer. Therefore, we combine the two frames and save them on your computer's memory, using the *frombuffer()* method.

The code cell below imports the *combine_frames()* function from the local *utils* package and calls the function to combine frames, like so:

```
[17]: from utils.ch11util import combine_frames

combined = combine_frames(frames,random_frames)
```

Next, we use the *imageio* library to convert the 200 combined frames into an animation, as follows:

```
[18]: import imageio
imageio.mimsave('files/ch11/compare_cartpole.gif',
                combined, fps=12)
```

After running the above code cell, if you open the file *compare_cartpole.gif*, you'll see an animation with 200 combined frames. In each frame, the left side shows the Cart Pole game with random moves while the right side shows the game with deep learning game strategies. The pole falls down after about 20 time steps in the random-move game. In contrast, in the game with deep learning game strategies, the pole stays upright for all 200 consecutive time steps.

11.5.3 Subplots of the Cart Pole Game Stages

We'll create subplots to show the game window in different stages of the game when random moves are used. Since there are a total of 200 time steps in each game, we select eight stages of the game with roughly equal spaces between them. Specifically, we select time steps 1, 30, 60, 90, 120, 150, 176, and 200 to create eight subplots in a four by two matrix.

To save space, in the *utils.ch11util.py* file, we define a *gen_subplots()* function to select eight frames for subplots. The code cell below imports the *gen_subplots()* function from the local *utils* package and calls the function to generate the eight frames. After that, we use the *matplotlib* library to create a picture with eight subplots in it, like so:

[19]:
```
from utils.ch11util import gen_subplots
from matplotlib import pyplot as plt

random_pics=gen_subplots(random_frames)
plt.figure(figsize=(28,30),dpi=200)
for i in range(8):
    plt.subplot(4,2,i+1)
    plt.imshow(random_pics[i])
    plt.axis('off')
plt.subplots_adjust(bottom=0.001,right=0.999,top=0.999,
        left=0.001, hspace=-0.26,wspace=-0.22)
plt.savefig("files/ch11/random_cartpole.png")
```

Figure 11.1 has eight subplots in it. The first one, at the top left, shows the game window at the first time step of the Cart Pole game with random moves. The top right subplot shows the game window at time step 30 and the pole is already falling down. Other subplots show that the pole swings up and down multiple times in the 200 time steps. The picture shows that with random moves, the cart pole is not able to stay upright for long.

For comparison, we also create subplots to show the game window in different stages when the deep learning game strategies are used to play the game. We use the same eight time steps 1, 30, 60, 90, 120, 150, 176, and 200 to create subplots in a four by two matrix.

In the *utils.ch11util.py* file, we define a *subplots()* function to generate eight frames for subplots. We then import the *subplots()* function from the local *utils* package and call the function to create eight frames. Similarly, we create a picture with eight subplots in it as follows:

[20]:
```
from utils.ch11util import subplots

pics=subplots(frames)
plt.figure(figsize=(28,30),dpi=200)
for i in range(8):
    plt.subplot(4,2,i+1)
    plt.imshow(pics[i])
    plt.axis('off')
plt.subplots_adjust(bottom=0.001,right=0.999,top=0.999,
        left=0.001, hspace=-0.26,wspace=-0.22)
plt.savefig("files/ch11/cartpole.png")
```

Figure 11.2 also has eight subplots in it. The cart pole stays upright in all eight subplots. The picture shows that with deep learning game strategies, the cart pole can successfully stay upright for more than 195 consecutive time steps.

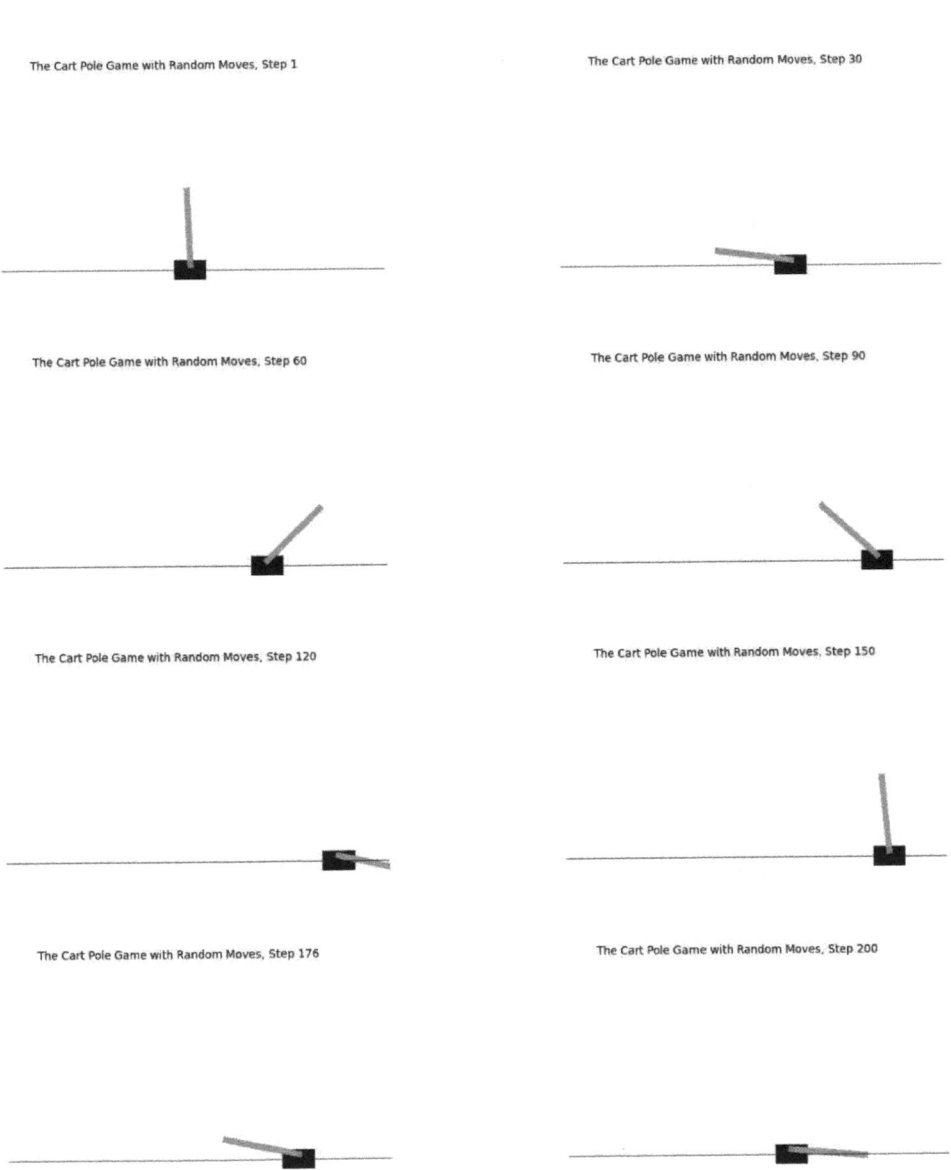

Figure 11.1 Different stages of the Cart Pole game with random moves

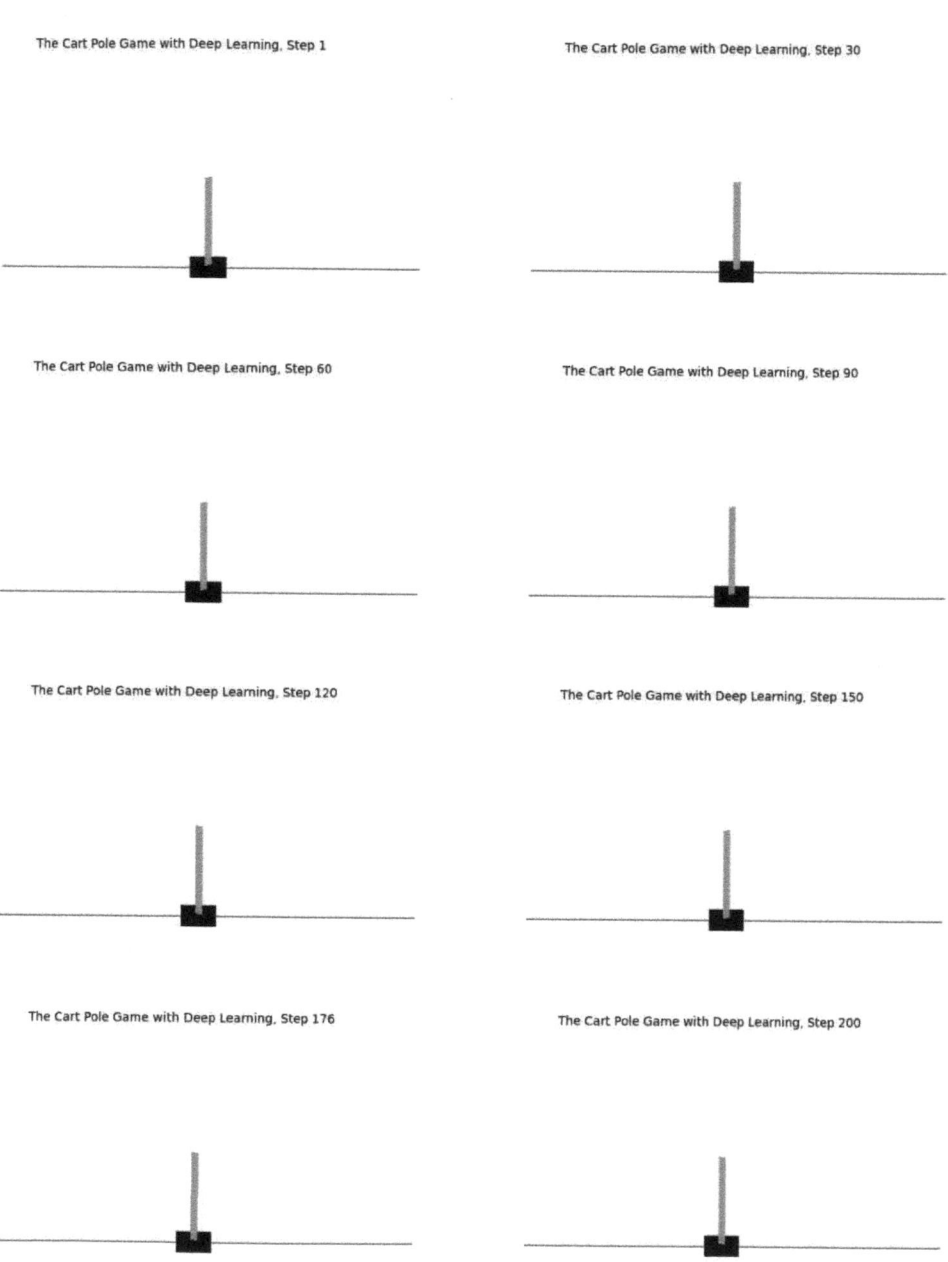

Figure 11.2 Different stages of the Cart Pole game with deep learning

11.6 GLOSSARY

- **Action Space:** The collection of all actions that can be taken by the agent in a game environment.
- **Observation Space:** The collection of all states that can occur in a game environment.

11.7 EXERCISES

11.1 What is the action space in a game environment? How many values are there in the action space in the Cart Pole game?

11.2 What is the observation space in a game environment? How many values are there in the observation space in the Cart Pole game?

11.3 Modify the code box in Section 11.1.2 so that the cart moves to the left in every time step. Run the code cell and see what happens.

11.4 Modify the second code box in Section 11.2.2 so that the last twelve time steps in a game are labeled as 0 and the remaining time steps as 1.

11.5 Modify the first code box in Section 11.3.2 so that the deep neural network has three hidden layers with 64, 32, and 16 neurons in them, respectively. Retrain the deep neural network.

11.6 Continue the previous question. Retrain the deep neural network with three hidden layers you just created. Modify the first code box in Section 11.4.2 so that you play a full game with the new deep neural network.

## CHAPTER 12

Deep Learning in Multi-Player Games

Oh, well, this would be one of those circumstances that people unfamiliar with the law of large numbers would call a coincidence.
–Sheldon Cooper, in The Big Bang Theory

SO FAR, YOU have applied deep learning to two games in OpenAI Gym, namely the Frozen Lake and the Cart Pole games. In this chapter, you'll learn how to create your own game environments so that you can use deep learning to develop game strategies in them. More important, by creating your own game environment, you learn how to convert a real-world problem into a game and provide a solution as if you are playing a game. A case in point is the Amazon delivery route problem we discussed in Chapter 3: later in the book, we'll convert the problem into a game and provide a solution to the problem in a self-made game environment.

To get your started, you'll learn in this chapter how to create your own game environment for a simple everyday game, Tic Tac Toe. We'll create all attributes and methods that game environments in OpenAI Gym have. Better yet, you'll add a graphical game window using the *turtle* library so that you can visualize the game board as the game progresses. Along the way, you'll learn the necessary skills to create a game environment, an agent, and how the agent interacts with the opponent and the environment. You'll code in how to change from one state to another based on agent's actions, how to determine rewards, and how to determine if the game has ended. Later in this book, you'll use these skills to create game environments for Connect Four and the Amazon delivery route problem.

Once the game environment is created, you'll apply deep learning to Tic Tac Toe with the aim of developing intelligent game strategies. You'll use simulated games as input data to feed into a deep neural network. After the model is trained, you'll use the trained model to play games. At each step of the game, you'll look at all possible next moves. You'll use the model to predict the probability of winning the game with each hypothetical next move. You'll pick the move with the highest probability of winning the game for the agent.

Finally, you'll animate the decision making process. You'll use the deep learning game strategy to play a full game. At each step, the animation will show the game board on the left, and the probability of winning with each hypothetical next move on the right. The best move will be highlighted.

New Skills in This Chapter

- Creating your own game environment
- Adding attributes and methods to a game environment
- Making moves and determining wins and losses in a game
- Training game strategies in self-made environments
- Designing deep learning game strategies in multi-player games

---

Before you start, open the Jupyter Notebook app in the virtual environment MLA on your computer. After that, open a blank Jupyter notebook and save it as *ch12.ipynb* in the directory /Desktop/mla/ on your computer. Next, we'll create a subdirectory /files/ch12/ to store files in this chapter. Start a new cell in *ch12.ipynb* and execute the following lines of code in it:

[1]:
```
import os

os.makedirs("files/ch12", exist_ok=True)
```

To convert a *ps* file to a *png* file, you need to conda install Ghostscript. We'll use it in this chapter and other chapters in this book.

Run the following line of command in the Anaconda prompt (Windows) or a terminal (MAC/Linux) with your virtual environment activated:

```
conda install -c conda-forge ghostscript==9.54.0
```

Follow the on-screen instructions to finish the installation.

After that, restart you Jupyter Notebook for it to take effect.

12.1 CREATE THE TIC TAC TOE GAME ENVIRONMENT

We'll create a Tic Tac Toe game environment, using the *turtle* library to generate graphical game windows. We'll create all the features and methods that a typical OpenAI Gym environment has.

12.1.1 Use a Python Class to Represent the Environment

We'll create a Python class to represent the Tic Tac Toe game environment. The class will have various attributes and methods to replicate those in a typical OpenAI Gym game environment.

Specifically, our self-made Tic Tac Toe game environment will have the following attributes:

- action_space: an attribute that provides the space of all actions that can be taken by the agent. The action space in Tic Tac Toe will have nine values, 1 to 9. We use 1 to 9 instead of 0 to 8 to avoid confusion.
- observation_space: an attribute that provides the list of all possible states in the environment. We'll use a NumPy array with 9 values to represent the nine cells on the game board.
- state: an attribute indicating which state the agent is currently in. Each of the nine cells can take values -1 (occupied by Player O), 0 (empty), or 1 (occupied by Player X).
- action: an attribute indicating the action taken by the agent. The action is a number between 1 and 9.
- reward: an attribute indicating the reward to the agent because of the action taken by the agent. The reward is 0 in each step, unless a player has won the game, in which case the winner has a reward of 1 and the loser a reward of -1.
- done: an attribute indicating whether the game has ended. This happens when one player wins or if the game is tied.
- info: an attribute that provides information about the game. We'll set it as an empty string.

Our self-made Tic Tac Toe game environment has a few methods as well:

- reset() is a method to set the game environment to the initial (that is, the starting) state. All cells on the board will be empty.
- render() is a method to show the current state of the game environment graphically.
- step() is a method that returns the new state, the reward, the value of the *done* variable, and the variable *info* based on the action taken by the agent.
- sample() is a method to randomly choose an action from the action space.
- close() is a method to close the game environment.

12.1.2 Create a Local Module for the Tic Tac Toe Game

We'll create a local module for the Tic Tac Toe game and place it inside the local package for this book: the package *utils* that we have created in Chapter 1.

Now let's code in a self-made Tic Tac Toe game environment using a Python class. To save space, we place the code in the file *ttt_env.py* in the folder *utils* you created in Chapter 1. Download the file from the book's GitHub repository and place it in the folder /Desktop/mla/utils/ on your computer.

Open the file *ttt_env.py* to familiarize yourself with the module. We outline the main structure of the module below:

[2]:
```python
# Define an action_space helper class
class action_space:
    ...

# Define an obervation_space helper class
class observation_space:
    ...

# the ttt class
class ttt():
    # initiate the class
    def __init__(self):
        ...
    # reset the board
    def reset(self):
        ...
    # place piece on board and update state
    def step(self, inp):
        ...

    # Determine if a player has won the game
    def win_game(self):
        ...
    # Show the graphical board
    def render(self):
        ...
    # Close the game environment
    def close(self):
        ...
```

First, we use two helper classes *action_space* and *observation_space* to create the action space and observation space for the Tic Tac Toe game. The main Python class is *ttt*, which generates an instance of the Tic Tac Toe game. The *ttt* class has several methods such as *reset()*, *step()*, *render()*, and *close()*.

Next, we'll learn how to access the attributes and methods of this game environment.

12.1.3 Verify the Custom-Made Game Environment

You can check the attributes and methods of the self-made game environment and make sure it has all the elements provided by a typical OpenAI Gym game environment.

First we'll initiate the game environment and show the game board.

```
[3]: from utils.ttt_env import ttt

env = ttt()
env.reset()
env.render()
```

We import the *ttt* class from the local package. We then create an instance of the game and call it *env*. The *reset()* method sets the game board to the initial state. The *render()* method generates a graphical game window using the *turtle* library.

If you run the above cell, you should see a separate turtle window, with a game board in it.

If you want to close the game window, use the *close()* method, like so:

```
[4]: env.close()
```

Next, we'll check the attributes of the game environment such as the observation space and the action space.

```
[5]: # check the action space
number_actions = env.action_space.n
print("the number of possible actions are",\
        number_actions)
# sample the action space ten times
print("the following are ten sample actions")
for i in range(10):
    print(env.action_space.sample())
# check the shape of the observation space
print("the shape of the observation space is", \
        env.observation_space.shape)
```

```
the number of possible actions are 9
the following are ten sample actions
2
...
3
7
the shape of the observation space is (9,)
```

Results above show that there are nine possible actions that can be taken by the agent. The meanings of the actions in this game are as follows:

- 1: Placing a game piece in cell 1
- 2: Placing a game piece in cell 2
- ...
- 9: Placing a game piece in cell 9

The *sample()* method returns an action from the action space randomly. The state space is a vector with 9 values. Each value can be either −1, 0, or 1, with the following meanings:

- 0 means the cell is empty
- −1 means the cell is occupied by Player O
- 1 means the cell is occupied by Player X.

12.1.4 Play a Game in the Tic Tac Toe Environment

Let's play a game in the custom-made environment, by randomly choosing an action from the action space each step.

```
[6]: import time
import random

env=ttt()
state=env.reset()
env.render()
# Play a full game
while True:
    action = random.choice(env.validinputs)
    time.sleep(1)
    print(f"Player X has chosen action {action}")
    state, reward, done, info = env.step(action)
    env.render()
    print(f"the current state is \n{state.reshape(3,3)[::-1]}")
    if done:
        if reward==1:
            print(f"Player X has won!")
        else:
            print(f"It's a tie!")
        break
    action = random.choice(env.validinputs)
    time.sleep(1)
    print(f"Player O has chosen action {action}")
    state, reward, done, info = env.step(action)
    env.render()
    print(f"the current state is \n{state.reshape(3,3)[::-1]}")
    if done:
        print(f"Player O has won!")
        break
env.close()
```

```
Player X has chosen action 7
the current state is
[[1 0 0]
 [0 0 0]
 [0 0 0]]
...
Player O has chosen action 5
the current state is
[[ 1  0  0]
 [-1 -1  1]
 [-1  0  1]]
Player X has chosen action 9
the current state is
[[ 1  0  1]
 [-1 -1  1]
 [-1  0  1]]
Player X has won!
```

We use the *render()* method to show the turtle game window. At the same time, we print out the game board as a NumPy array. We reshape the game board into a three by three matrix. We also use [::-1] to switch the top and bottom rows in the matrix so that the cell numbers match those appear in the turtle game window.

Note that the outcome is different each time you run it because the actions are randomly chosen.

12.2   TRAIN A DEEP LEARNING GAME STRATEGY

In this section, you'll learn how to use a deep neural network to train intelligent game strategies for Tic Tac Toe. In particular, you'll use the convolutional neural network that you used in image classifications to train the model. By treating the game board as a two-dimensional image instead of a one-dimensional vector, you'll greatly improve the effectiveness of your game strategies.

You'll learn how to prepare data to train the model, how to interpret the prediction from the model. How to use the prediction to play games, and how to check the efficacy of your strategies.

12.2.1   A Blueprint of the Deep Learning Game Strategy

Here is a summary of what we'll do to train the game strategy:

1. We'll let two computer players play a game with random moves, and record the whole game history. The game history will contain all the game board positions from the very first move to the very last move.

2. We then associate each board position with a game outcome (a win, a tie, or a loss). The game board position is similar to image pixels in our image classification problem, and the outcome is similar to the labels.
3. We'll simulate 100,000 games. By using the game boards and outcomes as *Xs* and *ys*, we feed the data into a deep neural network to train the model.
4. We use the trained model to play a game. At each step of the game, we look at all possible next moves and feed the hypothetical game board into the pre-trained model. The model will tell you the probabilities of a win, a loss, and a tie.
5. We select the action with the highest chance of winning for the agent who has the turn to make a move.

12.2.2 Simulate Tic Tac Toe Games

You'll learn how to generate data to train the deep neural network. We'll generate 100,000 games in which both players use random moves. We'll then record the board positions of all intermediate steps and the eventual outcomes of each board position.

First, let's simulate one game. The code in the cell below accomplishes that.

```
[7]: from pprint import pprint
import numpy as np

env=ttt()
# Define the one_game() function
def one_game():
    history=[]
    state=env.reset()
    while True:
        action=random.choice(env.validinputs)
        state,reward,done,info=env.step(action)
        history.append(np.array(state))
        if done:
            break
    return history, reward

# Simulate one game and print out results
history, outcome = one_game()
pprint(history)
pprint(outcome)
```

```
[array([0, 0, 0, 0, 1, 0, 0, 0, 0]),
 array([ 0,  0,  0,  0,  1,  0, -1,  0,  0]),
 array([ 0,  0,  0,  0,  1,  0, -1,  1,  0]),
 array([ 0,  0, -1,  0,  1,  0, -1,  1,  0]),
 array([ 0,  1, -1,  0,  1,  0, -1,  1,  0])]
1
```

The simulated game has five steps with the following moves by the two players: 5, 7, 8, 3, and 2. Player X has won the game by connecting cells 2, 5, and 8. The game outcome is 1, meaning Player X has won.

Now let's simulate 100,000 games and save the data.

[8]:
```python
# simulate 100000 games and record them
results = []
for x in range(100000):
    history, outcome = one_game()
    # Note here we associate each board with the game outcome
    for board in history:
        results.append((outcome, board))
```

There is an outcome associated with each game: 1 means Player X has won, −1 means Player O has won, and 0 means the game is tied. After each game is finished, we retroactively associate the game outcome with each board position in the game. By doing this, we train the model to predict the game outcome based on game board positions.

Now let's save the data on your computer for later use:

[9]:
```python
import pickle
# save the simulation data on your computer
with open('files/ch12/games_ttt100K.p', 'wb') as fp:
    pickle.dump(results,fp)
# read the data and print out the first 10 observations
with open('files/ch12/games_ttt100K.p', 'rb') as fp:
    games = pickle.load(fp)
pprint(games[:10])
```

```
[(1, array([0, 0, 0, 1, 0, 0, 0, 0, 0])),
 ...
 (1, array([ 1,  1, -1,  1,  1, -1, -1, -1,  1])),
 (0, array([0, 0, 0, 0, 1, 0, 0, 0, 0]))]
```

The first nine observations are from the first game in which Player X won. Therefore, you see the outcome 1 as the first element of the first nine observations. The tenth observation starts the second game. The first element in the tenth observation is 0, and this tells us that the second game is tied.

Next, you'll learn how to train a deep neural network based on the data you just generated.

The Law of Large Numbers

Even though the moves by both players are random, we repeat the game many times. The randomness in all these games is washed out by the law of large numbers. As a result, the outcome data is useful to predict the outcome of a move. In statistics, the law of large numbers says that if you perform the same experiment many times, the average outcome should be close to the expected value. In our setting, if the average outcome from playing move A is better than the average outcome from playing move B over a large number of trials, move A should be chosen over move B.

12.2.3 Train Your Tic Tac Toe Game Strategy

We create a deep neural network to train our game strategy. In particular, we include a convolutional layer in the model so that we can detect the spatial features on the game board and associate these features (such as three game pieces in a row) with game outcomes.

The following neural network trains the game strategy using the data you just created.

```
[10]:  from tensorflow.keras.utils import to_categorical
       from tensorflow.keras.layers import Dense, Conv2D, Flatten
       from tensorflow.keras.models import Sequential

       model = Sequential()
       model.add(Conv2D(filters=128,
       kernel_size=(3,3),padding="same",activation="relu",
                       input_shape=(3,3,1)))
       model.add(Flatten())
       model.add(Dense(units=64, activation="relu"))
       model.add(Dense(units=64, activation="relu"))
       model.add(Dense(3, activation='softmax'))
       model.compile(loss='categorical_crossentropy',
                       optimizer='adam',
                       metrics=['accuracy'])
```

We use Keras to create a deep neural network to train game strategies in Tic Tac Toe. Compared to the neural networks we used in Chapters 10 and 11, there are several changes. Specifically, the differences are 1) Instead of using just dense layers, we have added in a convolutional layer with a kernel size of three by three; 2) Since there are three possible game outcomes, instead of just two, we treat this as a multi-category classification instead of a binary classification problem. Therefore, we have three neurons in the output layer instead of just one. We use softmax as our activation function in the output layer; 3) The loss function is categorical cross entropy now instead of the binary cross entropy that we used in Chapters 10 and 11.

The outcome data is a variable with three possible values: -1, 0, and 1. We'll convert them into one-hot variables so that the deep neural network can process. We also convert the board position into a three by three matrix instead of a one-dimensional vector before we feed it into the deep neural network.

[11]:
```python
import tensorflow as tf

with open('files/ch12/games_ttt100K.p', 'rb') as fp:
    tttgames = pickle.load(fp)

boards = []
outcomes = []
for game in tttgames:
    boards.append(game[1])
    outcomes.append(game[0])

X = np.array(boards).reshape((-1, 3, 3, 1))
# one_hot encoder, three outcomes: -1, 0, and 1
y = tf.keras.utils.to_categorical(outcomes, 3)
```

We train the model for 100 epochs, as follows:

[12]:
```python
# Train the model for 100 epochs
model.fit(X, y, epochs=100, verbose=0)
model.save('files/ch12/trained_ttt100K.h5')
```

It takes several hours to train the model since we have close to a million observations. The trained model is saved on your computer. Alternatively, you can download the trained model from the book's GitHub repository.

12.3   USE THE TRAINED MODEL TO PLAY GAMES

Next, we'll use the trained model to design game strategies to play a game.

12.3.1   Best Moves Based on the Trained Model

First, we'll define a *best_move_X()* function for Player X. The function will go over each possible next move hypothetically, and use the trained deep neural network to predict the probability of Player X winning the game if the move were chosen. The function returns the move with the highest chance of Player X winning.

Specifically, the *best_move_X()* function works as follows: 1) It retrieves the current game board; 2) It retrieves all possible next moves, and adds a move to the current game board to form a hypothetical game board; 3) It uses the pre-trained model to predict the chance of Player X winning the game based on the hypothetical board; 4) It chooses the move with the highest probability of Player X winning the game.

[13]:
```python
from copy import deepcopy

def best_move_X(env):
    # if there is only one valid move, take it
    if len(env.validinputs)==1:
        return env.validinputs[0]
    # Set the initial value of bestoutcome
    bestoutcome=-2;
    bestmove=None
    #go through all possible moves hypothetically
    for move in env.validinputs:
        env_copy=deepcopy(env)
        state,reward,done,info=env_copy.step(move)
        state=state.reshape(-1,3,3,1)
        prediction=model.predict(state, verbose=0)
        # output is prob(X wins) - prob(O wins)
        win_lose_dif=prediction[0][1]-prediction[0][2]
        if win_lose_dif>bestoutcome:
            # Update the bestoutcome
            bestoutcome=win_lose_dif
            # Update the best move
            bestmove=move
    return bestmove
```

The function *best_move_X()* returns the move to maximize the value of prob(X wins) − prob(O wins). Note that the value of prob(X wins) − prob(O wins) and prob(X wins) are highly correlated, the results are almost identical no matter whether the function *best_move_X()* returns the move to maximize the value of prob(X wins) − prob(O wins) or the value of prob(X wins). Here we are using the former, but you can easily change it to the latter case and verify.

Similarly, we'll define a *best_move_O()* function for Player O. The function will go over each move hypothetically, and use the trained deep neural network to predict the probability of Player O winning the game. The function returns the move with the highest chance of winning for Player O.

[14]:
```python
def best_move_O(env):
    # Set the initial value of bestoutcome
    bestoutcome = -2;
    bestmove=None
    #go through all possible moves hypothetically
```

```
    for move in env.validinputs:
        env_copy=deepcopy(env)
        state,reward,done,info=env_copy.step(move)
        state=state.reshape(-1,3,3,1)
        prediction=model.predict(state, verbose=0)
        # output is prob(O wins) - prob(X wins)
        win_lose_dif=prediction[0][2]-prediction[0][1]
        if win_lose_dif>bestoutcome:
            # Update the bestoutcome
            bestoutcome = win_lose_dif
            # Update the best move
            bestmove = move
    return bestmove
```

The function *best_move_O()* is similar to the function *best_move_X()* we defined earlier. The key difference is that in the function *best_move_O()*, we choose the move to maximize the value of prob(O wins) − prob(X wins). In contrast, in the function *best_move_X()*, we choose the move to maximize the value of prob(X wins) − prob(O wins).

12.3.2 Test a Game Using the Trained Model

Now let's use the *best_move_X()* function to choose moves for Player X and play a game. We'll randomly choose moves for Player O.

```
[15]:  env=ttt()
       state=env.reset()
       env.render()
       # Play a full game manually
       while True:
           # Use the best_move_X() function to select move
           action=best_move_X(env)
           print(f"Player X has chosen action {action}")
           state,reward,done,info=env.step(action)
           print(f"the current state is \n{state.reshape(3,3)[::-1]}")
           env.render()
           if done:
               if reward==1:
                   print(f"Player X has won!")
               else:
                   print(f"It's a tie!")
               break
           action = random.choice(env.validinputs)
           print(f"Player O has chosen action {action}")
           state, reward, done, info = env.step(action)
```

```
print(f"the current state is \n{state.reshape(3,3)[::-1]}")
env.render()
if done:
    print(f"Player O has won!")
    break
```

The best strategy looks at each possible next move, and add that move to the current board to form a hypothetical board. We feed the hypothetical board to the trained model to make predictions. The prediction will have three values: the probability of tying, Player X winning, and Player O winning. The best strategy chooses the move with the highest probability of Player X winning the game.

In one example output, Player X uses the best moves recommended by the trained model and wins the game by occupying cells 4, 5, and 6, as shown in Figure 12.1.

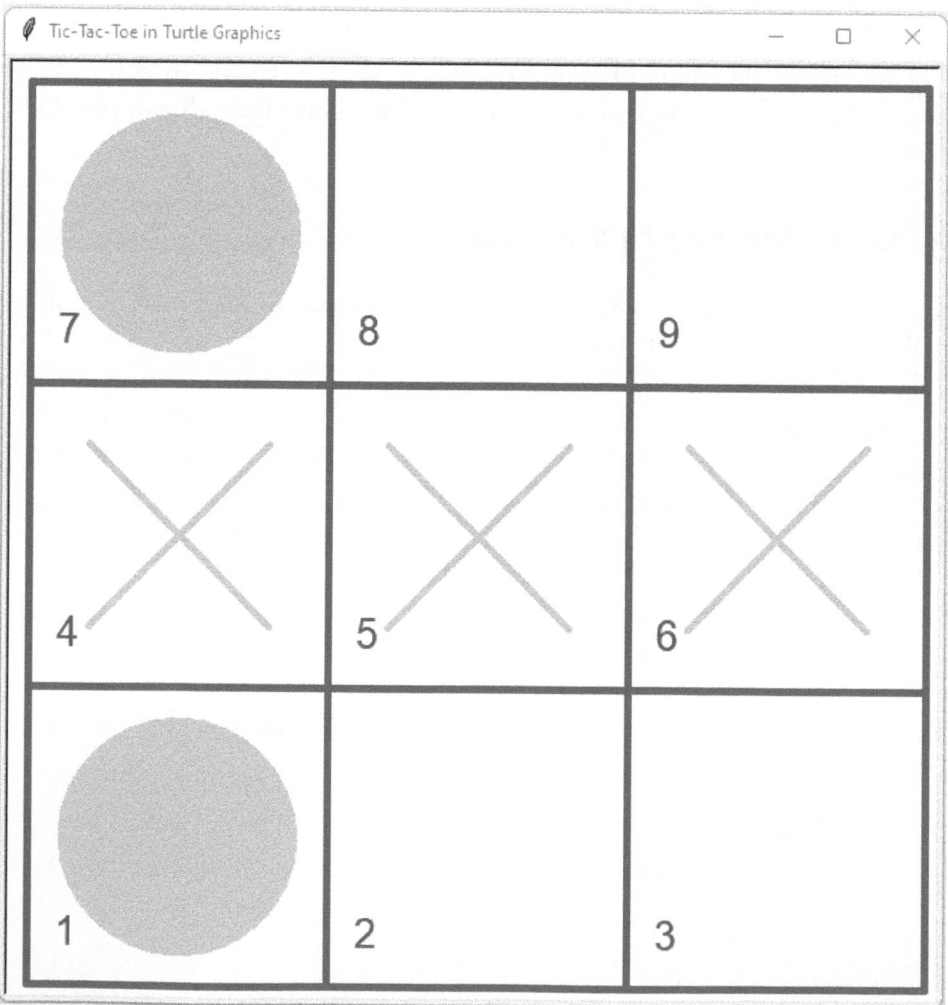

Figure 12.1 A Tic Tac Toe game with the deep learning game strategy

You can also test the best strategy for Player O by using the *best_move_O()* function, assuming Player X chooses random moves. I leave that as an exercise for you.

12.3.3 Test the Efficacy of the Trained Model

Next, we'll test how often the deep learning game strategy wins against a player who makes random moves. The following code cell does that:

```
[16]: # Initiate the game environment
env=ttt()
results=[]
for i in range(1000):
    state=env.reset()
    if i%2==0:
        action=random.choice(env.validinputs)
        state, reward, done, info = env.step(action)
    while True:
        if env.turn=="X":
            action = best_move_X(env)
        else:
            action = best_move_O(env)
        state, reward, done, info = env.step(action)
        if done:
            # result is 1 if the deep learning agent wins
            if reward!=0:
                results.append(1)
            else:
                results.append(0)
            break
        action = random.choice(env.validinputs)
        state, reward, done, info = env.step(action)
        if done:
            # result is -1 if the deep learning agent loses
            if reward!=0:
                results.append(-1)
            else:
                results.append(0)
            break
```

In Tic Tac Toe, Player X has a huge first-mover's advantage. Therefore, we test 1000 games and in 500 of them, we let the random-move agent go first. In the other 500 games, the deep learning agent moves first. We record game outcomes in a list *results*. If the deep learning agent wins, we record an outcome of 1 in the list *results*. If the deep learning agent loses, we record an outcome of −1. If the game is tied, we record an outcome of 0.

Next, we check how many times the deep learning agent has won:

```
[17]: # count how many times the deep learning agent won
      wins=results.count(1)
      print(f"the deep learning agent has won {wins} games")
      # count how many times the deep learning agent lost
      losses=results.count(-1)
      print(f"the deep learning agent has lost {losses} games")
      # count how many times the game ties
      losses=results.count(0)
      print(f"the game has tied {losses} times")
```

```
the number of winning games is 994
the number of tying games is 6
the number of losing games is 0
```

Whenever it's Player X's turn, the deep learning agent uses the *best_move_X()* function to select a move. Whenever it's Player O's turn, the deep learning agent uses the *best_move_O()* function to select a move. The opponent of the deep learning agent is the random-move agent. Results show that the deep learning agent has won 994 out of 1000 games. The remaining six games are tied. The deep learning agent didn't lose even one game. So the deep learning game strategy works really well!

12.4   ANIMATE THE DEEP LEARNING PROCESS

In this section, we'll create an animation to show how the agent makes a decision based on the trained deep neural network in each step of the game.

12.4.1   Probabilities of Winning for Each Hypothetical Move

In each stage of the game, we'll first draw the game board on the left of the screen. Player X, who uses deep learning game strategies here onwards, will look at all possible next moves and use the trained model to predict the probability of winning with each hypothetical next move. We'll draw the probabilities on the right. Finally, we'll highlight the action with the highest probability of winning. The action is Player X's next move. We'll repeat this step by step until the game ends.

This animation will let us look under the hood and understand how deep learning can help us design intelligent game strategies.

In the code cell below, we play a full game and record the game board and the winning probabilities in each step of the game. To save space, we defined a *record_ttt()* function in the local *utils* package. Download the file *ch12util.py* from the book's GitHub repository and save it in the folder /Desktop/mla/utils/ on your computer. The code cell below imports the *record_ttt()* function from the local *utils* package and calls the function to record the game board and winning probabilities, like so:

```
[18]:  from utils.ch12util import record_ttt

       history=record_ttt()
```

The *record_ttt()* function returns a list *history* that contains various information in each stage of the game. In particular, the second element in each stage has the probabilities of Player X winning the game with different hypothetical next moves. For illustration purposes, we require that Player X wins the game in three steps. If not, we start another game until Player X does win in three steps. The *record_ttt()* function also creates several *ps* files on your computer that we'll use later: *ttt_step0.ps*, *ttt_step1.ps*, and so on.

Before making the first move, Player X has nine hypothetical next moves: 1 to 9. The trained neural network tells us what's the probability of winning the game with each hypothetical move. We can print out the nine probabilities as follows:

```
[19]:  p_wins_step0=history[0][1]
       for key, value in p_wins_step0.items():
           print(f"If Player X chooses action {key}, \
           the probability of winning is {value:.4f}.")
```

```
If Player X chooses action 1, the probability of winning is 0.6460.
If Player X chooses action 2, the probability of winning is 0.5623.
If Player X chooses action 3, the probability of winning is 0.6474.
If Player X chooses action 4, the probability of winning is 0.5680.
If Player X chooses action 5, the probability of winning is 0.7345.
If Player X chooses action 6, the probability of winning is 0.5654.
If Player X chooses action 7, the probability of winning is 0.6453.
If Player X chooses action 8, the probability of winning is 0.5629.
If Player X chooses action 9, the probability of winning is 0.6471.
```

The above results show that the probability of Player X winning the game is the highest, at 73.45%, if action 5 is taken. That's why Player X occupies cell 5 in the first move.

Player O chooses cell 2 after that. Now it's Player X's turn again. When making the second move, Player X faces seven choices. We can also print out the probability of winning with each hypothetical next move as follows:

```
[20]:  p_wins_step1=history[1][1]
       for key, value in p_wins_step1.items():
           print(f"If Player X chooses action {key},\
           the probability of winning is {value:.4f}.")
```

```
If Player X chooses action 1, the probability of winning is 0.7908.
If Player X chooses action 3, the probability of winning is 0.7563.
If Player X chooses action 4, the probability of winning is 0.7577.
If Player X chooses action 6, the probability of winning is 0.7657.
```

If Player X chooses action 7, the probability of winning is 0.7784.
If Player X chooses action 8, the probability of winning is 0.6105.
If Player X chooses action 9, the probability of winning is 0.7951.

The above results show that the probability of Player X winning the game is the highest, at 79.51%, if action 9 is taken. That's why Player X occupies cell 9 in the second move.

You can also print out the probability of Player X winning the game when making the third move, but I'll leave that for you to finish as an exercise.

Let's save the game history data for later use. Run the code in the following cell:

[21]:
```
import pickle

# save the game history on your computer
with open('files/ch12/ttt_game_history.p','wb') as fp:
    pickle.dump(history,fp)
```

12.4.2 Animate the Whole Game

Next, you'll combine the pictures created in the last subsection into an animation. As a result, you'll see the game board step by step for the whole game.

[22]:
```
import imageio
from PIL import Image

frames=[]
for i in range(6):
    im=Image.open(f"files/ch12/ttt_step{i}.ps")
    frame=np.asarray(im)
    frames.append(frame)
imageio.mimsave("files/ch12/ttt_steps.gif",frames,fps=1)
```

If you open the file *ttt_steps.gif* on your computer, you'll see an animation showing the game board at each stage of the game.

12.4.3 Animate the Decision Making

Next, we'll animate the decision making process of Player X in each stage of the game. We'll draw the probabilities of Player X winning the game with each hypothetical next move. We'll then highlight the move with the highest probability of winning the game. We'll animate this step by step until the game ends.

The *gen_images()* function in the local *utils* package creates three images in each stage of the game: the game board before Player X makes a move, the probabilities of Player X winning the game with different hypothetical next moves, and the best move for Player X based on the highest probability.

```
[23]: from utils.ch12util import gen_images

gen_images()
```

The above code cell creates images to demonstrate the decision making process of Player X. For example, if you open the file *ttt_stage4step3.png*, you'll see a picture showing the probabilities of Player X winning the game with each hypothetical next move. In particular, the probability is 100% if Player X chooses Cell 1 in the fourth stage of the game. The cell is highlighted in blue, and that is also the move made by Player X as a result.

Next, we'll combine the pictures into an animation to show the decision-making process of Player X.

```
[24]: from PIL import Image
import imageio

frames=[]
for stage in [0, 2, 4]:
    for step in [1,2,3]:
        file=f"files/ch12/ttt_stage{stage*2}step{step}.png"
        im=Image.open(file)
        f1=np.asarray(im)
        frames.append(f1)
imageio.mimsave('files/ch12/ttt_DL_probs.gif',frames,fps=2)
```

If you open the file *ttt_DL_probs.gif*, you'll see the animation of the decision making process of Player X during the whole game.

12.4.4 Animate Board Positions and the Decision Making

You can combine the game board positions and the decision making process of Player X in each stage of the game. On the left of the screen, we'll draw the game board. On the right of the screen, we'll draw the probabilities of Player X winning the game with each hypothetical next move. We'll animate this step by step until the game ends.

```
[25]: from utils.ch12util import combine_animation

frames=combine_animation()
```

If you open the file *ttt_DL_steps.gif*, you'll see an animation with two frames in each step. The left frame shows the board position while the right frame shows the probabilities of Player X winning the game with each hypothetical next move. The best action is then highlighted in blue so that we know what's the best move for Player X at that stage of the game.

12.4.5 Subplots of the Decision-Making Process

We also create a figure with three subplots to include in the hard copy of the book. Specifically, we focus on the decision-making process of Player X when making the three moves. In each move, we'll display the current board position faced by Player X on the left. On the right, we'll display the probability of Player X winning the game with each hypothetical next move. The move with the highest probability of winning is then highlighted.

To do that, we obtain every third image from the list *frames*, like so:

```
[26]: subplot_frames=frames[2::3]
```

There are three images in the newly-created list *subplot_frames*. We plot the images in a three by one matrix as follows:

```
[27]: from matplotlib import pyplot as plt

plt.figure(figsize=(20,30),dpi=200)
for i in range(3):
    plt.subplot(3,1,i+1)
    plt.imshow(subplot_frames[i])
    plt.axis('off')
plt.subplots_adjust(bottom=0.001,right=0.999,top=0.999,
        left=0.001, hspace=-0.01,wspace=-0.22)
plt.savefig("files/ch12/subplots_ttt.png")
```

Figure 12.2 shows the resulting subplots. The top graph shows that Player X faces nine choices at the beginning of the game. Choosing cell 5 has the highest probability of winning for Player X and this explains why Player X's first move is 5. The middle graph shows that after Player O occupies cell 2, Player X has seven choices, and cell 9 leads to the highest probability of Player X winning. The bottom graph shows that after Player O occupies cell 3, Player X should choose cell 1 since doing so leads to a 100% probability of Player X winning the game.

12.5 GLOSSARY

- **Law of Large Numbers:** In statistics, the law of large numbers says that when you perform the same experiment many times, the average outcome should be close to the expected value.
- **Multi-Player Games:** Game environments in which there are more than one agent who can choose actions to interact with the environment and each other.

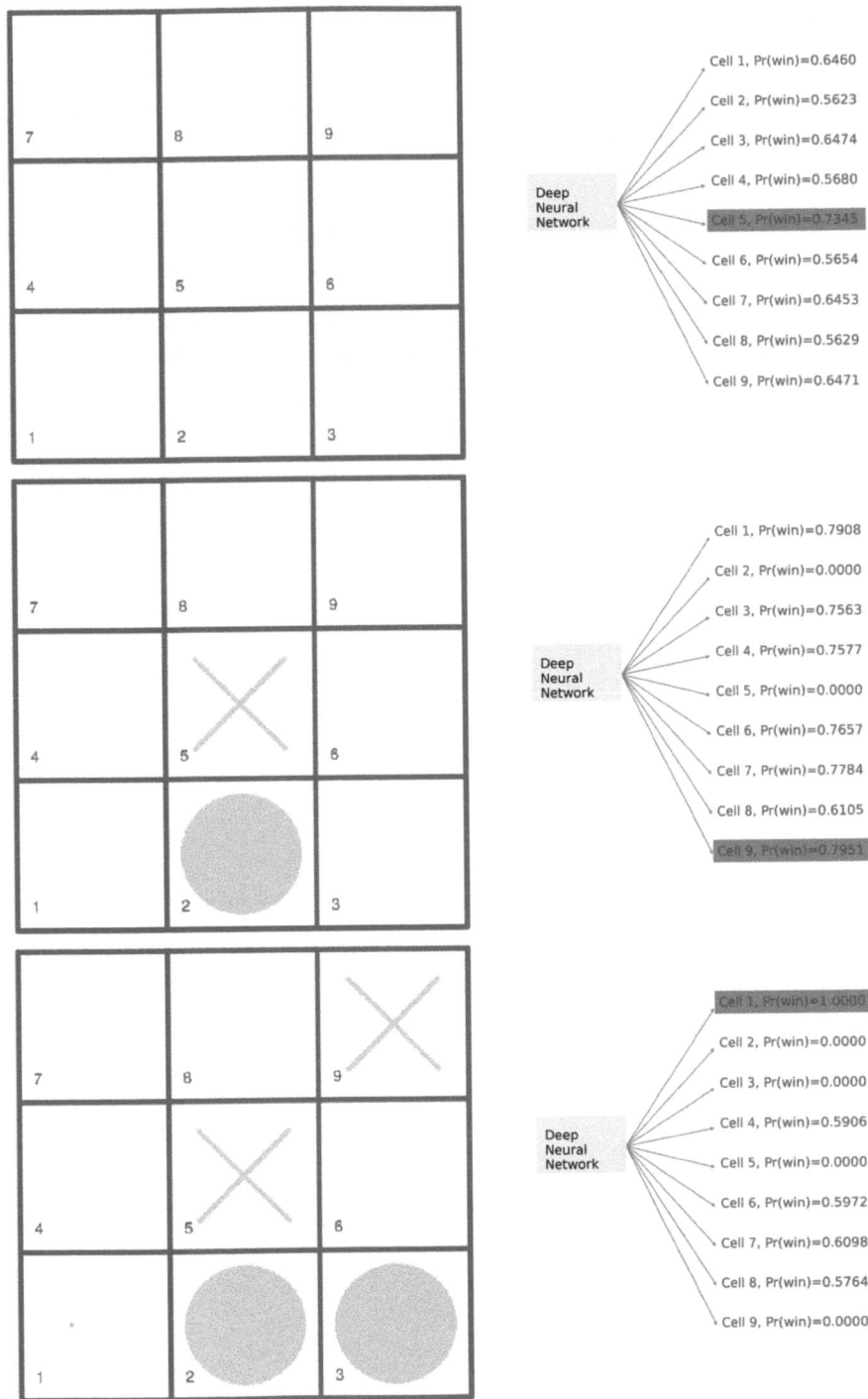

Figure 12.2 Deep learning game strategies in Tic Tac Toe

12.6 EXERCISES

12.1 Rerun the three code boxes in Section 12.1.3 to familiarize yourself with the Tic Tac Toe game environment.

12.2 Modify the first code box in Section 12.1.4 so that Player X chooses random moves, but you choose moves for Player O using your keyboard (hint, use the *input()* function).

12.3 Modify the first code box in Section 12.3.2 so that Player X chooses random moves while Player O selects moves using the *best_move()* function.

12.4 In Section 12.4.1, print out the probabilities of Player X winning the game when making the third move with different hypothetical next moves.

## CHAPTER 13

Deep Learning in Connect Four

Predicting better than pure guesswork, even if not accurately, delivers real value. A hazy view of what's to come outperforms complete darkness by a landslide.
Predictive Analytics: The Power to Predict Who Will Click, Buy, Lie, or Die
–Eric Seigel

IN THIS CHAPTER, you'll combine what you have learned in Chapters 10 to 12 and design deep learning game strategies for the Connect Four game. You'll first create a game environment for Connect Four with all the attributes and methods of a typical OpenAI Gym game environment. The game environment also has a graphical interface.

You'll use simulated games as input data to feed into a deep neural network. After the model is trained, you'll use it to play Connect Four games. At each step of the game, you'll look at all possible next moves. The model predicts the probability of winning the game for the deep learning agent with each hypothetical next move. You'll pick the move with the highest probability of winning.

Finally, you'll animate the decision-making process. You'll use the deep learning game strategy to play a full game. At each step, the animation will show the game board on the left, and all possible next moves and the associated probabilities of winning on the right. The best next move is highlighted.

New Skills in This Chapter

- Creating a Connect Four game environment
- Coding in complicated Connect Four game rules
- Simulating game data to train a deep neural network
- Designing deep learning game strategies for different players

---

DOI: 10.1201/b23383-13

Before you start, open the Jupyter Notebook app in the virtual environment MLA on your computer. After that, open a blank Jupyter notebook and save it as *ch13.ipynb* in the directory /Desktop/mla/ on your computer. Next, we'll create a subdirectory /files/ch13/ to store files in this chapter. Start a new cell in *ch13.ipynb* and execute the following lines of code in it:

```
[1]:  import os

      os.makedirs("files/ch13", exist_ok=True)
```

13.1 CREATE A CONNECT FOUR GAME ENVIRONMENT

Connect Four is a well-known board game. I'll go over the rules to clarify the logic in the upcoming code. In Connect Four, two players take turns dropping discs into one of seven columns, from the top. One player has red discs and the other yellow. The seven columns are on a six-row, vertically suspended grid. When a disc is dropped into a column, it will fall to the lowest available space in that column. Discs cannot move from one column to another. The first player who forms a direct line—either horizontally, vertically, or diagonally—with four of their game pieces wins. If all 42 slots have been filled and nobody has won, the game is tied.

We'll create a Connect Four game environment, using the *turtle* library to draw game boards. We'll create all the attributes and methods that a typical OpenAI Gym environment has.

13.1.1 A Connect Four Game Environment

We'll create a Python class to represent the Connect Four game environment. The class will have various attributes and methods to replicate those in a typical OpenAI Gym game environment.

Specifically, our self-made Connect Four game environment has the following attributes:

- action_space: an attribute representing all actions that can be taken by the agent. The action space has seven values, 1 to 7, representing the seven columns a player can drop discs in.
- observation_space: an attribute including all possible states in the environment. We'll use a NumPy array with seven rows and six columns to represent the 42 cells on a game board.
- state: an attribute indicating which state the agent is currently in. Each of the 42 cells can take values −1 (occupied by the yellow player), 0 (empty), or 1 (occupied by the red player).
- action: an attribute indicating the action taken by an agent. The action is an integer between 1 and 7.

- reward: an attribute indicating the reward to the agent because of the action taken by the agent. The reward is 0 in each step, unless a player has won the game, in which case the winner has a reward of 1 and the loser a reward of -1.
- done: an attribute indicating whether the game has ended. This happens when one player wins or if the game is tied.
- info: an attribute to provide information about the game. We'll set it as an empty string.

Our self-made Connect Four game environment has a few methods as well:

- reset() is a method to set the game environment to the initial (that is, the starting) state. All cells on the board will be empty.
- render() is a method to show the current state of the environment graphically.
- step() is a method that returns the new state, the reward, the value of the *done* variable, and the variable *info* based on the action taken by the agent.
- close() is a method to close the game environment.

We'll create a local module for the Connect Four game and place it inside the local package for this book: the package *utils* that we have created in Chapter 1.

Open the file *conn_env.py* to familiarize yourself with the module. The main Python class is *conn*, which generates an instance of the Connect Four game. The *conn* class has several methods such as *reset()*, *step()*, *render()*, and *close()*.

Next, we'll learn how to access the attributes and methods of the Connect Four game environment.

13.1.2 Verify the Connect Four Game Environment

To get acquainted with the game environment, you'll learn to access different attributes and methods of the self-made Connect Four game environment. First we'll initiate the game environment and show the game board, like so:

```
[2]: from utils.conn_env import conn

env = conn()
env.reset()
env.render()
```

We import the *conn* class from the local package and create an instance of the Connect Four game named *env*. The *reset()* method sets the game board to the initial state. The *render()* method creates a graphical game window. As a result, you should see a separate turtle window, with a Connect Four game board in it.

You can close the game window using the *close()* method, as follows:

```
[3]: env.close()
```

The code cell below prints out the observation space and action space of the game environment.

```
[4]: env=conn()
     # check the action space
     number_actions = env.action_space.n
     print("the number of possible actions is", number_actions)
     # check the shape of the observation space
     print("the shape of the observation space is",\
           env.observation_space.shape)
```

```
the number of possible actions is 7
the shape of the observation space is (7, 6)
```

There are seven possible actions that each agent can take: numbers 1 to 7. The meanings of the actions are as follows: 1 means placing a game piece in column 1; 2 means placing a game piece in column 2, and so on. The state space is a matrix with 7 columns and 6 rows. Each cell can take one of the three values: 0, meaning the cell is empty; −1, meaning the cell is occupied by the yellow player; 1, meaning the cell is occupied by the red player.

13.1.3 Play a Connect Four Game

Next, you'll learn how to manually interact with the Connect Four game. You'll use the keyboard to enter a number between 1 and 7 each step of the game until the game ends. The following lines of code show you how.

```
[5]: import time
     import random

     env=conn()
     state=env.reset()
     env.render()
     print(f"the current state is \n{state.T[::-1]}")
     print('enter a number between 1 and 7')
     while True:
         action=int(input("Player red, what's your move?"))
         time.sleep(1)
         print(f"Player red has chosen action {action}")
         state,reward,done,info=env.step(action)
         print(f"the current state is \n{state.T[::-1]}")
         env.render()
         if done:
             if reward==1:
                 print(f"Player red has won!")
             else:
```

```
                print(f"It's a tie!")
            break
    action=random.choice(env.validinputs)
    time.sleep(1)
    print(f"Player yellow has chosen action {action}")
    state,reward,done,info=env.step(action)
    env.render()
    print(f"the current state is \n{state.T[::-1]}")
    if done:
        if reward==-1:
            print(f"Player yellow has won!")
        else:
            print(f"It's a tie!")
        break
env.close()
```

```
...
Player yellow has chosen action 5
the current state is
[[ 0  0  0  0  0  0  0]
 [ 0  0  0  0  0  0  0]
 [ 0  0  0  0  0  0  0]
 [ 0  0  0  0  0  0  0]
 [ 0  0  0 -1  0  0  0]
 [ 0  1  1  1 -1 -1  0]]
Player red, what's your move?1
Player red has chosen action 1
the current state is
[[ 0  0  0  0  0  0  0]
 [ 0  0  0  0  0  0  0]
 [ 0  0  0  0  0  0  0]
 [ 0  0  0  0  0  0  0]
 [ 0  0  0 -1  0  0  0]
 [ 1  1  1  1 -1 -1  0]]
Player red has won!
```

I am the red player and move first. The opponent makes random moves. The above
output shows an example game in which I have won by connecting four pieces horizontally in columns 1 to 4.

13.2   TRAIN A DEEP NEURAL NETWORK

In this section, you'll use a deep neural network to train intelligent game strategies
for Connect Four. In particular, you'll use a convolutional neural network to train

the model. By treating the game board as a two-dimensional image instead of a one-dimensional vector, you'll greatly improve the intelligence of your game strategies.

You'll learn how to prepare data to train the model; how to interpret the predictions from the model; how to use the prediction to play games; and how to check the efficacy of your deep learning Connect Four game strategies.

13.2.1 The Game Plan

The steps involved in training a game strategy for Connect Four is similar to what we have done in Chapter 12 for Tic Tac Toe. Specifically, here is a summary of what we'll do to train the game strategy:

1. We'll let two computer players play a game with random moves, and record the whole game history. The game history will contain all the game board positions from the very first move to the very last move.
2. We then associate each board position with a game outcome (a win, a tie, or a loss). The game board position is similar to image pixels in our image classification problems earlier in this book, and the game outcome is similar to the image labels. Essentially we conduct a multi-category classification: classifying each board position into a win, a tie, or a loss.
3. We'll simulate 100,000 games. We then feed the board positions and the corresponding game outcomes into a deep neural network to train the model.
4. We can now use the trained model to play games. At each step of the game, we look at all possible next moves, and feed the hypothetical game board into the pre-trained model. The model will tell us the probabilities of a win, a tie, or a loss for the current player.
5. You select the move with the highest probability of the current player winning the game.

13.2.2 Simulate Connect Four Games

You'll learn how to generate data to train the deep neural network. Specifically, you'll generate 100,000 games in which both players use random moves. You'll then record the board positions of all intermediate steps and the eventual outcomes of each board position.

First, let's simulate one Connect Four game. The code in the cell below accomplishes that:

```
[6]: import numpy as np
     from pprint import pprint

     env=conn()
     def one_game():
         history=[]
```

```
        state=env.reset()
        while True:
            action=random.choice(env.validinputs)
            state,reward,done,info=env.step(action)
            history.append(np.array(state).reshape(7,6))
            if done:
                break
        return history, reward
    # Simulate one game and print out results
    history,outcome=one_game()
    pprint(history)
    pprint(outcome)
```

The *one_game()* function generates a full game, with both players choosing random moves. The function returns a list *history*, which contains all the board positions of the game, from the first step to the last step. The function also returns a variable *reward*, which indicates the game outcome: 1 means red won, −1 means yellow won, and 0 means a tie game.

We'll simulate 100,000 games and save the data so that we can later use the data to train our model.

[7]:
```
# Simulate 100000 games
results=[]
for x in range(100000):
    history,outcome=one_game()
    # Associate each board with the game outcome
    for board in history:
        results.append((outcome,board))
```

Each game has multiple board positions and a game outcome. After a game is finished, we retroactively associate the game outcome with each board position in the game. By doing this, we train the model to predict the game outcome based on game board positions early in the game.

[8]:
```
import pickle
# save the simulation data on your computer
with open('files/ch13/games_conn100K.p', 'wb') as fp:
    pickle.dump(results,fp)
# read the data and print out the first 10 observations
with open('files/ch13/games_conn100K.p', 'rb') as fp:
    games=pickle.load(fp)
pprint(games[:10])
```

```
. . .
 (1,
  array([[ 0,  0,  0,  0,  0,  0],
         [ 0,  0,  0,  0,  0,  0],
         [ 1,  0,  0,  0,  0,  0],
         [ 0,  0,  0,  0,  0,  0],
         [ 0,  0,  0,  0,  0,  0],
         [-1,  0,  0,  0,  0,  0],
         [ 0,  0,  0,  0,  0,  0]]))]
```

Each element in the saved file *games_conn100K.p* has two values: the first is the outcome associated with a board position, in the form of −1, 0, or 1; the second value is the board position, in the form of a 7 by 6 NumPy array.

As in Chapter 12 when we train game strategies for Tic Tac Toe, the moves by both players in simulated Connect Four games are random. Since we repeat the game many times, the randomness in all these games is washed out by the law of large numbers. As a result, the outcome data is useful to predict the outcome of a move. Of course, the predictions are not perfect. But if the predictions are better than random guesses, the game strategy will be relatively intelligent, as stated by the opening quote of this chapter by Eric Siegel [21].

Next, we'll feed the data into a deep neural network to train the model.

13.2.3 Train the Connect Four Game Strategy

The following neural network trains the Connect Four deep learning game strategy using the data you just created.

```
[9]: from tensorflow.keras.utils import to_categorical
     from tensorflow.keras.layers import Dense, Conv2D, Flatten
     from tensorflow.keras.models import Sequential

     model=Sequential()
     model.add(Conv2D(filters=128,kernel_size=(4, 4),padding="same",
                      activation="relu", input_shape=(7,6,1)))
     model.add(Flatten())
     model.add(Dense(units=64, activation="relu"))
     model.add(Dense(units=64, activation="relu"))
     model.add(Dense(3, activation='softmax'))
     model.compile(loss='categorical_crossentropy',
                   optimizer='adam',
                   metrics=['accuracy'])
```

We use the Keras API to create a deep neural network to train our game strategy. The network includes a convolutional layer so that we can detect the spatial features on the game board and associate these features (such as four game pieces in a row horizontally, vertically, or diagonally) with game outcomes. Unlike the convolutional layer in Chapter 12, the kernel size we use here is four by four instead of three by three. Similar to Chapter 12, we use softmax as our activation function in the output layer and the loss function is categorical cross entropy.

The outcome data is a variable with three possible values: -1, 0, and 1. We'll convert them into one-hot variables so that the deep neural network can process. We convert the board position into a seven by six matrix instead of a one-dimensional vector before we feed it into the deep neural network.

```
[10]: with open('files/ch13/games_conn100K.p', 'rb') as fp:
          games=pickle.load(fp)

      boards = []
      outcomes = []
      for game in games:
          boards.append(game[1])
          outcomes.append(game[0])

      X = np.array(boards).reshape((-1, 7, 6, 1))
      # one_hot encoder, three outcomes: -1, 0, and 1
      y = to_categorical(outcomes, num_classes=3)

      # Train the model for 100 epochs
      model.fit(X, y, epochs=100, verbose=1)
      model.save('files/ch13/trained_conn.h5')
```

We train the model for 100 epochs. It takes about 24 hours to train the model since we have several million observations. The trained model is saved on your computer. Alternatively, you can download the trained model from the book's GitHub repository. Now that we have a trained model, let's use it to design deep learning Connect Four game strategies.

13.3 USE THE TRAINED MODEL TO PLAY CONNECT FOUR

Next, we'll use the trained model to play a game. The red player will use the best move from the trained model. The yellow player will randomly select a move.

13.3.1 Best Moves

First, we'll define a *best_move_red()* function for the red player. The function takes the game environment as its argument and goes over each possible next move hypothetically. It then uses the trained deep neural network to predict the probability of the red player winning the game. The function returns the move with the highest chance of winning.

Specifically, the function works as follows:

1. Look at the current board.

2. Iterate through all possible next moves; at each iteration, it adds a move to the current board to form a hypothetical board.

3. Use the pretrained model to predict the chance of the red player winning.

4. Choose the move with the highest chance of the red player winning.

The *best_move_red()* function is defined as follows:

```
[11]:  def best_move_red(env):
           # if there is only one valid move, take it
           if len(env.validinputs)==1:
               return env.validinputs[0]
           # set the initial value of bestoutcome
           bestoutcome=-2;
           bestmove=None
           # go through all possible moves hypothetically
           for move in env.validinputs:
               env_copy=deepcopy(env)
               state,reward,done,info=env_copy.step(move)
               state=state.reshape(-1,7,6,1)
               prediction=reload.predict(state,verbose=0)
               # Prob of red wins
               p_win_red=prediction[0][1]
               if p_win_red>bestoutcome:
                   # Update the bestoutcome
                   bestoutcome=p_win_red
                   # Update the best move
                   bestmove=move
           return bestmove
```

Similarly, we define a *best_move_yellow()* function for the second player. The function goes over all possible next moves and hypothetically adds the move to the current board. It uses the trained deep neural network to predict the probability of the yellow player winning the game. The function returns the move with the highest chance of the yellow player winning the game.

```
[12]:  def best_move_yellow(env):
           # if there is only one valid move, take it
           if len(env.validinputs)==1:
               return env.validinputs[0]
           # set the initial value of bestoutcome
           bestoutcome=-2;
           bestmove=None
```

```
        # go through all possible moves hypothetically
    for move in env.validinputs:
        env_copy=deepcopy(env)
        state,reward,done,info=env_copy.step(move)
        state=state.reshape(-1,7,6,1)
        prediction=reload.predict(state,verbose=0)
        # Prob of yellow wins
        p_win_yellow=prediction[0][2]
        if p_win_yellow>bestoutcome:
            # Update the bestoutcome
            bestoutcome=p_win_yellow
            # Update the best move
            bestmove=move
    return bestmove
```

Next, we'll test how often our deep learning game strategy wins against a player who makes random moves.

13.3.2 Test Connect Four Deep Learning Game Strategies

Now let's use the *best_move_red()* and *best_move_yellow()* functions to choose moves for the red and yellow players, respectively. To level the playing field so that no agent has a first-mover's advantage, we simulate 100 games and let the deep learning agent move first in 50 games. In the other 50 games, the random-move agent goes first.

[13]:
```
from tensorflow.keras.models import load_model

reload=load_model('files/ch13/trained_conn.h5')

env=conn()
results=[]
for i in range(100):
    state=env.reset()
    if i%2==0:
        action=random.choice(env.validinputs)
        state, reward, done, info=env.step(action)
    while True:
        if env.turn=="red":
            action=best_move_red(env)
        else:
            action=best_move_yellow(env)
        state, reward, done, info=env.step(action)
        if done:
            # result is 1 if the deep learning agent wins
```

```
        if reward!=0:
            results.append(1)
        else:
            results.append(0)
        break
    action=random.choice(env.validinputs)
    state, reward, done, info=env.step(action)
    if done:
        # result is -1 if the deep learning agent loses
        if reward!=0:
            results.append(-1)
        else:
            results.append(0)
        break
```

We record game outcomes in a list *results*. If the deep learning agent wins, we record an outcome of 1 in the list *results*. If the deep learning agent loses, we record an outcome of −1. If the game is tied, we record an outcome of 0.

Next, we check how many times the deep learning agent has won:

[14]:
```
# count how many times the agent won
wins=results.count(1)
print(f"the deep learning agent has won {wins} games")
# count how many times the agent lost
losses=results.count(-1)
print(f"the deep learning agent has lost {losses} games")
# count how many times the game ties
losses=results.count(0)
print(f"the game has tied {losses} times")
```

```
the deep learning agent has won 100 games
the deep learning agent has lost 0 games
the game has tied 0 times
```

Results show that the deep learning agent has won all 100 games. The indicates that the deep learning game strategy works well!

13.4 ANIMATE DEEP LEARNING IN CONNECT FOUR

In this section, we'll create an animation to show how the agent makes a decision by using the best moves derived from the trained deep neural network. For simplicity, we assume the deep-learning agent moves first and the random-move agent moves second. As an exercise, you can animate the decision-making process if the deep-learning agent moves second instead.

13.4.1 Print Out Probabilities of Winning for Each Next Move

In each stage of the game, we'll first draw the game board on the left of the screen. The red player will look at all possible next moves and use the trained deep neural network to predict the probability of winning with each hypothetical next move. We'll draw the probabilities on the right. Finally, we'll highlight the action with the highest probability of winning. The action is red player's next move. We'll repeat this step by step until the game ends.

This animation will let us look under the hood and understand how deep learning helps us design intelligent game strategies in Connect Four.

In the code cell below, we play a full game and record the game board and the winning probabilities in each step of the game, with the deep learning agent moves first and the random-move agent moves second. To save space, we have defined a *record_conn()* function in the local *utils* package. Download the file *ch13util.py* from the book's GitHub repository and save it in the folder /Desktop/mla/utils/ on your computer. The code cell below imports the *record_conn()* function from the local *utils* package and calls the function to record the game board and winning probabilities, like so:

[15]:
```
from utils.ch13util import record_conn

history=record_conn()
```

The *record_conn()* function returns a list *history* that contains various information in each stage of the game. In particular, the second element in each stage is the probabilities of the red player winning the game with different hypothetical next moves. For illustration purposes, we require the red player to win the game in four steps. If not, we start another game until the red player does win in four steps. The *record_conn()* function also creates several *ps* files on your computer that we'll use later: *conn_step0.ps*, *conn_step1.ps*, and so on.

Figure 13.1 shows the final screenshot of the game. The deep learning agent, which is the red player, wins the game by connecting four red discs horizontally in columns 2 to 5.

Before making the first move, the red player has seven hypothetical next moves: 1 to 7. The trained neural network tells us what's the probability of winning the game with each hypothetical move. We can print out the seven probabilities by using the code below.

[16]:
```
p_wins_step0=history[0][1]
for key, value in p_wins_step0.items():
    print(f"If red chooses {key},\
  the probability of winning is {value:.4f}.")
```

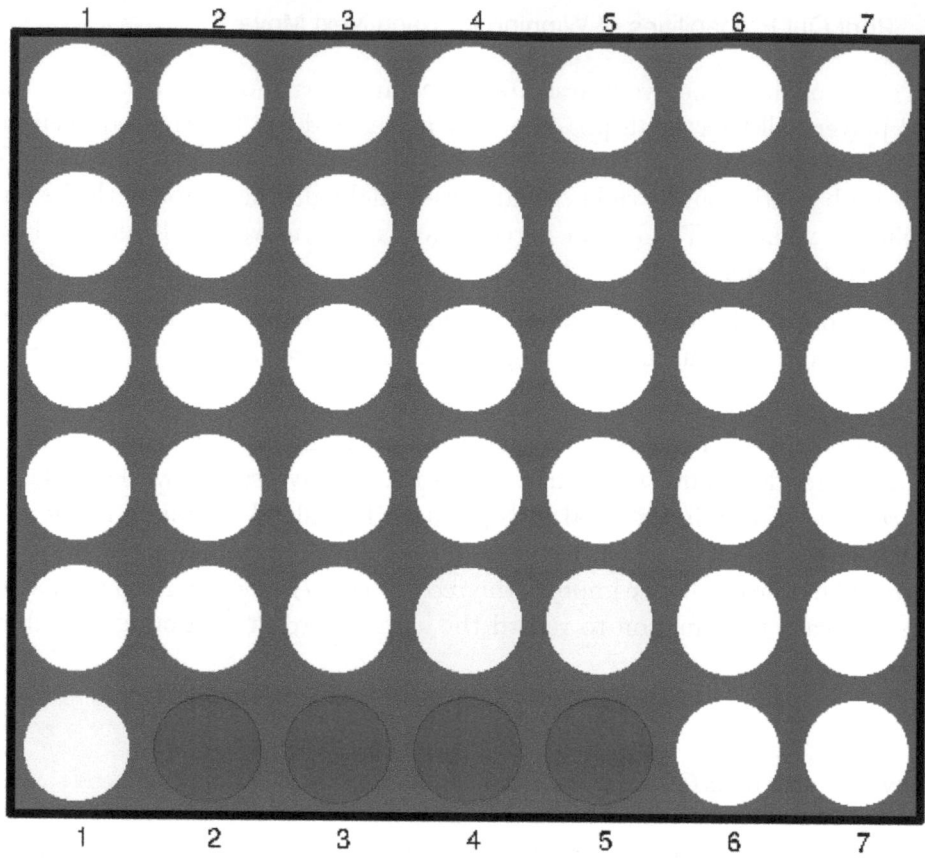

Figure 13.1 Deep learning agent wins a game in Connect Four

```
If red chooses 1, the probability of winning is 0.3281.
If red chooses 2, the probability of winning is 0.3718.
If red chooses 3, the probability of winning is 0.4599.
If red chooses 4, the probability of winning is 0.4793.
If red chooses 5, the probability of winning is 0.4599.
If red chooses 6, the probability of winning is 0.4495.
If red chooses 7, the probability of winning is 0.4096.
```

The above results show that the probability of the red player winning the game is the highest, at 47.93%, if action 4 is taken. That's why the red player chooses Column 4 in the first move.

You can also print out the probability of the red player winning the game in the next rounds, but I'll leave that for you to finish.

Let's save the game history data for later use. Run the code in the following cell:

```
[17]:  # save the game history on your computer
       with open('files/ch13/conn_game_history.p','wb') as fp:
           pickle.dump(history,fp)
```

13.4.2 Animate a Complete Connect Four Game

Next, you'll combine the pictures created in the last subsection into an animation. As a result, you'll see the game board step by step for the whole game.

```
[18]: import imageio
from PIL import Image

frames=[]
for i in range(8):
    im=Image.open(f"files/ch13/conn_step{i}.ps")
    frame=np.asarray(im)
    frames.append(frame)
imageio.mimsave("files/ch13/conn_steps.gif",\
                frames,fps=1)
```

We first use the *PIL* library to open the eight images created in the last subsection. We put the eight images in a list *frames* and use the *imageio* library to convert the images to an animation in *gif* format. If you open the file *conn_steps.gif*, you'll see the game board at each stage of the game.

13.4.3 Animate the Decision-Making Process

Next, we'll animate the decision-making process of the red player in each stage of the game. We'll draw the probabilities of the red player winning the game with each hypothetical next move and highlight the move with the highest probability of winning. We'll animate this process step by step until the game ends.

The *stage_pics()* function in the local *utils* package creates three images in each stage of the game: the game board before the red player makes a move, the probabilities of the red player winning the game with different hypothetical next moves, and the best move for the red player based on the highest probability.

```
[19]: from utils.ch13util import stage_pics

stage_pics()
```

Run the above code cell and twelve images will be saved on your computer. For example, if you open the file *conn_stage6step3.png*, you'll see the probabilities of the red player winning the game with each hypothetical move. In particular, the probability is 100% if the red player chooses Column 2 or Column 6. The highest probability, along with the best action (Column 2 in this case), is highlighted in blue.

Next, we'll combine the pictures into an animation to show the decision-making process of the red player.

[20]:
```
frames=[]

for stage in range(len(history)):
    for step in [1,2,3]:
        file=f"conn_stage{stage*2}step{step}.png"
        im = Image.open("files/ch13/"+file)
        f1=np.asarray(im)
        frames.append(f1)
imageio.mimsave('files/ch13/conn_DL_probs.gif',\
                frames,fps=2)
```

If you open the file *conn_DL_probs.gif*, you'll see the animation illustrating the decision-making process of the deep learning agent based on the predicted probabilities from the trained model.

13.4.4 Combine Board Positions and Decision Making

Next, we'll combine the game board positions and the decision making process of the red player in each stage of the game. On the left of the screen, we'll draw the game board. On the right of the screen, we'll draw the probabilities of the red player winning the game with each hypothetical next move. We'll animate this step by step until the game ends.

At each stage of the game, the *DL_steps()* function in the local *utils* package places the game board on the left and the probabilities of winning on the right and creates a combined image. After that, it creates an animation based on these images.

[21]:
```
from utils.ch13util import DL_steps

frames=DL_steps()
```

The above code cell first imports the *DL_steps()* function from the local *utils* package and then calls the function to create the images and animation. Further, the function returns a list *frames* with all the combined images.

If you open the file *conn_DL_steps.gif*, you'll see an animation with two frames in each step. The left frame shows the board position while the right frame shows the probabilities of the red player winning the game with each hypothetical next move. The best action is then highlighted in blue so that we know what's the best move for the red player.

13.4.5 Create Subplots of Deep Learning

We also create a figure with four subplots to include in the hard copy of the book. Specifically, we focus on the decision making process of the red player when making the four moves. In each move, we'll display the current board position faced by the red player on the left. On the right, we'll display the probability of the red player winning the game with each hypothetical next move. The move with the highest probability of winning is then highlighted.

To do that, we obtain every third image from the list *frames*, like so:

```
22]: frames_subplots=frames[2::3]
```

There are four images in the newly-created list *frames_subplots*. We plot the images in a four by one matrix as follows:

```
23]: from matplotlib import pyplot as plt

plt.figure(figsize=(20,28),dpi=200)
for i in range(4):
    plt.subplot(4,1,i+1)
    plt.imshow(frames_subplots[i])
    plt.axis('off')
plt.subplots_adjust(bottom=0.001,right=0.999,top=0.999,
        left=0.001, hspace=-0.1,wspace=-0.22)
plt.savefig("files/ch13/subplots_conn.png")
```

Figure 13.2 shows the resulting subplots. The top graph shows that the red player faces seven choices at the beginning of the game. Choosing Column 4 has the highest probability of winning for the red player and this explains why the red player's first move is 4. The second graph shows that after the yellow player places a disc in Column 4, the red player has seven choices, and Column 3 leads to the highest probability of winning. The third graph shows that after the yellow player places a disc in Column 1, the red player should choose Column 5, which leads to a 65.91% probability of winning. The bottom graph shows that the red player should choose Column 2 since doing so leads to a 100% probability of winning the game.

13.5 GLOSSARY

- **Connect Four:** A board game in which two players take turns dropping discs into one of seven columns, from the top. One player has red discs and the other yellow. The seven columns are on a six-row, vertically suspended grid. When a disc is dropped into a column, it will fall to the lowest available space in that column. Discs cannot move from one column to another. The first player who forms a direct line—either horizontally, vertically, or diagonally—with four of their game pieces wins. If all 42 slots have been filled and nobody has won, the game is tied.

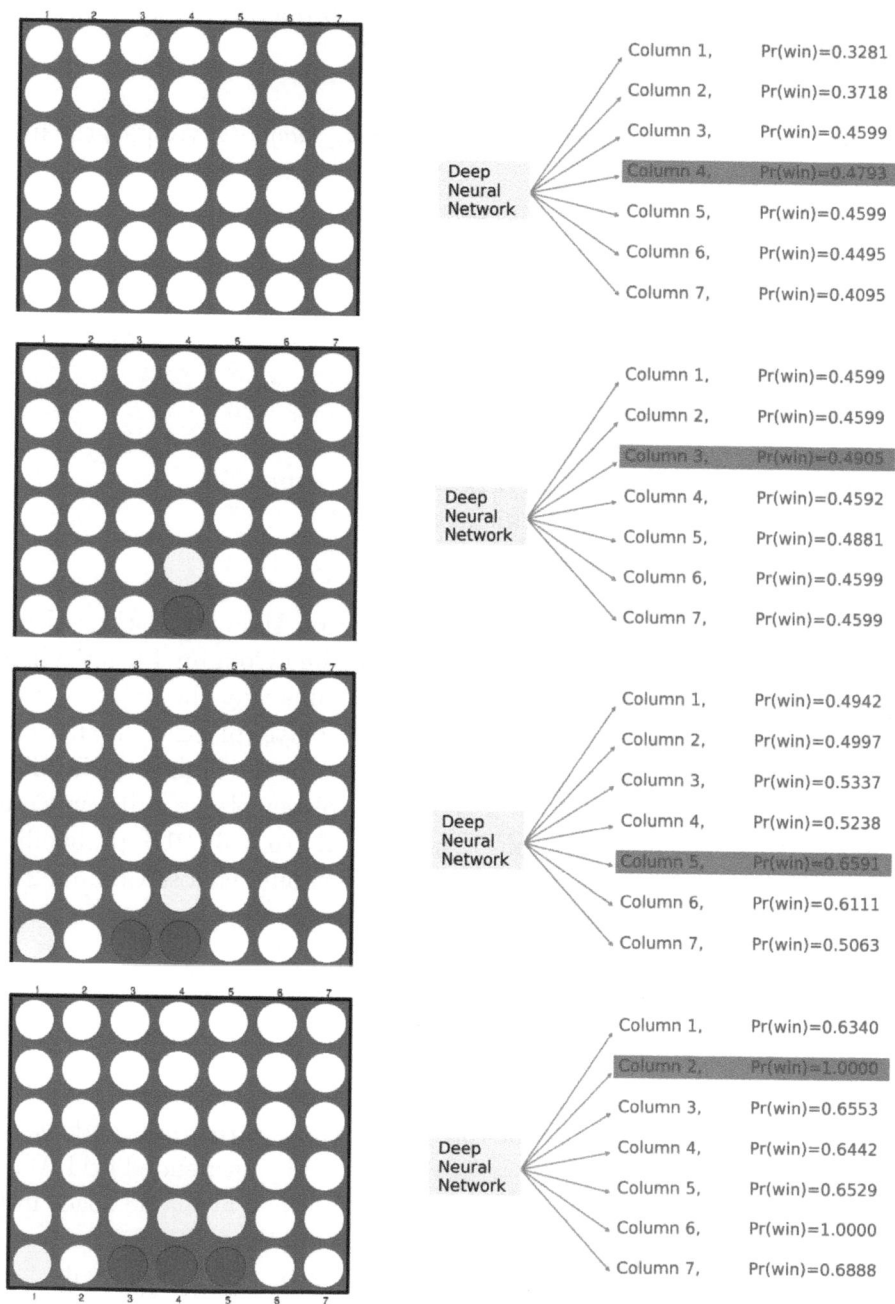

Figure 13.2 Decision-making process of the deep learning agent in Connect Four

13.6 EXERCISES

13.1 Rerun the three code boxes in Section 13.1.2 to familiarize yourself with the Connect Four game environment.

13.2 Modify the first code box in Section 13.1.3 so that the red player chooses random moves and you choose moves for the yellow player using your keyboard.

13.3 In Section 13.4.1, print out the probabilities of the red player winning the game with each hypothetical next move in the second, third, and fourth stage of the game.

V

Reinforcement Learning

## CHAPTER 14

Introduction to Reinforcement Learning

Like a human, our agents learn for themselves to achieve successful strategies that lead to the greatest long-term rewards. This paradigm of learning by trial-and-error, solely from rewards or punishments, is known as reinforcement learning (RL).
–DeepMind, 2016

AS WE DISCUSSED in Chapter 3, there are three different types of machine learning (ML): Supervised learning, unsupervised learning, and reinforcement learning. In supervised learning, we show a model many examples of input-output pairs. The model extracts features from the input data (e.g., images) and associate them with the output (e.g., image labels such as horses, deer, cats, or dogs). We then apply the trained model on new examples and make predictions on what the output should be (is the image a horse or a deer?). The deep neural networks we discussed in Chapters 5 to 12 are examples of supervised learning. In contrast, unsupervised learning models find naturally-occurring patterns from the data by using methods such as clustering, principal component analysis, and data visualization.

In reinforcement learning (RL), an agent operates in an environment through trial and error. The agent learns to achieve the optimal outcome by receiving feedback from the environment in the form of rewards and punishments. The opening quote of this chapter from DeepMind summarizes the idea behind RL [6]. For the rest of the book, we'll discuss various types of reinforcement learning methods, which include tabular Q-learning, deep Q-learning, policy gradients, and double deep Q-learning.

In this chapter, you'll learn how RL works. We'll use the Frozen Lake game in OpenAI Gym to illustrate the concept of dynamic programming and Bellman equation. Your'll learn to train the Q-table by trial and error. Specifically, the agent plays the game many times and adjusts the values in the Q-table based on the rewards: increase the

Q-value if an action leads to a positive reward and decrease the Q-value otherwise. You'll also learn to use the trained Q-table to solve the Frozen Lake game.

Additionally, you'll create an animation to demonstrate how tabular Q-learning works in each step of the Frozen Lake game. In particular, in each state, you'll put the game board on the left and the Q-table on the right. You'll highlight the row corresponding to the state and compare the Q-values under the four actions. You'll then highlight the best action in red. You'll repeat this process until the game ends.

New Skills in This Chapter

- Understanding how reinforcement learning works
- Implementing tabular Q-learning in Frozen Lake
- Creating a game environment for Frozen Lake
- Training a Q-table from scratch
- Using the trained Q-table to win a game

Before you start, open the Jupyter Notebook app in the virtual environment MLA on your computer. After that, open a blank Jupyter notebook and save it as *ch14.ipynb* in the directory /Desktop/mla/ on your computer. Next, we'll create a subdirectory /files/ch14/ to store files in this chapter. Start a new cell in *ch14.ipynb* and execute the following lines of code in it:

[1]:
```
import os

os.makedirs("files/ch14", exist_ok=True)
```

14.1 BASICS OF REINFORCEMENT LEARNING

Reinforcement Learning (RL) is one type of Machine Learning (ML). In a typical RL problem, an agent decides how to choose among a list of actions step by step in an environment to maximize the cumulative payoff.

RL is widely used in many different fields, from control theory, operations research, to statistics. The optimal actions are solved by using a Markov Decision Process (MDP). The agent uses trial and error to interact with the environment to see what rewards from those actions are. The agent then adjusts the decision based on the outcome: rewarding good choices and penalizing bad ones. Hence the name reinforcement learning.

14.1.1 Basic Concepts

Let's first discuss a few basic concepts related to RL: environment, agent, state, action, and reward.

- Environment: the world in which agent(s) live and interact with each other or with nature. More importantly, an environment is where the agent(s) can explore and learn the best strategies. Examples include the Frozen Lake game, the popular Breakout Atari game, or a real-world problem that we need to solve.
- Agent: the player of the game. In most games, there is one player and the opponent is embedded into the environment. But you have seen two-player games such as Tic Tac Toe or Connect Four earlier in this book.
- State: the current situation of the game. The current game board in the Connect Four game, for example, is the current state of the game.
- Action: what the player decides to do given the current game situation.
- Reward: the payoff to the agent from taking a certain action in a given state. Positive values are rewards and negative values penalties.

Next, we discuss the idea behind one type of RL: tabular Q-learning.

14.1.2 The Bellman Equation and Q-Learning

Q-learning is one way to solve the optimization problem in RL. It is a value-based approach. RL problems can also be solved by policy-based approaches such as policy gradients, which we'll discuss later in this book.

In RL, the agent is trying to learn the best strategy to maximize the expected payoff over time. A strategy (also called a policy) maps a certain state to a certain action. A strategy is basically a decision rule that tells the agent what to do in a given situation.

The Q-value, $Q(s, a)$, is the expected cumulative payoff based on the current state s and the action a. It measures how good a strategy is. You can interpret the letter Q as quality. The better the strategy, the higher the payoff to the agent, and the higher the Q-value. The agent is trying to find the best strategy that maximizes the Q-value.

An agent's action in time step t not only affects the reward in this period, but also rewards in future periods, $t+1$, $t+2$, and so on. Therefore, finding the best strategy can be complicated and involves dynamic programming.

In the setting of Q-learning, the Bellman equation is as follows:

$$Q(s, a) = Reward + Discount\_Factor * max\_Q(s', a')$$

where $Q(s, a)$ is the Q value to the agent in the current state s when an action a is taken. *Reward* is the payoff to the agent as a result of the action in the current state. *Discount_factor* is a constant between 0 and 1 that measures how much the agent discounts future rewards as opposed to the current reward. Lastly, $max\_Q(s', a')$ is the maximum future cumulative payoff, assuming optimal strategies will be applied in the future as well.

In order to find out the Q-values, we'll try different actions in each state multiple times. We'll adjust the Q-values based on the outcome: increase the Q-value if the reward is high and decrease the Q-value if the reward is low or even negative. We'll use a simple example, the Frozen Lake game, to demonstrate how Q-learning works.

14.2   USE Q-VALUES TO PLAY THE FROZEN LAKE GAME

You have learned how to play the Frozen Lake game using deep learning in Chapter 10. So I assume you know how the game works. If not, check Chapter 10 for details.

The OpenAI Gym environment is designed for training RL game strategies. In particular, in this chapter, you'll learn how to train a tabular Q-learning game strategy to win the Frozen Lake game.

14.2.1   The Logic Behind Q-Learning

What if you have a Q-table to guide you to successfully play the Frozen Lake game? The Q-table is a 16 by 4 matrix, with the rows representing the 16 states: 0 means the top left corner (that is, the starting position), 3 means the top right corner,..., and 15 means the bottom right corner (i.e., the winning position). The four columns represent the four actions that the agent can take in any state: 0 means going left, 1 going down, 2 going right, and 3 going up.

It turns out we do have such a table. Download the file *Qtable.csv* from the folder /files/ch14/ in the book's GitHub repository. Save it in the folder /Desktop/mla/files/ch14/ on your computer. Open the file and take a look so that you know the values in the 16 by 4 matrix.

With the guidance of the Q-table, reaching the destination (i.e., state 15, the lower right corner) safely is easy for the agent. Here are the steps:

1. The agent starts at state 0.
2. It looks at the above Q-table and consults the row corresponding to state 0 (in this case, the first row), which has four values: 0.531, 0.59, 0.59, and 0.531. The four values are the expected cumulative payoff to the agent from taking the four actions in state 0.
3. The agent chooses the action that leads to the highest Q-value: taking actions 1 or 2 both have a payoff of 0.59, higher than those from taking actions 0 or 3. We have a tie here, so the agent chooses action 1 (that is, going down) in this case (the first in the two tied actions, 1 and 2).
4. Since the agent has chosen going down in state 0, the new state is now the first column in the second row based on the map of the frozen lake. Therefore, the new state is state 4.
5. The agent now chooses the best action in state 4 based on the above Q-table, following the same reasoning as above. This means the agent takes action 1 again.

6. The agent repeats the above steps until the game ends (that is, either the agent falls into a hole or reaches the destination).

Based on the numbers in the Q-table and the logic in the above steps, the agent will take the following actions sequentially: down, down, right, down, right, and right. It will pass the following states: 0, 4, 8, 9, 13, 14, and finally 15.

As you can see, the agent has successfully reached the goal (state 15) without falling into one of the four holes (states 5, 7, 11, and 12).

We'll use a Python program to code in the above steps.

14.2.2   A Q-Table to Win the Frozen Lake Game

First, we load the Q-table into Python by using the *loadtxt*() method in NumPy, as follows:

```
[2]: import numpy as np

     Q=np.loadtxt('files/ch14/Qtable.csv', delimiter=",")
```

The *delimiter* option in the *loadtxt*() method indicates what separates elements in the *CSV* file. The Q-table is loaded up in Python as a 16 by 4 NumPy array.

Next, we define a *play_game*() function to play the Frozen Lake game using the Q-table. In each step, the agent goes to the row corresponding to the state in the Q-table. The action with the largest Q in the row is selected.

```
[3]: def play_game():
         state=env.reset()
         env.render()
         while True:
             action=np.argmax(Q[state,:])
             print(f'current state is {state} and action is {action}')
             state,reward,done,_=env.step(action)
             env.render()
             if done==True:
                 if reward==1:
                     print('Congratulations, you won!')
                 else:
                     print('Sorry, better luck next time.')
                 break
```

We use a *while* loop to iterate through different steps in the game. In each iteration, the agent chooses the action that leads to the highest Q-value in that state. The command *Q[state,:]* obtains the row in the Q-table corresponding to the current state. We then use the *argmax()* method in NumPy to obtain the index value of the largest Q in the row. We can now use the *play_game*() function to play a complete game, like so:

```
[4]: import gym

env=gym.make('FrozenLake-v0',is_slippery=False)
env.reset()
play_game()
env.close()
```

```
SFFF
FHFH
FFFH
HFFG
current state is 0 and action is 1
  (Down)
...
current state is 14 and action is 2
  (Right)
SFFF
FHFH
FFFH
HFFG
Congratulations, you won!
```

The agent has successfully reached state 15, taking the shortest possible path. You can run the above code cell multiple times, and the output will be the same every time, because the agent is using a deterministic game strategy and there is no randomness involved.

You may wonder: where did the numbers in the Q-table come from? That's what we'll discuss next: how to train a Q-table with tabular Q-learning.

14.3 TRAIN THE Q-VALUES

In this section, we'll first discuss what is Q-learning and the logic behind it. We then code in the logic and use a program to generate the Q-values that we have just used in the last section.

14.3.1 What is Q-Learning?

Let's use S to denote the number of possible states and A the number of possible actions. The Q-values form a table of S rows and A columns, and we call it the

Q-table. We need to find out the Q-values in each cell in the table so that the agent can use these values to figure out the optimal strategies in every situation.

Before Q-learning starts, we set all the values in the Q-table to 0. At each iteration, we'll update Q-values as follows:

$$Q(s,a) \Leftarrow learning\_rate * New\_Q(s,a) + (1 - learning\_rate) * Q(s,a)$$

Here the learning rate, which has a value between 0 and 1, determines how fast we update the Q-values. The updated $Q(s,a)$ is a weighted average of the new Q-value and the previous $Q(s,a)$. This is when updating (i.e., learning) happens. The new Q value is calculated as follows:

$$New\ Q(s,a) = Reward + discount\_factor * max\_Q(s',a')$$

The discount factor is a constant between 0 and 1 that measures how much the agent discounts future rewards as opposed to the current reward. Lastly, $max\_Q(s',a')$ is the maximum future cumulative payoff, assuming optimal strategies will be applied in the future as well.

After many rounds of trial and error, the updates in each iteration will be minimal, which means the Q-values converge to the equilibrium (i.e., the steady-state) values.

If you look at the above equations, when

$$Q(s,a) = Reward + discount\_factor * max\_Q(s',a'),$$

there is no update in the Q-table, and we have

$$New\_Q(s,a) = Q(s,a).$$

And those are the equilibrium Q-values we are looking for.

14.3.2   Let the Learning Begin

We'll write a Python program and let the agent randomly select moves to play the game for many episodes. Unavoidably, there will be many mistakes along the way. But we'll assign a low reward if the agent fails so that it assigns a low Q-value to the actions taken in the states along the failing path. On the other hand, if the agent makes the right choices and successfully reaches the destination, we'll assign a high reward to the actions that lead to this outcome so that the agent will choose these actions in the future. It's through such repeated rewards and punishments that the agent learns the correct Q-values.

The Credit Assignment Problem in RL

In reinforcement learning, agents learn the best actions through the feedback from rewards and punishments. However, rewards and punishments are sparse and delayed and the agent needs to figure out how to assign proper credits to a sequence of actions that lead to a good or a bad outcome. The discounted rewards are the solution. For example, in the above game, the sequence of moves are the following: 1 (down), 1 (down), 2 (right), 1 (down), 2 (right), and 2 (right). After these six moves, the agent has reached the destination and won the game. The rewards for the six steps made by the agent are 0, 0, 0, 0, 0, and 1, respectively. However, the sixth step alone didn't win the game, so we should give credits to the first five moves as well by discounting rewards. Assuming the discount rate is 0.9, the discounted rewards to the six steps made by agent are 0.59, 0.66, 0.73, 0.81, 0.9, and 1, respectively.

We define an *update_Q()* function to update the Q-table based on the moves made by the agent and the rewards, as follows:

```
[5]: def update_Q(episode):
         # The initial state is the starting position (state 0)
         state=env.reset()
         # The cutoff value for exploration
         cutoff=min_exp+(max_exp-min_exp)*episode/max_episode
         # Play a game
         for _ in range(max_steps):
             # Exploitation
             if np.random.uniform(0,1,1)>cutoff:
                 action=np.argmax(Q[state, :])
             # Exploration
             else:
                 action=env.action_space.sample()
             # Use the selected action to make the move
             new_state,reward,done,_=env.step(action)
             # Update Q values
             if done==True:
                 Q[state,action]=reward
                 break
             else:
                 Q[state,action]=lr*(reward+gamma*np.max(\
                     Q[new_state,:]))+(1-lr)*Q[state,action]
                 state=new_state
```

The *update_Q()* function lets the agent play a complete game. After each step, the agent updates the Q-table based on actions taken and the rewards: if an action leads to a high reward, the agent increases the Q-value associated with the action; if an action leads to a punishment, the agent decreases the corresponding Q-value. The agent balances exploitation versus exploration when choosing an action. With exploitation, the agent chooses the action based on the values in the current Q-table. With exploration, the agent randomly selects an action to explore different actions in case there is a better strategy than what's recommended by the current Q-table.

Exploitation versus Exploration in RL

An important hyper-parameter in the process of training a Q-table is the exploration rate. Exploration means that the agent randomly selects an action. This is important for training the Q-values because without it, the Q-values may get stuck in the wrong equilibrium. Exploration gives the agent the chance to explore new strategies and see if they lead to higher Q-values. Exploitation is the opposite of exploration: the agent chooses the action based on the values in the current Q-table. This increases the chance that a Q-table converges.

We set the learning rate to 0.6 and the discount factor to 0.9. We allow a maximum of 50 steps in each game and train the Q-table for 10,000 episodes, like so:

```
[6]: lr=0.6
gamma=0.9
max_exp=0.7
min_exp=0.3
max_steps=50
max_episode=10000

# Set Q-values to zeros at first
Q=np.zeros((16, 4))
# Train the Q-table for 10,000 episodes
env.reset()
for episode in range(max_episode):
    update_Q(episode)
# Print out and save the trained Q-table
Q=np.round(Q,4)
print(Q)
np.savetxt("files/ch14/trained_Q.csv",Q,delimiter=',')
```

```
[[0.5314 0.5905 0.5905 0.5314]
 [0.5314 0.     0.6561 0.5905]
 [0.5905 0.729  0.5905 0.6561]
 [0.6561 0.     0.5905 0.5905]
 [0.5905 0.6561 0.     0.5314]
 [0.     0.     0.     0.    ]]
```

```
[0.     0.81   0.     0.6561]
[0.     0.     0.     0.    ]
[0.6561 0.     0.729  0.5905]
[0.6561 0.81   0.81   0.    ]
[0.729  0.9    0.     0.729 ]
[0.     0.     0.     0.    ]
[0.     0.     0.     0.    ]
[0.     0.81   0.9    0.729 ]
[0.81   0.9    1.     0.81  ]
[0.     0.     0.     0.    ]]
```

When training the Q-table, we set the cutoff value for exploitation to $min\_exp = 0.3$ in the first episode of training. If a randomly distributed variable between 0 and 1 is greater than this cutoff value, the agent uses exploration; otherwise, the agent uses exploitation. This means with 30% probability, the agent chooses actions based on values in the Q-table; with the complementary probability of 70%, the agent randomly selects moves to explore different strategies. The cutoff value then gradually increases as training progresses. At the last episode of training, the cutoff value increases to $max\_exp = 0.7$.

After 10,000 episodes of training, we print out the trained Q-table. You'll notice that the Q-values are exactly the same as those in the file *Qtable.csv* that we used earlier. This answers our earlier question of where the Q-values came from. You can play the Frozen Lake game using the newly trained Q-table *trained_Q.csv*. You should get exactly the same outcome as earlier when you used the file *Qtable.csv*. I'll leave that as an exercise for you.

14.4 Q-LEARNING IN A SELF-MADE GAME ENVIRONMENT

Since there is no graphical window in the Frozen Lake game in OpenAI Gym, we'll create our own Frozen Lake game environment and add a graphical game window using the *turtle* library. After that, we test the trained Q-table from the last section and see if works in the self-made game environment.

14.4.1 A Self-Made Frozen Lake Game Environment

We represent a self-made Frozen Lake game environment using a Python class. Download the file *frozenlake_env.py* from the book's GitHub repository and save it in the folder /Desktop/mla/utils/ on your computer.

Next, we'll check the attributes and methods of the self-made game environment and make sure it has all the attributes and methods that are provided by OpenAI Gym. The code cell below imports the game environment and initializes the starting game state:

```
[7]:   from utils.frozenlake_env import Frozen

       env=Frozen()
       env.reset()
       env.render()
```

You should see a separate *turtle* window with 16 cells in it. There is a red dot in the top left corner, representing the starting position of the agent. Four gray circles represent holes in four cells. The right bottom cell is marked as *goal*. The game window is a graphical representation of the starting game state in Frozen Lake.

If you want to close the game window, use the *close()* method, like so:

```
[8]:   env.close()
```

Next, we'll check the attributes of the environment such as the observation space and action space.

```
[9]:   env=Frozen()
       # check the action space
       number_actions=env.action_space.n
       print("the number of possible actions are",number_actions)
       # check the shape of the observation space
       print("the shape of the observation space is",\
             env.observation_space.shape)
```

```
the number of possible actions are 4
the shape of the observation space is (16,)
```

The meanings of the four actions are exactly the same as those in OpenAI Gym: 0 means going left, 1 going down, 2 going right, and 3 going up. The 16 states are marked as 0 to 15.

14.4.2   Use the Q-Table in the Self-Made Game Environment

Next, we test our trained Q-table in the self-made Frozen Lake game environment and see if the agent can win the game.

```
[10]:  import time
       # Use the Q-table you just trained
       Q=np.loadtxt('files/ch14/trained_Q.csv',delimiter=",")
       def use_trained_Q():
           state=env.reset()
           env.render()
           while True:
               # Show the game board for 1 second
               time.sleep(1)
```

```
      # Choose the action with the highest Q
      action=np.argmax(Q[state,:])
      print(f'the state is {state}; the action is {action}')
      state, reward, done, _ = env.step(action)
      env.render()
      if done==True:
          if reward ==1:
              print('Congratulations, you won!')
          else:
              print('Sorry, better luck next time.')
          break

use_trained_Q()
time.sleep(5)
env.close()
```

```
the state is 0; the action is 1
the state is 4; the action is 1
the state is 8; the action is 2
the state is 9; the action is 1
the state is 13; the action is 2
the state is 14; the action is 2
Congratulations, you won!
```

The trained Q-table has guided the agent to choose the following actions: 1, 1, 2, 1, 2, 2 (down, down, right, down, right, right) and successfully reached the destination. This is one of the shortest paths that one can take to win the game. You can also see the game window changing in each step with the location of the agent. At the end of the game, the graphical rendering shows that the agent has successfully reached the goal, the bottom right corner, without falling into one of the holes.

Figure 14.1 shows the final game window when the agent has reached the bottom right corner. This demonstrates that our trained Q-table works in the self-made Frozen Lake game environment.

14.5 ANIMATE THE Q-LEARNING PROCESS

In this section, we'll create an animation to show how the agent makes a decision by consulting the Q-table at each step in the Frozen Lake game.

14.5.1 Highlight Values and Actions in the Q-Table

We'll first draw a Q-table at each step of the game to highlight in blue the row corresponding to the current state. We'll then highlight in red the action with the

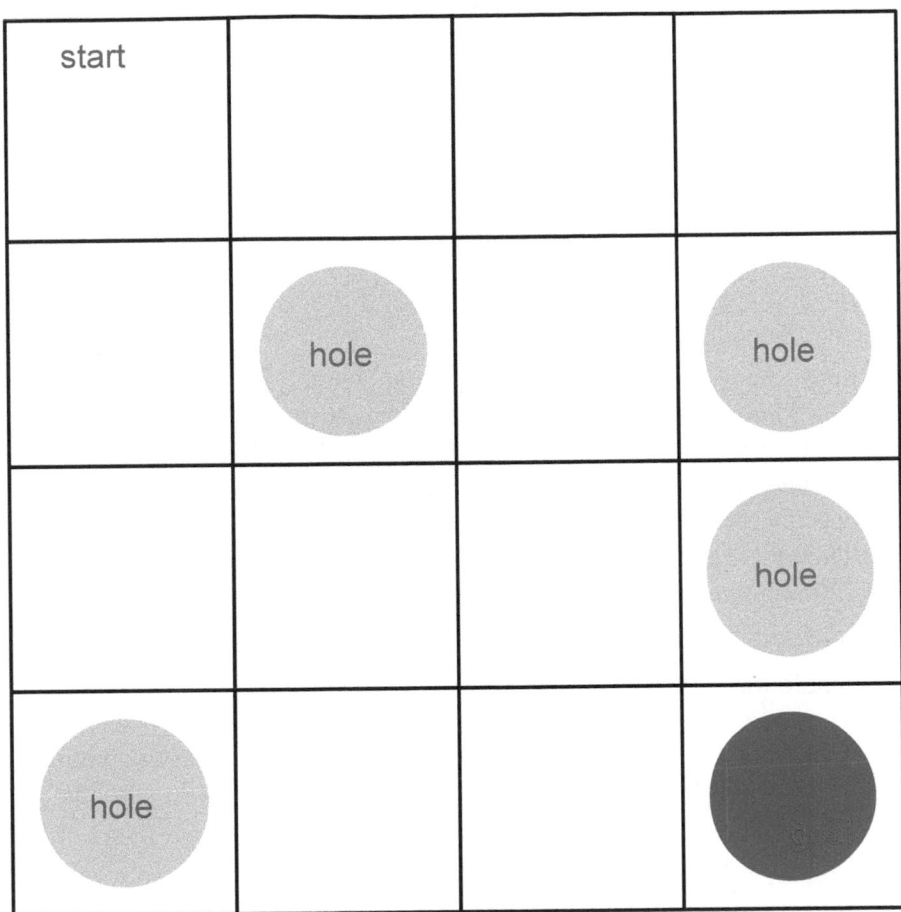

Figure 14.1 Solving the Frozen Lake game with tabular Q-learning

highest Q-value in that row, and use it as the best action. We'll repeat this step by step until the game ends.

We create a list *states* to contain all the states that the agent has visited along the winning path. We also create a list *actions* to contain all actions taken by the agent, as follows:

```
states=[0,4,8,9,13,14]
actions=[1,1,2,1,2,2]
```

In each state, we draw three pictures: the first one is the Q-table without any highlights; the second one is the Q-table with the row corresponding to the current state highlighted in blue; the third picture is the Q-table with the action corresponding to the highest Q-value highlighted in red.

To save space, we define a *Q_steps()* function in the local package. Download the file *ch14util.py* from the book's GitHub repository and place it in the folder /Desktop/mla/utils/ on your computer. The function iterates through the six steps along the path of the agent's successful route. In each step, it first draws the Q-table. It then looks up the game state in the list *states* and highlights the corresponding row in the Q-table. Finally, it looks up the best action in the list *actions* and highlights it in red. Three graphs are saved on your computer in each step. The code cell below imports the *Q_steps()* function from the local package and calls the function to generate a total of 18 graphs on your computer, like so:

[11]:
```
from utils.ch14util import Q_steps

Q_steps()
```

After running the above code cell, if you open, for example, the picture *plt_Qs_stepc2.png*, you'll see that the agent is in state 8. Therefore, the row corresponding to state 8 in the Q-table is highlighted in light blue. The agent compares the four Q-values under the four actions. The values are 0.656, 0.000, 0.729, 0.590, respectively. Obviously, the Q-value under action=2 is the largest among the four numbers. Therefore, the agent chooses action 2 in this state. You can see that the number 0.729 is highlighted in red in the picture.

14.5.2   Animate the Use of the Q-Table

Next, you'll combine the pictures created in the last subsection into an animation. As a result, you'll see how the agent takes the best action step by step with the guidance of the Q-table.

[12]:
```
from PIL import Image
import imageio

frames=[]
for i in range(6):
    for letter in ["a", "b", "c"]:
        im=Image.open(f"files/ch14/plt_Qs_step{letter}{i}.png")
        f1=np.asarray(im)
        frames.append(f1)
imageio.mimsave('files/ch14/plt_Qs_steps.gif',frames,fps=2)
```

We use the *PIL* library to open the 18 images we just created and put them in a list *frames*. We then use the *imageio* library to combine them into an animation in *gif* format. If you open the file *plt_Qs_steps.gif*, you'll see an animation of the decision-making process of the agent with the help of the Q-table. In each state, you see three frames: the Q-table, the Q-table with the row corresponding to the current state highlighted in blue, and Q-table with the best action highlighted in red.

14.5.3 Game Board Positions and Best Actions

We'll add the game board positions in each step to the above animation, and put them side by side with the Q-table. This way, we can visualize not only the use of the Q-table, but also the movement of the agent. The animation improves our understanding of how the Q-table guides the agent from one state to the next.

First, we'll record all the game positions. We define a *record_boards()* function, which is placed in the file *ch14util.py* you just downloaded. The function records the game board in each step of the game and saves them as *ps* files on your computer. The code cell below imports the function from the local package and calls it to generate the files.

```
[13]: from utils.ch14util import record_boards

      record_boards()
```

Next, we'll convert the game board position files from the *ps* format to the *png* format and combine them with the Q-table images. Specifically, we'll put the game board on the left and the Q-table on the right to form one frame. We'll repeat the frame three times per step. Finally, we'll combine them into an animation. All these are done in the *board_Q_table()* function in the file *ch14util.py* you just downloaded. The following cell imports the function and calls it to generate the animation:

```
[14]: from utils.ch14util import board_Q_table

      frames=board_Q_table()
```

The *board_Q_table()* function generates the animation. It also returns a list *frames* that contains all the images used to create the animation. If you open the file *frozen_Q_steps.gif*, you'll see an animation with both the game board and the Q-table in each frame. The game board shows the position of the agent in a red dot, while the Q-table highlights the row corresponding to the current state and the best action in that state.

14.5.4 Subplots of the Q-Learning Process

The agent has consulted the Q-table six times and taken six different actions to win the game. To illustrate how the Q-table has guided the agent step by step, we create two figures, each with three subplots in it. The first figure shows the decision-making process of the agent in the first three steps.

To do that, we obtain every third image from the list *frames* that was generated by the *board_Q_table()* function earlier, like so:

[15]:
```
subplot_frames=frames[2::3]
```

We take the first three images from the list *frames* and plot them into a picture in the format of a three by one matrix, as follows:

[16]:
```
from matplotlib import pyplot as plt

plt.figure(figsize=(20,30),dpi=200)
for i in range(3):
    plt.subplot(3,1,i+1)
    plt.imshow(subplot_frames[i])
    plt.axis('off')
plt.subplots_adjust(bottom=0.001,right=0.999,top=0.999,
        left=0.001, hspace=-0.01,wspace=-0.22)
plt.savefig("files/ch14/subplots_frozen1.png")
```

Figure 14.2 has three subplots. The top graph shows that the agent at the starting position (state 0). The first row (i.e., state 0) of the Q-table on the right is highlighted in blue. The action 1 (going down) in the first row has the greatest value among the four Q-values in the row. Action 1 is therefore highlighted in red and this explains why the agent's first move is to go down. The second and the third graphs work similarly and they explain why the agent chooses actions 1 and 2 subsequently.

We also take the last three images from the list *frames* and plot them into a picture, as follows:

[17]:
```
plt.figure(figsize=(20,30),dpi=200)
for i in range(3):
    plt.subplot(3,1,i+1)
    plt.imshow(subplot_frames[i+3])
    plt.axis('off')
plt.subplots_adjust(bottom=0.001,right=0.999,top=0.999,
        left=0.001, hspace=-0.01,wspace=-0.22)
plt.savefig("files/ch14/subplots_frozen2.png")
```

The three subplots in Figure 14.3 explain why the agent takes actions 1, 2, and 2 in the last three steps, respectively. For example, the top graph shows that the agent is in state 9 and the tenth row of the Q-table on the right is highlighted in blue. Action 1 (going down) has the greatest value, 0.810, among the four Q-values in the row. Action 1 is therefore highlighted in red and this explains why the agent's fourth move is to go down.

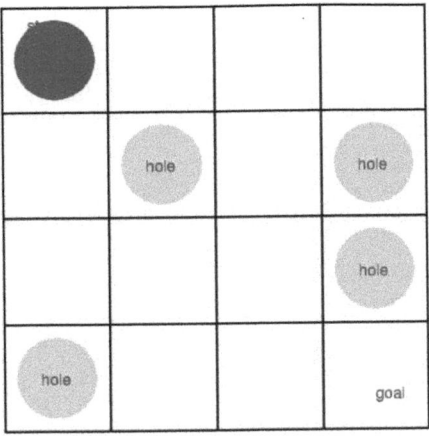

action=	0 left	1 down	2 right	3 up
state 0	0.531	0.591	0.591	0.531
state 1	0.531	0.000	0.656	0.591
state 2	0.591	0.729	0.591	0.656
state 3	0.656	0.000	0.591	0.591
state 4	0.591	0.656	0.000	0.531
state 5	0.000	0.000	0.000	0.000
state 6	0.000	0.810	0.000	0.656
state 7	0.000	0.000	0.000	0.000
state 8	0.656	0.000	0.729	0.591
state 9	0.656	0.810	0.810	0.000
state 10	0.729	0.900	0.000	0.729
state 11	0.000	0.000	0.000	0.000
state 12	0.000	0.000	0.000	0.000
state 13	0.000	0.810	0.900	0.729
state 14	0.810	0.900	1.000	0.810
state 15	0.000	0.000	0.000	0.000

action=	0 left	1 down	2 right	3 up
state 0	0.531	0.591	0.591	0.531
state 1	0.531	0.000	0.656	0.591
state 2	0.591	0.729	0.591	0.656
state 3	0.656	0.000	0.591	0.591
state 4	0.591	0.656	0.000	0.531
state 5	0.000	0.000	0.000	0.000
state 6	0.000	0.810	0.000	0.656
state 7	0.000	0.000	0.000	0.000
state 8	0.656	0.000	0.729	0.591
state 9	0.656	0.810	0.810	0.000
state 10	0.729	0.900	0.000	0.729
state 11	0.000	0.000	0.000	0.000
state 12	0.000	0.000	0.000	0.000
state 13	0.000	0.810	0.900	0.729
state 14	0.810	0.900	1.000	0.810
state 15	0.000	0.000	0.000	0.000

action=	0 left	1 down	2 right	3 up
state 0	0.531	0.591	0.591	0.531
state 1	0.531	0.000	0.656	0.591
state 2	0.591	0.729	0.591	0.656
state 3	0.656	0.000	0.591	0.591
state 4	0.591	0.656	0.000	0.531
state 5	0.000	0.000	0.000	0.000
state 6	0.000	0.810	0.000	0.656
state 7	0.000	0.000	0.000	0.000
state 8	0.656	0.000	0.729	0.591
state 9	0.656	0.810	0.810	0.000
state 10	0.729	0.900	0.000	0.729
state 11	0.000	0.000	0.000	0.000
state 12	0.000	0.000	0.000	0.000
state 13	0.000	0.810	0.900	0.729
state 14	0.810	0.900	1.000	0.810
state 15	0.000	0.000	0.000	0.000

Figure 14.2   Q-learning in the Frozen Lake game, part I

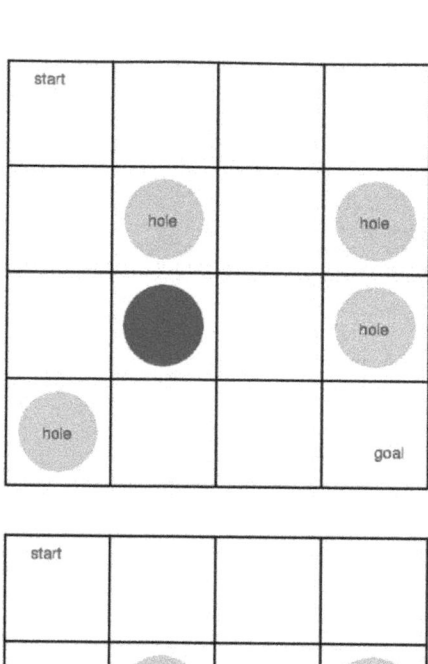

action=	0 left	1 down	2 right	3 up
state 0	0.531	0.591	0.591	0.531
state 1	0.531	0.000	0.656	0.591
state 2	0.591	0.729	0.591	0.656
state 3	0.656	0.000	0.591	0.591
state 4	0.591	0.656	0.000	0.531
state 5	0.000	0.000	0.000	0.000
state 6	0.000	0.810	0.000	0.656
state 7	0.000	0.000	0.000	0.000
state 8	0.656	0.000	0.729	0.591
state 9	0.656	0.810	0.810	0.000
state 10	0.729	0.900	0.000	0.729
state 11	0.000	0.000	0.000	0.000
state 12	0.000	0.000	0.000	0.000
state 13	0.000	0.810	0.900	0.729
state 14	0.810	0.900	1.000	0.810
state 15	0.000	0.000	0.000	0.000

action=	0 left	1 down	2 right	3 up
state 0	0.531	0.591	0.591	0.531
state 1	0.531	0.000	0.656	0.591
state 2	0.591	0.729	0.591	0.656
state 3	0.656	0.000	0.591	0.591
state 4	0.591	0.656	0.000	0.531
state 5	0.000	0.000	0.000	0.000
state 6	0.000	0.810	0.000	0.656
state 7	0.000	0.000	0.000	0.000
state 8	0.656	0.000	0.729	0.591
state 9	0.656	0.810	0.810	0.000
state 10	0.729	0.900	0.000	0.729
state 11	0.000	0.000	0.000	0.000
state 12	0.000	0.000	0.000	0.000
state 13	0.000	0.810	0.900	0.729
state 14	0.810	0.900	1.000	0.810
state 15	0.000	0.000	0.000	0.000

action=	0 left	1 down	2 right	3 up
state 0	0.531	0.591	0.591	0.531
state 1	0.531	0.000	0.656	0.591
state 2	0.591	0.729	0.591	0.656
state 3	0.656	0.000	0.591	0.591
state 4	0.591	0.656	0.000	0.531
state 5	0.000	0.000	0.000	0.000
state 6	0.000	0.810	0.000	0.656
state 7	0.000	0.000	0.000	0.000
state 8	0.656	0.000	0.729	0.591
state 9	0.656	0.810	0.810	0.000
state 10	0.729	0.900	0.000	0.729
state 11	0.000	0.000	0.000	0.000
state 12	0.000	0.000	0.000	0.000
state 13	0.000	0.810	0.900	0.729
state 14	0.810	0.900	1.000	0.810
state 15	0.000	0.000	0.000	0.000

Figure 14.3   Q-learning in the Frozen Lake game, part II

14.6 GLOSSARY

- **Dynamic Programming:** A method to optimize the cumulative payoff by choosing a sequence of actions through recursion.
- **Exploitation:** In RL, exploitation is when the agent selects a move based on Q-values in the current Q-table. It's the opposite of exploration. It's necessary in Q-learning to make the Q-table converge.
- **Exploration:** In RL, exploration is when the agent randomly selects a move to explore new strategies and see if they lead to higher Q values. It's the opposite of exploitation. It's necessary in Q-learning to make sure that the Q-values don't get stuck in the wrong equilibrium.
- **Q-Learning:** A value-based reinforcement learning algorithm. The agent learns the value of an action a in a state s, $Q(s, a)$, through trial and error.

14.7 EXERCISES

14.1 Modify the code cell(s) in Section 14.2.2 to use the file *trained_Q.csv* to play the Frozen Lake game.

14.2 Modify the code cell(s) in Section 14.3.2 so that the learning rate is 0.7 and the discount factor is 0.95. Train the Q-table and save it as *new_trained_Q.csv* on your computer.

14.3 Follow the previous question and modify code cell(s) in Section 14.4.2 to use the Q-table *new_trained_Q.csv* to play the Frozen Lake game. See if the outcome is the same as before.

## CHAPTER 15

Q-Learning with Continuous States

All exact science is dominated by the idea of approximation.
–Bertrand Russell

THE FROZEN LAKE game we solved with Q-learning in the last chapter has 16 different states and four possible actions in each state. Therefore, it is easy to create a Q-table with $16 \times 4 = 64$ values. However, in many real-world problems, the number of state-action combinations is either infinite or very large. In such cases, it is infeasible to create and train a Q-table.

To solve this problem, we can use a finite number of discrete states to approximate for the infinite number of states. The finite number of states cannot be too small, or else the true state cannot be accurately represented and the Q-learning fails. The finite number of states cannot be too large either, or else it's prohibitively costly or time-consuming to train the Q-values.

The Mountain Car game in OpenAI Gym is such an example. The game state is represented by two variables: the position of the car and the speed of the car. Both variables are continuous and can take an infinite number of values. You'll learn how to create a finite state space in Q-learning when the number of states is infinite. Specifically, you'll use 190 discrete values to represent the position of the car and 150 discrete values to represent the car speed. As a result, there are a total of $190 \times 150 = 28500$ different discrete state-action combinations. After 100,000 rounds of training, the trained Q-table wins the game 100% of the time.

At the end of this chapter, you'll create an animation to compare the Mountain Car game before and after Q-learning. In each frame in the animation, you can see the car position without Q-learning on the left and the car position with Q-learning on the right. With Q-learning, the agent drives the car to the mountain top in every episode. The animation shows Q-learning at work.

DOI: 10.1201/b23383-15

New Skills in This Chapter

- Discretizing a continuous state
- Implementing tabular Q-learning in Mountain Car
- Training a Q-table from scratch for Mountain Car
- Using the trained Q-table to win the Mountain Car game
- Increasing the resolution of an image or animation

Before you start, open the Jupyter Notebook app in the virtual environment MLA on your computer. After that, open a blank Jupyter notebook and save it as *ch15.ipynb* in the directory /Desktop/mla/ on your computer. Next, we'll create a subdirectory /files/ch15/ to store files in this chapter. Start a new cell in *ch15.ipynb* and execute the following lines of code in it:

[1]:
```
import os

os.makedirs("files/ch15", exist_ok=True)
```

15.1 THE MOUNTAIN CAR GAME ENVIRONMENT

You'll first learn how to control the Mountain Car game in the OpenAI Gym environment. You'll learn the parameter values, how to interact with the environment so that later you can train the model to learn the Q-table for the game.

15.1.1 The Mountain Car Game

If you go to the Mountain Car game site provided by OpenAI Gym via the link bit.ly/3J6JScj, you'll see the description for the game environment.

The agent tries to drive a car up to the mountain top on the right. There is a flag at the mountain top in the game window and the agent wins the game if the car reaches the mountain top within 200 attempts. The car starts at the bottom of the valley, and the agent needs to accelerate the car in either direction. The goal is to swing the car back and forth to build up enough momentum to reach the goal.

We'll write a Python program to access the Mountain Car game environment and learn its features.

[2]:
```
import gym
env = gym.make('MountainCar-v0')

# check the action space
number_actions = env.action_space.n
print("the number of possible actions are", number_actions)
```

```
# sample the action space ten times
print("the following are ten sample actions")
for i in range(10):
    print(env.action_space.sample())
# check the shape of the observation space
print("the shape of the observation space is",\
  env.observation_space.shape)
```

```
the number of possible actions are 3
the following are ten sample actions
0
1
2
2
2
0
0
2
2
0
the shape of the observation space is (2,)
```

There are three possible actions in this game: 0, 1, and 2, with the following meanings:

- 0: moving the car to the left
- 1: no movement
- 2: moving the car to the right

There are two state variables:

- the position of the car, which is a continuous variable with values between −1.2 and 0.6;
- the speed of the car, which is a continuous variable with values from −0.7 to 0.7. A negative value means the car is moving to the left, while a positive value means the car is moving to the right.

To win the game, the agent needs to reach the top of the mountain within 200 attempts: that is, the position of the car needs to be greater or equal to 0.5.

In the program in the code cell below, the agent tries to reach the mountain top in 200 attempts, by randomly selecting actions. The graphical rendering will show you the game windows.

```
[3]: import time

obs = env.reset()
for i in range(200):
    action = env.action_space.sample()
```

```
        obs, reward, done, info = env.step(action)
        env.render()
time.sleep(5)
env.close()
```

This is a difficult game. With random actions, the car stays at the bottom of the valley without much movement, let alone reaching the mountain top.

Next, you'll print out the state variables of the game, and learn how to convert them into discrete numbers to build a Q-table.

15.1.2 Convert a Continuous State into Discrete Values

Let's first have a look at the values of the state variables. The following code cell takes a random action and prints out the values of the state variables.

```
[4]: obs = env.reset()
     # print out the state
     print(obs)
     action = env.action_space.sample()
     # print the new state
     obs, reward, done, info = env.step(action)
     print(obs)
```

```
[-0.41920721  0.          ]
[-0.41997741 -0.0007702 ]
```

At the start of the game, the state variables are approximately -0.419 and 0, respectively: the position of the car is -0.419, and the speed of the car is 0. After a random action is taken, the state variables are approximately -0.420 and -0.0008, respectively: the position of the car is about the same and the car is moving slowly to the left.

Next, we define a variable *state*, which has discrete values. We multiply the first element in the observation, the car position, by 100, and take the integer value. The value is roughly between -120 and 60. We add 125 to it so that it becomes positive and can be used as an index value in the Q-table.

We then multiply the second element in the observation, the car speed, by 1000, and take the integer value as well. We add 75 to it so that it becomes positive and can be used as an index value in the Q-table as well.

The code cell below prints out ten examples of the variable *state*.

```
[5]: def obs_to_state(obs):
         state = [int(obs[0]*100)+125, int(obs[1]*1000)+75]
         return state
```

```
for i in range(10):
    action = env.action_space.sample()
    obs, reward, done, info = env.step(action)
    state = obs_to_state(obs)
    print(state)
```

```
[79, 70]
[78, 69]
...
[72, 67]
```

The function *obs_to_state()* converts the continuous state variables into discrete ones. The variable *state*, which is a list, now has two integers in it. The variable *state* can take roughly a maximum of $180 \times 140 = 25200$ different values. We create a Q-table with dimensions 190 by 150 by 3. The first dimension of the Q-table corresponds to the 180 or so discrete car positions; the second dimension corresponds to the 140 or so discrete car speeds; the third dimension corresponds to the three possible actions: 0, 1, and 2. We use 190 and 150 instead of 180 and 140 to have some margin of safety to avoid possible index errors.

15.1.3   The Reward Structure of the Game

Next, we'll play a game until it's finished and print out all the rewards, as well as the variables *done* and *info*.

```
[6]:  obs = env.reset()
      episode = 0
      while True:
          episode += 1
          action = env.action_space.sample()
          obs, reward, done, info = env.step(action)
          state = obs_to_state(obs)
          print(episode, state, reward, done, info)
          env.render()
          # play till a full episode is finished
          if done:
              break
      time.sleep(5)
      env.close()
```

```
1 [70, 75] -1.0 False {}
2 [70, 75] -1.0 False {}
...
198 [75, 65] -1.0 False {}
199 [74, 66] -1.0 False {}
200 [73, 66] -1.0 True {'TimeLimit.truncated': True}
```

Each episode of the Mountain Car game has a maximum of 200 time steps. An episode is considered finished when the mountain car reaches the mountain top or when the number of attempts reaches 200, whichever comes first.

In each time step, the reward is −1, unless the car reaches the mountain top, in which case the reward is 1.

15.2 Q-LEARNING IN THE MOUNTAIN CAR GAME

In this section, you'll learn to train the Q-table for the Mountain Car game.

15.2.1 How to Train the Q-Table

We first populate a 190 by 150 by 3 Q-table with zeros. In each step, unless the mountain car reaches the top, we use Q-learning to update the Q-values as follows:

$$New\_Q(s,a) = lr * [Reward + \gamma * max\_Q(s',a')] + (1 - lr) * Old\_Q(s,a),$$

where lr is the learning rate and γ the discount factor. If the car reaches the mountain top in a time step, we update the Q-value as follows.

$$New\_Q(s,a) = 1$$

After many rounds of trial and error, the updates will be minimal, which means the Q-values converge to the equilibrium values. At that point, the Q-table is considered trained and the Q-learning process is complete.

First, we set up some hyperparameters like this:

```
[7]:  import numpy as np

      learning_rate=0.2
      discount_rate=0.99
      max_exp=0.9
      min_exp=0.01
      max_episode=100000
      max_steps=200
      Q=np.zeros((190, 150, 3))
```

The learning rate is set to 0.2 and the discount factor 0.99. The exploration rate is set between 0.01 and 0.9. We'll train the model for 100,000 episodes. The Q-table is a 190 by 150 by 3 NumPy array with values 0 before training starts.

15.2.2 Update the Q-Table

Next, we define a *update_Q()* function to update the Q-table based on trial and error, as follows:

```
[8]: def update_Q(episode):
         obs=env.reset()
         epsilon=min_exp+(max_exp-min_exp)*episode/max_episode
         # Play a full game till it ends
         for _ in range(max_steps):
             state = obs_to_state(obs)
             # Exploitation
             if epsilon<np.random.uniform(0,1,1):
                 action=np.argmax(Q[state[0], state[1], :])
             # Exploration
             else:
                 action=env.action_space.sample()
             # Use the selected action to make a move
             new_obs,reward,done,info=env.step(action)
             new_state=obs_to_state(new_obs)
             # Update Q values
             if done==True:
                 if new_obs[0]>=0.5:
                     Q[state[0],state[1],action]=1
                     outcome.append(1)
                     break
                 else:
                     outcome.append(0)
                     break
             else:
                 Q[state[0],state[1],action]=learning_rate*\
     (reward+discount_rate*np.max(Q[new_state[0],new_state[1],:]))\
                     +(1-learning_rate)*Q[state[0],state[1],action]
                 obs=new_obs
                 continue
```

In this function, we play a full episode of the Mountain Car game, allowing a maximum of 200 time steps. After each time step, the agent receives a reward based on the current state s and the action taken a. The Q-value, $Q(s, a)$, in the Q-table is updated accordingly.

15.2.3 Train the Q-Table via Trial and Error

We can now go ahead and train the Q-table by letting the agent interact with the game environment, like this:

```
[9]:  outcome=[]
      for episode in range(max_episode):
          update_Q(episode)
          if episode%1000 == 0:
              print("this is episode", episode)
```

We create a list *outcome* to record the final result of each game episode: a value of 1 means the agent has successfully driven the car to the mountain top and a value of 0 indicates the agent has failed in the episode.

The training takes about 30 minutes. The exact amount of time depends on your computer hardware. We print out a short message after every 1000 episodes to keep track of the progress.

Once the training is over, we save the Q-table for later use:

```
[10]: import pickle

      with open('files/ch15/mountain_car_Qs.p','wb') as fp:
          pickle.dump((Q, outcome),fp)
```

The trained Q-table is saved as a *pickle* file on your computer. You can also download the file from the book's GitHub repository. Once the trained Q-table is saved on your computer, you can load up the model whenever you need to use it, like this:

```
[11]: import numpy as np

      # Load up the data
      with open('files/ch15/mountain_car_Qs.p','rb') as fp:
          (Q, outcome)=pickle.load(fp)
      # Print out information about the Q-table
      print("the shape of the Q-table is", Q.shape)
      print("the size of the outcome list is", len(outcome))
      # The mean value of the outcomes
      print("the average value in the outcome list is",\
       np.mean(np.array(outcome)))
```

```
the shape of the Q-table is (190, 150, 3)
the size of the outcome list is 100000
the average value in the outcome list is 0.12124
```

The above output shows that the dimension of the Q-table is (190, 150, 3) and there are 100,000 values in the list *outcome*, with an average value of 0.12124. This indicates that in 12.124% of the episodes during training, the agent has successfully driven the car to the mountain top.

15.3   TEST THE TRAINED Q-TABLE

Now that we have a trained Q-table, we'll test if the Q-table can successfully guide the agent to drive the car to the mountain top. For that purpose, we first define a *test_Q()* function. The function tests one episode of the game, with or without graphical rendering.

15.3.1   Define the Test_Q() Function

We define a *test_Q()* function to play one episode of the game using the trained Q-table. The function has an argument *rendering*, which takes a default value of *False*.

```
[12]:  def test_Q(rendering=False):
           obs=env.reset()
           # Play a full game till it ends
           for i in range(1,201):
               state=obs_to_state(obs)
               # Select the best action from the Q-table
               action=np.argmax(Q[state[0], state[1], :])
               # Use the selected action to make a move
               obs, reward, done, info=env.step(action)
               if rendering==True:
                   env.render()
               # Update Q values
               if done==True:
                   if obs[0]>=0.5:
                       print(f"congrats, you won in {i} steps!")
                       result=1
                   else:
                       print("sorry, better luck next time")
                       result=0
                   break
           return result
```

The function plays the game for a maximum of 200 time steps. In each time step, the agent obtains the best action from the trained Q-table. If the agent reaches the mountain top, the game stops and the function returns a value of 1. If the agent fails to reach the mountain top in 200 attempts, the function returns a value of 0.

15.3.2   The Effectiveness of the Trained Q-Table

Below, we play one game with the trained Q-table. We turn on the graphical rendering of the game so that you can see how the Q-table helps the agent drive the car to the mountain top.

[13]:
```
test_Q(rendering=True)
```

```
congrats, you won in 111 steps!
```

The above output shows that the agent has driven the car to the mountain top in 111 attempts. Separately, there is a game window showing that the car reaches the top of the mountain. This indicates that the trained Q-table can indeed help the agent win the game.

To test the average performance of the trained Q-table, we test ten games and see what's the average performance.

[14]:
```
results=[]
for _ in range(10):
    result=test_Q(rendering=False)
    results.append(result)
print("the average score from the ten games is",\
 np.mean(np.array(results)))
```

```
congrats, you won in 156 steps!
congrats, you won in 86 steps!
congrats, you won in 110 steps!
congrats, you won in 83 steps!
congrats, you won in 110 steps!
congrats, you won in 148 steps!
congrats, you won in 151 steps!
congrats, you won in 84 steps!
congrats, you won in 158 steps!
congrats, you won in 114 steps!
the average score from the ten games is 1.0
```

The Q-table has helped the agent drive the car to the mountain top in all ten games. It took the agent anywhere between 83 to 158 attempts to win the game each time.

15.4 ANIMATE THE GAME BEFORE AND AFTER Q-LEARNING

We'll first animate the mountain car game before Q-learning. You'll see that the mountain car stays in the valley without much movement. After Q-learning, the mountain car made to the top in every episode. We'll put the animation before and after the Q-learning side by side to show what a difference the Q-learning makes.

15.4.1 The Mountain Car Game without Q-Learning

First, let's animate the game before Q-learning. We'll play five games and record all game windows in a list called *frames*.

```
15]: frames=[]
     for _ in range(5):
         env.reset()
         frames.append(env.render(mode='rgb_array'))
         while True:
             action=env.action_space.sample()
             obs, reward, done, info=env.step(action)
             frames.append(env.render(mode='rgb_array'))
             if done:
                 break
```

Since each game has a maximum of 200 time steps, the list *frames* has a total of 1000 game windows, in the form of NumPy arrays.

Next, we combine the game windows into an animation, as follows:

```
16]: import imageio

     frames4=[]
     for frame in frames[::4]:
         frame4=frame.repeat(2,axis=0).repeat(2,axis=1)
         frames4.append(frame4)
     imageio.mimsave('files/ch15/beforeQ.gif',frames4,fps=5)
```

To reduce the number of frames, we take every fourth game window so that the total number of frames is 250 instead of 1000. The command *[::4]* takes every fourth element from a list.

Each game window is a picture with a resolution of 400 by 600 pixels. We use the *repeat()* method in NumPy to repeat the values in a certain dimension. For example, the command *repeat(2,axis=0)* repeats all rows in the NumPy array twice, and the command *repeat(2,axis=1)* repeats all columns in the NumPy array twice. As a result, we increase the resolution of the image from 400 by 600 pixels to 800 by 1200 pixels.

Finally, we combine the images into an animation in *gif* format. If you open the file *beforeQ.gif* on your computer, you should see an animation of the Mountain Car game without the help of the trained Q-table. The car gets stuck at the bottom of the valley, not able to reach the mountain top.

15.4.2 The Mountain Car Game with Q-Learning

Now, let's create an animation of the mountain car with the help of Q-learning. Below, we play the game ten times and record all game windows in a list called *Qframes*.

```
[17]: Qframes=[]
     for _ in range(10):
```

```
obs=env.reset()
Qframes.append(env.render(mode='rgb_array'))
while True:
    state=obs_to_state(obs)
    # Select the best action
    action=np.argmax(Q[state[0],state[1],:])
    # Use the selected action to make a move
    obs,reward,done,info=env.step(action)
    Qframes.append(env.render(mode='rgb_array'))
    if done:
        break
```

We have seen in the last section that with the help of the trained Q-table, it takes the agent anywhere between 83 to 158 attempts to win a game. Since we recorded ten games, the list *Qframes* should have around 1000 game windows, in the form of NumPy arrays.

Next, we combine the game windows into an animation, as follows:

[18]:
```
Qframes4=[]
for Qframe in Qframes[::4]:
    Qframe4=Qframe.repeat(2,axis=0).repeat(2,axis=1)
    Qframes4.append(Qframe4)
imageio.mimsave('files/ch15/afterQ.gif',Qframes4,fps=5)
```

Here we double the height and width of each frame so we have four times the resolution as before, using the *repeat()* method in NumPy.

If you open the file *afterQ.gif* on your computer, you should see an animation in which the mountain car reaches the mountain top in every episode without much effort.

15.4.3 The Mountain Car Game with and without Q-Learning

Next, we'll put the frames before Q-learning and after Q-learning side by side. As a result, you car compare the Mountain Car game in the same animation with and without Q-learning.

[19]:
```
combined=[]
num_frames=min(len(frames4),len(Qframes4))
for i in range(num_frames):
    frame4=frames4[i]
    Qframe4=Qframes4[i]
    frame=np.concatenate([frame4, Qframe4],axis=1)
    combined.append(frame)
```

```
imageio.mimsave('files/ch15/mountain_car.gif',\
                combined, fps=5)
```

If you open the file *mountain_car.gif* on your computer, you'll see an animation of the mountain car game with and without Q-learning. In each frame, the left side shows the car without Q-learning. The car gets stuck at the bottom of the valley without much movement. On the right side of each frame, you can see the movement of the mountain car with Q-learning. The car reaches the mountain top several times. The animation shows how Q-learning helps the agent drive the car to the mountain top.

We also create a picture with eight subplots before Q-learning. We select every 30-th frame from the list *frames4* and keep eight of them to form subplots, like this:

```
[20]: subplots=frames4[::30][:8]
```

The new list is called *subplots* and it has eight NumPy arrays in it. We'll use the *matplotlib* library to create a picture and put the eight images in it to form a four by two matrix, like this:

```
[21]: from matplotlib import pyplot as plt

plt.figure(figsize=(12,16),dpi=200)
for i in range(8):
    plt.subplot(4,2,i+1)
    plt.imshow(subplots[i])
    plt.axis('off')
plt.subplots_adjust(bottom=0.001,right=0.999,top=0.999,
        left=0.001, hspace=0.01,wspace=0.02)
plt.savefig("files/ch15/beforeQ.png")
```

Figure 15.1 shows that the mountain car is at the bottom of the valley in all eight subplots, even though the positions are slightly different from one subplot to the other. This shows that without the help of the Q-table, the agent cannot drive the car to the mountain top.

Similarly, we create a picture with eight subplots to show the Mountain Car game with Q-learning. We select every 30-th frame from the list *Qframes4* and keep eight of them to form subplots, like this:

```
[22]: Qsubplots=Qframes4[8::36][:8]
```

The list *Qsubplots* has eight NumPy arrays in it. We create a picture and put the eight images in it to form a four by two matrix, like so:

```
[23]: plt.figure(figsize=(12,16),dpi=200)
for i in range(8):
    plt.subplot(4,2,i+1)
```

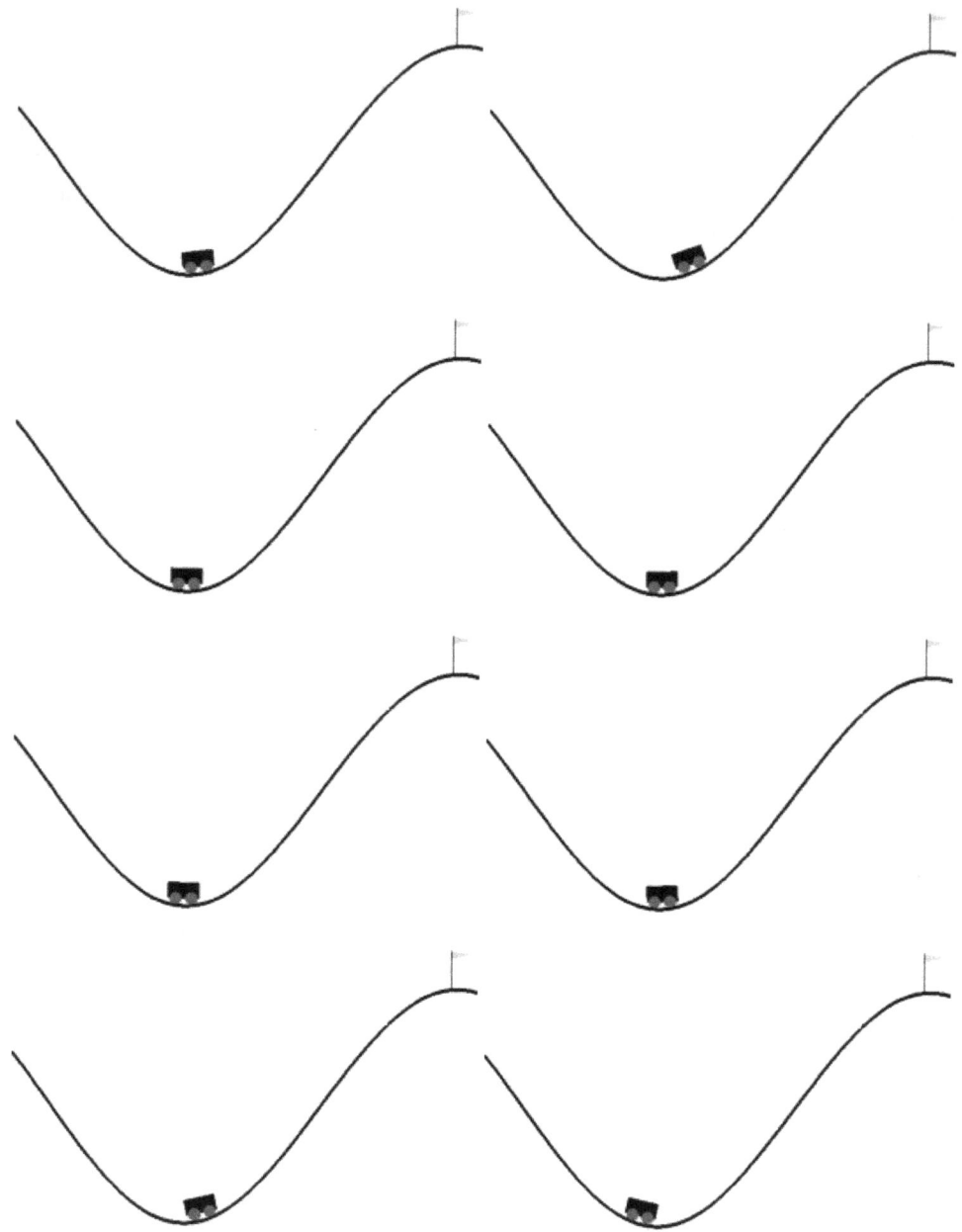

Figure 15.1 The Mountain Car game before Q-learning

```
    plt.imshow(Qsubplots[i])
    plt.axis('off')
plt.subplots_adjust(bottom=0.001,right=0.999,top=0.999,
      left=0.001, hspace=0.01,wspace=0.02)
plt.savefig("files/ch15/afterQ.png")
```

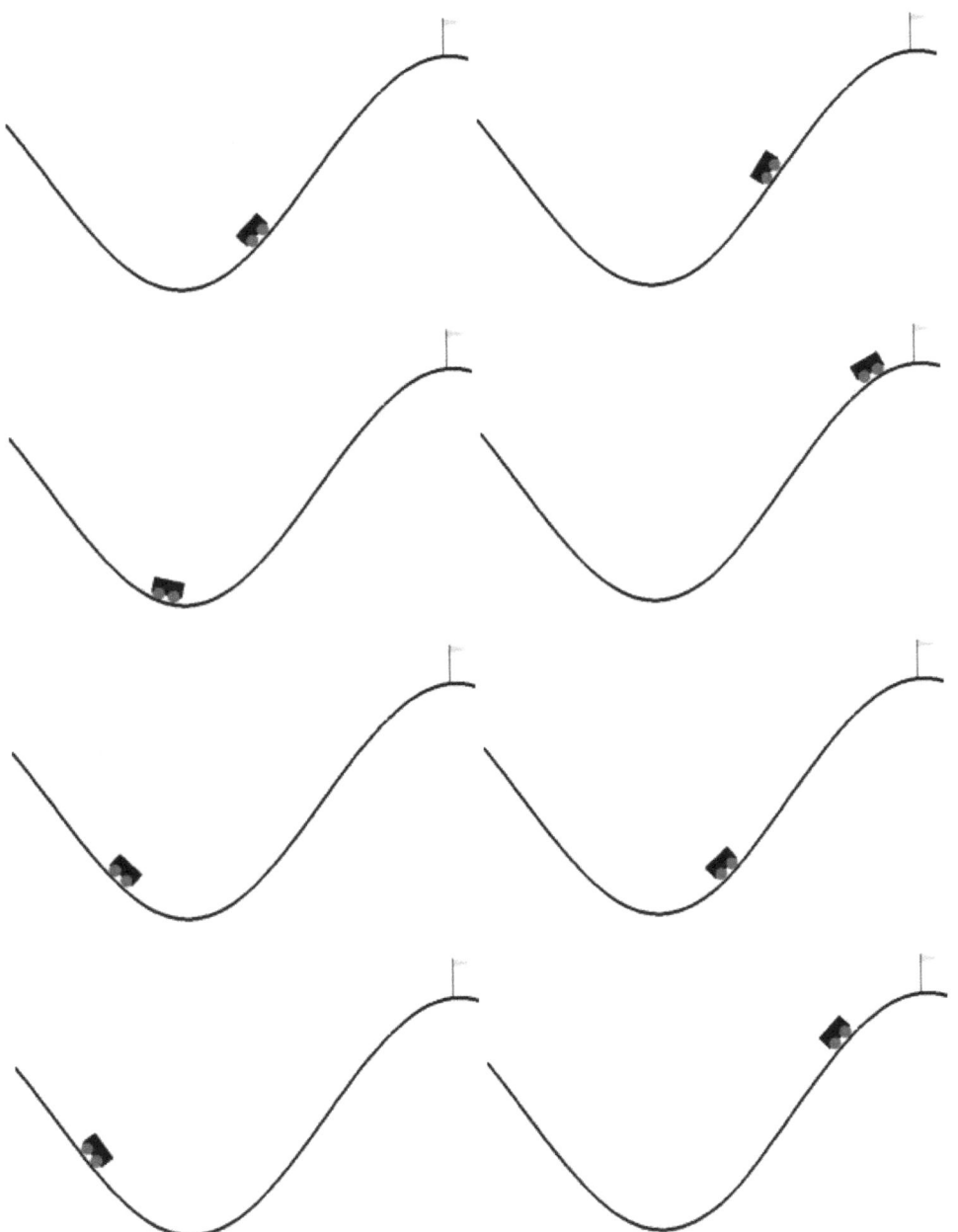

Figure 15.2 The Mountain Car game after Q-learning

In Figure 15.2, the car is in very different positions in the eight subplots. In some subplots, the car is to the left of frame high in the downward slope in order to build up momentum. In others, the car is close to the mountain top. This shows that with the help of the Q-table, the agent learns to drive to the left to build up momentum to reach the mountain top.

15.5 GLOSSARY

- **Continuous State:** A state in a game environment in which the variable representing the state is continuous. Hence the total number of states is infinite.
- **Discrete State:** A state in a game environment in which the variable representing the state is discrete. Hence the total number of states is finite.

15.6 EXERCISES

15.1 Modify the second code cell in Section 15.1.1 so that the agent uses action 0 in time steps 0, 3, 6, 9..., action 1 in time steps 1, 4, 7, 10, ..., and action 2 in time steps 2, 5, 8, 11,... That is, the action is the remainder of the time step value divided by three.

15.2 Modify the code cell in Section 15.3.1 to redefine the *test_Q()* function so that the agent selects the best action from the Q-table with 95% probability and selects a random move with 5% probability. Define the new function *new_test_Q()*.

15.3 Follow the previous question and modify code cell in Section 15.3.2 to use the *new_test_Q()* to play the Mountain Car game ten times. See what's the average performance of the agent.

## CHAPTER 16

Solving Real-World Problems with Machine Learning

The most obvious characteristic of science is its application, the fact that as a consequence of science one has a power to do things. And the effect this power has had need hardly be mentioned. The whole industrial revolution would almost have been impossible without the development of science.

The Meaning of It All: Thoughts of a Citizen-Scientist

– Richard P. Feynman

WITH SKILLS YOU have acquired in Chapters 4 to 15, you are ready to solve the Amazon Delivery Route problem that we laid out in Chapter 3. Specifically, you'll create your own game environment with the goal of finding the shortest route between any two households in town. This is similar to the Frozen Lake game that you solved in Chapter 14. You'll create a Q-table and use trial and error to find the steady-state Q-values. You'll then use the Q-table as a guide to go from one stop to the next by using the shortest route.

Once you have the solution to the shortest route between any two households in town, you'll use brute force to find the shortest route to deliver to any eight households each day. Let's call the eight houses/destinations D1, D2, ..., D8. You'll consider all possible routes, starting with the hub H. You deliver packages to the eight households one by one. Finally, you return to the hub and finish the day's work. You'll consider all possible routes such as H→D2→D8→D1→D7→D6→D3→D5→D4→H, or H→D7→D4→D1→D3→D6→D8→D5→D2→H... You'll calculate the total distance of each possibility and select the route with the shortest total distance as your delivery route of the day.

DOI: 10.1201/b23383-16

Now, instead of starting your day scratching your head to figure out the shortest route to go, you'll just enter the locations of the eight households into your Python program. After 30 seconds, the machine learning model tells you the shortest route, along with detailed instructions on which street to go first, which one second, and so on, till you finish your job for the day. You'll also create an animated instruction on the map: a blue dot lets you know which street to go next. The blue dot stops briefly at each intersection so that you can see the whole process in motion.

With this, the circle is complete: you started with a challenging real-world problem, knowing nothing about machine learning. You then learned how reinforcement learning works and how to create your own game environment to train your model. You converted the real-world problem into a game environment and used machine learning to solve it. You used the solution to guide the real-world problem and knew exactly what to do in the real-world situation. The opening quote of this book by Richard Feynman highlights the power of science in solving real-world problems [8]. That's exactly the purpose of this book: to master ML so that you can apply it in your daily lives.

New Skills in This Chapter

- Converting a real-world problem into a game
- Solving a real-world problem using machine learning
- Creating and using a multi-dimensional Q-table
- Finding out all possible permutations of a given list

Before you start, open the Jupyter Notebook app in the virtual environment MLA on your computer. After that, open a blank Jupyter notebook and save it as *ch16.ipynb* in the directory /Desktop/mla/ on your computer. Next, we'll create a subdirectory /files/ch16/ to store files for this chapter.

Start a new cell in *ch16.ipynb* and execute the following lines of code in it:

```
[1]: import os

os.makedirs("files/ch16", exist_ok=True)
```

You should see the new folder /Desktop/mla/files/ch16/ on your computer.

16.1   CREATE A DELIVERY ROUTE GAME ENVIRONMENT

In earlier chapters of this book, you have created your own environments for three different games: Frozen Lake, Tic Tac Toe, and Connect Four. In this section, you'll use the same skills to create an environment for the Amazon Delivery Route problem from scratch. The game environment will have all the attributes and methods of a typical game environment in OpenAI Gym. We then use reinforcement learning to solve the delivery route problem and find out the shortest route to deliver to the eight households.

16.1.1 Draw Delivery Routes

First, you'll draw a map of the town with streets and a park in it. We'll use the *turtle* library for this purpose.

Go to the book's GitHub repository, download the file *ch16util.py*, and place the file in /Desktop/mla/utils/ on your computer. In the file, we have defined the function *delivery_map()* to draw the map of streets and the park in town. In the code cell below, we import the function from the local package and call the function to draw the map, like this:

[2]:
```
from utils.ch16util import delivery_map

delivery_map()
```

The function *delivery_map()* creates a 10 by 10 grid to represent the streets in town. The households live on the street intersections. There are a total of 100 intersections. We also have a park in the city, which occupies a squared area with corner coordinates (2, 6), (6, 6), (6, 2), and (2, 2). There are households on the park border such as (2, 3), (5, 6) and so on. However, there is no household at the nine coordinates inside the park: (3, 3), (3, 4), (3, 5), (4, 3), (4, 4), (4, 5), (5, 3), (5, 4), and (5, 5).

The Amazon Hub is located in H=(x=6, y=6). There are a total of 90 households that you can potentially deliver packages to: there are a total of $10 \times 10 = 100$ intersections; nine intersections fall inside the park and the Amazon Hub occupies one. Therefore, you have a total of $100-9-1=90$ households as your potential destinations.

After you run the above code cell, you should see a game window with the town map, which is the same as Figure 3.1 that you have seen in Chapter 3.

Next, we'll create a game environment so that you can use tabular Q-learning to find the shortest route between any two households in town.

16.1.2 Create a Game Environment

We'll create a Python class to represent the Delivery Route environment. The class has various attributes and methods so that we can train the tabular Q-learning agent in it. Similar to the game environments that we have created before in this book and to those in OpenAI Gym, we code in several attributes. Specifically:

- action_space is the collection of all actions that can be taken by the agent. In this case, the action space has four values: 0, 1, 2, and 3, corresponding to going left, going down, moving right, and moving up, respectively.
- observation_space contains all possible states in the environment. In this case, the action space has 91 values: the 90 households plus the Amazon Hub.
- state is an attribute indicating which state the environment is currently in. In this case, the state is an integer between 0 and 90.

- action is the agent's move, which can take values 0, 1, 2, or 3.
- done is an attribute indicating whether the game has ended. In this case, it means that the agent has reached the intended destination.

The game environment has a few methods as well:

- reset() is a method to set the environment to the initial (that is, the starting) state.
- render() is a method showing the current state of the game environment in a graphical game window.
- step() is a method that returns the new state, the reward, and the value of the *done* variable based on the action taken by the agent.
- close() is a method to end the game environment, including the graphical game window.

We use a Python class *Route()* in the local package *utils* to represent the game environment. Open the file *ch16util.py* that you downloaded earlier and familiarize yourself with the class *Route()* in it. To initiate the game environment, you call the Python class and put in two arguments: *start* and *end*, the coordinates of the starting point and the end point.

Next, we test the Delivery Route game environment we just created.

16.1.3   Use the Delivery Route Game Environment

Next, you'll learn to initiate a Delivery Route game using the custom-made local module so that you have a better understanding of the game environment. This will prepare you for training the tabular Q-learning agent to find the shortest route between any two positions on the map.

As an example, let's say that the agent wants to go from the starting point (x=5, y=6) to the end point (x=1, y=3). In the code cell below, the agent randomly selects moves to play the game. The game stops when the agent reaches the end point or when the agent has made 20 moves, whichever comes first.

```
[3]: import numpy as np
import random, time
from utils.ch16util import Route

env=Route((5, 6), (1, 3))
state=env.reset()
env.render()
max_steps=20
# Try a maximum of 20 steps
for step in range(1,max_steps+1):
    # Select a random action
    action=random.choice(env.action_space)
    # Use the selected action to make the move
    new_state,reward,done,info=env.step(action)
```

```
    env.render()
    if done or step==max_steps:
        break
    else:
        state = new_state
time.sleep(5)
env.close()
```

We first import the *Route()* class that you just created. It sets (5, 6) as the starting point, and (1, 3) as the end point. The agent tries 20 random moves. We have turned on the *render()* method so that you can see the game window changes from step to step. The route traveled by the agent is highlighted in red. If you run the above code cell, you'll see a result similar to Figure 16.1. Your result is likely to be different since the actions are random.

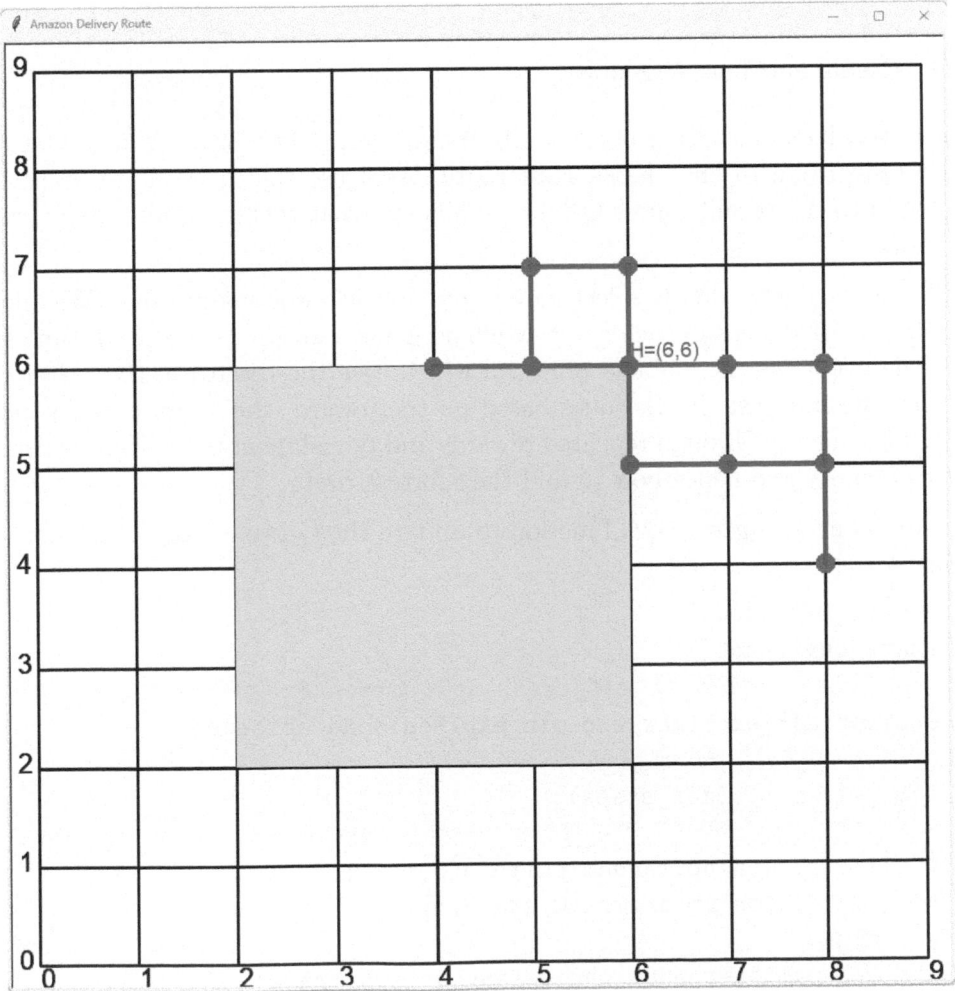

Figure 16.1   The Delivery Route problem before Q-learning

As you can see from the figure, the traveled route is highlighted in red. Note that the agent didn't reach the intended destination (1, 3) since the actions are chosen randomly. Also, you see less than 20 red segments because the agent traveled on the same segments of streets more than once due to the random nature of movements. You may wonder: how can we train the agent to go to the intended destination? We'll train a Q-table for that purpose by using tabular Q-learning.

16.2   TRAIN A Q-TABLE BETWEEN ANY TWO POSITIONS

The delivery route has many possible starting and end points. Further, when you have to drive to eight households and back to the Amazon Hub, you effectively have nine different pairs of starting and end points.

In this section, we'll learn how to train a Q-table when you have a given starting and end point. You'll then test if the Q-table indeed works as intended.

16.2.1   Create and Train A Q-table

Suppose you have a starting point (3, 9) and an end point (5, 0). You want to use tabular Q-learning to find the shortest route. We'll use the methods we learned in Chapter 14 to create and train a Q-table, similar to what we have done for the Frozen Lake game.

We'll let the agent randomly select moves to play the game many times. We allow a maximum of 1000 steps in each game. We'll assign a reward of −1 at each time step, unless the agent reaches the end point, in which case the reward is 100. After each time step, we'll adjust the Q-values based on the reward, the state, and the action taken by the agent. Through repeated rewards and punishments, the agent learns the correct Q-values and hence how to find the shortest route.

First, we define an *update_Q()* function to update the Q-table after each time step, as follows:

```
[4]:  def update_Q(episode):
          state=env.reset()
          # define epsilon to determine eploration/exploitation
          epsilon=min_exp+(max_exp-min_exp)*episode/episodes
          # Play a full game till it ends
          for _ in range(max_steps):
              # Select the best action or the random action
              if epsilon>np.random.uniform(0,1,1):
                  action=np.argmax(Q[state,:])
              else:
                  action=random.choice(env.action_space)
              # Use the selected action to make the move
              new_state,reward,done,info=env.step(action)
```

```
        # Update Q values
        if done==True:
            Q[state,action]=reward
            break
        else:
            Q[state,action]=lr*(reward+gamma*np.max\
              (Q[new_state,:]))+(1-lr)*Q[state,action]
            state=new_state
```

The *update_Q()* function lets the agent play a complete game. After each step, the agent updates the Q-table based on the action taken and the reward: if an action leads to a high reward, the agent increases the Q-value associated with the action; if an action leads to a punishment, the agent decreases the corresponding Q-value. The agent balances exploitation versus exploration when choosing an action. With exploitation, the agent chooses the action based on the values in the current Q-table. With exploration, the agent randomly selects an action to explore different actions in case there is a better strategy than what's recommended by the current Q-table.

We set the learning rate to 0.6 and the discount factor to 0.9. We allow a maximum of 1000 steps in each game and train the Q-table for 500 episodes, like so:

```
[5]: import pickle

# Set up hyperparameters
lr=0.6
gamma=0.9
max_exp=0.7
min_exp=0.0
max_steps=1000
episodes=500

# Train the Q-table
Q=np.zeros((91, 4))
env=Route((3,9),(5,0))
for episode in range(episodes):
    update_Q(episode)

# Save the Q-table and print it out
with open('files/ch16/Qs.pickle', 'wb') as fp:
    pickle.dump(Q,fp)
Q=np.round(Q,4)
print(Q)
```

```
[[ 54.9539   54.9539   62.171    48.4585]
 [ 48.4585   54.9539   54.9539   42.6127]
 ...
 [ 24.5191   24.5189   21.0635   17.9601]
 [ 21.0672   21.0651   17.9604   17.9604]]
```

When training the Q-table, we set the cutoff value of the epsilon, which governs exploration versus exploitation, to $min\_exp = 0.0$ in the first episode of training. If a uniformly distributed variable between 0 and 1 is greater than this cutoff value, the agent uses exploration; otherwise, the agent uses exploitation. The cutoff value then gradually increases as training progresses. At the last episode of training, the cutoff value increases to $max\_exp = 0.7$.

After 500 episodes of training, we print out the trained Q-table, which is a 91 by 4 NumPy array. Next, you'll use the trained Q table to guide the agent to successfully reach the goal in the Delivery Route game environment.

16.2.2   Test the Trained Tabular Q-Values

The trained Q-table is a 91 by 4 NumPy array, saved as *Qs.pickle* on your computer. Next, you'll use this trained Q-table to test if the agent can successfully reach the goal in our game environment.

The following code cell calls the *Route()* class from the local module and sets the starting and end points as (3, 9) and (5, 0). In each time step, the agent consults the trained Q-table and selects the action with the highest Q-value corresponding to the current game state. The game ends if the agent reaches the destination or when the number of time steps reaches 1000, whichever comes first.

```
[6]: env=Route((3,9),(5,0))
     env.render()
     for _ in range(max_steps):
         action = np.argmax(Q[state,:])
         # Use the selected action to make the move
         new_state, reward, done, info = env.step(action)
         state = new_state
         env.render()
         if done==True:
             break
     env.close()
```

```
exit turtle
```

If you run the above code cell, you'll see that the agent goes from the starting point to the end point using the shortest route possible. The game window also shows the route traveled in red step by step.

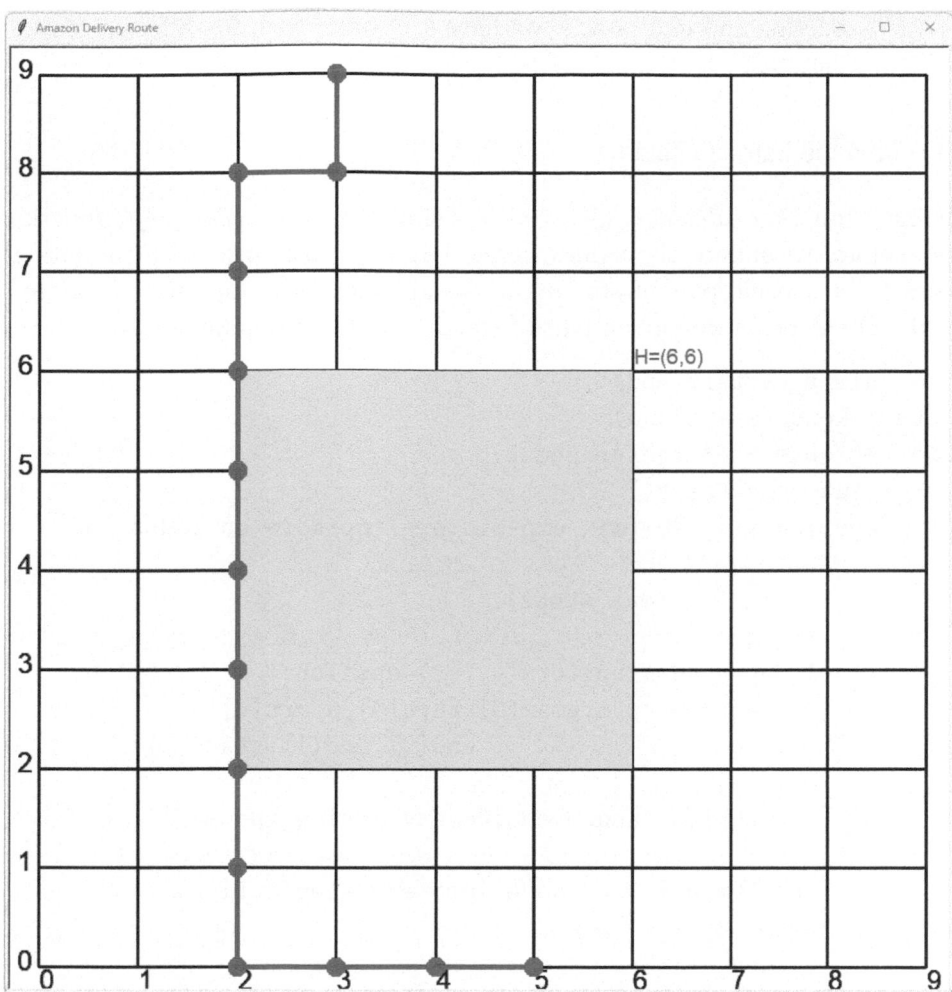

Figure 16.2 The Delivery Route Problem with Q-learning

Figure 16.2 shows the route used by the agent in red. There is a blue dot at each
stop as well. The route is the shortest possible from point (3, 9) to point (5, 0).

16.3 TRAIN THE Q-TABLE FOR ALL POSSIBLE ROUTES

Next, you'll train a large Q-table that gives you directions to any combination of
starting and end points: now matter where you start on the map, and no matter
where your destination is, you can use the Q table to find the directions and figure
out the shortest route. To do that, we'll create a Q-table with a size of 10 by 10 by
10 by 10 by 91 by 4, which has 3,640,000 elements in it. The reason we need such
a large Q-table is the starting position (*start_x*, *start_y*) can take 10 by 10 = 100
values. The end position (*end_x*, *end_y*) can also take 10 by 10 = 100 values. For

each pair of starting and end points, we have a Q-table with 91 different states and four different actions; hence the dimension (10, 10, 10, 10, 91, 4).

16.3.1 Train the Large Q-Table

We define a function *calculate_Q()*, which is similar to the *update_Q()* function we defined before, to update the values in the large Q-table. Instead of updating the Q-values for a specific pair of starting and end points, the function *calculate_Q()* trains the Q-values for any given pair of starting and end points:

```
[7]: def calculate_Q(start,end):
         env = Route(start,end)
         for episode in range(episodes):
             state=env.reset()
             epsilon=min_exp+(max_exp-min_exp)*episode/episodes
             # Play a full game till it ends
             for _ in range(max_steps):
                 # Select the best action or the random action
                 if np.random.uniform(0,1,1)<epsilon:
                     action=np.argmax(Q[start[0],start[1],\
                                        end[0],end[1],state,:])
                 else:
                     action=random.choice(env.action_space)
                 # Use the selected action to make the move
                 new_state,reward,done,info=env.step(action)
                 # Update Q values
                 if done==True:
                     Q[start[0],start[1],end[0],end[1],state,\
                        action] = reward
                     break
                 else:
                     Q[start[0],start[1],end[0],end[1],state,action]=\
                         lr*(reward+gamma*np.max\
                     (Q[start[0],start[1],end[0],end[1],new_state,:]))\
                 +(1-lr)*Q[start[0],start[1],end[0],end[1],state, action]
                 state=new_state
```

Next, we create a new Q-table, which has a dimension of (10,10,10,10,91,4), as follows:

```
[8]: Q=np.zeros((10, 10, 10, 10, 91, 4))
```

We populate the Q-table with zeros to start with. We also put the coordinates of the 91 positions in town in a list *grid*, like this:

```
[9]: park=[(3, 3), (3, 4), (3, 5),
           (4, 3), (4, 4), (4, 5),
           (5, 3), (5, 4), (5, 5)]
     grid=[]
     for x in range(10):
         for y in range(10):
             if (x,y) not in park:
                 grid.append((x,y))
```

The list *park* contains the coordinates of the intersections occupied by the park in the middle of the town. We then iterate the x-value from 0 to 9 and the y-value from 0 to 9. Any (x, y) pair that's not inside the park is added to the list *grid*. As a result, there are 91 (x, y) pairs in the list *grid*.

Next, we train the Q-table for any combination of starting and end points in the list *grid*, as follows:

```
[10]: for start in grid:
          for end in grid:
              if end!=start:
                  calculate_Q(start, end)
                  print(f"finished start {start} end {end}")
      with open('files/ch16/allQs.pickle', 'wb') as fp:
          pickle.dump(Q,fp)
```

The above code cell takes a couple of hours to run. However, once you have the table, you can use it every day after you know the eight destinations for the day, and you don't need to retrain it ever again.

16.3.2 Test the Large Q-Table

Next, we test the trained large Q-table that's saved in the file *allQs.pickle* on your computer. You can randomly pick two points on the map and test the Q-table. Below, we use the two points (8,9) and (3,1) as the starting and end points, respectively.

```
[11]: with open('files/ch16/allQs.pickle', 'rb') as fp:
          Q=pickle.load(fp)

      start=(8,9)
      end=(3,1)
      env=Route(start,end)
      state=env.reset()
      env.render()
      while True:
          # Select the action with the highest Q
          action=np.argmax(Q[start[0],start[1],end[0],\
                             end[1],state,:])
```

```
    # Use the selected action to make the move
    new_state, reward, done, _ = env.step(action)
    env.render()
    state=new_state
    if done==True:
        break
env.close()
```

Run the above code cell and you'll see a separate game window showing that the agent goes from the starting point (8,9) to the end point (3,1) using the shortest route possible. The route traveled is highlighted in red.

16.4   THE SHORTEST DELIVERY ROUTE TO EIGHT HOUSEHOLDS

Now that you have the solution to the shortest route between any two points on the map, you'll use brute force to find the shortest route to deliver to eight households each day. You'll first learn to find out all possible permutations of eight households. You'll calculate the total distance for each permutation and select the route with the shortest distance: that's your delivery route of the day.

16.4.1   Find All Possible Permutations in Python

First, you'll learn how to find all possible permutations if you have eight households. You can use the *itertools* library to do that. The code cell below finds all permutations of four elements when each element is a number from 0 to 4.

[12]:
```
from itertools import permutations

# Get all combination of [0, 1, 2, 3, 4]
perms=permutations(range(5), 4)
total=0
for i in perms:
    print(i)
    total+=1
print(total)
```

```
(0, 1, 2, 3)
(0, 1, 2, 4)
...
(4, 3, 2, 1)
120
```

Here we are trying to find out how many possible permutations of four numbers if you can choose each number from 0 to 4 without replacement. The output above prints out 120 possibilities. The first number has 5 possible values: 0, 1, 2, 3, and 4.

The second number has 4 possible values since there is no replacement. The third and fourth numbers have 3 and 2 possible values, respectively. So there are a total of $5\times4\times3\times2=120$ possibilities.

16.4.2 The Total Distance to Deliver to Eight Households

First, we calculate the total number of blocks the agent has to travel through for any given order of eight households. This is to prepare us for the next subsection when we consider all possible permutations. For now, assume you have to deliver to households D1, D2, ..., D8 and in that order. You'll start from the hub H, go to the first household H1, and then H2, and so on. After H8, you'll come back to H. So the sequence of destinations is H→D1→D2→D3→D4→D5→D6→D7→D8→H. You'll use the Q-table you generated in the last section to find the shortest route to deliver to the eight households.

Below we define the *cal_dis()* function to calculate the shortest distance between any two points:

```
[13]:  # Calculate the distance between any two points
       def cal_dis(start, end):
           env=Route(start, end)
           route=[]
           state=env.reset()
           # Go from start to end until you reach the end point
           for _ in range(max_steps):
               route.append(env.grid[state])
               action=np.argmax(Q[start[0],start[1],end[0],\
                               end[1],state,:])
               new_state,reward,done,info=env.step(action)
               state=new_state
               if done==True:
                   return len(route), route
                   break
```

The function uses the trained large Q-table to go from the starting position to the end position. The function returns the distance traveled as well as the sequence of intersections along the route. The distance is the number of blocks the agent needs to travel to go from the starting position to the end position.

Next, we randomly select eight households and use the *cal_dis()* function to calculate the total distance the agent needs to travel to deliver to these eight households, like this:

```
[14]:  while True:
           # Randomy pick 8 households
           indexes=np.random.choice(range(len(grid)),size=8)
```

```
    households=[grid[i] for i in indexes]
    # Make sure the hub is not selected
    if (6,6) not in households:
        break
# Print out the coordinates of the 8 households
print("the indexes of the 8 households are\n",indexes)
print("the coordinates of the 8 households are\n",households)
# Add H=(6,6) as the first stop and last stop
destinations = [(6,6)] + households + [(6,6)]
print("the coordinates of the 10 destinations are\n",destinations)
```

```
the indexes of the 8 households are
 [12 90 32 13 63 44 15  7]
the coordinates of the 8 households are
 [(1, 2), (9, 9), (3, 2), (1, 3), (7, 2), (5, 0), (1, 5), (0, 7)]
the coordinates of the 10 destinations are
 [(6, 6), (1, 2), (9, 9), (3, 2), (1, 3), (7, 2), (5, 0), (1, 5),
(0, 7), (6, 6)]
```

We randomly select eight households on the map. We then add the hub H as the starting point as well as the end point to the list so there are a total of ten positions in the list *destinations*. Next, we define a *total_dis* function to calculate the total distance the agent needs to travel to deliver to the eight households, in a particular order:

[15]:
```
# Calculate the total distance
def total_dis(destinations):
    totaldis=0
    routes=[]
    for i in range(len(destinations)-1):
        dis,route=cal_dis(destinations[i],\
                          destinations[i+1])
        totaldis+=dis
        routes.append(route)
    return totaldis,routes
totaldis,routes=total_dis(destinations)
print("# of blocks the agent needs to travel is",\
    totaldis)
print("destinations the agent needs to travel to is",\
    routes)
```

```
# of blocks the agent needs to travel is 70
destinations the agent needs to travel to is
[[(6, 6), (5, 6), (4, 6), (3, 6), (2, 6), (1, 6), (0, 6)],
[(0, 7), (0, 6), (0, 5)], [(1, 5), (1, 4), (1, 3), (1, 2),
(1, 1), (1, 0), (2, 0), (3, 0), (4, 0)], [(5, 0), (6, 0),
```

(7, 0), (7, 1)], [(7, 2), (6, 2), (5, 2), (4, 2), (3, 2),
(2, 2), (1, 2)], [(1, 3), (1, 2), (2, 2)], [(3, 2), (4, 2),
(5, 2), (6, 2), (7, 2), (8, 2), (9, 2), (9, 3), (9, 4),
(9, 5), (9, 6), (9, 7), (9, 8)], [(9, 9), (8, 9), (7, 9),
(6, 9), (5, 9), (4, 9), (3, 9), (2, 9), (1, 9), (1, 8),
(1, 7), (1, 6), (1, 5), (1, 4), (1, 3)], [(1, 2), (2, 2),
(3, 2), (4, 2), (5, 2), (6, 2), (6, 3), (6, 4), (6, 5)]]

The *total_dis()* function first calculates the shortest distance between any two destinations in the list using the *cal_dis()* function we defined earlier. The function then iterates through the nine pairs of starting and end points and adds up the total distances traveled as well as the sequence of intersections along the way.

For the selected eight households, the output above shows that the agent needs to travel 70 blocks to deliver the eight packages. Note here that the agent takes the ordering of the eight households as given. There could be a different ordering of the households that can reduce the total distance the agent needs to travel. We'll find out the best ordering of the eight households next.

16.4.3 The Shortest Route

We'll consider all possible orderings/permutations of the eight households. We then calculate the total distance the agent needs to travel for each permutation and select the permutation with the shortest distance.

First, we find out all permutations of the eight households and save them in a list *perms*:

```
[16]: perms=permutations(households, 8)
```

We then add the Amazon Hub as the starting and end positions of the day. With each permutation, there are ten destinations, as follows:

```
[17]: destination_perms=[]
      for perm in perms:
          destinations=[(6,6)]+list(perm)+[(6,6)]
          destination_perms.append(destinations)
```

We calculate the total distance traveled for each permutation and the corresponding route using the *total_dis()* function we defined earlier, like so:

```
[18]: dislist=[]
      routeslist=[]
      for d in destination_perms:
          dis,routes=total_dis(d)
          dislist.append(dis)
          routeslist.append(routes)
```

The collection of all possible routes are stored in a list *destination_perms*, which has $8\times7\times6\times5\times4\times3\times2\times1=40{,}320$ possibilities. For each permutation, we calculate the total distance by counting the total blocks the agent needs to drive through. The above cell takes less than one minute to run. Once done, we see which permutation has the shortest distance to travel:

[19]:
```
shortest_idx=np.argmin(np.array(dislist))
min_blocks=dislist[shortest_idx]
shortest_perm=destination_perms[shortest_idx]
shortest_route=routeslist[shortest_idx]
print("the minimum number of blocks to travel is",\
      min_blocks)
print("the destinations along the shortest route is")
print(shortest_perm)
print("the shortest route to travel for today is")
print(shortest_route)
```

```
the minimum number of blocks to travel is 38
the destinations along the shortest route is
[(6, 6), (9, 9), (7, 2), (5, 0), (3, 2), (1, 2), (1, 3), (1, 5),
(0, 7), (6, 6)]
the shortest route to travel for today is
[[(6, 6), (7, 6), (8, 6), (9, 6), (9, 7), (9, 8)], [(9, 9), (8, 9),
(7, 9), (7, 8), (7, 7), (7, 6), (7, 5), (7, 4), (7, 3)], [(7, 2),
(6, 2), (5, 2), (5, 1)], [(5, 0), (4, 0), (3, 0), (3, 1)], [(3, 2),
(2, 2)], [(1, 2)], [(1, 3), (1, 4)], [(1, 5), (0, 5), (0, 6)],
[(0, 7), (0, 6), (1, 6), (2, 6), (3, 6), (4, 6), (5, 6)]]
```

We use the *argmin()* method in NumPy to find out the index of the permutation with the shortest distance in the list of *dislist*. We print out the total number of blocks the agent needs to travel along the shortest route. We also print out the detailed instructions on which intersection to go to first, which one second, and so on.

16.5   ANIMATE THE DELIVERY ROUTE

We'll animate the entire route the agent takes to deliver to the eight households. Each frame will show the position of the agent at an intersection in town. The animation shows how the agent travels from one intersection to the next, starting at the Hub, then to each of eight households, finally returning to the hub.

First, we create a graph showing the agent at each intersection.

16.5.1   Create a Graph at Each Stop

To save space, we define a function *gen_ps()* in the local package. Open the file *ch16util.py* on your computer and take a look at the function. It saves an image of the town's map with the agent's position in a blue dot each time the agent travels to a different intersection. Further, each time the agent arrives at a household, it saves an image as well, so that we can create a subplot later.

```
[20]: from utils.ch16util import gen_ps

      gen_ps(perm,shortest_perm,shortest_route)
```

The function *gen_ps()* generates 39 *ps* files, each representing the agent at a different intersection of the town. If you open the file *route1.ps* after running the above code cell, for example, you'll see an image showing that the agent traveled from (6, 6) to (7, 6). Additionally, the function generates eight files *s0.ps*, *s1.ps* ... to show the map when the agent delivers to each of the eight households.

16.5.2 Animate the Shortest Route

We combine the 39 images *route0.ps*, *route1.ps*, ..., *route38.ps* into an animation and in that order, like this:

```
[21]: from PIL import Image
      import imageio

      frames=[]
      for i in range(min_blocks+1):
          file=f"files/ch16/route{i}.ps"
          im=Image.open(file)
          frame=np.asarray(im)
          frames.append(frame)
      imageio.mimsave('files/ch16/route.gif',frames,fps=2)
```

After running the above code cell, if you open the file *route.gif*, you'll see an animation with the town map and agent's traveling route. The agent starts at the hub (6, 6), travels to the intersection (7, 6) next, then intersection (8, 6), ..., intersection (5, 6), and finally back to the hub (6, 6). The route traveled is highlighted in red.

16.5.3 Subplots of the Eight Deliveries

We also create a picture with eight subplots to show the delivery to the eight households, by using the eight files *s0.ps*, *s1.ps* ... we generated earlier. The code cell below loads up the eight images, converts them to NumPy arrays, and places them in a list *subplots*:

```
[22]: subplots=[]
      for i in range(8):
          file=f"files/ch16/s{i}.ps"
```

```
im=Image.open(file)
frame=np.asarray(im)
subplots.append(frame)
```

Finally, we use the *matplotlib* library to create a picture and put the eight images in it to form a four by two matrix, like this:

[23]:
```
from matplotlib import pyplot as plt

plt.figure(figsize=(25,40),dpi=200)
for i in range(8):
    plt.subplot(4,2,i+1)
    plt.imshow(subplots[i])
    plt.axis('off')
plt.subplots_adjust(bottom=0.001,right=0.999,top=0.999,
left=0.001, hspace=-0.01,wspace=-0.02)
plt.savefig("files/ch16/deliveries.png")
```

Figure 16.3 shows the position of the agent when it delivers to each of the eight households. For example, the top left subplot shows that the agent has traveled to the household (9, 9), with the route traveled in red. The top right subplot shows that the agent then goes to the household (7, 2)... The bottom right subplot shows that the agent has delivered to the last household (0, 7).

16.6 GLOSSARY

- **Permutation:** An arrangement of objects in a certain order.

16.7 EXERCISES

16.1 Modify the first code cell in Section 16.1.3 so that the agent goes from the starting point $(7, 7)$ to the end point $(2, 1)$.

16.2 Modify the second code cell in Section 16.2.1 to train a Q-table to guide the agent to go from the starting point $(7, 7)$ to the end point $(2, 1)$. Save the trained Q-table as *newQs.pickle*.

16.3 Follow the previous question. Modify the code cell in Section 16.2.2 to use the *newQs.pickle* to guide the agent to go from the starting point to the end point.

16.4 Modify the code cell in Section 16.3.2 to use *allQs.pickle* to guide the agent to go from the starting point $(7, 7)$ to the end point $(2, 1)$.

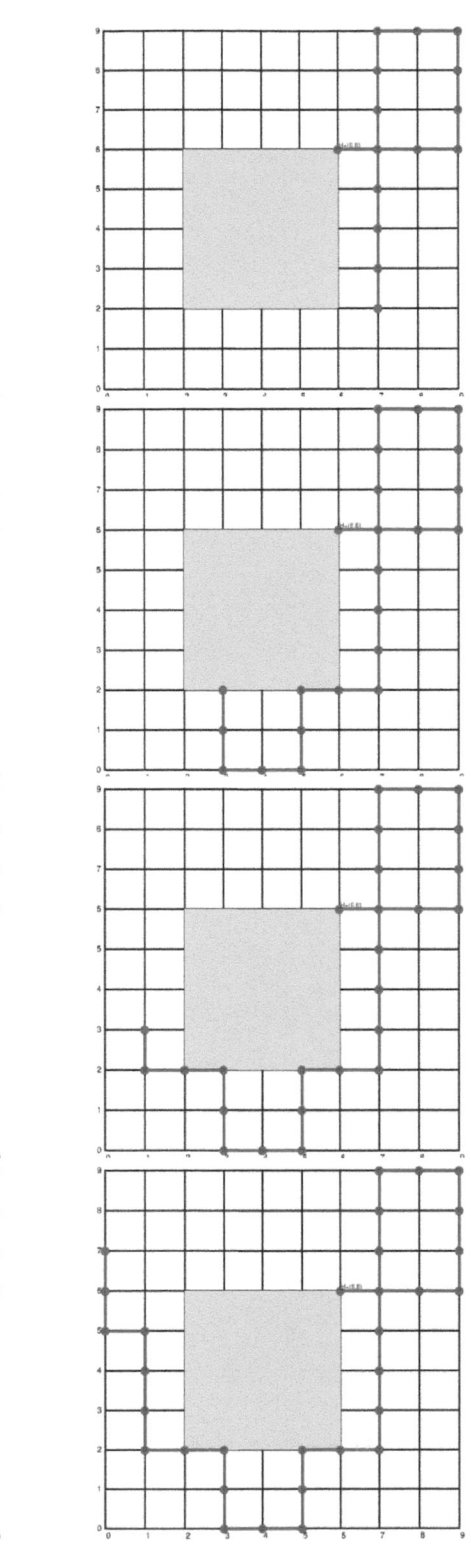

Figure 16.3 The deliveries to the eight households

VI

Deep Reinforcement Learning

## CHAPTER 17

Deep Q-Learning

It is best to think of feedforward networks as function approximation machines that are designed to achieve statistical generalization...
– Goodfellow, Bengio, and Courville (2016)

IN TABULAR Q-LEARNING, we create and train a Q-table with S rows and A columns, where S and A are the number of states and the number of actions, respectively. A tabular Q-learning agent chooses an action in a given state by consulting the Q-table: it looks at the Q-values corresponding to the current state and selects the action with the highest Q-value. In Chapters 13 and 14, you have used tabular Q-learning to successfully train game strategies for the Frozen Lake and Mountain Car games.

In many situations, however, the number of possible states is too large. Examples include Chess or the Go game: the number of possible board positions is astronomical. For example, there are roughly 10^{170} different board positions in Go [19]. It's impractical to create and train a Q-table for these types of games. None of the computer in the world can create a Q-table with so many different rows (each row represents a different game state), let alone calculating and updating values in it.

That's when deep neural networks can help. Neural networks are function approximating algorithms, as the opening quote of this chapter states [3]. We'll use a deep neural network to approximate the Q-table. The number of neurons in the input layer of the network is the *dimension* of the game state, not the *number* of all possible game states. A deep Q-learning agent chooses an action in a given state by feeding the current game state into the deep Q-network. The network returns A values, each representing a Q-value associated with an action. The agent selects the action with the highest Q-value. That's the idea behind deep Q-learning.

This chapter will apply deep Q-learning to a game that you have played before in Chapter 11: the Cart Pole game. You'll learn how to create a deep Q-network for the game, how to train the network by letting the agent take actions and interact with the game environment. We update the weights in the deep Q-network by minimizing

DOI: 10.1201/b23383-17

the difference between the current Q-values and the updated Q-values. You'll use the trained model to successfully win the game by keeping the cart pole upright for more than 195 consecutive time steps. Later in this book, you'll use deep Q-learning to tackle more complicated games such as Breakout, Space Invaders, and other Atari games.

At the end of this chapter, you'll create an animation to illustrate how deep Q-learning works. Specifically, at each time step, you'll put the image of the cart pole on the left. You'll draw on the right the current state of the game: the cart position, cart velocity, pole angle, and pole angular velocity. You'll feed the information to the trained deep Q-network to estimate the Q-values of moving the cart left and moving the cart right, respectively. The move with the higher Q-value is then highlighted in red on the graph, and that's the action taken by the agent. You'll repeat this in each of the 200 time steps in the game.

New Skills in This Chapter

- Creating a neural network to approximate a Q-table
- Training a deep Q-network
- Creating a replay buffer to store experience data
- Retrieving a batch of data from a replay buffer
- Using a trained Q-network to win the Cart Pole game

Before you start, open the Jupyter Notebook app in the virtual environment MLA on your computer. After that, open a blank Jupyter notebook and save it as *ch17.ipynb* in the directory /Desktop/mla/ on your computer. Next, we'll create a subdirectory /files/ch17/ to store files for this chapter.

Start a new cell in *ch17.ipynb* and execute the following lines of code in it:

```
[1]: import os

os.makedirs("files/ch17", exist_ok=True)
```

17.1   DEEP Q-LEARNING FOR THE CART POLE GAME

We'll create a neural network to approximate the Q-table. The dimension of the input in the neural network is the same as the dimension of the game state. In the Cart Pole game, the game state has four values, therefore, we'll create a neural network with four neurons in the input layer. The dimension of the output layer in the neural network is the same as the number of possible actions that can be taken by the agent. In the Cart Pole game, there are two possible actions: moving the cart to the left or moving the cart to the right. Therefore, we'll create a neural network with two neurons in the output layer. Generally speaking, the output from the neural network are the Q-values associated with the A actions that can be taken by the agent.

17.1.1 Create a Deep Q-Network

When training deep Q-networks, we feed the current state of the game to the model as the input. In Chapter 11, we learned that the game state in Cart Pole has four values and the agent can take two possible actions: moving the cart left and moving the cart right. Therefore, we create a neural network with four neurons in the input layer and two neurons in the output layer. We do have a lot of flexibility in terms of how many hidden layers to add in the network and how many neurons in each hidden layer. We choose two hidden layers with 32 neurons in each layer. Slightly changing the number of hidden layers and the number of neurons in each layer won't affect our results. I'll leave that as an exercise for you.

Therefore, we create a deep Q-network for the Cart Pole game as follows:

```
[2]: from tensorflow import keras

input_shape = [4]
num_actions = 2

def create_q_model():
    model = keras.models.Sequential([
    keras.layers.Dense(32, activation="elu",
                       input_shape=input_shape),
    keras.layers.Dense(32, activation="elu"),
    keras.layers.Dense(num_actions)
])
    return model
model = create_q_model()
optimizer = keras.optimizers.Adam(lr=1e-3)
loss_fn = keras.losses.mean_squared_error
```

Note that we don't use any activation function in the output layer in deep Q-networks because Q-values can potentially go from $-\infty$ to ∞. Further, we are using the Exponential Linear Unit (ELU) activation function instead of the usual ReLU activation function. This is due to the fact that in the Cart Pole game, all reward are positive numbers. In such situations, ELU activation functions return negative values for small values of inputs, and this allows the function to push the mean values closer to zero.

17.1.2   Train the Deep Q-Network

Now that we have a deep Q network for the Cart Pole game, we'll train the model by playing the game many times so that the agent can interact with the environment and receive feedback. We'll adjust the parameter values (that is, the weights) in the deep Q-network based on the actions taken by the agent and the resulting rewards.

Specifically, we'll train the model to minimize the difference between the current Q-value, $Q(s, a)$, and the updated Q-value, $New\_Q(s, a)$. We calculate the updated Q-value as follows:

$$New\_Q(s, a) = Reward + discount\_factor * max\_Q(s', a')$$

The discount factor is a constant between 0 and 1 that measures how much the agent discounts future rewards as opposed to the current reward; $max\_Q(s', a')$ is the maximum future reward, assuming optimal strategies will be applied in the future as well.

After many rounds of trial and error, the updates in each iteration will be minimal, which means the Q-values converge to the equilibrium (i.e., the steady-state) values and we have

$$New\_Q(s, a) = Q(s, a).$$

We create a replay buffer to train the deep Q-network. The replay buffer stores game histories from the agent's interactions with the environment. When training the model, we randomly select a subset of past experience to update model weights.

Below, we create a replay buffer with a maximum length of 2000 elements:

```
[3]:  import random
      from collections import deque
      import numpy as np
      import tensorflow as tf
      import gym
      gamma = 0.95
      env = gym.make("CartPole-v0")
      batch_size = 32
      # Create a replay buffer with a maximum length of 2000
      memory=deque(maxlen=2000)
      # Create a running rewards list with a length of 100
      running_rewards=deque(maxlen=100)
```

Instead of a list, we use a double ended queue (deque) in Python to store game experience data. A deque is a more efficient way of handling storage than a list when we need to constantly add and remove elements from the container. By setting the maximum length of the deque *memory* to 2000, we automatically delete the leftmost element whenever the length of the deque exceeds 2000. Similarly, we have created a deque *running_rewards* with a maximum length of 100 to store the total rewards from different episodes of the game. We use the deque *running_rewards* to keep track of the progress of training and to determine if the training is complete.

To train the model, we select a batch of observations from the replay buffer to update model parameters. The following function *gen_batch()* selects 32 observations and process them so that we can use the batch to update the model:

```
[4]: # Generate a batch
def gen_batch():
    # select a batch from the buffer memory
    samples = random.sample(memory,batch_size)
    dones = []
    frames = []
    new_frames = []
    rewards = []
    actions = []
    for sample in samples:
        frame, new_frame, action, reward, done = sample
        frames.append(frame)
        new_frames.append(new_frame)
        actions.append(action)
        if done==True:
            done=1.0
        else:
            done=0.0
        dones.append(done)
        rewards.append(reward)
    frames=np.array(frames)
    new_frames=np.array(new_frames)
    dones=tf.convert_to_tensor(dones)
    return dones,frames,new_frames,rewards,actions
```

Next, we define a function *update_Q()* to update model weights by selecting a batch from the replay buffer:

```
[5]: # Replay and update model parameters
def update_Q():
    dones,frames,new_frames,rewards,actions=gen_batch()
    # update the Q table
    preds = model.predict(new_frames, verbose=0)
    Qs = rewards + gamma * tf.reduce_max(preds, axis=1)
    # if done=1   reset Q to  -1; important
    new_Qs = Qs * (1 - dones) - dones
    # update model parameters
    onehot = tf.one_hot(actions, num_actions)
    with tf.GradientTape() as t:
        Q_preds=model(frames)
```

```
      # Calculate old Qs for the action taken
      old_Qs=tf.reduce_sum(tf.multiply(Q_preds,onehot),axis=1)
      # Calculate loss between new Qs and old Qs
      loss=loss_fn(new_Qs, old_Qs)
  # Update using backpropagation
  gs=t.gradient(loss,model.trainable_variables)
  optimizer.apply_gradients(zip(gs,model.trainable_variables))
```

We'll play the game many episodes so that the agent can interact with the environment and try different actions. The deep Q-learning agent adjusts the model weights based on the feedback from the environment in the form of rewards.

The function *play_episode()* below plays a full game:

[6]:
```
def play_episode():
    # reset state and episode reward before each episode
    state = np.array(env.reset())
    episode_reward = 0
    for timestep in range(1, 201):
        # Calculate current epsilon based on frame count
        epsilon = max(1 - episode / 500, 0.05)
        # Use epsilon-greedy for exploration
        if epsilon> np.random.rand(1)[0]:
            # Take random action
            action = np.random.choice(num_actions)
        else:
            state_tensor = tf.convert_to_tensor(state)
            state_tensor = tf.expand_dims(state_tensor, 0)
            action_probs = model(state_tensor, training=False)
            # Take best action
            action = tf.argmax(action_probs[0]).numpy()
        # Apply the sampled action in our environment
        state_next, reward, done, _ = env.step(action)
        state_next = np.array(state_next)
        episode_reward += reward
        # Save actions and states in replay buffer
        memory.append([state, state_next, action, reward, done])
        # current state becomes the next state in next round
        state = state_next
        # Update Q once batch size is over 32
        if len(memory) > batch_size:
            update_Q()
        if done:
            running_rewards.append(episode_reward)
            break
```

After each time step, we collect the experience data and put them in the replay buffer *memory*. The experience data contains five pieces of information: the old state, the new state, the action taken, the resulting reward, and the variable *done* indicating whether the game has ended. To help organize the data, we put the five pieces of information in a list and add it to the replay buffer *memory* after each time step. If the number of observations in the replay buffer is greater than 32, we update the model weights.

We train the model till the running reward is greater than 195: this means that in the past 100 games, the deep Q-learning agent keeps the cart pole upright for an average of 195 consecutive time steps.

```
[7]: for episode in range(1, 10001):
         play_episode()
         running_reward = np.mean(np.array(running_rewards))
         if episode%20==0:
             # Log details
             template = "running reward: {:.2f} at episode {}, "
             print(template.format(running_reward, episode ))
         if running_reward>=195:
             # Log details
             template = "running reward: {:.2f} at episode {}, "
             print(template.format(running_reward, episode))
             # Periodically save the model
             model.save("files/ch17/cartpole_deepQ.h5")
             print(f"solved at episode {episode}")
             break
```

The model is considered trained if the average score in the past 100 games is 195 or above, as stipulated by OpenAI Gym convention. That's the criteria used in our training process. Once the goal is achieved, the training stops.

The above program takes about an hour to run, depending on the speed of your computer. Here is the output from my computer:

```
. . .

. . .
running reward: 194.67 at episode 863,
running reward: 194.75 at episode 864,
running reward: 194.89 at episode 865,
running reward: 195.20 at episode 866,
solved at episode 866!
```

The model is trained after 866 episodes.

17.2   TEST THE TRAINED DEEP Q-NETWORK

Now that the model is trained, we can use it to play the OpenAI Gym Cart Pole game and see if it works. We'll also record the game history for animation in the next section.

17.2.1   Test and Record One Game

We first test one game, with the graphical rendering turned on.

```
[8]: import gym
     reload = tf.keras.models.load_model("files/ch17/cartpole_deepQ.h5")
     env = gym.make('CartPole-v0')
     state = env.reset()

     # We'll also save the game history for animation later
     history = []
     score = 0
     for i in range(1,201):
         # Save the screen for later use
         frame=env.render(mode='rgb_array')
         # Use the trained model to predict the prob of winning
         X_state = np.array(state).reshape(-1,4)
         prediction = reload.predict(X_state)
         # pick the action with higher probability of winning
         action = np.argmax(prediction)
         new_state, reward, done, info = env.step(action)
         history.append([frame, state, action, prediction])
         state = new_state
         score += 1
         if done == True:
             print(f"score is {score}")
             break
     env.close()
```

```
score is 200
```

The output above shows that the score is 200. Separately, you should have seen a Cart Pole game window in which the cart pole stays upright in all 200 time steps. This means the trained deep Q-learning agent has kept the cart pole upright in all 200 time steps. The trained deep Q-network works as intended.

Note that we have recorded the game history in every time step, including the game window, the state, the predicted Q-values from the trained model, and the action taken by the agent. We'll need the recorded information later when we create an animation of the deep Q-learning decision-making process.

17.2.2 Test the Efficacy of the Deep Q-Network

Next, we play the game 100 times using the trained deep Q-network and see how effective it is on average.

We first define a *test_cartpole()* function to test one complete game and return the score in the game.

```
[9]: def test_cartpole():
         state=env.reset()
         score=0
         for i in range(1,201):
             # Predict the prob of winning
             X_state=np.array(state).reshape(-1,4)
             prediction=reload.predict(X_state,verbose=0)
             # Pick the action with higher prob of winning
             action=np.argmax(prediction)
             new_state, reward, done, info=env.step(action)
             state=new_state
             score += 1
             if done:
                 break
         return score
```

We create an empty list *results* to keep track of the scores from the games. We call the function *test_cartpole()* we just defined 100 times and append the score from each game to the list *results*. We then calculate and print out the average score in the 100 games, like this:

```
[10]: # Repeat the game 100 times and record results
      results=[]
      for x in range(100):
          result=test_cartpole()
          results.append(result)
      #print out the average score
      average_score=np.array(results).mean()
      print("the average score is", average_score)
      env.close()
```

the average score is 200.0

The output shows that the average score is 200. This means that the trained deep Q-network keeps the cart pole upright for all 200 time steps in every single game.

17.3 ANIMATE DEEP Q-LEARNING

Next, we'll animate how the agent uses the trained deep Q-network to select a move in each time step to win the Cart Pole game.

Specifically, in each time step, the agent looks at the current game state, which is a list of four values: the position of the cart, the velocity of the cart, the angle of the pole, and the angular velocity of the pole. The agent feeds the game state, which is represented by the four values, into the trained deep Q-network and obtains two Q-values: the first is the Q-value for taking action 0 (i.e., moving left), and the second is the Q-value for taking action 1 (i.e., moving right). The agent compares the two values and takes the action with the higher Q-value. The agent repeats the process until the game ends.

To create an animation of the decision-making process of the deep Q-learning agent, we'll first create a sequence of images. In each time step, you'll draw a picture with the cart pole on the left. You'll draw on the right the current state of the game: cart position, cart velocity, pole angle, and pole angular velocity. You'll also draw the Q-values of moving the cart left and moving the cart right, respectively. The move with a higher Q-value is then highlighted in red, and that's the action taken by the agent.

Once you have a graph for each time step, you'll combine them into an animation.

17.3.1 Draw the Current Game State and Q-Values

Each Cart Pole game has a maximum of 200 time steps. In each time step, you'll draw a picture, with the cart pole on the left and the current game state and the predicted Q-values from the trained model on the right.

To save space, we define a function *save_graph()* in the local module *ch17util*. Download the file *ch17util.py* from the book's GitHub repository and place it in the folder /Desktop/mla/utils/ on your computer. The function takes five arguments: the first one, *step*, is the index of the time step in the game. The value of the argument *step* ranges from 0 to 199 since there are a maximum of 200 time steps in a Cart Pole game. The other four arguments of the function *save_graph()* are four lists: *frames*, *states*, *actions*, and *predictions*, which we create in the following code cell.

```
[11]: frames = []
states = []
actions = []
predictions = []
# Unpack the information in each time step
for item in history:
    frame, state, action, prediction = item
    frames.append(frame)
    states.append(state)
```

```
        actions.append(action)
        predictions.append(prediction[0])
```

Recall that we have recorded the game history in every time step when the agent plays a full game using the trained deep Q-network. The list *history* contains four pieces of information in each time step: the game window in the format of a NumPy array, the current game state, and the action taken by the agent, and the predicted Q-values associated with the current state from the trained model. In the above code cell, we unpack the four pieces of information from each time step and store them in the four lists *frames*, *states*, *actions*, and *predictions*, respectively.

We now import the function *save_graph()* from the local module and call it to create and save five pictures on your computer, like this:

```
[12]:  from utils.ch17util import save_graph

       for step in [0,49,99,149,199]:
           save_graph(step,frames,states,actions,predictions)
```

The five graphs correspond to time steps 1, 50, 100, 150, and 200 of the Cart Pole game played by the deep Q-learning agent. The graphs are saved in the folder /Desktop/mla/files/ch17/ as *cartpole_DeepQ1.png*, *cartpole_DeepQ50.png*,..., on your computer. If you open the file *cartpole_DeepQ1.png*, you'll see a picture as shown in Figure 17.1.

In Figure 17.1, the Cart Pole game window is on the left. The current state, [−0.0356, 0.0492, 0.0424, −0.0058], is also shown on the graph. The Q-values for moving up and moving down are 21.27932 and 22.46861, respectively. Since the second Q-value is greater, it's highlighted in red. The agent therefore takes action 1 (moving down) in the first step.

The other four pictures are similar but in different time steps. We'll use them to create a picture with four subplots in the next section.

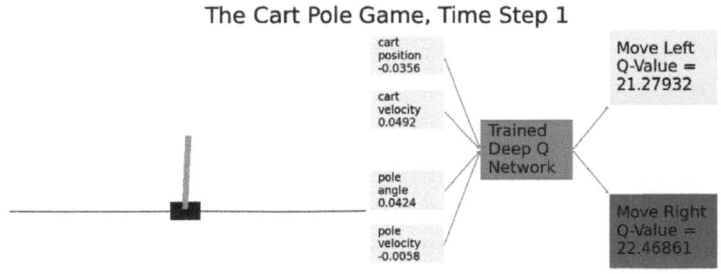

Figure 17.1   Decision-making process of the deep Q-learning agent

17.3.2 Create A Graph for Each Time Step

Next, we'll create a graph for each of the 200 time steps. Since we have so many pictures, we'll save them on your computer's random access memory (RAM) instead of on your computer's hard drive. This helps you save space on your computer.

We define a function *memory_graphs()* in the local module *ch17util* that you just downloaded from the book's GitHub repository. The function first creates an empty list *graphs*. In each time step, it places the game window on the left and the current state of the game on the right. It also draws the Q-values of moving the cart left and moving the cart right, respectively. The move with higher Q-value is highlighted in red. The function then adds the picture for the time step to the list *graphs*. It does this for all 200 time steps.

Below, we import the function *memory_graphs()* from the local module and call the function to create the 200 graphs, like so:

```
[13]: from utils.ch17util import memory_graphs

      graphs=memory_graphs(frames,states,actions,predictions)
```

The function returns the list *graphs*, which contains 200 pictures in the format of NumPy arrays. Each array is a picture in one of the 200 time steps.

17.4 AN ANIMATION AND A PICTURE WITH SUBPLOTS

We'll use the *imageio* library to convert the 200 graphs into an animation, like so:

```
[14]: import imageio

      imageio.mimsave('files/ch17/cartpole_deepQ.gif',graphs,fps=12)
```

The animation is saved as *cartpole_deepQ.gif* on your computer. If you open the file, you'll see how the trained deep Q-learning agent decides whether to move the cart to the left or to the right in each time step. In the middle of each frame are the four values in the current game state. On the right are the Q-values associated with moving left and moving right, respectively. The higher of the two Q-values is highlighted in red.

We'll also create a picture with four subplots in it to illustrate the decision-making process of the deep Q-learning agent in four different time steps: 50, 100, 150, and 200. The four subplots form a four by one matrix in the picture. We first extract the four corresponding NumPy arrays from the list *graphs* we created earlier, like so:

```
[15]: subplot_frames=[]
      for step in [49,99,149,199]:
          subplot_frames.append(graphs[step])
```

The NumPy arrays associated with the four time steps are stored in a new list *subplot_frames*. We then use the *matplotlib* library to create a picture with four subplots, like this:

```
16]:  from matplotlib import pyplot as plt

      plt.figure(figsize=(25,40),dpi=100)
      for i in range(4):
          plt.subplot(4,1,i+1)
          plt.imshow(subplot_frames[i])
          plt.axis('off')
      plt.subplots_adjust(bottom=0.001,right=0.999,top=0.999,
              left=0.001, hspace=-0.2)
      plt.savefig("files/ch17/subplots_deepQ.png")
```

We take the four images from the list *subplot_frames* and plot them into a picture in the format of a four by one matrix. The picture is saved on your computer. If you open the file *subplot_deepQ.png*, you should see an image as shown in Figure 17.2.

The top subplot in Figure 17.2 shows the decision-making process of the deep Q-learning agent in time step 50. The game state, $[-0.0140, -0.1316, -0.0184, -0.0291]$, is in the middle of the subplot. The Q-values for moving up and moving down are 22.70042 and 22.66498, respectively. Since the first Q-value is greater, it's highlighted in red. The agent therefore takes action 0 (i.e., moving left) in the 50-th time step. The second subplot illustrates the decision-making process at time step 100: the agent moves the cart pole to the left since the Q-value associated with moving left is greater. The last two subplots show that in time steps 150 and 200, the agent moves the cart to the left and to the right, respectively, based on the two Q-values from the trained deep Q-network.

17.5 GLOSSARY

- **Deep Q-Network:** A neural network with hidden layers to approximate Q-values in value-based reinforcement learning.
- **ELU Activation Function:** ELU is short for exponential linear unit activation function. It has the form

$$ELU(x) = \begin{cases} x & \text{for } x > 0 \\ \alpha(exp(x) - 1) & \text{for } x \leq 0 \end{cases}$$

It returns negative values when the value of x is small.
- **Replay Buffer:** A collection of game experience in reinforcement learning. When training the model, a subset of observations is retrieved from the replay buffer to update model weights.

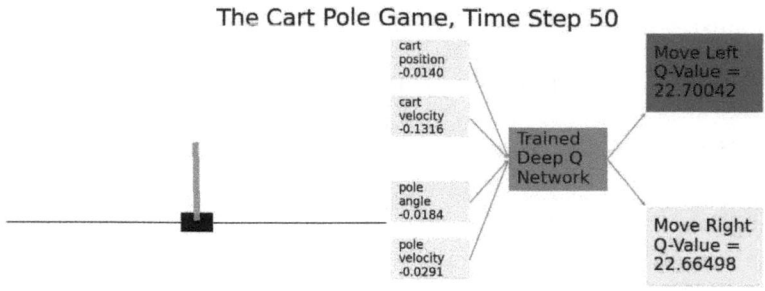

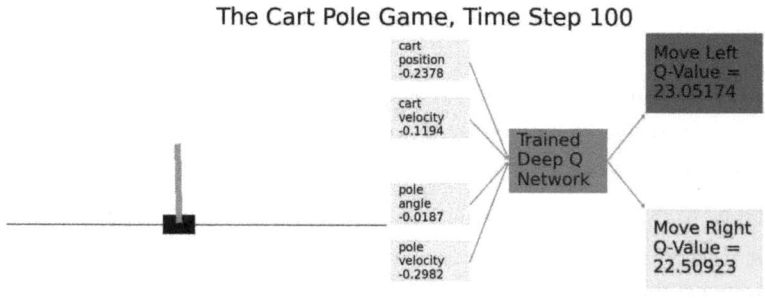

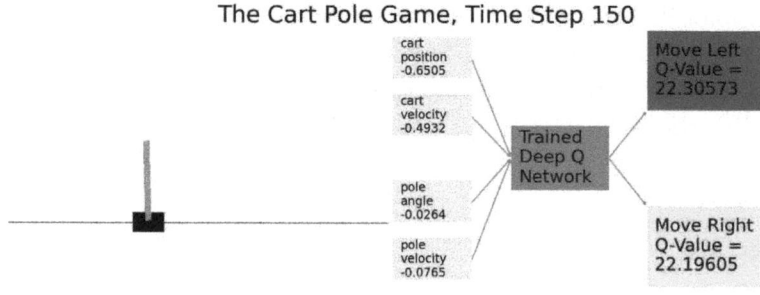

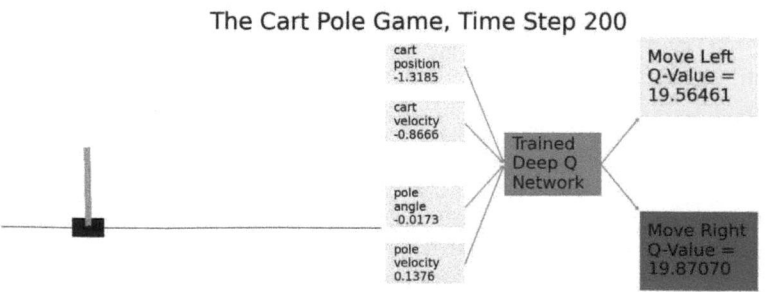

Figure 17.2 Subplots of deep Q-learning in the Cart Pole game

17.6 EXERCISES

17.1 Modify the code cell in Section 17.1.1 so that the deep Q-network has just one hidden layer with 24 neurons in it.

17.2 Follow the previous question. Rerun all code cells in Section 17.1.2 and save the newly trained model as *new_deepQ.h5* on your computer.

17.3 Follow the previous questions. Modify the code cell in Section 17.2.1 to use the newly trained model *new_deepQ.h5* to test and record one Cart Pole game.

17.4 Follow the previous questions. Modify the code cells in Section 17.2.2 to play 100 Cart Pole games and print out the average score.

## CHAPTER 18

Policy-Based Deep Reinforcement Learning

The idea behind reinforcement learning is you don't necessarily know the actions you might take, so you explore the sequence of actions you should take by taking one that you think is a good idea and then observing how the world reacts. Like in a board game where you can react to how your opponent plays.

– Jeff Dean, Head of Google AI

WHEN TRAINING REINFORCEMENT learning (RL) algorithms, we have focused exclusively on value-based approaches so far (such as tabular Q-learning and deep Q-learning). There is another branch of RL that takes a different approach in training an RL agent: instead of estimating the value functions associated with different actions, we can directly train a *policy* that tells the agent which action to take in a given state. We call such approaches policy-based RL. The policy-based approach can be a fast, direct, and effective way to train RL algorithms in many situations. In this chapter, you'll learn the policy gradient method, one type of policy-based RL. You'll use the policy gradient method to play the Atari Pong game.

The idea behind the policy gradient method is different from Q-learning that we discussed in the last few chapters: the agent selects actions to interact with the environment and tweaks the policy directly based on the rewards to reach the optimum. Specifically, if the prediction from the policy model is smaller than the desired outcome, the agent adjusts the model parameters so that the prediction will increase the next time the agent encounters a similar situation. Conversely, if the prediction from the policy model is greater than the desired outcome, the agent tweaks the model so that the prediction will decrease. Further, the magnitude of the adjustment is directly proportional to the rewards: the greater the reward, the greater the adjustment.

DOI: 10.1201/b23383-18

In this chapter, you'll first learn how to install and play the Atari Pong game in Python. You'll then implement the policy gradient method in the Pong game. Specifically, you'll create a deep neural network as the policy for the agent. The agent selects actions based on the policy to interact with the game environment. The agent tweaks the model weights after observing rewards until the policy can guide the agent to win the game. Instead of using the Keras API from TensorFlow, you'll create a neural network using only the NumPy library to represent the policy. This way, you'll have a much deeper understanding of how the deep RL model works.

At the end of the chapter, you'll create an animation to show that the agent learns to play the Pong game perfectly, beating the opponent 21-0 in every game, the best possible score. The left frame shows what happens if there is no training. The right frame shows how the agent plays after training.

New Skills in This Chapter

- Creating a neural network to represent a policy
- Preprocessing raw pixels from the Atari Pong game
- Selecting actions based on recommendations from the policy network
- Training the policy network based on observed rewards
- Playing the Pong game using the trained policy network

Before you start, open the Jupyter Notebook app in the virtual environment MLA on your computer. After that, open a blank Jupyter notebook and save it as *ch18.ipynb* in the directory /Desktop/mla/ on your computer. Next, we'll create a subdirectory /files/ch18/ to store files for this chapter.

Start a new cell in *ch18.ipynb* and execute the following lines of code in it:

```
[1]: import os

os.makedirs("files/ch18", exist_ok=True)
```

18.1 POLICY-BASED REINFORCEMENT LEARNING

This section introduces you to policy-based RL. In particular, we'll explain the intuition behind the policy gradient method with some simple mathematical equations. The Python code used in this chapter is largely based on Stanford University computer science professor Andrej Karpathy's bog [1] and the companion GitHub repository. I strongly encourage you to read through Andrej's blog to understand the intuition behind the idea of the policy gradient method.

18.1.1   What is a Policy?

A policy can be any algorithm that tells the agent what action to choose in a given situation. Let's use the Atari Pong game as an example: we'll create a deep neural network that takes the current state as the input. We'll put one single neuron in the output layer so the output from the deep neural network is a single number. Further, we'll use the Sigmoid activation in the output layer so the output is a number between 0 and 1. As you'll see later, for all practical purposes, the agent only needs to decide whether to move the paddle up (action 2) or down (action 3) to win the game. So we can treat the Pong game as a binary classification problem.

One policy could be: if the output from the neural network is greater than or equal to 0.5, we'll move the paddle up (i.e., take action 2); otherwise, we'll move the paddle down (i.e., take action 3). This is called a deterministic policy in the sense that the action is determined once we know the output from the policy neural network. A policy can be stochastic as well: since the output from the neural network, p, is a number between 0 and 1, we can have a stochastic policy as follows:

- Move the paddle up with probability p;
- Move the paddle down with probability 1-p.

The advantage of a stochastic policy is that it naturally allows for both exploitation and exploration. It allows for exploitation in the sense that the probability of *action=2* is high when the value of p is high. It also allows for exploration in the sense that the action is random. There is a chance that the recommended action is not taken. So this allows the agent to explore different game strategies.

18.1.2   What is the Policy Gradient Method?

Policy gradient method is an algorithm to adjust the model parameters to train the optimal policy in RL.

Imagine in a game environment, an agent is trying to learn the best strategy to maximize its expected payoff over time. A strategy (also called a policy) maps a certain state to a certain action. A policy is basically a decision rule that tells the agent what to do in a certain situation.

Let's say that the policy we are considering is $\pi_\theta(a_t|s_t, \theta)$. That is, the agent chooses an action a_t in time step t in the current state s_t, based on model parameters θ. Suppose the agent needs to choose a sequence of actions $(a_0, a_1, \ldots, a_{T-1})$ to maximize its expected cumulative rewards. In time step t, after observing the state s_t, the agent takes an action a_t and receives a reward of $r(a_t, s_t)$ as a result. If the discount factor is γ, the expected cumulative reward to the agent is

$$R(s_0, a_0, \ldots, a_{T-1}, s_T) = \sum_{t=0}^{T-1} \gamma^t r(s_t, a_t) + \gamma^T r(s_T)$$

where s_T is the terminal state.

The objective of the agent is to find the parameter values θ to maximize the expected cumulative reward

$$\max_{\theta} E[R(s_0, a_0, \ldots, a_{T-1}, s_T)|\pi_\theta]$$

The above maximization problem can be solved by using a gradient ascent algorithm. That is, we can update the model parameters θ by using the following formula until the parameters converge:

$$\theta \leftarrow \theta + Learning\ Rate * \nabla_\theta E[R|\pi_\theta]$$

where *Learning Rate* is the learning rate hyperparameter that controls how fast we update the model weights. This boils down to training the model to predict the probability of the correct action based on the state. The solution is

$$\theta \leftarrow \theta + Learning\ Rate \times E[\sum_{t=0}^{T-1} \nabla_\theta log\pi_\theta(a_t|s_t)R|\pi_\theta]$$

Interested readers can find the proof provided by OpenAI [18].

18.2   GET STARTED WITH ATARI GAMES

In this section, you'll start to play the Atari Pong game in the OpenAI Gym environment and learn its features.

First, you need to install Atari games in OpenAI Gym in Python. Activate the virtual environment *MLA* on your computer and enter the following command in the Anaconda prompt (Windows) or a terminal (MAC or Linux):

```
conda install -c conda-forge atari_py==0.2.9
```

After conda installing Atari games, you need to install *ROMS* on your computer as well. Go to the link below

http://www.atarimania.com/rom_collection_archive_atari_2600_roms.html

and download the file *Roms.rar* to your computer. Extract the two folders, *ROMS* and *HC Roms*, and place them in a folder on your computer. For example, I place them in *C:\temp* on my computer.

After that, run the following command in the Anaconda prompt (Windows) or a terminal (MAC or Linux) with the virtual environment *MLA* activated:

```
python -m atari_py.import_roms <path to folder>
```

Since I saved the files in *C:\temp* on my computer, I ran:

```
python -m atari_py.import_roms C:\temp
```

to install ROMS.

Also make sure that the version of gym installed on your computer is 0.15.7. See Chapter 10 on how to install the correct version of gym.

Finally, you need to restart the Jupyter Notebook on your computer for the installed packages to take effect.

18.2.1   The Pong Game

The following lines of code will get you started on the Pong game:

```
[2]: import gym
     env = gym.make("Pong-v0")
     env.reset()
     env.render()
```

You should see a Pong game frame in a separate window.

You can check the action space and observation space of the game as follows:

```
[3]: # Print out all possible actions in this game
     actions = env.action_space
     print(f"The action space in the Pong game is {actions}")
     # Print out the observation space in this game
     obs_space = env.observation_space
     print(f"The observation space in the Pong game is {obs_space}")
```

The action space in the Pong game is Discrete(6)
The observation space in the Pong game is Box(210, 160, 3)

There are six possible actions the agent can take. But for all practical purposes, we only need to decide whether the paddle should go up (action 2) or down (action 3). So we can treat this as a binary classification problem.

Each observation is a color picture of 210 pixels tall and 160 pixels wide. The following cell displays an observation.

```
[4]: import matplotlib.pyplot as plt
     import numpy as np

     env.reset()
     # Run 20 steps so the pong appears in the picture
     for _ in range(20):
         action = np.random.choice(range(6))
         obs, reward, done, info = env.step(action)
     plt.imshow(obs)
     plt.show()
```

18.2.2 Preprocess the Game Pictures

The input size of the game picture is too large, we'll preprocess the image to reduce the size while retaining vital information to train the model to win the game.

Specifically, we'll perform cropping, downsizing, and differencing before we feed the data into the model to train the agent.

We'll remove the top and bottom of the game frame (cropping) to reduce input size as follows:

```
[5]:  obs_cropped = obs[35:195]
      plt.imshow(obs_cropped)
      plt.show()
```

The size of the picture is now reduced from 210 by 160 by 3 to 160 by 160 by 3. We need to further reduce the size of the picture.

We'll use every other row and every other column so that the input size is 75% smaller. Further, we'll use just one of the three color channels to reduce size. After that, we remove the background colors and change the raw pixels to 1s and 0s only, like so:

```
[6]:  obs_downsized=obs_cropped[::2,::2,0]
      obs_downsized[obs_downsized==144]=0
      obs_downsized[obs_downsized==109]=0
      obs_downsized[obs_downsized!=0]=1
      plt.imshow(obs_downsized)
      plt.show()
```

The size of the preprocessed picture is now 80 by 80 by 1, a small fraction of the original size. However, the picture doesn't tell us the movement of the Pong ball. We can potentially use two consecutive pictures, but a more efficient way is to use the difference between two consecutive frames. This way, the input size is 6400 instead of 128000 and the training of the model will be faster.

To visualize how we preprocess the game pictures, we define a *preprocess()* function in the local module *ch18util*. Download the file *ch18util.py* from the book's GitHub repository and save it under /Desktop/mla/utils/ on your computer. The function randomly selects four game frames and creates a picture with 12 subplots of the original, cropped, and downsized game windows. We import the function from the local module and call it to generate a picture and save it on your computer.

```
[7]:  from utils.ch18util import preprocess

      preprocess()
```

After running the above code cell, the picture *preprocess.png* is saved on your computer. If you open the file, you should see a picture similar to Figure 18.1. The four subplots in the top row are the four original game windows. The middle row shows

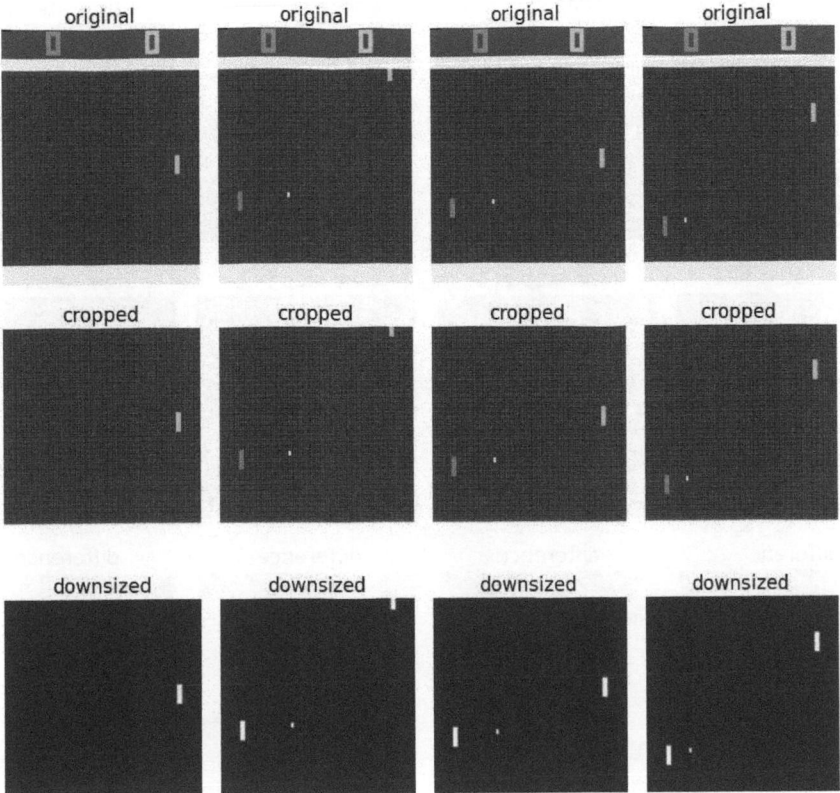

Figure 18.1 Preprocessing Atari Pong game pictures

the cropped game windows. The bottom row shows the downsized images but you can clearly see the paddles on each side and the Pong ball in each frame.

18.2.3 Use the Difference of Game Windows

The preprocessed game windows don't tell us which direction the Pong ball is moving to. To let the agent know the movement of the Pong ball, we'll get the difference of the two consecutive game windows after preprocessing. We'll use the difference as the input to the deep RL model later when training the policy gradient agent.

```
[8]: from utils.ch18util import prepro

next_obs, reward, done, info = env.step(2)
next_obs_downsized = prepro(next_obs).reshape(80,80)

dif = next_obs_downsized - obs_downsized
plt.imshow(dif)
plt.show()
```

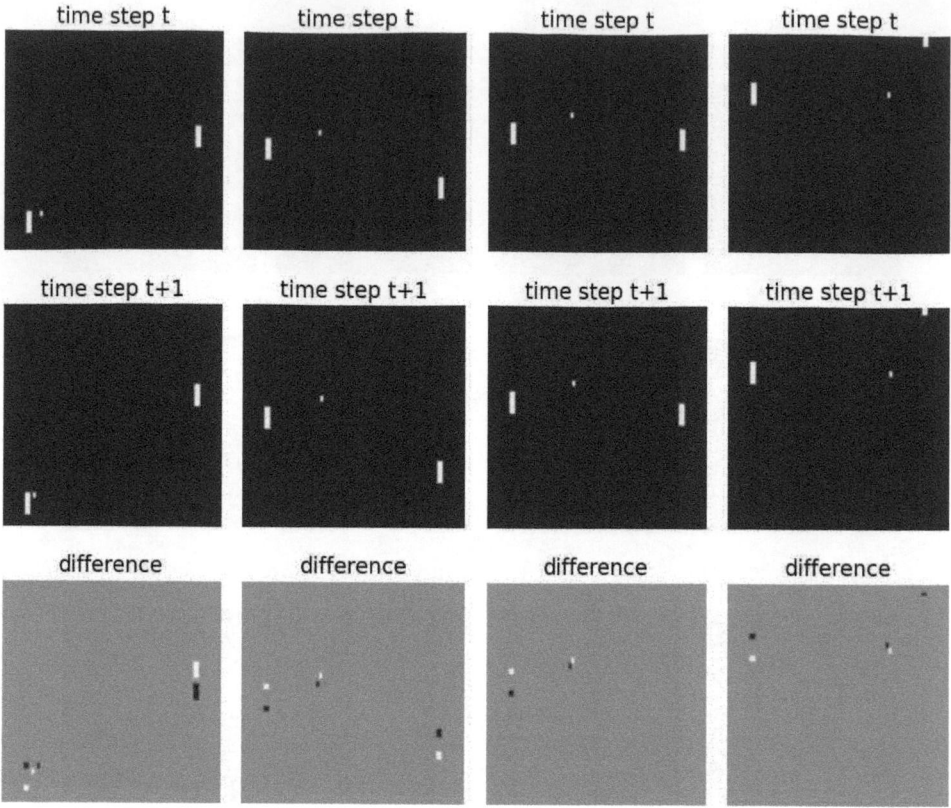

Figure 18.2 Obtaining the difference of two consecutive game windows

In the code cell above, we generate the next game window by choosing *action=2*. We then use the *prepro()* function defined in the local module *ch18util* to preprocess it so that it also has a size of 80 by 80 pixels. The difference between the two consecutive game windows is then shown as the output.

We define a *difference()* function in the local module *ch18util*. The function selects four game frames and creates a picture with 12 subplots in it. The top row shows the preprocessed pictures of four game windows. The middle row shows the processed pictures of the next time step of the four game windows. The bottom row shows the difference between the first two rows. Next, we import the *difference()* function from the local module and call it to generate the picture.

```
[9]: from utils.ch18util import difference

difference()
```

If you open the file *difference.png* on your computer, you'll see a picture similar to Figure 18.2. The first two rows are preprocessed game windows in time steps *t* and *t+1*, respectively. The bottom row shows the difference of the first two rows. If you look at the first column, for example, you can tell that the Pong ball is moving towards the bottom left corner. In the second column, in contrast, the Pong ball is moving away from the bottom left corner and moving towards the top right corner of the screen.

18.3 TRAIN THE POLICY GRADIENT AGENT

We'll use the policy gradient method to train the agent. To save space, we'll place most of the code in the local module *ch18util* that you just downloaded. In this section, we'll explain the logic behind the training process.

18.3.1 Create a Policy Network

We'll create a policy neural network using the NumPy library. We'll feed the difference of preprocessed images from two consecutive time steps into the neural network. The input layer of the network has 6400 neurons in it because the preprocessed images have a size of 80 by 80 pixels. There is one hidden layer with 200 neurons in it. The output layer has just one neuron in it with Sigmoid activation. Below, we define some hyperparameters for the model:

```
10]: H = 200
     learning_rate = 1e-4
     gamma = 0.99
     decay_rate = 0.99
     D = 80 * 80
     def sigmoid(x):
         return 1.0 / (1.0 + np.exp(-x))
```

This is essentially a binary classification problem: the agent needs to decide to move the paddle up or down. We can interpret the output from the neural network, p, as the probability that the agent moves the paddle up. The agent moves the paddle down with probability *1-p*.

During training, the policy network generates a value p to guide the agent's action by passing the input image forward using the following *policy_forward()* function:

```
11]: def policy_forward(model,x):
         h = np.dot(model['W1'], x)
         h[h<0] = 0
         logp = np.dot(model['W2'], h)
         p = sigmoid(logp)
         return p, h
```

The agent tweaks the model parameters periodically based on the rewards and actions taken, using the following *policy_backward()* function:

```
[12]: def policy_backward(model,eph, epdlogp, epx):
          dW2 = np.dot(eph.T, epdlogp).ravel()
          dh = np.outer(epdlogp, model['W2'])
          dh[eph <= 0] = 0
          dW1 = np.dot(dh.T, epx)
          return {'W1':dW1, 'W2':dW2}
```

In reinforcement learning, actions affect not only current period rewards, but also future rewards. We therefore use discounted rewards to assign credits properly. The rewards are discounted so that a sequence of actions, not a single action, get the credit/blame for the game outcome in the form of rewards. This is done through the *discount_rewards()* function below:

```
[13]: def discount_rewards(r):
          discounted_r = np.zeros_like(r)
          running_add = 0
          for t in reversed(range(0, len(r))):
              if r[t] != 0:
                  running_add = 0
              running_add = running_add * gamma + r[t]
              discounted_r[t] = running_add
          return discounted_r
```

We let the agent interact with the game environment for one episode and collect data for training. The details are defined in the *training()* function in the local module *ch18util*. We calculate the gradients as well as the episode reward after each episode of the game. To make the training more table, we update model parameters after every ten games instead of after each game. The details are defined in the *create_batch()* function in the local module *ch18util*.

18.3.2 Train the Model

We define the *policy_pong()* function in the local module *ch18util* for both training and testing of the model. The function is defined as follows:

```
[14]: def policy_pong(test=False,resume=False,render=False,cutoff=-14):
          rewards=deque(maxlen=100)
          if test:
              env = gym.make("PongDeterministic-v4")
              batch_size=1
          else:
              env = gym.make("Pong-v0")
              batch_size=10
          if resume:
              model = pickle.load(open('files/ch18/pg_pong.p','rb'))
```

```
    else:
        model = {}
        model['W1'] = np.random.randn(H,D) / np.sqrt(D)
        model['W2'] = np.random.randn(H) / np.sqrt(H)
    episode_count = 0
    while True:
        batchrewards=create_batch(env,render,model,batch_size)
        rewards += batchrewards
        episode_count += batch_size
        running_reward=np.mean(np.array(rewards))
        if episode_count % 100 == 0 or test==True:
            template = "running reward: {:.6f} at episode {}"
            print(template.format(running_reward,episode_count))
            pickle.dump(model,open('files/ch18/pg_pong.p','wb'))
        if test==False and running_reward>=cutoff:
            break
        if test==True and episode_count>=3:
            break
    env.close()
```

For games in the OpenAI Gym environment, there are different versions:

- v0: there is a 25% chance that the previous action will be repeated instead of the issued action;
- v4: 0% probability of repeating the previous action; but skip 2-5 frames randomly;
- Deterministic-v4: 0% probability of repeating the previous action; skip a fixed 4 frames.

When we train the model, we use version v0 to allow for exploration. Later, we'll use the version Deterministic-v4 when testing the trained model.

After every 100 episodes, the model is saved on your computer. You can stop training and resume training later by turning on the *resume=True* argument in the function. If you want to see the graphical renderings of the game windows, simply turn on the *render=True* argument in the function.

Let's first import the *policy_pong()* function from the local module and train the model for one batch (ten games) with the graphical rendering turned on, as follows:

```
[15]: from utils.ch18util import policy_pong

      policy_pong(test=False,resume=False,render=True,cutoff=-21)
```

By turning on the *render=True* argument in *policy_pong()*, you can see the graphical renderings of the game windows. By setting *cutoff=-21* in the function, the training stops after one batch because the lowest possible score is −21.

Next, you can turn off the graphical rendering of the game windows and train the model until the average score reaches −14, like so:

```
[16]: from utils.ch18util import policy_pong

policy_pong(test=False,resume=False,render=False,cutoff=-14)
```

The training takes about 24 hours, or you can download the trained model from the book's GitHub repository. If the agent can have an average score of −14 when playing in the v0 version of the game, it can have a perfect score when playing the Deterministic-v4 version.

18.4 TEST THE POLICY GRADIENT AGENT

We can now test the trained policy gradient agent. We'll first test three games to see the scores of the agent in these games. After that, we'll record the game windows to prepare for the animation in the next section.

First, we test three games by calling the *policy_pong()* function and setting the *test* argument to *True*:

```
[17]: policy_pong(test=True,resume=True,render=True)
```

```
running reward: 21.000000 at episode 1
running reward: 21.000000 at episode 2
running reward: 21.000000 at episode 3
```

The results show that the trained policy gradient agent has scored 21 points, the highest possible score, in each of the three games.

Next, we'll test one game and record the game windows so that we can animate the whole game in the next section:

```
[18]: from utils.ch18util import policy_forward
import numpy as np
import pickle
import gym

D = 80 * 80
model = pickle.load(open('files/ch18/pg_pong.p', 'rb'))
env = gym.make("PongDeterministic-v4")
frames = []
observation = env.reset()
prev_x = None
reward_sum=0
while True:
    cur_x = prepro(observation)
```

```
        x = cur_x - prev_x if prev_x is not None else np.zeros(D)
        prev_x = cur_x
        aprob, h = policy_forward(model,x)
        action = 2 if 0.5 < aprob else 3
        observation, reward, done, info = env.step(action)
        env.render()
        reward_sum += reward
        frames.append(observation)
        if done:
            print(f"the score is {reward_sum}")
            break
env.close()
```

```
the score is 21.0
```

We have played a full game using the trained model. All the game windows are saved as NumPy arrays in the list *frames*. The agent has scored 21 points again.

18.5 ANIMATE THE PONG GAMES

Next, we'll animate how the agent performs before and after training. We'll put the two games side by side so that you can compare them.

18.5.1 Record Games with Random Moves

We'll record game frames when the agent makes random moves. We'll use them for comparison later in the animation.

```
19]:  random_frames = []
      observation = env.reset()
      for _ in range(len(frames)):
          action = np.random.choice([2,3])
          observation, reward, done, info = env.step(action)
          random_frames.append(observation)
      env.close()
```

By using the command

```
for _ in range(len(frames))
```

we ensure that we get the same number of frames here as in the game with the trained agent. Later when we combine the frames, we don't have to worry about matching the number of frames in the two scenarios.

18.5.2 Combine the Animations

We'll combine the two games and form one single animation. The game windows with random moves are on the left of the combined frames, and those with the trained policy gradient agent are on the right.

```
[20]:
import imageio

fs = []
for i in range(len(frames)):
    if i%2==0:
        f = frames[i]
        rf = random_frames[i]
        middle = np.full(f.shape, 255).astype("uint8")
        frf = np.concatenate([rf, middle, f], axis=1)
        fs.append(frf)
imageio.mimsave('files/ch18/pong_compare.gif', fs, fps=24)
```

Run the above code cell and open the file *pong_compare.gif* on your computer. You'll see an animation of the Pong games. On the left of the screen, you should see the untrained agent (with the green paddle) loses to the opponent (with the orange paddle) 0-21, the worst possible score. On the right of the screen, you should see the trained policy gradient agent beat the opponent 21-0, the best possible score. The animation demonstrates that the policy gradient method is effective in training the agent.

18.5.3 Subplots of the Policy Gradient Agent

We also create a figure with 25 subplots to include in the hard copy of the book. Specifically, we select 25 images out of the thousands of NumPy arrays in the list *frames* we just created and put them in a five by five matrix to form a single picture.

First we take one image out of every 100 images in the list *frames* and put them in a new list *plots*, like so:

```
[21]:
plots=frames[::100]
```

There are roughly 26 images in the list *plots*, and we take images 2 to 26 to form a five by five matrix in a picture using the *matplotlib* library, like this:

```
[22]:
import matplotlib.pyplot as plt
plt.figure(figsize=(12,16),dpi=100)
for i in range(25):
    plt.subplot(5,5,i+1)
    plt.imshow(plots[i+1])
    plt.axis('off')
```

```
plt.subplots_adjust(bottom=0.001,right=0.999,top=0.999,
left=0.001, hspace=-0.1,wspace=0.1)
plt.savefig("files/ch18/trained_pg.png")
```

If you open the file *trained_pg.png* on your computer, you'll see a picture similar to Figure 18.3. It has 25 subplots in it. In each subplot, you can see the score of the two players at the top of the screen. While the score of the opponent remains at 0

Figure 18.3 A Pong game with the trained policy gradient agent

at all 25 subplots, the score of the trained policy gradient agent increases gradually from 1 to 2,..., then to 20 in the last image. The picture shows that the trained policy gradient agent plays the game perfectly, which demonstrates the effectiveness of the policy-based deep RL algorithm.

18.6 GLOSSARY

- **Policy:** In reinforcement learning, a policy is a decision rule to guide the agent which action to take in a given state.
- **Policy-Based RL:** A branch of reinforcement learning in which the algorithm directly trains a policy to guide the agent to take an action in a given state, rather than estimating the value functions associated with different actions.
- **Policy Gradient Method:** A reinforcement learning method in which the parameterized policy guides the agent to take actions in a given state. During the learning process, the agent tweaks the parameters in the policy model based on actions and observed rewards.

18.7 EXERCISES

18.1 Modify the third code cell in Section 18.2.1 so that the agent chooses 30 random moves. Draw a picture of the last game window using the *matplotlib* library.

18.2 Follow the previous question. Rerun the first two code cells in Section 18.2.2 and show the cropped and downsized game window.

18.3 Modify the last code cell in Section 18.3.2 and change the *resume* argument to *True* and rerun the cell.

## CHAPTER 19

The Policy Gradient Method in Breakout

An idea is always a generalization, and generalization is a property of thinking. To generalize means to think.

– Georg Wilhelm Friedrich Hegel

NOW THAT YOU understand how the policy gradient method works from the last chapter, you'll generalize the method to other Atari games such as Breakout. You'll modify the algorithm based on the differences between Pong and Breakout to make the policy gradient method work in the Breakout game.

Specifically, in the Atari Pong game, the agent only needs to choose between one of the two actions: moving the paddle up or down. Therefore, the agent essentially faces a binary classification problem. In contrast, in Breakout, there are four possible actions that the agent can take in each time step. You'll modify the policy neural network so that the output layer has four neurons, one for each possible action.

You also need to modify the rewards in Breakout to train the policy gradient agent effectively. Specifically, in the Pong game, the reward is already structured correctly for you: the agent has a reward of 1 every time it scores a point and a reward of −1 every time it loses a point; otherwise, the reward is 0 in a time step. In contrast, in Breakout, the agent has five lives in each episode of the game. The reward is 0 in all time steps except when the agent loses all five lives, in which case the reward is −1. You'll count the number of lives the agent has in each time step. You'll change the reward from 0 to −1 every time the agent loses a life (i.e., fails to catch the ball with the paddle at the bottom of the screen).

After about 500,000 episodes of training, the agent learns to dig a tunnel on the side to send the ball to the back of the wall to score more efficiently. You'll capture such episodes and create an animation of the tunnel-digging process. Further, you'll also learn the limitations of the policy gradient method in training the Breakout game agent: when taking the difference of two consecutive frames, the layers of bricks disappear and this means the agent cannot remove all bricks in the game.

New Skills in This Chapter

- Creating a policy neural network with multiple outputs
- Modify the rewards in the Atari Breakout game
- Training and testing a policy network for Breakout
- Zeroing in on certain time steps of a game episode

Before you start, open the Jupyter Notebook app in the virtual environment MLA on your computer. After that, open a blank Jupyter notebook and save it as *ch19.ipynb* in the directory /Desktop/mla/ on your computer. Next, we'll create a subdirectory /files/ch19/ to store files for this chapter.

Start a new cell in *ch19.ipynb* and execute the following lines of code in it:

```
[1]: import os

     os.makedirs("files/ch19", exist_ok=True)
```

19.1 GET STARTED WITH THE BREAKOUT GAME

In this section, you'll learn the special features of the Atari Breakout game. We'll focus on the features that are different from those in the Pong game.

19.1.1 The Breakout Game

Run the lines of code below to start the Breakout game:

```
[2]: import gym
     env = gym.make("Breakout-v0")
     env.reset()
     env.render()
```

```
[2]: True
```

You should see a Breakout game frame in a separate game window. On the top of the screen, the current score and the number of lives left are displayed.

You can check the action space and observation space of the game as follows:

```
[3]: actions = env.action_space
     print(f"The action space for Breakout is {actions}")
```

```
obs_space = env.observation_space
print(f"The observation space for Breakout {obs_space}")
```

The action space for Breakout is Discrete(4)
The observation space for Breakout Box(210, 160, 3)

There are four possible actions the agent can take:

- action 0: doing nothing
- action 1: firing the ball
- action 2: moving the paddle to the right
- action 3: moving the paddle to the left

In the Pong game, the ball is automatically fired. In Breakout, the agent needs to trigger the firing action. So we have to treat this as a multi-category classification problem.

Similar to the Pong game, each observation is a color picture of 210 pixels tall and 160 pixels wide. The following cell displays a game window:

[4]:
```
import matplotlib.pyplot as plt
import numpy as np

env.reset()
# Run 20 steps so the ball appears in the picture
for _ in range(20):
    action = np.random.choice([0,1,2,3])
    obs, reward, done, info = env.step(action)
plt.imshow(obs)
plt.show()
```

If you don't see a ball in the picture, rerun the above cell until you see one.

19.1.2 Preprocess the Game Frames

The input size of the game frame is too large, we'll process the image like we did for the Pong game in the last chapter to reduce the size while retaining vital information to train the model to win the game.

Specifically, we'll perform cropping, downsizing, and differencing before we feed the raw pixels into the model to train the agent.

Cropping means we remove the top and the bottom of the game frame to reduce the input size, like so:

[5]:
```
obs_cropped = obs[35:195]
plt.imshow(obs_cropped)
plt.show()
```

The size of the picture is now 160 by 160 pixels with three color channels. To further reduce the size of the picture, we'll use every other row and every other column. Additionally, we'll use just one of the three color channels to reduce the image size. We also remove the background colors and change the raw pixels to 1s and 0s only, like this:

```
[6]:  obs_downsized=obs_cropped[::2,::2,0]
      obs_downsized[obs_downsized==144]=0
      obs_downsized[obs_downsized==109]=0
      obs_downsized[obs_downsized!=0]=1
      plt.imshow(obs_downsized)
      plt.show()
```

The processed picture now has a size of 80 by 80 pixels. To let the agent know the direction of the movement of the Breakout ball, we'll use the difference between two consecutive frames, like we did in Chapter 18.

19.1.3   Obtain the Difference of Two Game Windows

We'll obtain the difference of two consecutive time steps after processing. Similar to what we have done in the last chapter, we define a *prepro()* function in the local module *ch19util*. Download the file *ch19util.py* from the book's GitHub repository and save it under /Desktop/mla/utils/ on your computer. The function *prepro()* preprocesses the Breakout game frame so that the size decreases from 210 by 160 pixels with three color channels to 80 by 80 pixels with one color channel.

We import the function from the local module and call it to preprocess the game window. We'll obtain the difference of two consecutive game windows and use it as the input to the policy network later when training the policy gradient agent.

```
[7]:  from utils.ch19util import prepro

      next_obs, reward, done, info = env.step(3)
      next_obs_downsized = prepro(next_obs).reshape(80,80)

      dif = next_obs_downsized - obs_downsized
      plt.imshow(dif)
      plt.show()
```

In the code cell above, we generate the next game window by choosing *action=3*. We then use the *prepro()* function defined in the local module *ch19util* to preprocess it so that it also has a size of 80 by 80 pixels. The difference between the two consecutive game windows is then shown as the output.

Note the limitations in processing the game windows by differencing two consecutive time steps. The layers of the bricks disappear from the picture. This is not a problem in early stages of the game since as long as the ball is caught by the paddle at the bottom, it will bounce up and hit a brick on the way up and you'll score no matter what. But in later stages of the game when many bricks are gone, the agent doesn't know where the remaining bricks are. It's impossible for the agent to aim at the bricks and score points. We'll address this limitation in Chapter 20 by using the Baselines game wrapper.

We define a *dif_breakout()* function in the local module *ch19util*. The function selects four game frames and creates a picture with 12 subplots in it. The top row shows the preprocessed pictures of the four game windows. The middle row shows the processed pictures of the next time step of the four game windows. The bottom row shows the difference between the first two rows. In the code cell below, we import the *dif_breakout()* function from the local module and call it to generate the picture, like this:

```
[8]: from utils.ch19util import dif_breakout

dif_breakout()
```

After running the above code cell, the picture *dif_breakout.jpg* is saved on your computer. If you open the file, you should see a picture similar to Figure 19.1. In the

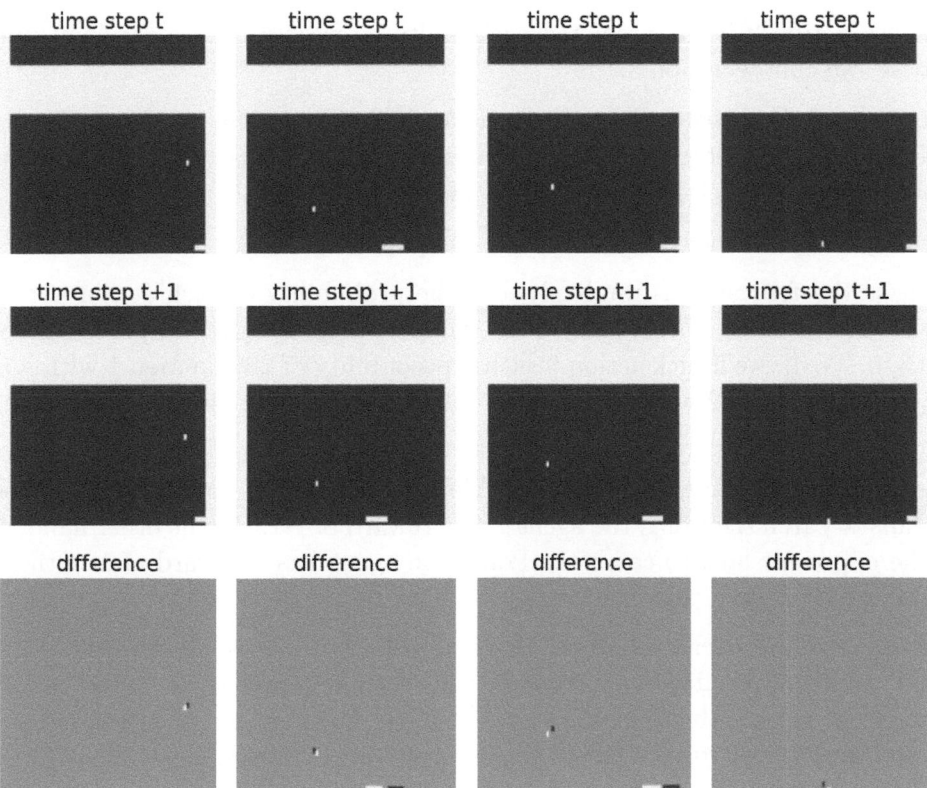

Figure 19.1 Differences of two time steps in Breakout

last row, you can tell the movement of the ball: it moves from the black spot to the white spot. For example, in the first column, the ball is moving from the top right corner to the bottom left corner. In the second column, the ball is moving from the top left corner to the bottom right corner. The agent, therefore, is able to see the ball movement from the images from the third row alone.

Again, you'll notice that the brick walls have disappeared in the difference images. But this is not a concern for early stages of the game since the ball can hit a brick and score points when most of the bricks are in place.

19.2   TRAIN THE POLICY GRADIENT MODEL IN BREAKOUT

We'll use the policy gradient method to train the agent in the Breakout game.

19.2.1   Changes Needed

The first thing we need to change is how the actions are determined. In the Pong game, we used the following line of code:

```
action = 2 if np.random.uniform() < aprob else 3
```

We choose action 2 if the predicted probability is greater than a random number; otherwise, we choose action 3.

In contrast, in the Breakout game, the agent has four actions to choose from. The model will make a prediction with four values, corresponding to the probabilities of the four actions. Therefore, we'll use this line of code:

```
action=np.random.choice([0,1,2,3], p=aprob)
```

We choose the four actions randomly, but the probability of each action is proportional to the predicted probability. For example, if the prediction probabilities are [0.2, 0.3, 0.1, 0.4], we'll pick action 0 with a probability of 20%, action 1 with a probability of 30%, action 2 with a probability of 10%, and action 3 with a probability of 40%.

In the Pong game, there are three possible rewards: -1, 0, and 1. Every time the agent fails to catch the Pong, the agent gets a reward of -1. On the other hand, every time the opponent fails to catch the Pong, the agent has a reward of 1. Otherwise, the reward is 0 in each time step.

In contrast, in the Breakout game, there are only two possible rewards: 0 and 1. Further, the agent has five lives, and each time the agent fails to catch the ball at the bottom of the screen, the number of lives decreases by one, but the reward is still 0. The agent gets a reward of -1 only when it loses all five lives.

Run the code cell below to see the reward structure in Breakout:

```
[9]:  env = gym.make("Breakout-v0")
      env.reset()
      env.render()

      while True:
          action = np.random.choice([0,1,2,3])
          obs, reward, done, info = env.step(action)
          print(reward, done, info)
          env.render()
          if info["ale.lives"]==4:
              break
```

```
0.0 False {'ale.lives': 5}
...
0.0 False {'ale.lives': 5}
0.0 False {'ale.lives': 5}
0.0 False {'ale.lives': 4}
```

You should see from the game window that the paddle just missed the ball. However, the reward is still 0 in the last time step. The number of lives changed from 5 to 4. We therefore will hard code in a reward of -1 whenever the number of lives decreases by 1.

19.2.2 Create a Policy Network

We'll create a policy neural network using the NumPy library without the help of the Keras API. We'll feed the difference of preprocessed images from two consecutive time steps into the neural network. The input layer of the network has 6400 neurons in it because the preprocessed images have a size of 80 by 80 pixels. There is one hidden layer with 200 neurons in it. The output layer has four neurons in it with softmax activation. Below, we define some hyperparameters for the model:

```
[10]:  H = 200
       learning_rate = 1e-4
       gamma = 0.99
       decay_rate = 0.99
       D = 80 * 80
       num_actions = 4
```

This is essentially a multi-category classification problem: the agent needs to decide which one of the four actions to take. We'll define a softmax function as the activation function in the model. Further, we'll define a one-hot encoder to compare the output from the policy model with the action taken:

```
[11]:  # Define the one-hot encoder and softmax functions
       def onehot_encoder(action):
           onehot=np.zeros((1,num_actions))
           onehot[0,action]=1
           return onehot

       def softmax(x):
           xi=np.exp(x)
           return xi/xi.sum()
```

During training, the policy network generates a vector p to guide the agent's action by using the following *policy_forward()* function:

```
[12]:  def policy_forward(model,x):
           h = np.dot(model['W1'], x)
           h[h<0] = 0
           logp = np.dot(model['W2'], h)
           p = sigmoid(logp)
           return p, h
```

The agent tweaks the model parameters periodically based on the rewards and actions taken, using the following *policy_backward()* function:

```
[13]:  def policy_backward(model,eph, epdlogp, epx):
           dW2 = np.dot(eph.T, epdlogp).ravel()
           dh = np.outer(epdlogp, model['W2'])
           dh[eph <= 0] = 0
           dW1 = np.dot(dh.T, epx)
           return {'W1':dW1, 'W2':dW2}
```

We use discounted rewards to assign credits properly. The rewards are discounted so that a sequence of actions, not a single action, get the credit/blame for the game outcome in the form of rewards. This is done through the *discount_rewards()* function below:

```
[14]:  def discount_rewards(r):
           discounted_r = np.zeros_like(r)
           running_add = 0
           for t in reversed(range(0, len(r))):
               if r[t] != 0:
                   running_add = 0
               running_add = running_add * gamma + r[t]
               discounted_r[t] = running_add
           return discounted_r
```

We let the agent interact with the game environment for one episode and collect data for training. The details are defined in the *training()* function in the local module *ch19util.* We calculate the gradients as well as the episode reward after each episode of game. To make the training more table, we update model parameters after every ten games instead of after each game. The details are defined in the *create_batch()* function in the local module *ch19util.*

19.2.3 Train the Policy Gradient Agent in Breakout

We define the *policy_breakout()* function in the local module *ch19util* for both training and testing of the model. The function is defined as follows:

```python
15]: def policy_breakout(test=False,resume=False,render=False,\
                     cutoff=25):
        rewards=deque(maxlen=100)
        env = gym.make("Breakout-v0")
        if test:
            batch_size=1
        else:
            batch_size=10
        if resume==True or test==True:
            model=pickle.load(open('files/ch19/pg_breakout.p','rb'))
        else:
            model={}
            model['W1']=np.random.randn(H,D) / np.sqrt(D)
            model['W2']=np.random.randn(num_actions,H) / np.sqrt(H)
        episode_count=0
        while True:
            batchrewards=create_batch(env,render,model,batch_size)
            rewards += batchrewards
            episode_count += batch_size
            running_reward=np.mean(np.array(rewards))
            if episode_count % 100 == 0 or test==True:
                template = "running reward: {:.6f} at episode {}"
                print(template.format(running_reward,episode_count))
                pickle.dump(model,\
                        open('files/ch19/pg_breakout.p','wb'))
            if test==False and running_reward>=cutoff:
                break
            if test==True and episode_count>=3:
                break
        env.close()
```

After every 100 episodes, the model is saved on your computer. You can stop training and resume training later by turning on the *resume=True* argument in the function. If you want to see the graphical renderings of the game windows, simply turn on the *render=True* argument in the function.

Let's first import the *policy_breakout()* function from the local module and train the model for one batch (ten games) with the graphical rendering turned on, as follows:

[16]:
```
from utils.ch19util import policy_breakout

policy_breakout(test=False,resume=False,render=True,cutoff=-5)
```

By turning on the *render=True* argument in *policy_pong()*, you can see the graphical renderings of the game windows. By setting *cutoff=−5* in the function, the training stops after one batch because the lowest possible score is −5.

Next, you can turn off graphical renderings of the game windows and train the model until the averge score is 40, like so:

[17]:
```
policy_breakout(test=False,resume=False,render=False,cutoff=40)
```

The training takes about about 24 hours and 500,000 episodes, or you can download the trained model *pg_breakout.p* from the book's GitHub repository. If the agent can have an average score of 40, you can capture an episode of the game in which the agent digs a tunnel at the side of the wall.

19.3   TEST THE POLICY GRADIENT AGENT IN BREAKOUT

We can now test the trained policy gradient agent in Breakout. If the agent sends the ball to the back of the wall, the ball can remove multiple bricks and have a high score in the episode. We therefore look for an episode with total rewards above, say, 100. In such episodes, you are likely to capture an incidence of tunnel digging.

We'll first test three games to see the scores of the agent in these games. After that, we'll search for an episode in which the total reward is above 100.

19.3.1   Test the Trained Policy Gradient Agent

First, we test three games by calling the *policy_breakout()* function and setting the *test* argument to *True*:

[18]:
```
policy_breakout(test=True,resume=True,render=True)
```

```
running reward: 17.000000 at episode 1
running reward: 36.500000 at episode 2
running reward: 37.333333 at episode 3
```

The results show that the trained policy gradient agent has scored 17, 36.5, and 37.33 points in the three games, respectively.

19.3.2 Search for Successful Episodes

Next, we start an infinite *while* loop. In each iteration, we play a complete game and record all game windows. If the score from an episode exceeds 100, we stop the *while* loop and save the frames in the episode on your computer as *above100.p*, like this:

```
[19]: from utils.ch19util import policy_forward
      import pickle

      while True:
          frames = []
          observation = env.reset()
          prev_x = None
          reward_sum=0
          while True:
              cur_x = prepro(observation)
              x = cur_x - prev_x if prev_x is not None else np.zeros(D)
              prev_x = cur_x
              aprob, h = policy_forward(model,x)
              action = np.random.choice([0,1,2,3], p=aprob)
              observation, reward, done, info = env.step(action)
              env.render()
              reward_sum += reward
              frames.append(observation)
              if done:
                  print(f"the score is {reward_sum}")
                  break
          if reward_sum>=100:
              file=f'files/ch19/above100.p'
              pickle.dump(frames, open(file,'wb'))
              break
      env.close()
```

It usually takes a couple of minutes for you to have an episode with rewards above 100. You can also change the criteria and keep only an episode with rewards above, say, 300. I'll leave that as an exercise for you.

In the next section, we'll zero in on the time steps in which the agent digs a tunnel on the side and sends the ball to the back of the wall. Since each episode of the game is different, we'll use the two episodes that I have generated as examples in the next section. You must modify the code cells in the next section if you want to use the episode that you created yourself.

19.4   ZERO IN ON INTERESTING TIME STEPS

Next, we'll zero in on the time steps of the game when the agent sends the ball to the back of the wall. We'll first use two episodes that I have recorded: download the file *above100.zip* from the book's GitHub repository. Unzip it and you'll see two files: *above100a.p* and *above100b.p*.

19.4.1   Animate Interesting Time Steps

To find out which frames contain images of the ball going to the back of the wall, we'll first convert all NumPy arrays into individual images, as follows:

```
[20]: frames=pickle.load(open('files/ch19/above100a.p','rb'))
      for i in range(len(frames)):
          frame=frames[i]
          plt.imshow(frame)
          plt.savefig(f"files/ch19/frame{i}.jpg")
```

This generates hundreds of individual images on your computer, and you can browse through these images to find out which time steps you should keep to highlight how the agent digs a tunnel on the side to send the ball to the back of the wall.

For frames in *above100a.p*, we remove the first 800 frames and the last ten frames, and convert the remaining frames into an animation, like this:

```
[21]: import imageio

      imageio.mimsave("files/ch19/tunnel_a.gif",frames[800:-10],fps=240)
```

Run the above code cell and open the file *tunnel_a.gif* on your computer. You'll see an animation of the policy gradient agent digging a tunnel on the side of the wall and sending the ball to the back through the tunnel. On the top of the screen, you can see the score increasing as the ball removes many bricks at the back of the wall. At the beginning of the animation, the score is 41. At the end, the score is 216. The animation demonstrates that the policy gradient agent has scored 175 points with one single return of the ball.

You can use the same method on the file *above100b.p* and keep only the interesting frames and convert them into an animation, like so:

```
[22]: images = pickle.load(open('files/ch19/above100b.p','rb'))

      imageio.mimsave("files/ch19/tunnel_b.gif", images[600:],fps=240)
```

The resulting animation *tunnel_b.gif* is saved on your computer. In the animation, the trained policy gradient agent manages to send the ball to the back of the wall twice.

19.4.2 Subplots of the Interesting Time Steps

Even though we cannot show animations in the hard copy of the book, we can create a figure with multiple subplots to show how the policy gradient agent sends the ball to the back of the wall. For that purpose, we showcase 25 pictures in different stages.

First we zero in on the frames that we want to use as subplots, like so:

```
[23]:  plots=frames[880::2]
```

Starting from the 881th frame, we select every other image from the list *frames* and put them in a new list *plots*. We then select 25 images and plot them in a five by five matrix, as follows:

```
[24]:  plt.figure(figsize=(12,16),dpi=100)
       for i in range(25):
           plt.subplot(5,5,i+1)
           plt.imshow(plots[i+1])
           plt.axis('off')
       plt.subplots_adjust(bottom=0.001,right=0.999,top=0.999,
       left=0.001, hspace=-0.1,wspace=0.1)
       plt.savefig("files/ch19/tunnel.jpg")
```

After running the above code cell, the picture *tunnel.jpg* is saved on your computer. If you open the file, you should see a picture similar to Figure 19.2. The five images in the first row show that the ball moves closer and closer to the tunnel at the left side of the wall. In the second row, the ball goes through the tunnel and moves to the back of the wall. In the last three rows, the ball gradually removes bricks at the back of the wall, and the score has increased from 41 to 83 as a result.

19.5 EXERCISES

19.1 Rerun the code cells in Section 19.1.1 to familiarize yourself with the Atari Breakout game.

19.2 Rerun the last code cell in Section 19.1.3. Go to your computer and open the file *dif_breakout.jpg* and figure out which direction the ball is moving to in each of the four columns.

19.3 Modify the code cell in Section 19.3.2 and capture a game episode in which the policy gradient agent has scored at least 300 points. Save the game windows in the episode as *above300.p*.

19.4 Continue the previous question. Modify the first two code cells in Section 19.4.1 and create an animation to highlight the time steps in which the agent sends the ball to the back of the wall.

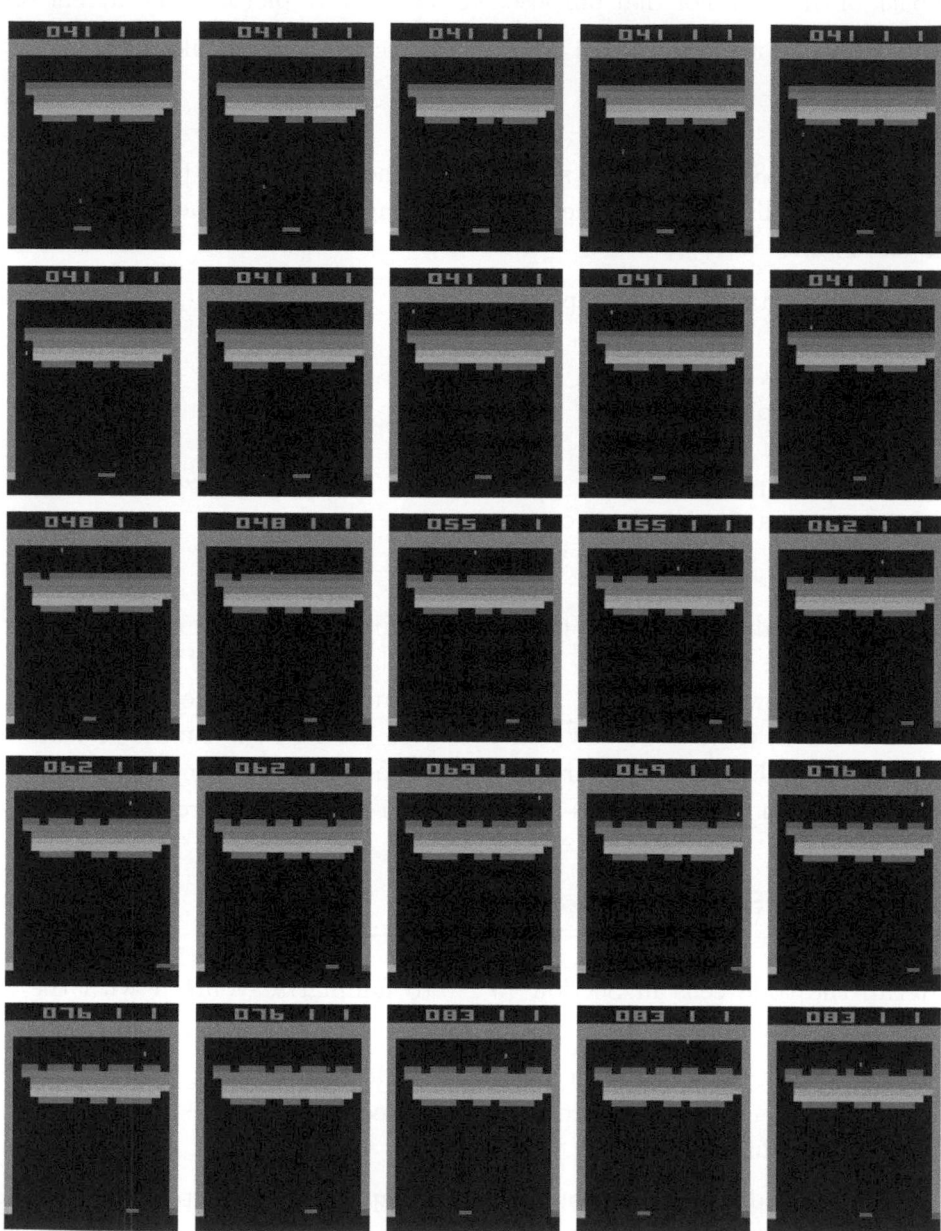

Figure 19.2 Subplots of game windows in Breakout

## CHAPTER 20

Double Deep Q-Learning

> These overestimations result from a positive bias that is introduced because
> Q-learning uses the maximum action value as an approximation for the maximum
> expected action value.
>
> Double Q-learing
>
> – *Hado van Hasselt, 2010, NeurIPS Proceedings*

DEEP Q-LEARNING has a well-known problem of overestimating Q values, as stated by the opening quote of this chapter [10]. In most cases, the overestimation bias is not a serious issue since the agent only cares about the relative magnitude of the Q-values for different actions. However, in complicated situations such as Atari games, this poses a problem and leads to wrong actions in certain scenarios.

To overcome this problem, we'll use the double Q-learning method proposed by Hado van Hasselt [10]. Specifically, we'll use one deep Q-network for training (the training network) and another deep Q-network for prediction (the target network), and periodically update the weights in the target network with the weights from the training network.

The double deep Q-learning algorithm can train the agent to play Atari Games very effectively. You'll learn to create a deep neural network with convolutional layers to extra features from the Atari gameplay screenshots. We'll use the Atari Breakout game as the example in this chapter. The trained agent can eliminate almost all bricks on the screen.

More importantly, the trained agent sends the ball to the back of the wall multiple times once there is at least one tunnel on either side of the screen. The agent has "learned" that it's more efficient to earn points that way than directly aiming at the bricks.

DOI: 10.1201/b23383-20

Furthermore, the model is highly scalable, and you can tweak the model slightly and apply it to other Atari games such as Space Invaders, Seaquest, and Beam Rider, as you'll see in the next two chapters.

An article in the journal *Nature* in 2015 demonstrates that a deep Q-network can train multiple Atari games to super human levels [17]. The model used in this chapter is largely based on the article, as well as the modifications made in the Keras example script by Jacob Chapman and Mathias Lechner [12]. I strongly encourage you to read through the explanations provided by these two sources to gain more intuition on double deep Q-learning.

At the end of the chapter, you'll create an animation of the time steps in the Atari Breakout game in which the trained double deep Q-learning agent sends the ball to the back of the wall five consecutive times. It's clear that the agent has "learned" to do this on purpose because this is a more efficient way of scoring points than aiming at the bricks directly.

New Skills in This Chapter

- Creating a double deep Q-learning model
- Obtaining the weights from a deep neural network
- Assigning weights to a deep neural network
- Training a double Q-network for Breakout
- Playing Breakout with the trained double Q-network

Before you start, open the Jupyter Notebook app in the virtual environment MLA on your computer. After that, open a blank Jupyter notebook and save it as *ch20.ipynb* in the directory /Desktop/mla/ on your computer. Next, we'll create a subdirectory /files/ch20/ to store files for this chapter.

Start a new cell in *ch20.ipynb* and execute the following lines of code in it:

[1]:
```
import os

os.makedirs("files/ch20", exist_ok=True)
```

We'll use the OpenAI *Baselines* library to train several Atari games from this chapter onwards. The *Baselines* library provides an Atari Gym wrapper for various games to make the training of RL models easier. For more details, go to their GitHub repository https://github.com/openai/baselines.

To install *Baselines*, make sure that you have installed *atari_py* and *ROMS* on your computer. If not, refer to Chapter 18 on how to install.

Also, make sure you are using version 0.15.7 of the OpenAI Gym environment. In case you accidentally installed a different version, run the following lines of code to correct it.

```
pip uninstall gym
```

```
pip install gym==0.15.7
```

Here are the steps to install *Baselines*:

- Step 1: Make sure you have *Git* installed on your computer; if not, see instructions via the link below https://git-scm.com/book/en/v2/Getting-Started-Installing-Git.
- Step 2: Open the Anaconda prompt (Windows) or a terminal (MAC or Linux) and activate the virtual environment *MLA*. Clone the OpenAI Baselines repository by running the following line of command:
  ```
  git clone https://github.com/openai/baselines.git
  ```
- Step 3: Go into the baselines directory by running the following line of command:
  ```
  cd baselines
  ```
- Step 4: Install the *Baselines* library in the virtual environment by running the following command:
  ```
  pip install -e .
  ```
  Make sure you don't miss the dot at the end of the above command.

After installation, restart your Jupyter Notebook for the library to take effect.

20.1 GET STARTED WITH OPENAI BASELINES

In this section, you'll learn the special features of the Breakout game with the *Baselines* game wrapper. I'll focus on the features that are different from the Atari Breakout game without using the game wrapper.

20.1.1 The Breakout Game with OpenAI Baselines

If you recall, in Chapter 19 we need to reconfigure the rewards by counting the number of lives remaining for the agent? Well, with the *Baselines* game wrapper, the agent has one life in each episode. That is, each time the agent loses a life (i.e., the paddle misses the ball at the bottom), the episode ends. In the original Atari Breakout game, the agent starts with 5 lives and the episode ends only when the agent loses all 5 lives.

This makes re-configuring the reward system much easier. Each time the game ends (i.e., *done==True*), we set the Q-value to -1. This is crucial for the success of the training. This is equivalent to setting the reward to -1 whenever the agent loses a life, as we did in Chapter 19.

To see how the variable *done* is related to the number of lives remaining, run the code in the cell below.

[2]:
```
from baselines.common.atari_wrappers import make_atari
from baselines.common.atari_wrappers import wrap_deepmind

# Use the Baseline Atari environment
env = make_atari("BreakoutNoFrameskip-v4")
# Process and stack the frames
env = wrap_deepmind(env, frame_stack=True, scale=True)

obs = env.reset()
while True:
    # randomly pick actions
    action = env.action_space.sample()
    obs, reward, done, info = env.step(action)
    print(action, reward, done, info)
    # Render the env
    env.render()
    if done:
        break
```

```
2 0.0 False {'ale.lives': 5}
2 0.0 False {'ale.lives': 5}
...
2 0.0 False {'ale.lives': 5}
2 0.0 True {'ale.lives': 4}
```

As you can see from the output, the agent starts with five lives. Once the agent loses one life, the variable *done* becomes *True* and the episode ends. Note that the reward is still 0, but we can code it as −1 by using the following line of code; you'll see it in the script for training later:

```
# Each time the agent loses a life, set Q to -1; important
new_Qs = Qs * (1 - dones) - dones
```

Run the following to close the game window.

[3]:
```
env.close()
```

20.1.2 Preprocessed Frames from Baselines

In Chapters 18 and 19, we need to preprocess raw images from the Pong and Breakout games by cropping and downsizing the game windows. The *Baselines* game wrapper does all those steps for us automatically. The game wrapper returns four consecutive frames of preprocessed images, each with a size of 84 by 84.

Let's visualize the preprocessed images from the library. Run the code in the cell below:

```
[4]:   import matplotlib.pyplot as plt
       import numpy as np

       npobs=np.array(obs)
       for i in range(4):
           plt.imshow(npobs[:,:,i])
           plt.show()
```

You should see four consecutive game windows. The number of lives is five in the first three frames and changes to four in the last frame. The four consecutive game windows tell the agent the movement of the ball so we don't need to use the difference of two consecutive game windows as we did in Chapters 18 and 19. The wall of bricks is clearly visible in the four preprocessed frames so the agent can aim at them and remove these bricks to earn high scores.

20.1.3   Subplots of Preprocessed Frames

We define a *four_frames()* function in the local module *ch20util*. Download the file *ch20util.py* from the book's GitHub repository and place it in the folder /Desktop/mla/utils/ on your computer. The function selects three game states. Since each game state has four consecutive game frames, we have a total of 12 subplots in a picture. Each row has four consecutive game windows so we can infer the movement of the ball. In the code cell below, we import the *four_frames()* function from the local module and call it to generate the picture with subplots.

```
[5]:   from utils.ch20util import four_frames

       four_frames()
```

If you run the above code cell and open the file *four_frames.jpg* on your computer, you should see a picture similar to Figure 20.1. For example, the top row in Figure 20.1 shows that the ball is moving from the bottom left corner to the top right corner. In the middle and the bottom rows, however, the ball is moving from the top left corner to the bottom right corner.

20.2   TRAIN THE DOUBLE DEEP Q AGENT

We'll train the agent to play the Atari Breakout game with a double deep Q-network in this section. The network is based on the 2015 *Nature* article [17]. However, Chapman and Lechner show that with an Adam optimizer instead of the RMSProp optimizer, the training is faster [12]. We therefore use the Adam optimizer as well.

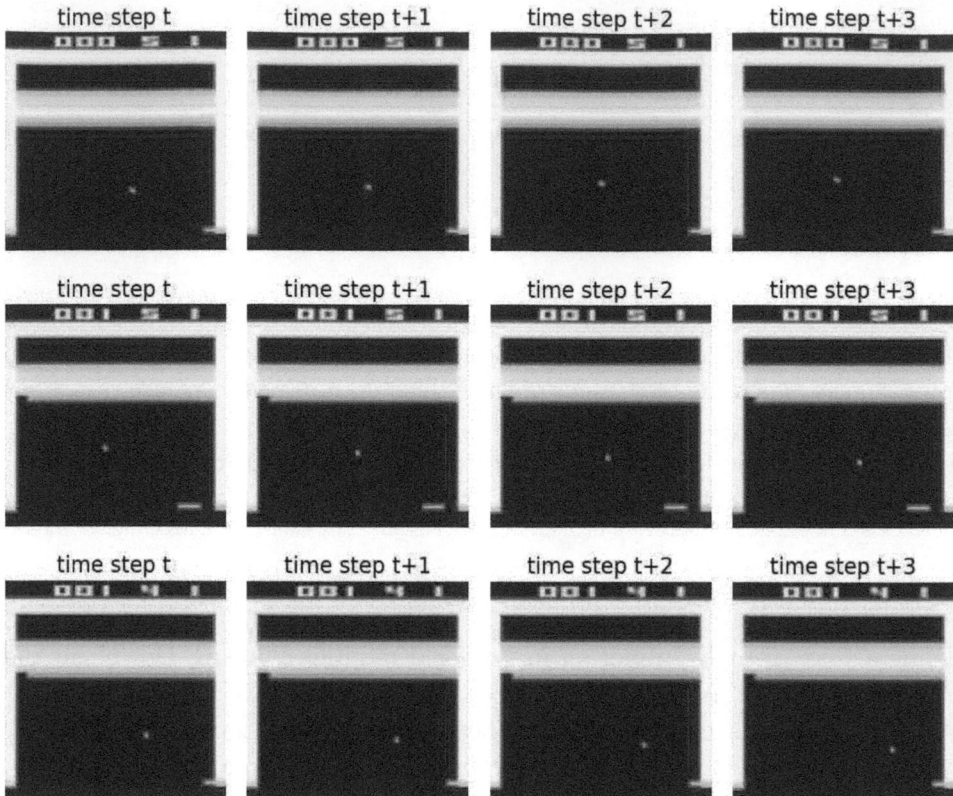

Figure 20.1 Four consecutive game windows by Baselines game wrapper

20.2.1 Create a Double Deep Q-Network

Q-learning has a well-known problem of overestimating the Q values. To overcome this, we use double deep Q-learning: we'll use one deep Q-network for training and another for prediction. We call the latter the target network and periodically update weights in the target network by using the weights from the training network.

The deep Q-network we use has convolutional layers since the inputs are two-dimensional pictures. We can use convolutional layers to extract spatial features from the graphs and associate them with game strategies.

```
[6]: import tensorflow as tf
from tensorflow import keras

# Input and output shape
input_shape = (84, 84, 4,)
num_actions = 4
def create_model():
    model=keras.models.Sequential()
    model.add(keras.layers.Conv2D(filters=32,kernel_size=8,
```

```
        strides=(4,4), activation="relu",
        input_shape=input_shape))
    model.add(keras.layers.Conv2D(filters=64,kernel_size=4,
        strides=(2,2), activation="relu"))
    model.add(keras.layers.Conv2D(filters=64,kernel_size=3,
        strides=(1,1), activation="relu"))
    model.add(keras.layers.Flatten())
    model.add(keras.layers.Dense(512, activation="relu"))
    model.add(keras.layers.Dense(num_actions))
    return model
```

The input to the model is four consecutive game windows so the agent can tell the movement of the ball. The output has four neurons in it, each representing the Q-value associated with an action. To overcome the overestimation problem in Q-learning, we create a training network and a target network. The two networks have the same model structure but different weights. We first initiate the two networks, as follows:

[7]:
```
# Network for training
dnn=create_model()
# Network for predicting (target network)
target_dnn=create_model()
```

To train the model, we use the Adam optimizer and the Huber loss function:

[8]:
```
lr=0.00025
optimizer=keras.optimizers.Adam(learning_rate=lr,clipnorm=1)
loss_function=keras.losses.Huber()
```

20.2.2 Train the Deep Q Network

Now that we have a double deep-Q network for Breakout, we'll train the model by letting the agent interact with the game environment. We'll adjust the model weights in the deep Q-network based on the actions and the resulting rewards, similar to what we did in Chapter 17 with the Cart Pole game.

We create a replay buffer to train the deep Q-network. The replay buffer stores game histories from the agent's interaction with the environment. When training the model, we randomly select a batch of past experience to update the model weights.

Below, we create a replay buffer with a maximum length of 50,000 elements:

[9]:
```
import random
from collections import deque

# Discount factor for past rewards
gamma = 0.99
```

```
# batch size
batch_size = 32
# Create a replay buffer
memory=deque(maxlen=50000)
# Create a running rewards list
running_rewards=deque(maxlen=100)
```

We have also created a list *running_rewards* to store the total rewards from each episode. The list has a maximum length of 100 and we'll use the average value in the list to determine when the training is complete.

To train the model, we select 32 observations from the replay buffer to update model parameters. The following function *gen_batch()* randomly chooses 32 observations and processes them so that they are ready for training:

[10]:
```
# Generate a batch
def gen_batch():
    # select a batch from the buffer memory
    samples = random.sample(memory,batch_size)
    dones = []
    frames = []
    new_frames = []
    rewards = []
    actions = []
    for sample in samples:
        frame, new_frame, action, reward, done = sample
        frames.append(frame)
        new_frames.append(new_frame)
        actions.append(action)
        dones.append(done)
        rewards.append(reward)
    frames=np.array(frames)
    new_frames=np.array(new_frames)
    dones=tf.convert_to_tensor(dones)
    return dones,frames,new_frames,rewards,actions
```

Next, we define a function *update_Q()* to update model weights based on a batch of game experience. Specifically, we'll adjust the weights so that the difference between the current Q-value, $Q(s, a)$, and the updated Q-value, *New* $Q(s, a)$ is minimized. See Chapter 17 for the idea behind deep Q-learning. The function *update_Q()* is defined as follows:

[11]:
```
# Replay and update model parameters
def update_Q():
    dones,frames,new_frames,rewards,actions=gen_batch()
    # update the Q table
```

```
preds = target_dnn.predict(new_frames, verbose=0)
Qs = rewards + gamma * tf.reduce_max(preds, axis=1)
# if done=1  reset Q to  -1; important
new_Qs = Qs * (1 - dones) - dones
# update model parameters
onehot = tf.one_hot(actions, num_actions)
with tf.GradientTape() as t:
    Q_preds=dnn(frames)
    # Calculate old Qs for the action taken
    old_Qs=tf.reduce_sum(tf.multiply(Q_preds,onehot),axis=1)
    # Calculate loss between new Qs and old Qs
    loss=loss_function(new_Qs, old_Qs)
# Update using backpropagation
gs=t.gradient(loss,dnn.trainable_variables)
optimizer.apply_gradients(zip(gs,dnn.trainable_variables))
```

We'll play the game many episodes so that the agent can interact with the environment and try different actions and observe the rewards. The deep Q-learning agent adjusts the model weights based on the feedback from the environment to maximize cumulative rewards.

We define some hyper-parameters below:

[12]:
```
# Let the game begin
running_reward = 0
frame_count = 0
# Number of frames to take random actions
epsilon_random_frames = 50000
# Train the model after 4 actions
update_after_actions = 4
# How often to update the target network
update_target_network = 10000
```

In the first 50,000 frames, the agent takes random actions before using predictions from the trained Q-network to select actions. Since we use four consecutive game windows as inputs, we'll train the model after every four actions. Finally, after every 10,000 frames, we'll update the weights of the target network.

The function *play_episode()* below plays a full episode of the Breakout game:

[13]:
```
def play_episode():
    global frame_count
    # reset state and episode reward before each episode
    state = np.array(env.reset())
    episode_reward = 0
    # Allow 10,000 steps per episode
```

```
for timestep in range(1, 10001):
    frame_count += 1
    # Calculate current epsilon based on frame count
    epsilon = max(0.1, 1 - frame_count * (1-0.1) /1000000)
    # Use epsilon-greedy for exploration
    if frame_count < epsilon_random_frames or \
        epsilon > np.random.rand(1)[0]:
        # Take random action
        action = np.random.choice(num_actions)
    # Use exploitation
    else:
        state_tensor = tf.convert_to_tensor(state)
        state_tensor = tf.expand_dims(state_tensor, 0)
        action_probs = dnn(state_tensor, training=False)
        action = tf.argmax(action_probs[0]).numpy()
    # Apply the sampled action in our environment
    state_next, reward, done, _ = env.step(action)
    state_next = np.array(state_next)
    episode_reward += reward
    # Change done to 1.0 or 0.0 to prevent error
    if done==True:
        done=1.0
    else:
        done=0.0
    # Save actions and states in replay buffer
    memory.append([state, state_next, action, reward, done])
    # current state becomes the next state in next round
    state = state_next
    # Update Q once batch size is over 32
    if len(memory) > batch_size and \
        frame_count % update_after_actions == 0:
        update_Q()
    if frame_count % update_target_network == 0:
        # update the target network with new weights
        target_dnn.set_weights(dnn.get_weights())
        # Periodically save the model
        dnn.save("files/ch20/DoubleQ_Breakout.h5")
    if done:
        running_rewards.append(episode_reward)
        break
```

After each time step, we collect the experience data and put them in the replay buffer. The experience data contains five pieces of information: the old state, the new state, action taken, reward, and the variable *done* indicating whether the game has ended. To help organize the data, we put the five pieces of information in a list and add to the replay buffer *memory*. After every four time steps, if the number of observations in the replay buffer *memory* is greater than 32, we update the model weights.

We train the model till the running reward is greater than 20: this means that in the past 100 games, the double deep Q-learning agent has earned an average reward of more than 20.

```
14]:  episode=0
      frame_count=0
      while True:
          episode += 1
          play_episode()
          running_reward = np.mean(np.array(running_rewards))
          if episode%20==0:
              # Log details
              msg="running reward: {:.2f} at episode {} and frame {}"
              print(msg.format(running_reward,episode,frame_count))
          if running_reward>20:
              dnn.save("files/ch20/DoubleQ_Breakout.h5")
              print(f"solved at episode {episode}")
              break
```

The above program takes two to three days to run on a regular computer. Once done, the trained model is saved as *DoubleQ_breakout.h5* on your computer. Alternatively, you can download the trained model from the book's GitHub repository.

20.3   TEST THE TRAINED BREAKOUT AGENT

In this section, you'll first play five episodes of Breakout using the trained model, so that you can visualize the trained double deep Q-agent in action.

After that, you'll play 100 episodes of the game and see what the average score is, without the graphical rendering of the game windows.

20.3.1   Testing One Original Episode

In each episode of the original Atari Breakout game, the agent has five lives. But the Baselines game wrapper breaks it down to five smaller episodes. In each new episode, the agent has one life.

Here you'll play five consecutive episodes of the game with the Baselines game wrapper and that's equivalent to one full original episode of the game without the game wrapper.

You'll turn on the graphical rendering of the game windows so that you can visualize the game in action, like so:

```
[15]: from tensorflow.keras import models

      reload=models.load_model("files/ch20/DoubleQ_Breakout.h5")
      for i in range(5):
          state=env.reset()
          for j in range(10000):
              if np.random.rand(1)[0]<0.01:
                  action=np.random.choice(4)
              else:
                  state_tensor=tf.convert_to_tensor(state)
                  state_tensor=tf.expand_dims(state_tensor,0)
                  action_Qs=reload(state_tensor,training=False)
                  action=tf.argmax(action_Qs[0]).numpy()
              state, reward, done, info = env.step(action)
              env.render()
              if done:
                  break
      env.close()
```

The trained model is able to remove most, if not all, bricks in the game. More importantly, the agent sends the ball to the back of the wall multiple times once there is at least one opening to the back of the wall. The agent has definitely "learned" that it's more efficient to earn points that way than directly aiming at the bricks.

20.3.2   Play Multiple Games and Test the Average Score

We now play 100 games and turn off the graphical rendering. We'll see what the average score is. To save space, we have defined a function *test_breakout()* in the local module *ch20util*. You can see the definition of the function in the file *ch20util.py* you just downloaded from the book's GitHub repository. The function plays 100 episodes of the Breakout game using the trained model. The agent takes the action with the highest Q-value in each time step with a 99% probability; it takes a random action with a 1% probability. We use exploration here to avoid repetitive actions in certain episodes: when there are very few bricks left on the wall, the trajectory of the ball is exactly the same without hitting any brick in each time step if we use only exploitation. This can go on for thousands of time steps and it delays the testing process. Below, we import and call the function *test_breakout()* to test 100 games:

```
[16]: from utils.ch20util import test_breakout

      test_breakout()
```

```
the score in episode 1 is 23.0
the score in episode 2 is 20.0
...
the score in episode 99 is 17.0
the score in episode 100 is 13.0
the average score is 16.62
```

The function prints out the score in each episode as well as the average score. The output above shows that the average score is 16.62. Your output is likely to be different.

20.4   ANIMATE INTERESTING TIME STEPS

We'll highlight time steps in an episode in which the agent purposefully sends the ball to the back of the wall multiple times.

20.4.1   Collect a Successful Episode

We'll first record an episode with high scores. If the episode score is above, say 125, you are likely to see time steps in which the agent sends the ball to the back of the wall multiple times. Since each game is different, I'll use the episode I collected as the example below. As an exercise, you can find your own episode and zero in on the interesting time steps.

To save time, we have defined the function *collect_episode()* in the local module *ch20util*. We import the function and call it to capture an episode with a score of at least 125.

```
[17]:   from utils.ch20util import collect_episode

        collect_episode()
```

After running the above code cell, you'll see a file *breakout_frames.p* on your computer. It contains all the game windows in the episode, in the form of NumPy arrays. You can then zero in on the steps of the game when the agent sends the ball to the back of the wall multiple times. To do that, you can convert the game windows in the episode into individual pictures so that you know which time steps to focus on.

Since each game is different, I'll use the episode I collected as the example. Download the file *breakout_frames1.zip* from the book's GitHub repository and unzip the file and place it in /Desktop/mla/files/ch20/ on your computer. After that, run this code cell:

```
[18]: import matplotlib.pyplot as plt
      import pickle

      frames=pickle.load(open("files/ch20/breakout_frames1.p","rb"))
      for i in range(len(frames)):
          plt.imshow(frames[i])
          plt.axis("off")
          plt.savefig(f"files/ch20/photo{i}")
```

The above code cell takes about ten minutes to run. Once done, go to your local
folder to browse through the individual pictures. It seems that the agent has sent the
ball to the back of the wall from photos numbered 100 to 294. We therefore keep only
those time steps and convert them into an animation, like so.

```
[19]: import imageio

      imageio.mimsave("files/ch20/breakout_highlight.gif",
                      frames[100:294], fps=240)
```

If you run the above code cell and open the file *breakout_highlight.gif* on your computer, you should see an animation of the double deep Q-learning agent sends the
ball to the back of the wall five consecutive times. At the beginning of the animation,
the score is 220. At the end, the score is 343. The agent has scored 123 points without
losing one single life. Further, the agent never aims at any brick directly. All bricks
are removed by the ball bouncing off the wall at the top of the screen. It's clear that
the agent has "learned" to do this on purpose to earn points more efficiently.

20.4.2   A Picture with Subplots

Next, we create a figure with multiple subplots to show how the agent purposefully
sends the ball to the back of the wall multiple times. We first select 25 game windows
from the list *frames*, like so:

```
[20]: plots=frames[100:294][::8]
```

We have selected every eighth game window in the list *frames* and we have exactly 25
images in the new list *plots*. Then we plot them into a five by five matrix, as follows:

```
[21]: plt.figure(figsize=(12,16),dpi=100)
      for i in range(25):
          plt.subplot(5,5,i+1)
          plt.imshow(plots[i])
          plt.axis('off')
      plt.subplots_adjust(bottom=0.001,right=0.999,top=0.999,
      left=0.001, hspace=-0.1,wspace=0.1)
      plt.savefig("files/ch20/DoubleQ_plots.jpg")
```

Figure 20.2 Time steps in which the agent sends the ball to the back of the wall

Run the above code cell and open the picture *DoubleQ_plots.jpg* on your computer. You should see a picture similar to Figure 20.2. The 25 images show that the agent has sent the ball to the back of the wall multiple times. The top left subplot shows that the agent has a score of 220 and three lives. The bottom right subplot shows that the agent has a score of 343 and the number of lives is still three. The number of bricks remaining has also decreased significantly. The picture shows that the double deep Q-learning agent has learned a way to earn points efficiently.

20.5 GLOSSARY

- **Double Q-Learning:** A Q-learning algorithm in which one set of Q-values are used for training and another set for prediction.
- **Overestimation Bias:** In Q-learning, the estimated Q-values are generally greater than the true Q-values because Q-learning uses the maximum action value as the expected action value.
- **Training Network:** The deep network for training in double deep Q-learning. The weights in the training network are updated by using the game experience.
- **Target Network:** The deep network for prediction purpose in double deep Q-learning. The weights in the target network are updated periodically by using the weights in the training network.

20.6 EXERCISES

20.1 Install the *Baselines* library on your computer, by following instructions at the beginning of this chapter.

20.2 Rerun the code cell in Section 20.1.2 to visualize the preprocessed game windows from the OpenAI Baselines game wrapper. Determine which direction the ball is moving in the game windows.

20.3 Rerun the code cells in Section 20.4.1 and capture a successful game episode. Then zero in on time steps in which the agent sends the ball to the back of the wall multiple times.

20.4 Continue the previous question. Use the *imageio* library to convert the time steps your collected in the last question into an animation.

## CHAPTER 21

Space Invaders with Double Deep Q-Learning

We demonstrate that the deep Q-network agent, receiving only the pixels and the game score as inputs, was able to surpass the performance of all previous algorithms and achieve a level comparable to that of a professional human games tester across a set of 49 games, using the same algorithm, network architecture and hyperparameters.

Human-level control through deep reinforcement learning
– *Mnih et al, 2015, Nature*

IN 2015, THE DeepMind team published a paper on the journal *Nature* demonstrating that a deep Q-network agent is capable of achieving human-level control of 49 different Atari games such as Breakout, Space Invaders, Seaquest, Boxing... [17]. The team achieved this by using the same network structure and model hyperparameter values. The only inputs to the model are raw pixels of gameplay screenshots and the scores earned by the agent.

In Chapter 20, you have learned how to use a double deep Q-network to train an agent in one of the Atari games, namely Breakout, to achieve human-level control of the game. In fact, the deep Q-network agent has learned a strategy that human players didn't know before: digging a tunnel on the side of the wall and sending the ball to the back to score more efficiently. In this chapter and the next, you'll learn to generalize the idea and scale up the deep Q-network. Our ultimate goal is to create one single algorithm and apply it to all Atari games, as the DeepMind team did. We'll accomplish this goal in Chapter 22. In this chapter, you'll tweak the model we used in Chapter 20 so that you can apply it to another Atari game, Space Invaders. In each step, you'll learn how you can apply the same deep Q-network to Space Invaders. You'll understand the changes we need to make to the model and why. This way, you'll know which parts of the algorithm can be applied to all Atari games and which parts are specific to individual games. After this chapter, you'll be prepared to move on to Chapter 22, in which you'll create a single function to train all Atari games and use the name of the game as the only argument of the function.

Specifically, in this chapter, you'll learn the features of the Space Invaders game that are different from Breakout and other Atari games so you know how to tweak the training process. You then feed the raw pixels of the gameplay screenshots to the double deep Q-network to train the agent. Even though the agent does not know the rules of the Space Invaders game, it can manage to eliminate all invaders (i.e., aliens) on the screen, just by learning from the reward system (i.e., scores) via repeated interactions with the game environment. At the end of the chapter, you'll learn how to capture an episode of the game in which the trained agent eliminates all aliens and create an animation to highlight interesting time steps in the game.

New Skills in This Chapter

- Playing Space Invaders with and without the Baselines game wrapper
- Modifying an existing Q-network to apply to Space Invaders
- Playing Space Invaders with the trained double Q-network
- Capturing time steps that the agent eliminates all invaders

---

Before you start, open the Jupyter Notebook app in the virtual environment MLA on your computer. After that, open a blank Jupyter notebook and save it as *ch21.ipynb* in the directory /Desktop/mla/ on your computer. Next, we'll create a subdirectory /files/ch21/ to store files for this chapter.

Start a new cell in *ch21.ipynb* and execute the following lines of code in it:

```
[1]: import os

os.makedirs("files/ch21", exist_ok=True)
```

21.1 GETTING STARTED WITH SPACE INVADERS

In this section, you'll learn how to play the Space Invaders game, both with and without the Baselines game wrapper. I'll focus on the features that are important in terms of training game strategies and features that are specific to Space Invaders.

21.1.1 Space Invaders in OpenAI Gym

You'll first learn to play the Space Invaders game in OpenAI Gym, without the Baselines game wrapper.

The lines of code below will get you started.

```
[2]: import gym

     env = gym.make("SpaceInvaders-v0")
     env.reset()
     env.render()
```

[2]: True

You should see a Space Invaders game frame in a separate window. There are different rows of invaders on the screen. There is a number three at the bottom of the screen, indicating that the number of lives remaining for the agent is three at the beginning of the game.

You can check the action space and observation space of the game as follows:

```
[3]: # Action space
     action_space = env.action_space
     print(f"The action space for Space Invaders is {action_space}")
     # Meanings of the actions
     meanings = env.env.get_action_meanings()
     print(f"The meanings of the actions are\n {meanings}")
     # Print out the observation space in this game
     obs_space = env.observation_space
     print(f"The observation space is {obs_space}")
```

```
The action space for Space Invaders is Discrete(6)
The meanings of the actions are
 ['NOOP', 'FIRE', 'RIGHT', 'LEFT', 'RIGHTFIRE', 'LEFTFIRE']
The observation space is Box(210, 160, 3)
```

There are six possible actions the agent can take. In the above code cell, we use the *get_action_meanings()* method to print out the meanings of each action. The meanings of actions 0 to 5 are the following:

- action 0: doing nothing
- action 1: firing bullets
- action 2: moving to the right
- action 3: moving to the left
- action 4: moving to the right and firing bullets
- action 5: moving to the left and firing bullets

Each observation is a color picture of 210 pixels tall and 160 pixels wide. The following code cell generates an image of an observation by using the *matplotlib* library.

```
[4]: import matplotlib.pyplot as plt
     import numpy as np

     env.reset()
```

```
num_actions = env.action_space.n
for _ in range(200):
    action = np.random.choice(num_actions)
    obs, reward, done, info = env.step(action)
plt.imshow(obs)
plt.show()
env.close()
```

The agent randomly selects a move in each time step. We repeat this for 200 time steps. The game state *obs* is represented as NumPy arrays and we use the *imshow()* method in *matplotlib* to convert the game state into an image. After running the above code cell, you should see a game window of Space Invaders.

Next, we see how the reward system works in Space Invaders. Specifically, we print out the rewards in each time step, along with the number of lives left for the agent.

[5]:
```
from pprint import pprint

env.reset()
history = []
while True:
    action = np.random.choice(num_actions)
    obs, reward, done, info = env.step(action)
    env.render()
    history.append([reward, done, info])
    if info["ale.lives"]==2:
        break
env.close()
pprint(history[-10:])
```

```
[[0.0, False, {'ale.lives': 3}],
 [0.0, False, {'ale.lives': 3}],
 [0.0, False, {'ale.lives': 3}],
 [0.0, False, {'ale.lives': 3}],
 [0.0, False, {'ale.lives': 3}],
 [0.0, False, {'ale.lives': 3}],
 [0.0, False, {'ale.lives': 3}],
 [0.0, False, {'ale.lives': 3}],
 [0.0, False, {'ale.lives': 3}],
 [0.0, False, {'ale.lives': 2}]]
```

In the above code cell, we print out the reward, the value of the variable *done*, as well as the number of lives left for the agent. We stop the game when the agent loses a life. As you can see from the above output, the agent has three lives at the beginning of the game. In the last time step, the number of lives changes to two, which indicates that the agent has lost a life. The reward to the agent is 0 in the last time step even though the agent has lost a life. Further, the variable *done* is still *False* in the last time step when the agent loses a life. You don't see it in the above output, but the variable *done* turns *True* only after the agent loses all three lives.

Therefore, we need the help of the Baselines game wrapper to break an episode into smaller episodes so that we can effectively train the agent.

21.1.2 Space Invaders with the Baselines Game Wrapper

With the Baselines game wrapper, the agent has one life in each episode. That is, each time the agent loses a life, the episode ends and the variable *done* turns *True*. This makes re-configuring the reward system much easier. Each time the agent loses a life, we set the Q-value to −1. This is crucial for the success of training: by punishing actions that lead to losing a life, the model trains the agent to select actions to avoid being attacked by invaders.

Let's examine the game with the Baselines game wrapper and the modified reward structure in the game, as follows:

```
[6]:  from baselines.common.atari_wrappers import make_atari
      from baselines.common.atari_wrappers import wrap_deepmind

      # Use the Baseline Atari environment
      env = make_atari("SpaceInvadersNoFrameskip-v4")
      # Process and stack the frames
      env = wrap_deepmind(env, frame_stack=True, scale=True)

      obs = env.reset()
      history = []
      while True:
          action = env.action_space.sample()
          obs, reward, done, info = env.step(action)
          history.append([reward, done, info])
          env.render()
          if done:
              break
      pprint(history[-10:])
```

```
[[0.0, False, {'ale.lives': 3}],
 [0.0, False, {'ale.lives': 3}],
 [0.0, False, {'ale.lives': 3}],
 [0.0, False, {'ale.lives': 3}],
 [0.0, False, {'ale.lives': 3}],
 [0.0, False, {'ale.lives': 3}],
 [0.0, False, {'ale.lives': 3}],
```

```
[0.0, False, {'ale.lives': 3}],
[0.0, False, {'ale.lives': 3}],
[0.0, True, {'ale.lives': 2}]]
```

As you can see, in the very last time step above, the number of lives changes from 3 to 2 and the variable *done* becomes *True*. The episode ends as a result. Note that the reward is still 0, but we can code it as −1 by using this line of code during training later:

```
# Each time the agent loses a life, set Q to -1; important
new_Qs = Qs * (1 - dones) - dones
```

Run the following line of code to close the game window.

[7]:
```
env.close()
```

21.1.3   Preprocessed Space Invaders Game Windows

The Baselines game wrapper preprocesses the game windows for us and returns four consecutive images of preprocessed game windows, each with a size of 84 by 84 pixels.

Let's visualize the preprocessed game windows with the Baselines game wrapper. Run the code in the cell below.

[8]:
```
import matplotlib.pyplot as plt
import numpy as np

npobs=np.array(obs)
for i in range(4):
    plt.imshow(npobs[:,:,i])
    plt.show()
```

You should see four consecutive preprocessed Space Invaders game windows. Together, they tell the agent the movement of the invaders so the agent can select actions accordingly to avoid being attacked, eliminate aliens on the screen, and earn high scores. To visualize the preprocessed game windows, we define an *invaders_windows()* function in the local module *ch21util*. Download the file *ch21util.py* from the book's GitHub repository https://github.com/markhliu/MLA and place it in the folder /Desktop/mla/utils/ on your computer. The function selects three game states and creates a picture with three rows of subplots in it. Each row shows the preprocessed images of four consecutive game windows. In the code cell below, we first import the *invaders_windows()* function from the local module and then call the function to create the picture with subplots, like so:

[9]:
```
from utils.ch21util import invaders_windows

invaders_windows()
```

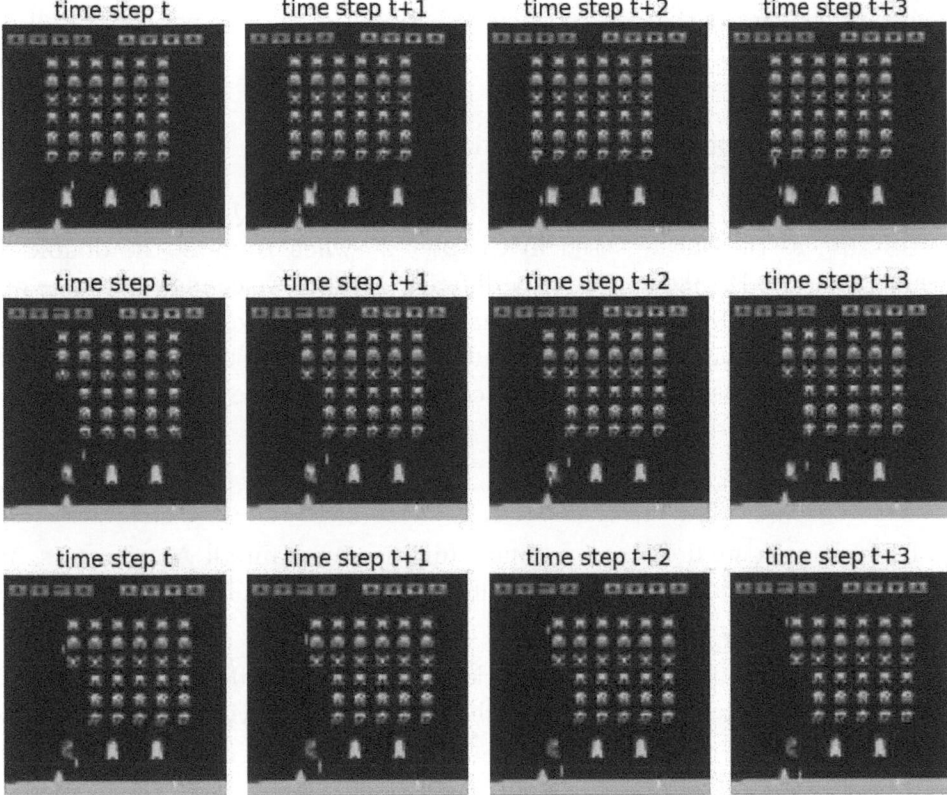

Figure 21.1   Four consecutive preprocessed Space Invaders game windows

If you run the above code cell and open the file *invaders_windows.jpg* on your computer, you should see a picture similar to Figure 21.1. Each row has four consecutive preprocessed Space Invaders game windows. The agent in the game must avoid being hit by the bullets fired by the invaders. The agent can fire bullets to eliminate invaders on the screen. The preprocessed game windows show the positions of the aliens and bullets. The agent can tell if a bullet is moving up or down by comparing the positions of the bullets in the four consecutive game windows.

In the first row in Figure 21.1, for example, the first two game windows show that a bullet is moving down and hits the shelter on the left. In the second row, a bullet moves down between the left and the middle shelter. In the bottom row, there are two bullets: one bullet moves up to the left of the screen and the other moves down close to the left shelter.

21.2   TRAIN THE DOUBLE DEEP Q-NETWORK

We can use the same Double Deep Q-Network from Chapter 20 to train the agent in the Space Invaders game, with a few modifications. In this chapter, we'll go through the necessary changes so that we know how to apply the same Q-network to all Atari games in Chapter 22.

21.2.1 The Same Double Deep Q-Network

In the local module *ch21util*, we first create a double deep Q-network that has the same structure as the one we used in Chapter 20 when training the double deep Q-learning agent for Breakout. The only difference is that we change the value of the variable *num_actions* from 4 to 6 since the agent must choose one of the six actions in each time step in Space Invaders. Instead of hard-coding in the number of actions, we'll retrieve the number of actions in Space Invaders from the action space by using the following line of code:

```
[10]: num_actions = env.action_space.n
```

In the next chapter, we'll define one single function to train all Atari games. We'll use the above line of code to automatically retrieve the number of actions in each game.

Next, we create the double deep Q-network in the local module *ch21util*. The model structure and hyperparameter values are the same for all Atari games, as we'll see in Chapter 22.

```
[11]: input_shape = (84, 84, 4,)
def create_model():
    model=keras.models.Sequential()
    model.add(keras.layers.Conv2D(filters=32,kernel_size=8,
        strides=(4,4), activation="relu",
        input_shape=input_shape))
    model.add(keras.layers.Conv2D(filters=64,kernel_size=4,
        strides=(2,2), activation="relu"))
    model.add(keras.layers.Conv2D(filters=64,kernel_size=3,
        strides=(1,1), activation="relu"))
    model.add(keras.layers.Flatten())
    model.add(keras.layers.Dense(512, activation="relu"))
    model.add(keras.layers.Dense(num_actions))
    return model
```

As in Breakout, the input to the double deep Q-network is four consecutive preprocessed game windows. The number of neurons in the output layer is equal to the number of actions that the agent can take in each time step. Each value in the output layer represents the Q-value associated with one of the actions. The trained agent will select the action with the highest Q-value, as in any deep Q-learning model. To overcome the overestimation bias in Q-learning, we create a training network and a target network (hence the name double deep Q-learning), as follows:

```
[12]: # Network for training
      dnn=create_model()
      # Network for predicting (target network)
      target_dnn=create_model()
```

We'll periodically update the weights on the target network by using the weights from the training Q-network. To train the model, we use the Adam optimizer and the Huber loss function as we did in Chapter 20:

```
[13]: lr=0.00025
      optimizer=keras.optimizers.Adam(learning_rate=lr,clipnorm=1)
      loss_function=keras.losses.Huber()
```

We'll also use the same optimizer and loss function in Chapter 22 so we can apply them to all Atari games.

21.2.2 The Same Training Process

The training process for Space Invaders is similar to that for Breakout. We'll let the deep Q-learning agent choose different actions to interact with the game environment. We'll adjust the model parameters in the deep Q-network based on the actions and the feedback from the game environment, in the form of rewards.

For that purpose, we create a replay buffer with a maximum length of 50,000 elements to train the deep Q-network. The replay buffer stores game histories from the agent's interaction with the environment. When training the model, we randomly select a batch of past experience to update the model weights.

In the local module *ch21util*, we use the same hyperparameters that we used in Chapter 20. We'll use these hyperparameters again for all Atari games in Chapter 22:

```
[14]: # Discount factor for past rewards
      gamma=0.99
      # batch size
      batch_size=32
      # Create a replay buffer
      memory=deque(maxlen=50000)
      # Create a running rewards list
      running_rewards=deque(maxlen=100)
```

The list *running_rewards* is created to record the total rewards from each of the last 100 episodes of games. We use it to determine if the training is complete. In Breakout, we stop training when the average score is at least 20. In Space Invaders, we'll do the same.

To train the model, we select 32 observations from the replay buffer to update model parameters. The function *gen_batch()* defined in the local module *ch21util* selects 32 observations and process them so that they are ready for training. Further, we define a function *update_Q()* in the local module to update model weights by using the output from the function *gen_batch()*. Go to the file *ch21util.py* and you'll see the exact definition of the functions. The two functions are the same as those we defined in Chapter 20, and we'll use them again in Chapter 22.

In the local module *ch21util*, we also define a function *play_episode()* to play a full episode of the Space Invaders game. We allow a maximum of 10,000 time steps in each episode. When selecting actions, the agent uses a combination of exploitation and exploration. Specifically, in the first 50,000 frames, the agent takes random actions before using predictions from the trained Q-network to select actions. Because the model uses four consecutive game windows as inputs, model parameters are updated after every four actions. To overcome the overestimation bias in Q-learning, we update the weights in the target Q-network after every 10,000 frames by using the weights from the training Q-network. The function *play_episode()* is defined below and we'll use a similar version of the function in Chapter 22 when we generalize it to all Atari games:

[15]:
```python
def play_episode():
    global frame_count
    # reset state and episode reward before each episode
    state = np.array(env.reset())
    episode_reward = 0
    # Allow 10,000 steps per episode
    for timestep in range(1, 10001):
        frame_count += 1
        # Calculate current epsilon based on frame count
        epsilon = max(0.1, 1 - frame_count * (1-0.1) /1000000)
        # Use epsilon-greedy for exploration
        if frame_count < epsilon_random_frames or \
            epsilon > np.random.rand(1)[0]:
            # Take random action
            action = np.random.choice(num_actions)
        # Use exploitation
        else:
            state_tensor = tf.convert_to_tensor(state)
            state_tensor = tf.expand_dims(state_tensor, 0)
            action_probs = dnn(state_tensor, training=False)
            action = tf.argmax(action_probs[0]).numpy()
        # Apply the sampled action in our environment
        state_next, reward, done, _ = env.step(action)
        state_next = np.array(state_next)
        episode_reward += reward
        # Change done to 1.0 or 0.0 to prevent error
        if done==True:
```

```
            done=1.0
        else:
            done=0.0
        # Save actions and states in replay buffer
        memory.append([state, state_next, action, reward, done])
        # current state becomes the next state in next round
        state = state_next
        # Update Q once batch size is over 32
        if len(memory) > batch_size and \
            frame_count % update_after_actions == 0:
            update_Q()
        if frame_count % update_target_network == 0:
            # update the target network with new weights
            target_dnn.set_weights(dnn.get_weights())
            # Periodically save the model
            dnn.save("files/ch21/DoubleQ_Invaders.h5")
        if done:
            running_rewards.append(episode_reward)
            break
```

The function collects gameplay experience data and store them in the replay buffer *memory* we created earlier. In each time step, if the number of observations in the replay buffer *memory* is greater than 32, we update the model weights after every four actions (i.e., four gameplay screenshots).

To train the model, we define a function *train_invaders()* in the local module *ch21util*. The function starts the training process until the average score in the past 100 games exceeds 20. The definition of the function is as follows:

```
[16]: def train_invaders():
        global frame_count
        episode=0
        frame_count=0
        while True:
            episode += 1
            play_episode()
            running_reward = np.mean(np.array(running_rewards))
            if episode%20==0:
                # Log details
                m="running reward: {:.2f} at episode {} and frame {}"
                print(m.format(running_reward,episode,frame_count))
            if running_reward>20:
                dnn.save("files/ch21/DoubleQ_Invaders.h5")
                print(f"solved at episode {episode}")
                break
```

We then import the function *train_invaders()* from the local module and call the function to train the double deep Q-network agent in Space Invaders, like so:

```
[17]: from utils.ch21util import train_invaders

train_invaders()
```

The model is considered trained if the average score exceeds 20. The above code cell takes two to three days to run on a regular computer. The trained model is saved as *DoubleQ_Invaders.h5* on your computer. Alternatively, you can download the trained model from the book's GitHub repository.

21.3 TEST THE TRAINED AGENT IN SPACE INVADERS

To test the trained model, you'll first play three episodes of the game so that you can visualize the trained double deep-Q agent in action in Space Invaders. Three episodes of the game with the Baselines game wrapper is equivalent to one original episode in Space Invaders without the game wrapper. The trained agent can potentially eliminate all space invaders on the screen before losing all three lives.

We'll also test the average effectiveness of the trained model by playing 100 episodes of the game and print out the average score, without the graphical rendering of game windows.

21.3.1 Testing One Full Original Episode

In the original Atari Space Invaders game, the agent has three lives in each episode. To make sure that the reward is −1 every time the agent loses a life, the Baselines game wrapper breaks it down to three small episodes.

Next, we define a function *invaders_episode()* in the local module *ch21util*. The function plays the game for three consecutive episodes with the Baselines game wrapper so we can test the trained agent in one full original episode. Further, the function turns on the graphical rendering of game windows so we can visualize the double deep Q-network in action.

The code cell below imports the function *invaders_episode()* from the local module and calls the function to test the trained double deep Q-network agent in Space Invaders for a full original episode, as follows:

```
[18]: from utils.ch21util import invaders_episode

invaders_episode()
```

When testing the trained model, we let the agent select actions randomly with a 1% probability. With a 99% probability, the agent selects the action with the highest Q-value predicted by the trained Q-network in each time step. After you run the above code cell, you should see a separate game window in which the agent eliminates most, if not all, invaders on the screen before losing all three lives.

21.3.2 Average Performance of the Trained Model

We now play 100 games and turn off the graphical rendering of game windows. We'll see what's the average score. To save space, we have defined a function *test_invaders()* in the local module *ch21util*. Open the file *ch20util.py* on your computer and take a look at the definition. The function plays 100 episodes of the Space Invaders game with the Baselines game wrapper using the trained model. The agent takes the action with the highest Q-value in each time step with a 99% probability; it takes a random action with a 1% probability. After each episode, the function prints out the score and the episode number. At the end, the program calculates the average score in the 100 episodes. Below, we import and call the function *test_invaders()*:

```
[19]:  from utils.ch21util import test_invaders


       test_invaders()
```

```
the score in episode 1 is 12.0
the score in episode 2 is 16.0
...
the score in episode 99 is 16.0
the score in episode 100 is 9.0
the average score is 13.37
```

The output above shows that the average score is 13.37. Your output is likely different since each game is different and there is randomness involved in the action taken by the agent.

21.4 ANIMATE SPACE INVADERS

We'll highlight an episode of the Space Invaders game in which the trained double deep Q-network agent manages to eliminate all invaders on the screen.

21.4.1 Collect Space Invaders Episodes

To capture an episode in which the agent has eliminated all space invaders on the screen, we'll collect three consecutive episodes of the game since one original game episode is split into three smaller episodes with the Baselines game wrapper. We put all game windows in a list *invaders*. We also use the *imageio* library to animate each episode so that we can visualize the game windows and determine if all space invaders are eliminated.

For that purpose, we have defined the function *collect_invaders()* in the local module *ch21util* as follows:

```
[20]: def collect_invaders():
          frames = []
          state = env.reset()
          for i in range(3):
              episode_frames = []
              for j in range(10000):
                  if np.random.rand(1)[0]<0.01:
                      action = np.random.choice(4)
                  else:
                      state_tensor = tf.convert_to_tensor(state)
                      state_tensor = tf.expand_dims(state_tensor,0)
                      action_probs = reload(state_tensor,
                                            training=False)
                      action = tf.argmax(action_probs[0]).numpy()
                  obs, reward, done, info = env.step(action)
                  state=obs
                  episode_frames.append(env.render(mode='rgb_array'))
                  if done:
                      frames.append(episode_frames)
                      imageio.mimsave(f"files/ch21/episode{i+1}.gif",
                                      episode_frames[::5], fps=240)
                      break
          env.close()
          pickle.dump(frames, open(f'files/ch21/invaders.p', 'wb'))
```

We allow for a maximum of 10,000 time steps in each episode and we collect a total of three consecutive episodes. Each individual episode is converted to an animation and saved on your computer.

Next, we import the function *collect_invaders()* from the local module and calls the function to collect a full original episode of the game:

```
[21]: from utils.ch21util import collect_invaders

collect_invaders()
```

Run the above code cell and then go to your local folder to see the animations *episode1.gif*, *episode2.gif*, and *episode3.gif*. If there is no episode in which all invaders are eliminated, rerun the above cell until you collect at least one episode in which all space invaders are eliminated from the screen.

21.4.2 Zero in on the Interesting Time Steps

Next, we'll zero in on the time steps of the game when the agent eliminates all space invaders on the screen.

Since each game is different, I'll use the episode I collected as the example. Download the file *invaders1.zip* from the book's GitHub repository and unzip the file. Place the unzipped file *invaders1.p* in /Desktop/mla/files/ch21/ on your computer.

First, let's create an animation of the three episodes, which corresponds to one full episode of the Space Invaders game without the Baselines game wrapper:

```
22]: import pickle
     import imageio
     frames = pickle.load(open(r'files/ch21/invaders1.p', 'rb'))
     fs = frames[0]+frames[1]+frames[2]
     imageio.mimsave("files/ch21/invaders1.gif", fs[::5], fps=24)
```

The file *invaders1.p* contains three lists. Each list contains the game windows from an individual episode of Space Invaders. We first combine the three lists into one single list *fs*. We then convert the NumPy arrays in the list into an animation, *invaders1.gif*. To speed up the animation, we use every fifth game window in the list *fs*.

To zero in on the time steps that the agent successfully eliminates all space invaders on the screen, we use only game windows 800 to 1354. We convert the highlighted part into a shorter animation *highlight.gif* as follows:

```
23]: highlights = fs[800:1355]
     imageio.mimsave("files/ch21/highlight.gif",
                     highlights[::5], fps=240)
```

Run the above code cell and open the animation on your computer. You can see that the agent has successfully eliminated all space invaders on the screen. The agent is also able to avoid attacks from the invaders and manage to capture the moving red dot at the top of the screen to score more points.

21.4.3 Subplots of Space Invaders

We also create a picture with subplots to visualize how the trained agent eliminates all invaders, avoids being attacked, and earns high scores.

For that purpose, we select one picture from every 23 game windows in the list *highlights*. The newly generated list *plots* contains 25 game windows:

```
24]: plots=highlights[::23]
```

Then we create a picture with 25 subplots in it, and the 25 game windows form a five by five matrix in the picture, as follows:

```
[25]: import matplotlib.pyplot as plt

      plt.figure(figsize=(12,16),dpi=100)
      for i in range(25):
          plt.subplot(5,5,i+1)
          plt.imshow(plots[i])
          plt.axis('off')
      plt.subplots_adjust(bottom=0.001,right=0.999,top=0.999,
      left=0.001, hspace=-0.1,wspace=0.1)
      plt.savefig("files/ch21/invaders_plots.jpg")
```

Run the above code cell and open the picture *invaders_plots.jpg* on your computer. You should see a picture similar to Figure 21.2. The 25 subplots show that the agent

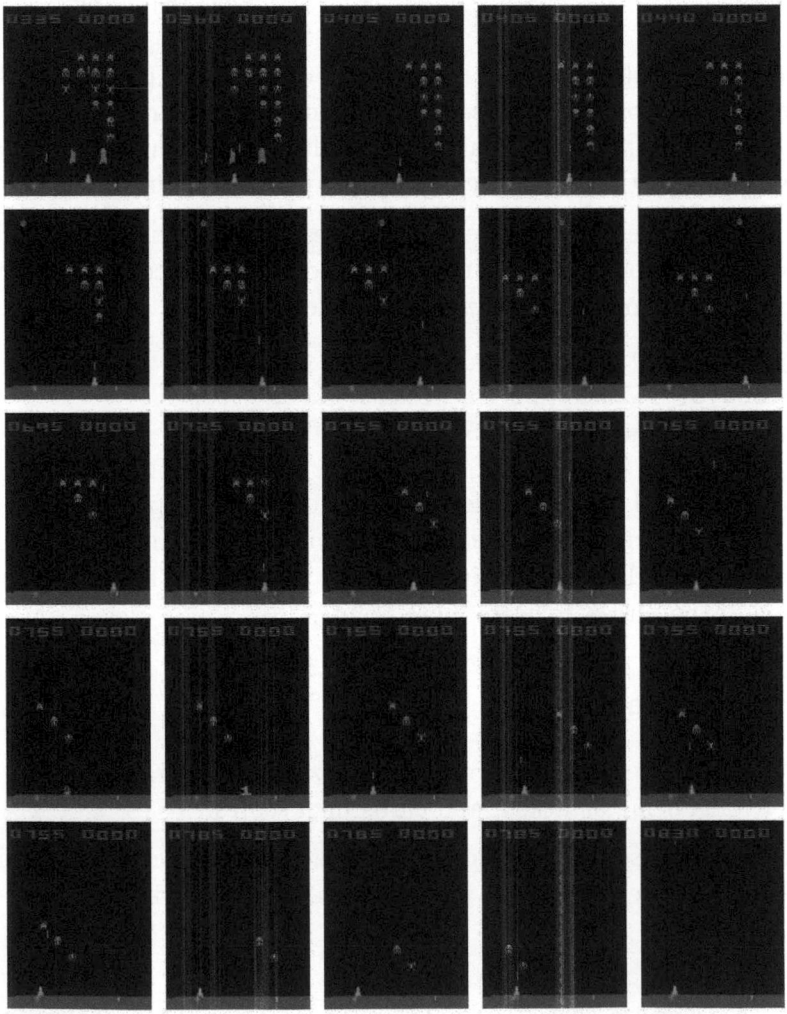

Figure 21.2 Time steps in which the agent eliminates all aliens

has eliminated all invaders on the screen and earned high scores. Specifically, the top left subplot shows that the score is 335 and there are many aliens left on the screen. The top right subplot shows that the number of aliens on the screen has decreased and the score is now 440. In the five subplots in the second row, there is a red dot at the top of the screen. The first subplot in the third row shows no red dot: the agent has captured the red dot and earned high scores because of it.

The first subplot in the bottom row shows that there are three aliens left on the screen. The number is reduced to two in the middle three subplots at the bottom row. The bottom right subplot shows that all aliens have been eliminated. The total score is 830 in the last subplot. The subplots in the picture show that the trained agent is able to move to the left or right to avoid being attacked by the bullets fired by aliens. It can also fire bullets to eliminate aliens on the screen. It also has learned to capture the moving red dot at the top of the screen to earn more points. The agent achieved all these without knowing the rules of the game. Instead, the agent acquired all these skills by interacting with the game environment and receiving feedback in the form of rewards, and that's the miracle of deep reinforcement learning!

21.5 EXERCISES

21.1 Rerun code cells in Sections 21.1.1 and 21.1.2 to familiarize yourself with the Space Invaders game with and without the *Baselines* game wrapper.

21.2 Rerun the second code cell in Section 21.1.3 and open the newly generated file *invaders_windows.jpg* on your computer to visualize the preprocessed game windows. In each row, determine whether a bullet is moving up or down in the game windows.

21.3 Rerun the second code cell in Section 21.4.1 until you capture an episode in which the agent eliminates all aliens on the screen.

## CHAPTER 22

Scaling Up Double Deep Q-Learning

> At DeepMind we have pioneered the combination of these approaches - deep reinforcement learning - to create the first artificial agents to achieve human-level performance across many challenging domains.
>
> *– DeepMind, 2016*

IN CHAPTER 20, you learned the basics of double deep Q-learning and used it to play the Atari Breakout game. In Chapter 21, you tweaked the same deep Q-network to play another Atari game, Space Invaders. Along the way, you learned what changes you need to make in the deep Q-network to apply it to a new Atari game. In this chapter, you'll learn to generalize and scale up the same deep Q-network to play any Atari game. To drive home the message, you'll define a function to apply to any Atari game with the same deep Q-network, same hyperparameters, and same training procedure. All you need is to put in the name of the Atari game as the only argument in the function, and the trained network will play the game at the super human level in any of the 49 Atari games.

Once the function is defined, you'll test it on two Atari games: Seaquest and Beam Rider. You'll see that the defined function can train the two games successfully by just taking one piece of information, the name of the game, as the input. Even though the agent does not know the rules of Seaquest or Beam Rider, it manages to earn high scores, just by learning from repeated interactions with the game environment and the rewards it receives as a result. This shows that machine learning models are highly scalable in the same domain. Better yet, as the opening quote of this chapter states [6], the idea behind deep reinforcement learning can be (and has been) applied to many other domains with great success. Indeed, DeepMind's AlphaGo algorithm, which is also powered by deep reinforcement learning, beat the World Go Champion Lee Sedol in March 2016. The news generated much media attention and made deep reinforcement learning the most promising field in ML.

At the end of this chapter, you'll also capture episodes of the Seaquest and Beam Rider games in which the double deep Q-network agent earns high scores. You'll create animations of the successful episodes to visualize the trained agent in action. With these skills, you are ready to train and test any Atari game by using deep reinforcement learning.

New Skills in This Chapter

- Playing an Atari game with and without the Baselines game wrapper
- Creating a Q-network to train all Atari games
- Defining A function to test any Atari game
- Capturing a game episode with high scores in an Atari game

Before you start, open the Jupyter Notebook app in the virtual environment MLA on your computer. After that, open a blank Jupyter notebook and save it as *ch22.ipynb* in the directory /Desktop/mla/ on your computer. Next, we'll create a subdirectory /files/ch22/ to store files for this chapter.

Start a new cell in *ch22.ipynb* and execute the following lines of code in it:

```
[1]: import os

os.makedirs("files/ch22", exist_ok=True)
```

22.1   GET STARTED WITH THE SEAQUEST GAME

In this section, you'll learn how to play the Seaquest game, both with and without the Baselines game wrapper.

22.1.1   The Seaquest Game in OpenAI Gym

You'll first learn to play the Seaquest game in OpenAI Gym without the Baselines game wrapper.

To initiate the game, run these lines of code in the cell below:

```
[2]: import gym

env1 = gym.make("Seaquest-v0")
env1.reset()
env1.render()
```

```
[2]: True
```

You should see a Seaquest game frame in a separate window, in which a submarine appears on the screen. The agent's score is at the top with a value of 0 at the beginning. The oxygen level appears at the bottom of the screen.

You can check the action space and observation space of the game as follows:

```
[3]: actions = env1.action_space
     print(f"The action space for the Seaquest game is {actions}")
     meanings = env1.env.get_action_meanings()
     print(f'''The meanings of the actions for the Seaquest game are
         \n {meanings}''')
     # Print out the observation space in this game
     obs_space = env1.observation_space
     print(f"The observation space for Seaquest game {obs_space}")
```

```
The action space for the Seaquest game is Discrete(18)
The meanings of the actions for the Seaquest game are
 ['NOOP', 'FIRE', 'UP', 'RIGHT', 'LEFT', 'DOWN', 'UPRIGHT',
 'UPLEFT', 'DOWNRIGHT', 'DOWNLEFT', 'UPFIRE', 'RIGHTFIRE',
 'LEFTFIRE', 'DOWNFIRE','UPRIGHTFIRE', 'UPLEFTFIRE',
 'DOWNRIGHTFIRE', 'DOWNLEFTFIRE']
The observation space for Seaquest game Box(210, 160, 3)
```

In Seaquest, there are 18 possible actions the agent can take. However, the agent doesn't even need to understand the game rules to learn to play it at a super-human level. All it needs is the right reward system. So we won't discuss the meanings of above 18 actions in the output.

Each observation is a color picture that is 210 pixels tall and 160 pixels wide, the same as that in any other Atari game. Run the following code cell and the output displays an example of a game window:

```
[4]: import matplotlib.pyplot as plt
     import numpy as np

     num_actions1 = env1.action_space.n
     env1.reset()
     for _ in range(20):
         action = np.random.choice(num_actions1)
         obs1, reward, done, info = env1.step(action)
     plt.imshow(obs1)
     plt.show()
     env1.close()
```

Next, you'll print out the outputs from each time step in the game to understand the reward system.

```
[5]:  from pprint import pprint

      env1.reset()
      env1.render()
      history = []
      while True:
          action = np.random.choice(num_actions1)
          obs1, reward, done, info = env1.step(action)
          env1.render()
          history.append([reward, done, info])
          if len(history)>1:
              if info["ale.lives"]<history[-2][2]["ale.lives"]:
                  pprint(history[-10:])
                  break
      env1.close()
```

```
[[0.0, False, {'ale.lives': 4}],
 [0.0, False, {'ale.lives': 4}],
 [0.0, False, {'ale.lives': 4}],
 [0.0, False, {'ale.lives': 4}],
 [0.0, False, {'ale.lives': 4}],
 [0.0, False, {'ale.lives': 4}],
 [0.0, False, {'ale.lives': 4}],
 [0.0, False, {'ale.lives': 4}],
 [0.0, False, {'ale.lives': 4}],
 [0.0, False, {'ale.lives': 3}]]
```

The agent starts with four lives in the game. When one life is lost, the reward is still 0, not −1. Further, the variable *done* is still *False* after a life is lost: the variable *done* turns *True* only after all four lives are lost.

Therefore, we need the help of the Baselines game wrapper to break an original episode into four smaller episodes.

22.1.2 Seaquest with the Baselines Game Wrapper

With the Baselines game wrapper, the agent has one life in each episode. That is, each time the agent loses a life, the episode ends and the variable *done* turns *True*. This makes reconfiguring the reward system easy: each time the agent loses a life, we set the Q-value to −1. This is crucial for the success of the training process: the agent is punished for losing a life. Therefore, the agent learns to avoid taking actions that lead to a loss of life. The trained agent is, therefore, able to live for many time steps and earn high scores.

Run the code in the cell below so you can see the reward structure with the Baselines game wrapper:

```
[6]: from baselines.common.atari_wrappers import make_atari
     from baselines.common.atari_wrappers import wrap_deepmind

     env1 = make_atari("SeaquestNoFrameskip-v4")
     env1 = wrap_deepmind(env1, frame_stack=True, scale=True)
     obs1 = env1.reset()
     history = []
     while True:
         action = env1.action_space.sample()
         obs1, reward, done, info = env1.step(action)
         history.append([reward, done, info])
         env1.render()
         if done:
             pprint(history[-10:])
             break
     env1.close()
```

```
[[0.0, False, {'ale.lives': 4}],
 [0.0, False, {'ale.lives': 4}],
 [0.0, False, {'ale.lives': 4}],
 [0.0, False, {'ale.lives': 4}],
 [0.0, False, {'ale.lives': 4}],
 [0.0, False, {'ale.lives': 4}],
 [0.0, False, {'ale.lives': 4}],
 [0.0, False, {'ale.lives': 4}],
 [0.0, False, {'ale.lives': 4}],
 [0.0, True, {'ale.lives': 3}]]
```

As you can see, when the number of lives changes from 4 to 3, the variable *done* becomes *True* and the episode ends. Note that the reward is still 0, not −1, when a life is lost. But we can code it as −1 by using this line of code later:

```
# Each time the agent loses a life, set Q to -1; important
new_Qs = Qs * (1 - dones) - dones
```

Run the following to close the game window:

```
[7]: env1.close()
```

22.1.3 Preprocessed Seaquest Game Windows

The Baselines game wrapper preprocesses the game windows for you. In each time step, it returns four consecutive preprocessed game windows, all with a size of 84 by 84 pixels.

Let's visualize the preprocessed game windows with the Baselines game wrapper. Run the code in the cell below:

```
[8]: npobs1=np.array(obs1)
     for i in range(4):
         plt.imshow(npobs1[:,:,i])
         plt.show()
```

You should see four slightly different game windows as the output. In particular, the first three windows should have three spare submarines at the top of the screen, meaning that the agent has three extra lives in reserve besides the life the agent currently has. In contrast, the fourth game window has only two spare submarines at the top of the screen. This means that in the very last time step, the agent has lost a life. The agent can infer movements of objects from the four preprocessed game windows during the training process.

22.1.4   Subplots of Seaquest Game Windows

We define a *seaquest_pixels()* function in the local module *ch22util*. The function selects three trajectories of the preprocessed game windows and creates a picture with 12 subplots in it. Each row represents a different trajectory and each row shows the preprocessed images of four consecutive game windows in the trajectory. Download the file *ch22util.py* from the book's GitHub repository and place it in the folder */Desktop/mla/utils/* on your computer, and take a look at the *seaquest_pixels()* function in the file.

The code cell below imports the *seaquest_pixels()* function from the local module and calls it to generate the picture with 12 subplots, like so:

```
[9]: from utils.ch22util import seaquest_pixels

     seaquest_pixels()
```

Run the above code cell and open the file *seaquest_pixels.jpg* on your computer, you should see a picture similar to Figure 22.1. Each row has four consecutive preprocessed Seaquest game windows. There are three spare submarines at the top of the screen in the first three images of the first row. There are only two spare submarines in the fourth image of the first row. This indicates that the agent just lost a life in the last time step. The middle and bottom rows show the same pattern: the fourth image in each row has one less life compared to the first three images in the row.

22.2   GET STARTED WITH BEAM RIDER

In this section, you'll learn how to play another Atari game, Beam Rider, both with and without the Baselines game wrapper.

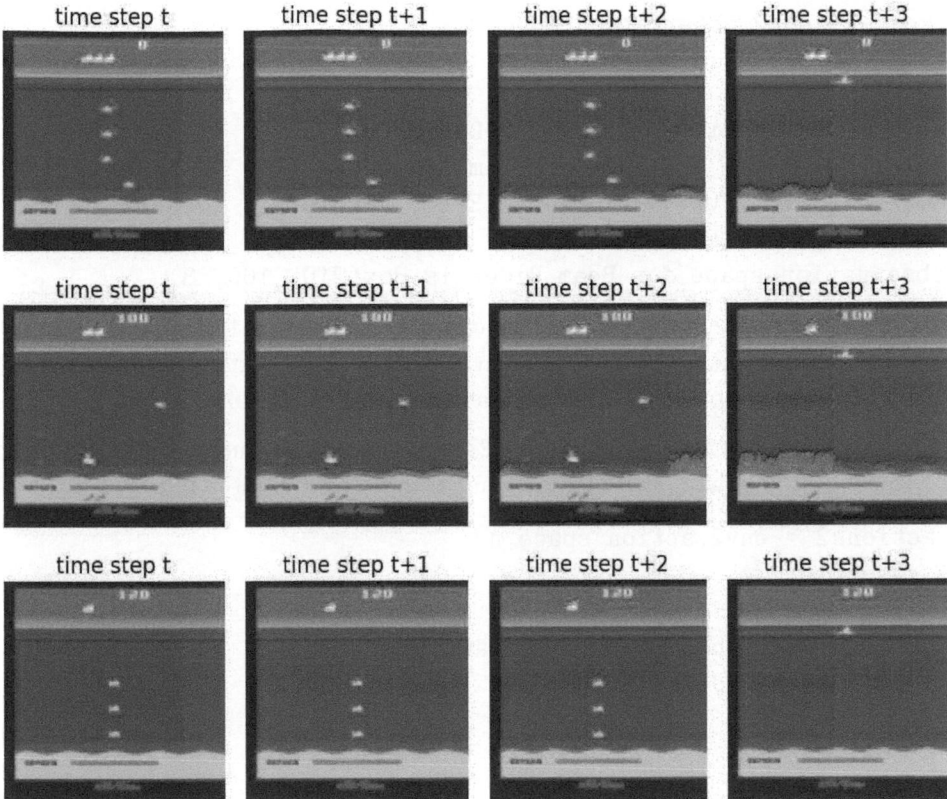

Figure 22.1 Preprocessed Seaquest game windows

22.2.1 Beam Rider without the Game Wrapper

You'll first learn to play the Beam Rider game in OpenAI Gym without the Baselines game wrapper.

The code cell below will initiate the game:

```
[10]: env2 = gym.make("BeamRider-v0")
      env2.reset()
      env2.render()
```

[10]: True

You should see a Beam Rider game frame in a separate window. The following code cell checks the action space and observation space of the game:

```
[11]: actions = env2.action_space
      print(f"The action space for Beam Rider is {actions}")
      meanings = env2.env.get_action_meanings()
      print(f'''The meanings of the actions for Beam Rider are
            \n {meanings}''')
```

```
obs_space = env2.observation_space
print(f"The observation space for Beam Rider is {obs_space}")
```

The action space for Beam Rider is Discrete(9)
The meanings of the actions for Beam Rider are
 ['NOOP', 'FIRE', 'UP', 'RIGHT', 'LEFT', 'UPRIGHT', 'UPLEFT',
 'RIGHTFIRE', 'LEFTFIRE']
The observation space for Beam Rider is Box(210, 160, 3)

There are nine possible actions the agent can take. However, the agent doesn't even need to understand the game rules to learn to play it perfectly. All we need is the right reward system. So I won't discuss the meanings of the nine possible actions.

Each observation is a color picture of size 210 by 160 pixels, the same as that in other Atari games. The following cell displays an example of a game window:

[12]:
```
num_actions2 = env2.action_space.n
env2.reset()
for _ in range(20):
    action = np.random.choice(num_actions2)
    obs2, reward, done, info = env2.step(action)
plt.imshow(obs2)
plt.show()
env2.close()
```

Next, you'll print out the outputs of the game to understand the reward structure:

[13]:
```
env2.reset()
env2.render()
history = []
while True:
    action = np.random.choice(num_actions2)
    obs2, reward, done, info = env2.step(action)
    env2.render()
    history.append([reward, done, info])
    if len(history)>1:
        if info["ale.lives"]<history[-2][2]["ale.lives"]:
            pprint(history[-10:])
            break
env2.close()
```

```
[[0.0, False, {'ale.lives': 3}],
 [0.0, False, {'ale.lives': 3}],
 [0.0, False, {'ale.lives': 3}],
 [0.0, False, {'ale.lives': 3}],
 [0.0, False, {'ale.lives': 3}],
 [0.0, False, {'ale.lives': 3}],
```

```
[0.0, False, {'ale.lives': 3}],
[0.0, False, {'ale.lives': 3}],
[0.0, False, {'ale.lives': 3}],
[0.0, False, {'ale.lives': 2}]]
```

The agent has three lives in this game. When one life is lost, the reward is still 0, not −1. Further, the variable *done* is still *False* after a life is lost. The variable *done* turns *True* only after all three lives are lost.

In the next subsection, we'll use the Baselines game wrapper to break each original episode into three smaller episodes.

22.2.2 Beam Rider with the Baselines Game Wrapper

With the Baselines game wrapper, the agent has one life in each episode. That is, each time the agent loses a life, the episode ends and the variable *done* turns *True*. Below, we look at the outputs from the game with the Baselines game wrapper:

```
14]:  env2 = make_atari("BeamRiderNoFrameskip-v4")
      env2 = wrap_deepmind(env2, frame_stack=True, scale=True)
      obs2 = env2.reset()
      history = []
      while True:
          action = env2.action_space.sample()
          obs2, reward, done, info = env2.step(action)
          history.append([reward, done, info])
          env2.render()
          if done:
              pprint(history[-10:])
              break
      env2.close()
```

```
[[0.0, False, {'ale.lives': 3}],
 [0.0, False, {'ale.lives': 3}],
 [0.0, False, {'ale.lives': 3}],
 [0.0, False, {'ale.lives': 3}],
 [0.0, False, {'ale.lives': 3}],
 [0.0, False, {'ale.lives': 3}],
 [0.0, False, {'ale.lives': 3}],
 [0.0, False, {'ale.lives': 3}],
 [0.0, False, {'ale.lives': 3}],
 [0.0, True, {'ale.lives': 2}]]
```

The above output shows that when the number of lives changes from 3 to 2 in the very last time step, the variable *done* becomes *True* and the episode ends. However, the reward is still 0, not −1, when a life is lost. We'll code the reward as −1 by using this line of code later:

```
# Each time the agent loses a life, set Q to -1; important
new_Qs = Qs * (1 - dones) - dones
```

Run the following code cell to close the game window:

[15]:
```
env2.close()
```

22.2.3   Preprocessed Beam Rider Game Windows

As in the Atari games we have seen before, the Baselines game wrapper preprocesses the game windows for us. The game wrapper returns four consecutive preprocessed game windows, each with a size of 84 by 84 pixels.

Let's visualize the preprocessed images from the Baseline game wrapper. Run the code in the cell below:

[16]:
```
npobs2=np.array(obs2)
for i in range(4):
    plt.imshow(npobs2[:,:,i])
    plt.show()
```

You should see the four consecutive preprocessed images of Beam Ridder game windows. The four images look slightly different from each other.

22.2.4   Subplots of Beam Rider Game Windows

We define a *beamrider_pixels()* function in the local module *ch22util*. The function selects three trajectories of the preprocessed game windows and creates a picture with 12 subplots in it. Each row represents a different trajectory and the four images in each row show the preprocessed images of four consecutive game windows. Take a look at the definition of the function in the file *ch22util.py* you just downloaded.

The code cell below imports the *beamrider_pixels()* function from the local module and calls it to generate the picture with 12 subplots, like so:

[17]:
```
from utils.ch22util import beamrider_pixels

beamrider_pixels()
```

If you run the above code cell and open the file *beamrider_pixels.jpg* on your computer, you should see a picture similar to Figure 22.2. Each row has four consecutive preprocessed game windows and they are different from each other slightly. At the top of each subplot, you can see the agent's score as well as the sector that the agent is currently in. The number in green at the top left corner of the screen indicates how many more alien spaceships the agent needs to destroy before upgrading to the next sector. The agent needs to destroy a total of 15 spaceships in each sector to enter the next sector. We'll feed four preprocessed images in each time step into the

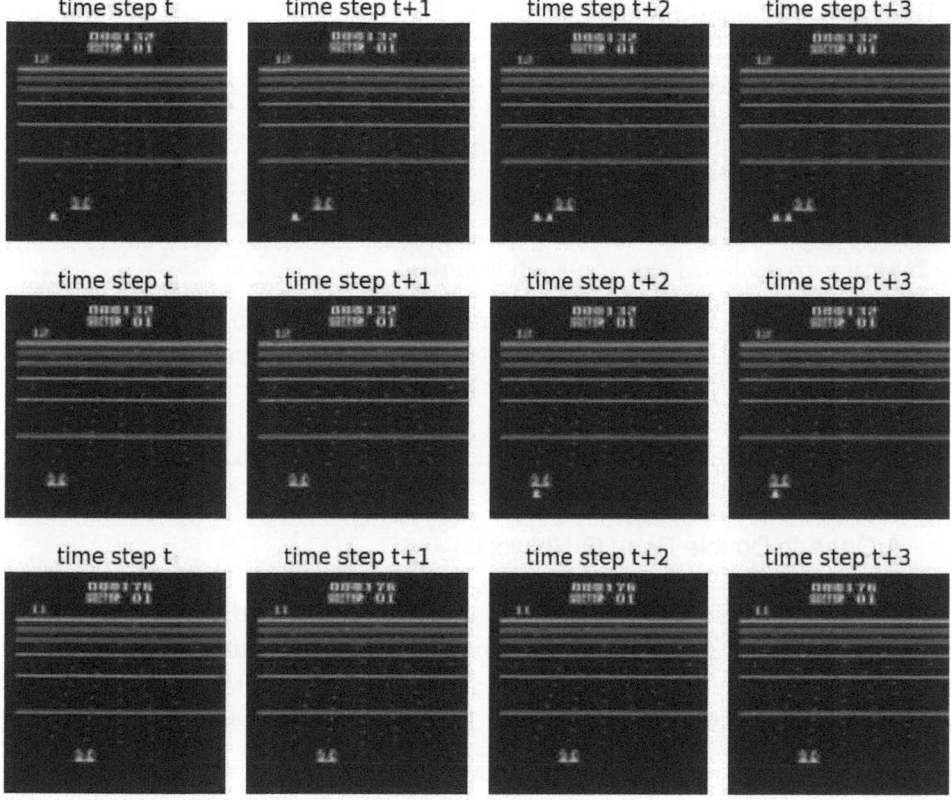

Figure 22.2   Preprocessed Beam Rider game windows

deep Q-network during training, and the agent can infer movements of objects by comparing their positions in the four consecutive game windows.

22.3   SCALING UP THE DOUBLE DEEP Q-NETWORK

Next, we'll scale up the double deep Q-network to train any Atari game. Specifically, we'll define a function to train all games, and the only input needed is the name of the game.

22.3.1   Differences among Atari Games

Our goal is to create a function to train a double deep Q-network agent in any Atari game, with the same network architecture, same hyperparameter values, and same training procedure. To that end, we first need to understand the differences among various Atari games.

Obviously, the name of the game is different. But there is a pattern. For the four games we have seen so far, Breakout, Space Invaders, Seaquest, and Beam Rider, their environment names are the following:

- BreakoutNoFrameskip-v4
- SpaceInvadersNoFrameskip-v4
- SeaquestNoFrameskip-v4
- BeamRiderNoFrameskip-v4

Therefore, we can use this line of code

```
f"{name}NoFrameskip-v4"
```

in the function to scale up the game environment.

The number of actions is different in different games. The numbers of actions in the above four games are 4, 6, 18, and 9, respectively. However, we can use the code:

```
num_actions = env.action_space.n
```

in the function to retrieve the number of actions from each game automatically.

22.3.2 A Generic Double Deep Q-Network

First, we create a double deep Q-network that can be applied to all Atari games in the local module *ch22util*. The function *create_model()* creates a deep Q-network. Since the number of actions the agent can take varies in different games, we'll use the variable *num_actions* as an argument in the function *create_model()*, like this:

```
[18]:  input_shape = (84, 84, 4,)
       def create_model(num_actions):
           model=keras.models.Sequential()
           model.add(keras.layers.Conv2D(filters=32,kernel_size=8,
             strides=(4,4),activation="relu",input_shape=input_shape))
           model.add(keras.layers.Conv2D(filters=64,kernel_size=4,
             strides=(2,2),activation="relu"))
           model.add(keras.layers.Conv2D(filters=64,kernel_size=3,
             strides=(1,1),activation="relu"))
           model.add(keras.layers.Flatten())
           model.add(keras.layers.Dense(512,activation="relu"))
           model.add(keras.layers.Dense(num_actions))
           return model
```

Later, we'll retrieve the number of actions in each game based on the name of the game. The model structure is the same as the one we used in Chapters 20 and 21 except the number of neurons in the output layer. The values in the output layer represent the Q-values associated with different actions the agent can take. Once the model is trained, the double deep Q-network agent selects the action with the highest Q-value as the best action in each time step.

To train the model, we'll use the same optimizer and loss function, which are the same as those we used in Chapters 20 and 21:

```
19]: lr=0.00025
     optimizer=keras.optimizers.Adam(learning_rate=lr,clipnorm=1)
     loss_function=keras.losses.Huber()
```

22.3.3 The Training Process for any Atari Game

To train the deep Q-learning agent in any Atari game, we'll use the same training process that we used in Space Invaders and Breakout. Specifically, we'll let the agent choose different actions to interact with the game environment. We'll adjust the weights in the deep Q-network based on the actions taken by the agent as well as the resulting rewards.

As in the paper published in the journal *Nature* by the DeepMind team, we'll use the same hyperparameters to train all Atari games. For example, we use the same discount rate of 0.99 and batch size of 32, as follows:

```
20]: gamma=0.99
     batch_size=32
```

Similar to what we did in Chapters 20 and 21, we create a replay buffer with a maximum length of 50,000 elements to store game histories from the agent's interaction with the environment. When training the model, we randomly select a batch of past experience to update the model weights.

```
21]: # Create a replay buffer
     memory=deque(maxlen=50000)
     # Create a running rewards list
     running_rewards=deque(maxlen=100)
```

We create the list *running_rewards* to determine when to stop training the model. The list stores the total rewards from each of the last 100 episodes of games. When the average score exceeds 20 in any Atari game, we consider the model trained and stop the training process. We select 32 observations from the replay buffer *memory* by using the function *gen_batch()* defined in the local module *ch22util*. We then use the function *update_Q()* in the local module to update model weights. Since the number of actions varies in different Atari games, we'll use the variable *num_actions* as the input to the function *update_Q()*, as follows:

```
22]: # Replay and update model parameters
     def update_Q(num_actions):
         global dnn,target_dnn
         dones,frames,new_frames,rewards,actions=gen_batch()
         # update the Q table
         preds = target_dnn.predict(new_frames, verbose=0)
         Qs = rewards + gamma * tf.reduce_max(preds, axis=1)
         # if done=1  reset Q to  -1; important
```

```
    new_Qs = Qs * (1 - dones) - dones
    # update model parameters
    onehot = tf.one_hot(actions, num_actions)
    with tf.GradientTape() as t:
        Q_preds=dnn(frames)
        # Calculate old Qs for the action taken
        old_Qs=tf.reduce_sum(tf.multiply(Q_preds,onehot),axis=1)
        # Calculate loss between new Qs and old Qs
        loss=loss_function(new_Qs, old_Qs)
    # Update using backpropagation
    gs=t.gradient(loss,dnn.trainable_variables)
    optimizer.apply_gradients(zip(gs,dnn.trainable_variables))
```

Further, since different functions defined in the local module need access to the double deep Q-networks, we make the Q-networks *dnn* and *target_dnn* global objects by using the keyword *global* in the function above.

To let the agent interact with the game environment, we define a function *play_episode()* to play a full episode of the game. As we did in Chapters 20 and 21, we allow a maximum of 10,000 time steps in each episode. The agent uses a combination of exploitation and exploration when selecting actions. Specifically, we define the function *play_episode()* in the local module *ch22util* as follows:

```
[23]:  def play_episode(num_actions,name):
           global frame_count,env,dnn,target_dnn
           # reset state and episode reward before each episode
           state = np.array(env.reset())
           episode_reward = 0
           # Allow 10,000 steps per episode
           for timestep in range(1, 10001):
               frame_count += 1
               # Calculate current epsilon based on frame count
               epsilon = max(0.1, 1 - frame_count * (1-0.1) /1000000)
               # Use epsilon-greedy for exploration
               if frame_count < epsilon_random_frames or \
                   epsilon > np.random.rand(1)[0]:
                   # Take random action
                   action = np.random.choice(num_actions)
               # Use exploitation
               else:
                   state_tensor = tf.convert_to_tensor(state)
                   state_tensor = tf.expand_dims(state_tensor, 0)
                   action_probs = dnn(state_tensor, training=False)
                   action = tf.argmax(action_probs[0]).numpy()
               # Apply the sampled action in our environment
```

```
        state_next, reward, done, _ = env.step(action)
        state_next = np.array(state_next)
        episode_reward += reward
        # Change done to 1.0 or 0.0 to prevent error
        if done==True:
            done=1.0
        else:
            done=0.0
        # Save actions and states in replay buffer
        memory.append([state, state_next, action, reward, done])
        # current state becomes the next state in next round
        state = state_next
        # Update Q once batch size is over 32
        if len(memory) > batch_size and \
            frame_count % update_after_actions == 0:
            update_Q(num_actions)
        if frame_count % update_target_network == 0:
            # update the target network with new weights
            target_dnn.set_weights(dnn.get_weights())
            # Periodically save the model
            dnn.save(f"files/ch22/{name}.h5")
        if done:
            running_rewards.append(episode_reward)
            break
```

To generalize the function to all Atari games, we use the name of the game, *name*, as an argument in the function. The function *play_episode()* collects gameplay experience data and stores them in the replay buffer *memory*. In each time step, we call *update_Q()* to update the model weights. The training stops if the running reward exceeds 20. After every 10,000 frames, we update the weights in the target network by extracting the weights from the training network. We periodically save the trained model in the local folder. The name of the trained model is the same as the name of the Atari game. For example, when we train the Seaquest game, the trained model is saved as *Seaquest.h5*; when we train the Beam Rider game, the trained model is saved as *BeamRider.h5*.

Finally, we define a function *train_atari()* in the local module to train an Atari game. The function starts the training process until the average score in the past 100 games exceeds 20. Here is the definition of the function:

```
[24]: def train_atari(name):
          global frame_count,env,num_actions,dnn,target_dnn
          # Use the Baseline Atari environment
          env = make_atari(f"{name}NoFrameskip-v4")
          # Process and stack the frames
```

```
env = wrap_deepmind(env, frame_stack=True, scale=True)
num_actions = env.action_space.n

# Network for training
dnn=create_model(num_actions)
# Network for predicting (target network)
target_dnn=create_model(num_actions)
episode=0
frame_count=0
while True:
    episode += 1
    play_episode(num_actions,name)
    running_reward = np.mean(np.array(running_rewards))
    if episode%20==0:
        # Log details
        m="running reward: {:.2f} at episode {} and frame {}"
        print(m.format(running_reward,episode,frame_count))
    if running_reward>20:
        dnn.save(f"files/ch22/{name}.h5")
        print(f"solved at episode {episode}")
        break
```

The function *train_atari()* takes the name of the game, *name*, as the only argument. It creates a game environment based on the argument *name* and extracts the number of actions that the agent can take, *num_actions*, accordingly. The function then initiates a training Q-network and a target Q-network for the Atari game. The function starts an infinite *while* loop to train the model, until the agent earns an average score of above 20 in the past 100 games.

We are now ready to use this function to train any Atari game: all we need to do is to import the function *train_atari()* from the local model and put the name of the game as the only argument in the function.

22.4   TRY IT ON SEAQUEST

Next, you'll apply the scaled up double deep Q-network on the Seaquest game. You'll use the function *train_atari()* we defined in the last section to train the double deep Q-network agent. After that, you'll test how effective the trained model is.

22.4.1   Train the Model in Seaquest

The following line of code will train the agent in the Seaquest game:

```
25]: from utils.ch22util import train_atari

     train_atari("Seaquest")
```

We import the function *train_atari()* from the local module *ch22util* and call the function. We put the name of the game, *Seaquest*, as the argument in the function. The training takes a couple of days. But you can use a pre-trained model that I put on the book's GitHub repository, saved as *Seaquest.h5*.

In the original Atari Seaquest game without the Baselines game wrapper, the agent has four lives in each episode. The Baselines game wrapper breaks it down to four smaller episodes: in each episode, the agent has one life.

Here you'll play the game for four consecutive episodes with the Baselines game wrapper. This is equivalent to one full original episode without the game wrapper. You'll turn on the graphical rendering of game windows so you can see the trained double deep Q-network agent in action.

```
26]: import tensorflow as tf

     reload1 = tf.keras.models.load_model("files/ch22/Seaquest.h5")
     state = env1.reset()
     for i in range(4):
         score = 0
         for j in range(10000):
             if np.random.rand(1)[0]<0.01:
                 action = np.random.choice(num_actions1)
             else:
                 state_tensor = tf.convert_to_tensor(state)
                 state_tensor = tf.expand_dims(state_tensor, 0)
                 action_probs = reload1(state_tensor, training=False)
                 action = tf.argmax(action_probs[0]).numpy()
             state, reward, done, info = env1.step(action)
             score += reward
             env1.render()
             if done:
                 print("the score is", score)
                 break
     env1.close()
```

```
the score is 3.0
the score is 30.0
the score is 29.0
the score is 0.0
```

As you can see, the trained model is able to have high scores in some episodes. The output above shows that the agent has earned 3, 30, 29, and 0 points in the four episodes, respectively.

22.4.2 Test the Average Score in Seaquest

We define a function *test_atari()* in the local model *ch22util* to test any Atari game by using a trained model. The function takes the name of the game as the only argument. It plays 100 episodes of the game without the graphical rendering of game windows. After each episode, the function prints out the episode number and the score. After 100 episodes, the function prints out the average score. The function *test_atari()* is defined as follows:

```
[27]: def test_atari(name):
          reload = tf.keras.models.load_model(f"files/ch22/{name}.h5")
          env = make_atari(f"{name}NoFrameskip-v4")
          env = wrap_deepmind(env, frame_stack=True, scale=True)
          scores = []
          num_actions = env.action_space.n
          for i in range(100):
              state = env.reset()
              score = 0
              for j in range(10000):
                  if np.random.rand(1)[0]<0.01:
                      action = np.random.choice(num_actions)
                  else:
                      state_tensor = tf.convert_to_tensor(state)
                      state_tensor = tf.expand_dims(state_tensor, 0)
                      action_probs = reload(state_tensor, training=False)
                      action = tf.argmax(action_probs[0]).numpy()
                  state, reward, done, info = env.step(action)
                  score += reward
                  if done:
                      print(f"the score in episode {i+1} is {score}")
                      scores.append(score)
                      break
          env.close()
          print(f"the average score is {np.array(scores).mean()}")
```

To test the trained model in Seaquest, we import the function from the local module and call it to test 100 episodes of the game, like so:

```
[28]: from utils.ch22util import test_atari

      test_atari("Seaquest")
```

```
the score in episode 1 is 44.0
the score in episode 2 is 1.0
the score in episode 3 is 0.0
the score in episode 4 is 9.0
...
the score in episode 99 is 41.0
the score in episode 100 is 0.0
the average score is 18.8
```

The output above shows the agent's score in each episode. Your output is likely to be different. The average score in most cases is around 20.

22.4.3 Animate a Successful Episode

We'll highlight episodes where the agent performs well. To that end, we'll first record 20 episodes of the game, and this is equivalent to five full original Atari Seaquest games.

The code cell below accomplishes that:

```
[29]: import imageio
      import pickle

      for i in range(20):
          state = env1.reset()
          frames = []
          for j in range(10000):
              if np.random.rand(1)[0]<0.01:
                  action = np.random.choice(num_actions1)
              else:
                  state_tensor = tf.convert_to_tensor(state)
                  state_tensor = tf.expand_dims(state_tensor, 0)
                  action_Qs = reload1(state_tensor, training=False)
                  action = tf.argmax(action_Qs[0]).numpy()
              state, reward, done, info = env1.step(action)
              frames.append(env1.render(mode='rgb_array'))
              if done:
                  pickle.dump(frames,\
                      open(f'files/ch22/{name}{i+1}.p', 'wb'))
                  imageio.mimsave(f"files/ch22/{name}{i+1}.gif",\
                              frames, fps=240)
                  break
      env1.close()
```

You'll see 20 short animations in your local folder. If you display them as extra large icons on your computer, you'll see the starting score in each episode from the thumbnail picture of the animation. You can calculate the points earned in most episodes by looking at the starting scores of this episode and the next episode.

Next, we'll select a successful episode to further examine it. In my case, the starting score of episode 2 is 600, and the starting score of episode 3 is 1200. Therefore, I can infer that the agent has earned 1200−600=600 points in episode 2. I will zero in on episode 2, and the episode number for you may be different.

How to select successful episodes

First, make sure you view the *gif* files as extra large icons in the local folder on your computer. You'll see the starting score in each episode from the thumbnail picture of the animation. You can calculate the points earned in most episodes by looking at the starting scores of this episode and the next episode. If the next episode has a much higher score than the current episode, the agent has earned high scores in the current episode.

Go to the book's GitHub repository and download the file *Seaquest2.zip*. Unzip the file and save the unzipped file *Seaquest2.p* in the folder /Desktop/mla/files/ch22/ on your computer. Then convert the game windows in the episode into an animation as follows:

[30]:
```
Seaquest2=pickle.load(open("files\ch22\Seaquest2.p","rb"))
imageio.mimsave("files\ch22\seaqueste2.gif",Seaquest2[::5],fps=24)
```

Run the above code cell and open the animation *Seaquest2.gif* on your computer. You can see that the agent has successfully warded off attacks from both left and right. At the beginning of the episode, the score on the top of the screen is 600. At the end of the episode, the score increases to 1200, indicating the agent has scored a total of 600 points in this episode.

We can also create a picture with 25 subplots to show the effectiveness of the trained double deep Q-network agent in Seaquest. For that purpose, we first select 24 game windows throughout the episode. We then add in the last game window and put the 25 images in a list *Seaquest_plots*, like this:

[31]:
```
plots=Seaquest2[::22]
last=Seaquest2[-1].reshape(1,210,160,3)
Seaquest_plots=np.concatenate([plots,last],axis=0)
```

We then create a picture with 25 subplots in it, and the 25 game windows form a five by five matrix in the picture, as follows:

[32]:
```
plt.figure(figsize=(12,16),dpi=100)
for i in range(25):
    plt.subplot(5,5,i+1)
```

```
    plt.imshow(Seaquest_plots[i])
    plt.axis('off')
plt.subplots_adjust(bottom=0.001,right=0.999,top=0.999,
left=0.001, hspace=-0.1,wspace=0.1)
plt.savefig("files/ch22/Seaquest_plots.jpg")
```

Run the above code cell and open the picture *Seaquest_plots.jpg* on your computer. You should see a picture similar to Figure 22.3. The 25 subplots show that the agent has warded off attacks from the left and the right and earned high scores. For example, in the third subplot in the first row, the agent is trying to ward off attacks from the left; in the fourth subplot in the first row, the agent is trying to ward off attacks from

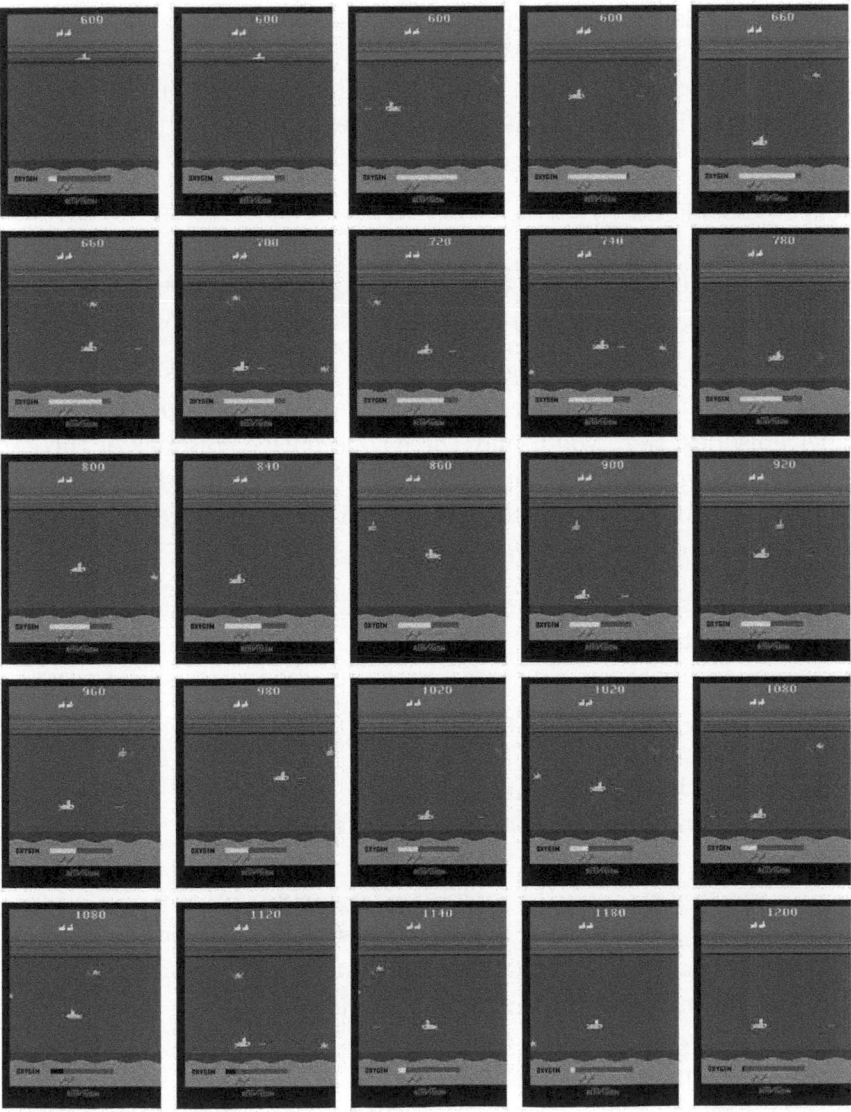

Figure 22.3 An episode of the Seaquest game

the right. The last subplot in the first row shows that the agent's score has increased to 660. In the second row, the agent's score increased from 660 to 780. After that, the score keeps on increasing from one subplot to the next. The very last subplot in the picture shows that the agent's score has increased to 1200.

22.5   TRY IT ON BEAM RIDER

Next, you'll apply the scaled up double deep Q-network on the Beam Rider game. You'll use the function *train_atari()* we defined earlier to train the agent. After that, you'll test how effective the trained model is.

22.5.1   Train the Model in Beam Rider

We have already imported the *train_atari()* from the local module in the last section. Now we can call the function again and put "BeamRider" as the argument in the function, like so:

[33]:
```
train_atari("BeamRider")
```

The training takes a couple of days. Alternatively, you can download a pre-trained model, *BeamRider.h5*, that I placed on the book's GitHub repository.

In the original Atari Beam Rider game without the Baselines game wrapper, the agent has three lives in each episode. The Baselines game wrapper breaks it down to three smaller episodes. Here you'll play three consecutive episodes of the game with the Baselines game wrapper. This is equivalent to one full original episode without the game wrapper. You'll turn on the graphical rendering of game windows so you can see the trained double deep Q-network agent in action.

[34]:
```
reload2 = tf.keras.models.load_model("files/ch22/BeamRider.h5")
state = env2.reset()
for i in range(3):
    score = 0
    for j in range(10000):
        if np.random.rand(1)[0]<0.01:
            action = np.random.choice(num_actions2)
        else:
            state_tensor = tf.convert_to_tensor(state)
            state_tensor = tf.expand_dims(state_tensor, 0)
            action_Qs = reload2(state_tensor, training=False)
            action = tf.argmax(action_Qs[0]).numpy()
        state, reward, done, info = env2.step(action)
        score += reward
        env2.render()
        if done:
```

```
                print("the score is", score)
                break
env2.close()
```

```
the score is 36.0
the score is 15.0
the score is 8.0
```

The trained agent has scored 36, 15, and 8 points in the three episodes, respectively.

22.5.2 The Average Score in Beam Rider

We have defined a *test_atari()* function in the local module in the last section to test the average score in any Atari game. We'll use the same function to test the performance of the trained double deep Q-network agent in Beam Rider. Since we have already imported the *test_atari()* from the local module in the last section, we can just call the function again and put "BeamRider" as the argument in the function, like so:

[35]:
```
test_atari("BeamRider")
```

```
the score in episode 1 is 40.0
the score in episode 2 is 15.0
the score in episode 3 is 27.0
...
the score in episode 99 is 8.0
the score in episode 100 is 21.0
the average score is 19.79
```

The above output shows the agent's score in each of the 100 episodes, as well as the average score.

22.5.3 A Successful Episode in Beam Rider

We'll highlight an episode in which the agent performs well. We'll first record 15 episodes, and this is equivalent to five full original Atari Beam Rider games.

The code cell below accomplishes that:

[36]:
```
for i in range(15):
    state = env2.reset()
    frames = []
    for j in range(10000):
        if np.random.rand(1)[0]<0.01:
            action = np.random.choice(num_actions2)
        else:
            state_tensor = tf.convert_to_tensor(state)
```

```
            state_tensor = tf.expand_dims(state_tensor, 0)
            action_Qs = reload2(state_tensor, training=False)
            action = tf.argmax(action_Qs[0]).numpy()
        state, reward, done, info = env2.step(action)
        frames.append(env2.render(mode='rgb_array'))
        if done:
            pickle.dump(frames,\
                open(f'files/ch22/{name}{i+1}.p', 'wb'))
            imageio.mimsave(f"files/ch22/{name}{i+1}.gif",\
                        frames, fps=240)
            break
env2.close()
```

You'll see 15 short animations in your local folder. Make sure you view them as extra large icons on your computer. You can see the score at the beginning of the episode from the thumbnail picture of the video. If the next episode has a much higher score than the current episode, the current episode is successful.

For example, I will zero in on episode 4 because the agent earned a high score. Go to the book's GitHub repository and download the file *BeamRider4.zip*. Unzip the file and save the unzipped file *BeamRider4.p* in the folder /Desktop/mla/files/ch22/ on your computer. Then convert the game windows in the episode into an animation as follows:

[37]:
```
BeamRider4=pickle.load(open("files\ch22\BeamRider4.p","rb"))
imageio.mimsave("files\ch22\BeamRider4.gif",\
                BeamRider4[::5],fps=24)
```

Run the above code cell and open the animation *BeamRider4.gif* on your computer. You can see that the agent has a score of 996 at the beginning and 3028 at the end. The agent has scored 3028−996=2032 points in the episode.

We can also create a picture with 25 subplots to show the effectiveness of the trained agent in Beam Rider. We first select 24 game windows throughout the episode. We then add in the last game window and put the 25 images in a list *BeamRider_plots*, like this:

[38]:
```
plots=BeamRider4[::73]
last=BeamRider4[-1].reshape(1,210,160,3)
BeamRider_plots=np.concatenate([plots,last],axis=0)
```

We then create a picture with 25 subplots in it, and the 25 game windows form a five by five matrix in the picture, as follows:

[39]:
```
plt.figure(figsize=(12,16),dpi=100)
for i in range(25):
    plt.subplot(5,5,i+1)
```

```
    plt.imshow(BeamRider_plots[i])
    plt.axis('off')
plt.subplots_adjust(bottom=0.001,right=0.999,top=0.999,
left=0.001, hspace=-0.1,wspace=0.1)
plt.savefig("files/ch22/BeamRider_plots.jpg")
```

Run the above code cell and open the picture *BeamRider_plots.jpg* on your computer. You should see a picture similar to Figure 22.4. The 25 subplots show that the agent has destroyed enemy spaceships and earned high scores. The top left subplot shows that the agent has a score of 996. The agent is currently in sector 2. The number 8 in green at the top left of the screen indicates that the agent needs to destroy eight

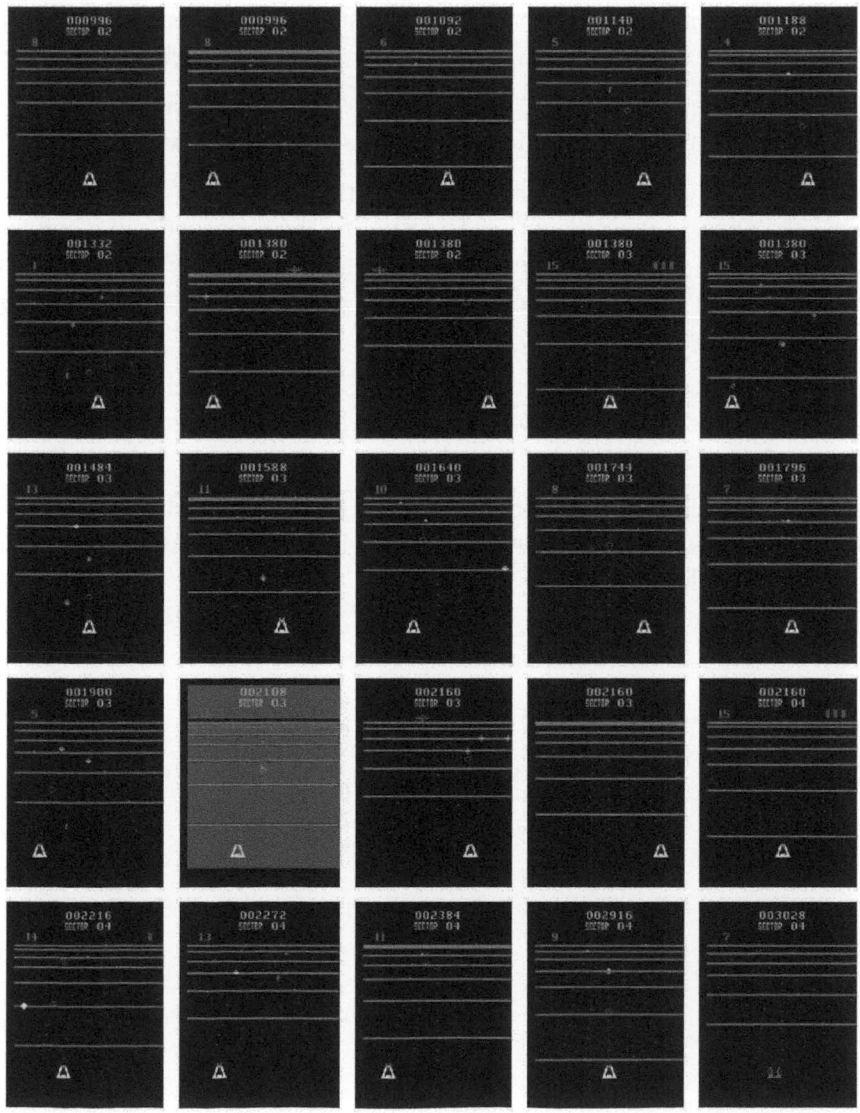

Figure 22.4 An episode of the Beam Rider game

more alien spaceships before the agent can enter into the next sector. In the first subplot in the second row, the number of spaceships the agent needs to destroy is 1, and the score has increased to 1332. The fourth subplot in the second row shows that the agent has entered sector 3. The last subplot at the bottom right corner shows that the agent has a score of 3028 and is currently in sector 4.

22.6 EXERCISES

22.1 Rerun code cells in Sections 22.1.1 and 22.1.2 to familiarize yourself with the Seaquest game with and without the *Baselines* game wrapper.

22.2 Rerun the code cell in Section 22.1.4 and open the newly generated file *seaquest_pixels.jpg* on your computer to visualize the preprocessed game windows. In each subplot, determine how many spare submarines the agent has.

22.3 Rerun code cells in Sections 22.2.1 and 22.2.2 to familiarize yourself with the Beam Rider game with and without the *Baselines* game wrapper.

22.4 Rerun the code cell in Section 22.2.4 and open the newly generated file *beam-rider_pixels.jpg* on your computer to visualize the preprocessed game windows. In each subplot, determine the agent's score, which sector the agent is in, and how many more alien spaceships the agent needs to destroy for the agent to enter the next sector.

22.5 Rerun the first code cell in Section 22.4.3. Go to the local folder to see the 20 short animations and select the episode in which the agent has scored the most points in Seaquest.

22.6 Rerun the first code cell in Section 22.5.3. Go to the local folder to see the 15 short animations and select the episode in which the agent has scored the most points in Beam Rider.

Bibliography

[1] Andrej Karpathy. Blog: http://karpathy.github.io/2016/05/31/rl/, 2016.

[2] Richard Bellman. *Adaptive Control Processes: A Guided Tour*. Princeton University Press, 1961.

[3] Ian Goodfellow Yoshua Bengio and Aaron Courville. *Deep Learning*. The MIT Press, 2016.

[4] Saheli Roy Choudhury. bit.ly/43QnZWB. *CNBC*, 2016.

[5] Martin Coulter and Greg Bensiger. Alphabet shares dive after google ai chatbot bard flubs answer in ad: bit.ly/4602vc2, 2023.

[6] DeepMind. Blog: deepmind.com/blog/deep-reinforcement-learning, 2016.

[7] History.com Editors. https://www.history.com/this-day-in-history/deep-blue-defeats-garry-kasparov-in-chess-match. *HISTORY*, 2009.

[8] Richard Feynman. *The Meaning of It All: Thoughts of a Citizen-Scientist*. Basic Books, 2015 Reprint.

[9] Y.W. Teh G.E. Hinton, S. Osindero. A fast learning algorithm for deep belief nets. *Neural Computation*, 2006.

[10] Hado Hasselt. Double q-learning. In J. Lafferty, C. Williams, J. Shawe-Taylor, R. Zemel, and A. Culotta, editors, *Advances in Neural Information Processing Systems*, volume 23. Curran Associates, Inc., 2010.

[11] Institutional Investor. CFA Institute Makes Biggest Single Package of Changes in Its History: bit.ly/42AyFb4, 2023.

[12] Jocob Chapman and Mathias Lechner. Deep Q-Learning for Atari Breakout: https://keras.io/examples/rl/deep_q_network_breakout/, 2020.

[13] Leaders. https://www.economist.com/leaders/2017/05/06/the-worlds-most-valuable-resource-is-no-longer-oil-but-data. *The Economist*, 2017.

[14] Mark Liu. *Make Python Talk: Build Apps with Voice Control and Speech Recognition*. No Starch Press, 2021.

[15] Scott MacFarland. https://www.huffpost.com/entry/if-a-picture-video-production_b_4996655/. *The Huffington Post*, 2014.

[16] Bernard Marr. `https://www.forbes.com/sites/bernardmarr/2018/12/31/the-most-amazing-artificial-intelligence-milestones-so-far/?sh=6698f5c37753`. *Forbes*, 2018.

[17] Volodymyr Mnih, Koray Kavukcuoglu, David Silver, Andrei A. Rusu, Joel Veness, Marc G. Bellemare, Alex Graves, Martin Riedmiller, Andreas K. Fidjeland, Georg Ostrovski, Stig Petersen, Charles Beattie, Amir Sadik, Ioannis Antonoglou, Helen King, Dharshan Kumaran, Daan Wierstra, Shane Legg, and Demis Hassabis. Human-level control through deep reinforcement learning. *Nature*, 518(7540):529–533, February 2015.

[18] OpenAI. `https://spinningup.openai.com/en/latest/spinningup/rl_intro3.html`, 2018.

[19] Max Pumperla and Kevin Ferguson. *Deep Learning and the Game of Go*. Manning, 2019.

[20] Barry Schwartz. *The Paradox of Choice: Why More Is Less*. Harper Perennial, 2005.

[21] Eric Seigel. *Predictive Analytics: The Power to Predict Who Will Click, Buy, Lie, or Die*. Wiley, 2015.

[22] Charles Severance. *Python for Everyone: Exploring Data in Python 3*. 2016.

[23] Daniel J. Siegel. *The Developing Mind: Toward a Neurobiology of Interpersonal Experience*. The Guilford Press, 1999.

[24] J.F. Gusella T. Green, S.F. Heinemann. Molecular neurobiology and genetics: Investigation of neural function and dysfunction. *Neuron*, 1998.

[25] The Data Team. `econ.st/43PiY0b`. *The Economist*, 2018.

[26] The CFA Institute. Hands-On Learning: `evolve.cfainstitute.org/practical-skills-modules.html`, 2023.

Index

Page numbers in **bold** refer to tables and those in *italic* refer to figures.

Milton Keynes UK
Ingram Content Group UK Ltd.
UKHW02845141024
449569UK00003B/77